THE LEGITIMACY AND RESPONSIVENESS OF INDUSTRY RULE-MAKING

Rule-making is no longer an activity undertaken exclusively by public actors. Private actors are increasingly allowed by legislatures and regulatory bodies to take part in (and in some cases assume responsibility for) the formation of legally binding rules, for example in the US, UK, Australia and the EU.

Departing from traditional forms of rule-making by involving private actors may enhance the ability of regulatory systems to achieve social goals, as regulatory scholars argue. However, because private actors are permitted to act in their own best interests, their involvement also raises doubts about the legitimacy of the underlying rule-making processes and the rules that are formulated.

The principal aim of this book is to highlight that the tension between the responsiveness that leading international regulatory scholars advocate in order to improve regulatory effectiveness, and the law and its formal, substantive, procedural and institutional values, is not as great as may first appear. Drawing on three in-depth case studies of the experience of the Australian telecommunications industry with self-regulatory rule-making—a form of rule-making that bears the hallmarks of 'responsive regulation', 'democratic experimentalism', 'smart regulation' and other strategies of proceduralization—it is argued that industry rule-making can, as a matter of practice, be responsive and legitimate at the same time. In doing so, the book formulates and applies criteria against which industry rule-making should be evaluated and identifies a number of indicia that point to when industry rule-making is likely to be simultaneously legitimate and responsive.

The Legitimacy and Responsiveness of Industry Rule-making

Karen Lee

• HART •
OXFORD • LONDON • NEW YORK • NEW DELHI • SYDNEY

HART PUBLISHING
Bloomsbury Publishing Plc
Kemp House, Chawley Park, Cumnor Hill, Oxford, OX2 9PH, UK

First published in Great Britain 2018

A catalogue record for this book is available from the British Library.

Library of Congress Cataloging-in-Publication data

Names: Lee, Karen, 1971- author.

Title: The legitimacy and responsiveness of industry rule-making / Karen Lee.

Description: Oxford, UK; Portland, Oregon : Hart Publishing, [2018] |

Identifiers: LCCN 2018016498 (print) | LCCN 2018016649 (ebook) | ISBN 9781509918102 (Epub) | ISBN 9781509918096 (hardback : alk. paper)

Subjects: LCSH: Administrative procedure. | Legislation.

Classification: LCC K3402 (ebook) | LCC K3402 .L44 2018 (print) | DDC 346/.06—dc23

LC record available at https://lccn.loc.gov/2018016498

ISBN: HB: 978-1-50991-809-6
ePDF: 978-1-50991-811-9
ePub: 978-1-50991-810-2

Typeset by Compuscript Ltd, Shannon

ACKNOWLEDGEMENTS

This book, which is based on my PhD thesis, completed on a part-time basis at the University of New South Wales, would not have been possible without the help and support of many individuals within the telecommunications field; academic and other professional colleagues; and friends. First, I would like to thank Anne Hurley and John Stanton of the Communications Alliance for agreeing to let me look through the organisation's internal files at its Sydney headquarters and for providing me with copies of much documentation, including all of the paperwork related to the development of the three 'consumer' codes of practice that form the heart of the book. Without their permission, it would have been much more difficult to shed light on the process of Part 6 rule-making. Additional thanks are owed to the administrative staff of the Communications Alliance, who were tasked with providing me with the information and answered numerous questions about the organisation, its history, its procedures and the reasons for particular decisions. I am much the wiser for it. They also helpfully forwarded letters requesting interviews to certain industry delegates, making the process of tracking down working committee representatives much easier.

Further, I am indebted to the individuals who served on code working committees who agreed to make time in their busy schedules to meet and share with me their experiences and perspectives on code development. The case studies and the project overall are much richer for their insights.

Thanks must also be given to my 'academic and professional support team'. My principal PhD supervisors, Professor and Dean of the Faculty of Law, University of Technology, Sydney (UTS), Lesley Hitchens, and Angus Corbett, now Adjunct Professor of Law, University of Pennsylvania Law School; and Adjunct Associate Professor, Australian Institute of Health Innovation, Macquarie University, were exceedingly generous with their time. They offered constructive criticism as well as much needed encouragement throughout the drafting of the thesis and gave helpful advice about converting the thesis into a book. My thinking about Part 6 rule-making and regulation more generally was helped tremendously by their involvement. Professor Kathy Bowrey, Faculty of Law, University of New South Wales (UNSW), provided helpful comments on certain draft chapters of the thesis and book; and gave me advice and encouragement while transforming the thesis into a book. The Faculty of Law at UNSW awarded me a grant of $5,000 to support my fieldwork. The grant was funded by the Law Society of NSW's Legal Scholarship Support Scheme/Public Purpose Fund, and I gratefully acknowledge the support provided by the Law Society.

My PhD examiners, Professor Christine Parker, University of Melbourne, and Professor Tony Prosser, Bristol University, provided insightful comments on the thesis; encouraged me to turn the thesis into a book and offered helpful advice on that process. Dr Mark Hannah, School of Law, Queen's University Belfast, shared his insights about transnational rule-making. Professor Veronica Taylor, then Director of the Regulatory Institutions Network (now the RegNet School of Regulation and Global Governance) at the Australian National University gave me the opportunity to be a departmental visitor at RegNet in 2012 and an office to work on my thesis. The RegNet experience exposed me to some of the best minds working in the regulatory field and conversations with RegNet colleagues have undoubtedly improved the thesis and the book. Professors Ian Walden and Andrew Kenyon gave me access to the law library facilities at Queen Mary, University of London, and the University of Melbourne, respectively, while I worked on my thesis. At Hart, Bill Asquith, who commissioned the book, was very supportive of the project from the outset. Olivia D'Cruz designed the book's wonderful cover. Sinead Moloney, Linda Staniford and Helen Kitto provided excellent editorial, production and copy-editing assistance.

Finally, the members of my 'personal support team' deserve special commendation. Mark Lunney offered much love and encouragement throughout the writing of the thesis and the book. My friends in Armidale, including all of the members of the Breakfast Club, reminded me to have some fun while working on the thesis and the book. Julie Ayling and Imelda Deinla gave support and friendship in Canberra. Sadly, Nick Higham died while I was working on the thesis but he was a wonderful mentor when I was in private practice and friend. He gave me my first opportunity to work in the wonderfully interesting world of telecommunications. I continue to be most thankful that he did.

TABLE OF CONTENTS

Part III. Substantive Analysis of Case Studies

GLOSSARY AND TABLE OF ABBREVIATIONS

2002 industry guideline	ACIF, *Industry Guideline ACIF G601: Consumer Contracts* (December 2002)
2003 determination	Telecommunications (Standard Form of Agreement Information) Determination 2003 (Cth)
2G	Second Generation
3G	Third Generation
ABA	Australian Broadcasting Authority
ACA	Australian Communications Authority
ACA determination	Telecommunications (Standard Form of Agreement Information) Determination 2003 (Cth)
ACCAN	Australian Communications Consumer Action Network
ACCC	Australian Competition and Consumer Commission
ACIF	Australian Communications Industry Forum Limited (now known as the Communications Alliance)
ACMA	Australian Communications and Media Authority
ADMA	Australian Direct Marketing Association
AEEMA	Australian Electrical and Electronic Manufacturers Association
AIIA	Australian Information Industry Association
AMTA	Australian Mobile Telecommunications Association
ANAO	Australian National Audit Office
AOTC	Australian and Overseas Telecommunications Corporation Limited
ARATA	Australian Rehabilitation and Assistive Technology Association
ASIC	Australian Securities and Investment Commission
ASX	Australian Securities Exchange Limited
ATUG	Australian Telecommunications User Group
AUSSAT	AUSSAT Pty Limited
Austel	Australian Telecommunications Authority
CAC	ACIF's Consumer Advisory Council
CAV	Consumer Affairs Victoria
Consumer Council	The Consumer Council of ACIF and the Communications Alliance (it replaced CAC)
CECRP	ACIF's Customer Equipment and Cabling Reference Panel
CEO	chief executive officer
CLC	Communications Law Centre

CLI	calling line identification
CMC	Code Monitoring Committee
Communications Alliance	Communications Alliance Limited (formerly known as ACIF)
COAG	Council of Australian Governments
Consumer Contracts code	ACIF, *Industry Code ACIF C620: Consumer Contracts* (2005)
CoT	Casualties of Telecom
CTN	Consumers' Telecommunications Network
CTRAC	Communications Technical Regulation Advisory Committee
CTRAC-DSWG	Communications Technical Regulation Advisory Committee-Disability Standards Working Group
DAB	ACIF's Disability Advisory Body
DBCDE	Department of Broadband, Communications and the Digital Economy (subsequently renamed the Department of Communications and now known as the Department of Communications and the Arts)
Disability Council	The Disability Council of ACIF and the Communications Alliance (it replaced DAB)
DCITA	Department of Communications, Information Technology and the Arts (subsequently renamed DBCDE, the Department of Communications and now known as the Department of Communications and the Arts)
DDA	Disability Discrimination Act 1992 (Cth)
DDP	directly deliberative polyarchy
Determination	Telecommunications Service Provider (Mobile Premium Services) Determination 2005 (No 1)
DOCA	Department of Communications and the Arts (subsequently renamed DCITA, DBCDE, the Department of Communications and now known (again) as the Department of Communications and the Arts)
DSWG	Disability Standard Working Group
equipment suppliers	manufacturers and importers of telephone handsets and other customer equipment
FCC	US Federal Communications Commission
GARI	Global Accessibility Reporting Initiative
HFC	hybrid fibre coaxial cable
HREOC	Human Rights and Equal Opportunity Commission
IAF code	ACIF, *Industry Code ACIF C625: Information on Accessibility Features for Telephone Equipment Code* (2005)
ICT	Information and Communications Technology
IIA	Internet Industry Association
ISPs	Internet Service Providers
IT	Information Technology

MCASG	The Communications Alliance's Mobile Content and Services Group
MCSP	mobile carriage service provider
Minister	Depending on the context, the Minister for DOCA, DCITA or DBCDE
MMS	Multimedia Messaging Service
MPS	mobile premium services
Mobile Premium Services code or MPS code	Communications Alliance, *Industry Code C637: Mobile Premium Services* (2009)
MPSI guideline	*Guideline to the Mobile Premium Services Self-Regulatory Scheme* (22 August 2006)
MPSI Scheme	Mobile Premium Services Self-Regulatory Scheme
MVNOs	Mobile Virtual Network Operators
NBN	National Broadband Network
OECD	Organisation for Economic Co-operation and Development
OPC	Office of the Privacy Commissioner (now Office of the Australian Information Commissioner)
OTC	Overseas Telecommunications Commission
PAC	Privacy Advisory Committee
Part 6	Part 6 of the Telecommunications Act 1997 (Cth)
SETEL	Small Enterprise Telecommunications Centre Limited
SFOAs	Standard Forms of Agreement
SMS	Short Message Service
SPAN	Service Providers Association Incorporated
Steering Group	The TCP Code Review Steering Group
TCP	Telecommunications Consumer Protections
Tedicore	Telecommunication and Disability Consumer Representation
Telecom	The company known as Telstra since 1 July 1995
TIO	Telecommunications Industry Ombudsman
TPC	Telecommunications Privacy Committee
VHA	Vodafone Hutchison Australia
xDSL	Digital Subscriber Line

TABLE OF CASES

Australia

United Kingdom

United States

TABLE OF PRIMARY AND SECONDARY LEGISLATION, AND BILLS

Australia

Commonwealth

Primary Legislation

Secondary Legislation

Bills

Victoria

European Union

United Kingdom

United States

Primary Legislation

Secondary Legislation

1

Introduction

The well-documented failures of 'command and control' regulation are radically altering the way that legislatures, governments and regulators worldwide seek to accomplish public policy goals. Instead of relying solely on the formal legal mechanisms of the state, they are increasingly making use of an ever-expanding suite of regulatory techniques that involve the direct participation of the 'targets of regulation'[1] and other parties in all aspects of the regulatory process. For example, in the US, Congress has authorised 'negotiated rulemaking' and 'audited self-regulation.' The former enables representatives from affected interest groups and independent agencies to negotiate and formulate collectively draft rules of conduct;[2] the latter permits third parties to implement federal law, subject to approval by federal regulators.[3] In Australia, bodies such as the Australian Securities and Investment Commission (ASIC) and the Australian Competition and Consumer Commission (ACCC) may elect to accept 'enforceable undertakings'—agreements reached following 'negotiation and settlement with (alleged offenders)'[4] rather than enforce statutory rules in courts of law.[5] They are also relying on 'third party-audits' to verify compliance with these undertakings.[6] Like a number of other countries, the UK continues to experiment with the instruments of 'mandated self-regulation',[7] 'co-regulation'[8] and 'delegation'.[9] All permit private actors to take

[1] C Parker and J Braithwaite, 'Regulation' in P Cane and M Tushnet (eds), *The Oxford Handbook of Legal Studies* (Oxford, Oxford University Press, 2003) 119, 128.

[2] See, eg, PJ Harter, 'Negotiating Regulations: A Cure for Malaise' (1982) 71 *Georgetown Law Journal* 1.

[3] DC Michael, 'Federal Agency Use of Audited Self-Regulation as a Regulatory Technique' (1995) 47 *Administrative Law Review* 171, 174–76.

[4] See, eg, C Parker, 'Restorative Justice in Business Regulation? The Australian Competition and Consumer Commission's Use of Enforceable Undertakings' (2004) 67 *MLR* 209, 209.

[5] See, eg, C Parker, 'Regulating Self-Regulation' in S Bell (ed), *Economic Governance and Institutional Dynamics* (Oxford, Oxford University Press, 2002) 244–61; K Yeung, *Securing Compliance: A Principled Approach* (Oxford, Hart Publishing, 2004) 191–242.

[6] See, eg, C Parker, 'Regulator-Required Corporate Compliance Program Audits' (2003) 25 *Law & Policy* 221.

[7] J Black, 'Constitutionalising Self-Regulation' (1996) 58 *MLR* 24, 27.

[8] See, eg, C Scott, 'Self-Regulation and the Meta-Regulatory State' in F Cafaggi (ed), *Reframing Self-Regulation in European Private Law* (Alphen aan den Rijn, Kluwer Law International, 2006) 131, 138–39.

[9] See, eg, ibid 136–37; CM Donnelly, *Delegation of Governmental Power to Private Parties: A Comparative Perspective* (Oxford, Oxford University Press, 2007) 3–5.

part in (and in some cases assume responsibility for) the formation, enforcement and/or monitoring of legally binding rules, activities once seen as the exclusive duties of the state.

Advocates of these so-called strategies of 'proceduralization',[10] which trade under the 'banners'[11] of 'reflexive law',[12] 'responsive regulation',[13] 'smart regulation',[14] 'democratic experimentalism',[15] 'collaborative governance'[16] and more recently 'really responsive regulation',[17] argue that 'democratization'[18] of the regulatory process overcomes the limitations of command and control regulation and enhances the ability of regulatory systems to achieve social goals. Permitting private actors and other third parties to participate in regulatory activities, it is said, enables the state to draw on their greater expertise of the underlying industry sectors in question.[19] Harnessing their knowledge and skills leads to regulatory interventions that are more flexible, innovative[20] and cost-effective.[21] Advocates suggest that any rules that are produced are likely to be better targeted to the relevant individual and/or group. These rules are also more likely to be more reasonable. Better targeted and more reasonable rules are two factors that are said to enhance the likelihood of industry compliance with them.[22] Similarly, proceduralization sanctions discussion with regulatory targets that have breached the law before enforcement action is taken. The multiplicity of enforcement strategies it endorses have a better chance of 'constrain[ing] noncompliance',[23] 'build[ing] business cultures of social responsibility'[24] and resulting in 'win-win outcomes'.[25] Moreover, the problems

[10] J Black, 'Proceduralizing Regulation: Part 1' (2000) 20 *OJLS* 597, 598.

[11] ibid.

[12] See, eg, G Teubner, *Law as an Autopoietic System* (Oxford, Blackwell, 1993); G Teubner, 'Substantive and Reflexive Elements in Modern Law' (1983) 17 *Law and Society Review* 239.

[13] I Ayres and J Braithwaite, *Responsive Regulation: Transcending the Deregulation Debate* (Oxford, Oxford University Press, 1992). See also J Braithwaite, *Regulatory Capitalism: How It Works, Ideas for Making It Work Better* (Cheltenham, Edward Elgar, 2008) and 'The Essence of Responsive Regulation' (2011) 44 *University of British Columbia Law Review* 475.

[14] N Gunningham and P Grabosky, *Smart Regulation: Designing Environmental Policy* (Oxford, Oxford University Press, 1998).

[15] MC Dorf and CF Sabel, 'A Constitution of Democratic Experimentalism' (1998) 98 *Columbia Law Review* 267.

[16] See, eg, C Ansell and A Gash, 'Collaborative Governance in Theory and Practice' (2008) 18 *Journal of Public Administration Theory and Practice* 543.

[17] R Baldwin and J Black, 'Really Responsive Regulation' (2008) 71 *MLR* 59.

[18] Black, 'Proceduralizing Regulation: Part 1', above n 10, 599.

[19] See, eg, A Ogus, 'Rethinking Self-Regulation' (1995) 15 *OJLS* 97, 97–98; C Coglianese and E Mendelson (eds), 'Meta-Regulation and Self-Regulation' in R Baldwin, M Cave and M Lodge, *The Oxford Handbook of Regulation* (Oxford, Oxford University Press, 2010) 146, 152.

[20] Ayres and Braithwaite, above n 13, 111. See also CF Sabel and J Zeitlin, 'Learning from Difference: The New Architecture of Experimentalist Governance in the EU' (2008) 14 *European Law Journal* 271.

[21] Ogus, above n 19, 98; Coglianese and Mendelson, above n 19, 152.

[22] Ayres and Braithwaite, above n 13, 110–16; Coglianese and Mendelson, above n 19, 152.

[23] Ayres and Braithwaite, above n 13, 20.

[24] ibid 51.

[25] Gunningham and Grabosky, above n 14, 413.

of over and under-inclusiveness, 'indeterminacy' and interpretation inherent in traditional rule enforcement are minimised (if not eliminated).[26]

Lawyers, on the other hand, question whether use of these new instruments of regulation is consistent with the notion of law itself and the underlying formal, substantive, procedural and institutional values[27] that give law its legitimacy. They argue that techniques of proceduralization enhance the risk of arbitrary decision-making because, rather than relying on clearly prescribed rules, they give significant discretion to private entities and/or expand the already considerable freedom that public actors enjoy in the regulatory arena.[28] The absence of such rules makes the law uncertain and unpredictable, making it difficult for citizens and others to know what the law is and how to behave accordingly.[29] Moreover, these new regulatory techniques permit the state to 'differentiate' between regulatees, an approach that is at odds with notions of 'generality' and non-discrimination, both of which are central to formal conceptions of legal equality.[30] Further, they allege that the negotiation between interested parties, which is characteristic of these mechanisms, permits private and public actors alike to ignore human rights,[31] thus posing significant challenges for achieving and preserving 'substantive equality'.[32] The emphasis on agreement also negates the importance of procedural fairness concerns, as parties strive to obtain particular regulatory outcomes.[33] Participating private parties are permitted to act in their best interests and are not legally accountable for their actions before a court of law.[34] While, in theory, state actors remain subject to legal constraints, negotiations are often not conducted publicly, making it difficult to evaluate if they have acted within the limitations of the law[35]—a problem that is exacerbated by the absence of detailed rules that delineate the scope of their authority.

This book considers one of the most legally controversial tools in the expanded regulatory 'tool kit': industry rule-making. The principal aim is to highlight that

[26] On the 'nature of rules', see J Black, *Rules and Regulators* (Oxford, Clarendon Press, 1997) 6–19.

[27] See generally PP Craig, 'Formal and Substantive Conceptions of the Rule of Law: An Analytical Framework' (1997) *PL* 467; J Jowell, 'The Rule of Law and Its Underlying Values' in J Jowell and D Oliver (eds), *The Changing Constitution* 7th edn (Oxford, Oxford University Press, 2011) 11, 16–22; J Waldron, 'The Rule of Law and the Importance of Procedure' in JE Fleming (ed), *Getting to the Rule of Law: Nomos L* (New York, New York University Press, 2011) 3; J Waldron, 'Principles of Legislation' in Richard W Bauman and Tsvi Kahana (eds), *The Least Examined Branch: The Role of Legislatures in the Constitutional State* (Cambridge, Cambridge University Press, 2006) 15.

[28] D Kingsford Smith, 'Beyond the Rule of Law? Decentred Regulation in Online Investing' (2004) 26 *Law & Policy* 439, 453–54, 458.

[29] Yeung, above n 5, 38–39.

[30] See generally P Westerman, 'Pyramids and the Value of Generality' (2013) 7 *Regulation & Governance* 80.

[31] Kingsford Smith, 'Beyond the Rule of Law?', above n 28, 454–55.

[32] Jowell, above n 27, 19.

[33] Yeung, above n 5, 185.

[34] See, eg, Ogus, above n 19, 98; R Baldwin, M Cave and M Lodge, *Understanding Regulation: Theory, Strategy and Practice* 2nd edn (Oxford, Oxford University Press, 2011) 142–44.

[35] Yeung, above n 5, 186.

the tension between the 'responsiveness' that regulatory scholars advocate in order to improve regulatory effectiveness, on the one hand, and the law and its formal, substantive, procedural and institutional values, on the other, is not as great as either camp asserts. The book is directed at lawyers, some of the harshest critics of proceduralized rule-making, who believe that the coherence of law is being sacrificed in the quest for enhanced regulatory effectiveness. Drawing on three in-depth case studies of the experience of the Australian telecommunications industry with self-regulatory rule-making in accordance with Part 6 of the Telecommunications Act 1997 (Cth), a form of rule-making that bears the hallmarks of various strategies of proceduralization, it is argued that industry rule-making, which is both responsive and effective in achieving public policy goals, can accord with the values that confer legitimacy in 'traditional' legislative and administrative rule-making contexts. The rules drafted by industry can be incorporated into the existing system of law without undermining its coherence. The book is also directed at regulatory scholars who argue (implicitly if not explicitly) that the need to maintain a coherent system of law should give way to the exigencies of responsiveness and effectiveness. It is argued that, rather than hindering the drive for responsiveness and effectiveness they seek, the principles supporting legal legitimacy can best be seen as regulatory tools that are central to the achievement of both of these objectives and are important in their own right if recourse to the formalised mechanisms of state and administrative law-making is to be avoided.

I. Approach and Scope of Book

A. Empirical Research of Industry Rule-making

Concerns have been raised for decades in a number of regulatory contexts and jurisdictions that industry rule-making is too responsive to the needs of industry to the detriment of consumer and public interests. The initial hostility of the US federal courts in the 1930s towards the delegation of Congressional rule-making authority to private entities, seen in cases such as *Carter v Carter Coal Co*[36] and *Schechter Poultry Corporation v US*,[37] was fuelled, in large part, by scepticism that private actors would act in the public interest.[38] The courts may have subsequently softened their opposition to delegation[39] but the debate about whether industry can formulate rules that go against its interests persists. Assertions that industry fails to formulate rules to address public harms continue to be made.[40]

[36] *Carter v Carter Coal Co* 298 US 238 (1936).
[37] *Schechter Poultry Corporation v US* 295 US 495 (1935).
[38] See generally LL Jaffe, 'Law Making by Private Groups' (1937) 51 *Harvard Law Review* 201.
[39] Donnelly, above n 9, 119.
[40] See, eg, JA Taylor and LT Frey, 'The Need for Industry and Occupation Standards in Hospital Discharge Data' (2013) 55 *Journal of Occupational and Environmental Medicine* 495; LL Sharma,

The rules that self-regulatory organisations draft are perceived to be weak by the general public, a response intensified by reports that industry-formulated rules contributed to the global financial crisis.[41] In the UK, the proliferation of codes of practice during the mid- to late 1970s and 1980s in diverse areas such as industrial relations, consumer protection and insurance brokerage sparked questions of whether industry rule-making worked against the public interest.[42] Industry rule-making may have since become commonplace in Britain[43] but the 2013 horsemeat scandal has renewed apprehension that industry cannot formulate robust rules even within a co-regulatory framework.[44] The same suspicion has arisen in Australia in the telecommunications[45] and broadcasting[46] sectors, the latter of which was beset by the 'Cash for Comment' affair[47] from 1999 to 2005.

However, in contrast to its application in enforcement and compliance,[48] there is surprisingly little empirical research about proceduralization in rule-making and its ability (or otherwise) to account for and address non-industry concerns. Novel means of rule-formulation permitted by the state and the rules they generate have, of course, generated academic attention.[49] However, the ability of industry

SP Teret and KD Brownell, 'The Food Industry and Self-Regulation: Standards to Promote Success and to Avoid Public Health Failures' (2010) 100 *American Journal of Public Health* 240, 240–42; DL Kunkel, JS Castonguay and CR Filer, 'Evaluating Industry Self-Regulation of Food Marketing to Children' (2015) 49 *American Journal of Preventive Medicine* 181.

[41] See, eg, ST Omarova, 'Wall Street as Community of Fate: Toward Financial Industry Self-Regulation' (2011) 159 *University of Pennsylvania Law Review* 411, 413–16.

[42] See, eg, AC Page, 'Self-Regulation and Codes of Practice' (1980) *Journal of Business Law* 24; AC Page, 'Self-Regulation: The Constitutional Dimension' (1986) 49 *MLR* 141.

[43] On the growth of self-regulation in the UK, see, eg, R Baggott, 'Regulatory Reform in Britain: The Changing Face of Self-Regulation' (1989) 67 *Public Administration* 435; M Moran, *The British Regulatory State: High Modernism and Hyper-Innovation* (Oxford, Oxford University Press, 2003).

[44] See, eg, AA Laverty (Imperial College), S Capewell (Liverpool University) and C Millett (Imperial College), 'Letter to the Editor' (2013) 381 *The Lancet* 1901.

[45] K MacNeill, 'Self Regulation: Rights and Remedies—the Telecommunications Experience' in C Finn (ed), *Sunrise or Sunset? Administrative Law in the New Millennium: Papers Presented at the 2000 National Administrative Law Forum* (Canberra, Australian Institute of Administrative Law, 2000) 249, 257–59, 260–61; S Horrocks and R Hill, 'Protecting the Consumer Interest in Network Standards and Operations Codes in Practice' in Communications Research Unit (ed), *Communications Research Forum Proceedings* (Canberra, DCITA, vol 4, 1999) 527.

[46] See, eg, L Hitchens, 'Commercial Broadcasting—Preserving the Public Interest' (2004) 32 *Federal Law Review* 79; D Wilding, 'In the Shadow of the Pyramid: Consumers in Communications Self-Regulation' (2005) 55(2) *Telecommunications Journal of Australia* 37.

[47] The scandal centred around the practice by leading Australian talkback radio presenters, including John Laws and Alan Jones, of accepting money from commercial sponsors in return for making positive comments about them during radio programmes without adequately disclosing the existence of such arrangements to their listeners.

[48] See, eg, Yeung, above n 5; Parker, 'Restorative Justice in Business Regulation', above n 4.

[49] In Australia, see, eg, W Pengilley, 'Competition Law and Voluntary Codes of Self-Regulation: An Individual Assessment of What Has Happened to Date' (1990) 13 *University of New South Wales Law Journal* 212; D Kingsford Smith, 'Governing the Corporation: The Role of "Soft Regulation"' (2012) 35 *University of New South Wales Law Journal* 378. In the UK, see, eg, Black, *Rules and Regulators*, above n 26. In the US, see, eg, L Susskind and G McMahon, 'The Theory and Practice of Negotiated Rulemaking' (1985) 3 *Yale Journal on Regulation* 133; LI Langbein and CM Kerwin, 'Regulatory Negotiation versus Conventional Rule Making: Claims, Counterclaims, and Empirical Evidence' (2000) 10 *Journal of Public Administration Research and Theory* 599; Michael, above n 3.

rule-making to be a legitimate law-making process has not been a focus for the vast majority of its scholars. Their work, some of which is empirically informed, clearly acknowledges the importance of the procedures used by industry and others to draft rules but is directed to issues such as costs, proposed benefits and capacity to produce 'better' rules—rules that improve outcomes in specific areas of regulation and stimulate change.[50] Only a few scholars have researched industry rule-making and attempted to evaluate if the rules generated can be integrated into the existing legal order without conflicting with its central principles and values. Moreover, as is discussed in more detail below, the data from which these scholars drew their conclusions were limited to a small number of industry sectors. The methodology they used contained some weaknesses or their analysis blurred the issues of rule-making, enforcement and compliance.

Hamilton conducted work in the 1970s on the 'reasonableness' of US federal agencies relying on 'voluntary standards' related to health and safety. While informed by interviews with some participants and observations of some working committees, his work did not contain any specific case studies.[51] Rather the approach adopted was anecdotal. Funk's conclusion that negotiated rule-making undermined the public interest was based on one case study of its use by the US Environmental Protection Agency.[52] It was not informed by direct observation of the process, the documentation exchanged between or interviews with actual participants. MacNeill's suggestion that self-regulatory rule-making by the Australian telecommunications sector does not serve consumer interests, which formed part of a wider discussion of the 'adequacy' of self-regulation to protect Australian telecommunications consumers, was based on brief analysis of the development of a single code of practice. It relied solely on publicly available documentation and comments made by consumer advocates involved in the process.[53] No interviews with industry, for example, were conducted. In the UK, Marsden has suggested that Internet regulation is a 'paradigm of constitutionally responsive co-regulation'[54] but his summary, discussion and analysis of his data are broad brush. They do not clearly distinguish between the rule-making, enforcement and compliance aspects of regulation, a problem also seen in the case studies of 'regulated self-regulation' undertaken by European scholars Schulz and Held[55] and the

[50] See, eg, C Coglianese, 'Assessing Consensus: The Promise and Performance of Negotiated Rule-making' (1997) 46 *Duke Law Journal* 1255; CC Caldart and NA Ashford, 'Negotiation as a Means of Developing and Implementing Environmental and Occupational Health and Safety Policy' (1999) 23 *Harvard Environmental Law Review* 141.

[51] RW Hamilton, 'The Role of Nongovernmental Standards in the Development of Mandatory Federal Standards Affecting Safety or Health' (1978) 56 *Texas Law Review* 1329, 1377–86.

[52] W Funk, 'When Smoke Gets in Your Eyes: Regulatory Negotiation and the Public Interest-EPA's Woodstove Standards' (1987) 18 *Environmental Law* 55.

[53] MacNeill, above n 45, 257–61.

[54] CT Marsden, *Internet Co-Regulation: European Law, Regulatory Governance and Legitimacy in Cyberspace* (Cambridge, Cambridge University Press, 2011) 3.

[55] W Schulz and T Held, *Regulated Self-Regulation as a Form of Modern Government: An Analysis of Case Studies from Media and Telecommunications Law* (Eastleigh, University of Luton Press, 2004) 9–11.

study of industry codes of practice regulating digital media content by Tambini, Leonardi and Marsden.[56]

This book begins the process of filling the empirical gap in our understanding of industry rule-making and its capacity to address consumer and public interests. In doing so, it formulates and applies criteria against which industry rule-making should be evaluated and identifies a number of indicia that suggest when industry rule-making is likely to be simultaneously legitimate and responsive.

B. Part 6 Rule-making

The experience of the Australian telecommunications sector with Part 6 of the Telecommunications Act 1997 (Cth) (Part 6) provides the empirical basis from which the questions of the legitimacy and responsiveness of industry rule-making are explored in this book. Part 6 was selected because it is a form of proceduralized rule-making. Under the Act, 'sections of the telecommunications industry' are permitted to formulate and seek the registration of codes of practice dealing with a variety of matters, including consumer protection, relating to their 'telecommunications activities',[57] with the Australian Communications and Media Authority (ACMA). Upon registration by ACMA, codes acquire the state's 'monopoly of force',[58] ie they are enforceable by ACMA. If industry fails to develop codes that 'provide appropriate community safeguards' or otherwise adequately regulate its participants, then ACMA may, in specified circumstances, adopt an industry standard.[59] The telecommunications sector in Australia (as it does worldwide) also has certain market characteristics common to a number of sectors where the state has deployed strategies of proceduralized rule-making. It is technically complex and is subject to and undergoing rapid change. In addition, the telecommunications industry in Australia has been permitted to formulate (and has, in fact, formulated) numerous codes of practice since 1997 when Part 6 was enacted, thus providing an excellent source of data. Further, controversy has surrounded (and continues to surround) the process by which the industry formulates codes of practice.[60] Consumer and public interest representatives involved in code development have alleged and continue to maintain[61] that industry has far greater

[56] D Tambini, D Leonardi and C Marsden, *Codifying Cyberspace: Communications Self-Regulation in the Age of Internet Convergence* (London, Routledge, 2007).

[57] Telecommunications Act 1997 (Cth) s 117.

[58] M Taggart, 'The Nature and Functions of the State' in P Cane and M Tushnet (eds), *The Oxford Handbook of Legal Studies* (Oxford, Oxford University Press, 2003) 101, 113.

[59] Telecommunications Act 1997 (Cth) ss 123–25.

[60] On the importance of selecting controversial case studies, see C Coglianese, 'Empirical Analysis of Administrative Law' (2002) 2002 *University of Illinois Law Review* 1111.

[61] See, eg, SETEL, Submission to Taskforce on Industry Self-Regulation, 13 December 1999; CTN, Submission to Taskforce on Industry Self-Regulation, 10 January 2000; Consumer Driven Communications Group, *Consumer Driven Communications: Strategies for Better Representation (Final Report)* (December 2004); ACCAN, Submission to ACMA, *Reconnecting the Customer Inquiry*, 10 September 2010.

bargaining power that it uses to the disadvantage of individual and small business consumers. Finally, Part 6 rule-making has attracted the attention of the Organisation for Economic Co-operation and Development (OECD) and the Australian National Audit Office (ANAO). In its report *Industry Self-Regulation: Role and Use in Supporting Consumer Interests*, the OECD cites Part 6 rule-making as an example of how government may promote multi-stakeholder dialogue in industry self-regulation.[62] The ANAO's 'Better Practice Guide' also cites the Mobile Premium Services (MPS) code,[63] the 2009 version of which is the focus of chapter seven, as an example of effective regulation.[64] Therefore, in addition to addressing directly the empirical gap in the academic literature, experience with Part 6 rule-making offers some important insights that could be of benefit to government and other industry sectors where industry rule-making has been deployed or is being contemplated as a solution to identified regulatory problems.

i. The Communications Alliance

The three case studies that inform the analysis of legitimacy and responsiveness in this book examine codes of practice developed by working committees established under the auspices of the Communications Alliance (formerly known as the Australian Communications Industry Forum (ACIF)).[65] It represents 'sections of the telecommunications sector' that have drafted codes of practice that have been registered by ACMA in accordance with Part 6. ACIF was established in 1997. In 2006, it merged with the Service Providers Association (SPAN) to form the Communications Alliance. In 2014, the Communications Alliance assumed the responsibilities of the Internet Industry Association (IIA). Prior to assuming the responsibilities of the IIA, the Communications Alliance was seen as the 'peak' self-regulatory body in the Australian telecommunications sector. Since assuming the responsibilities of the IIA, it is now seen as the peak self-regulatory body in the Australian communications sector.

When data collection for the book commenced, 28 Part 6 codes[66] had been prepared from scratch by working committees convened by the Communications Alliance and registered by ACMA or its predecessor, the Australian Communications Authority (ACA).[67] Most of these codes had also been revised numerous times and earlier versions of them deregistered by either the ACA or ACMA.

[62] OECD, *Industry Self-Regulation: Role and Use in Supporting Consumer Interests* (23 March 2015) 13.

[63] Communications Alliance, *Industry Code C637: Mobile Premium Services* (2009).

[64] ANAO, *Administering Regulation: Achieving the Right Balance* (June 2014) 5–6.

[65] Unless otherwise indicated, a reference to the Communications Alliance in this book includes a reference to ACIF.

[66] This figure, compiled from 'Status Reports' of ACIF and 'Publication Reports' of the Communications Alliance, excludes the Telecommunications Consumer Protections Code (C628) which amalgamated five codes in 2007.

[67] When Part 6 was first enacted, the power to register codes was bestowed on the ACA. ACMA was created in 2005 following the merger of the ACA with the Australian Broadcasting Authority (ABA).

ii. Consumer Codes

Each of the three case studies centres on the development of what the Communications Alliance classifies as a 'consumer' code, one of three different types of codes it categorises. 'Network' and 'operations' codes comprise the other two. The criteria the Communications Alliance uses to categorise codes have never been precisely defined. However, as a general rule, consumer codes generally relate to the goods and services that are delivered to consumers—the residential customers and small businesses who enter into contracts with providers of telecommunications services for the supply of those services and related goods—and grant some form of rights or protections to them.[68] Network codes deal with technical matters; operations codes govern the operational relationships, including the 'interworking of … "back office" systems, such as inter-operator billing …' between members of the telecommunications industry.[69]

The distinctions that the Communications Alliance draws between the three types of codes are neither accepted by the consumer and public interest organisations that participate in Communications Alliance code development processes[70] nor are they clear cut. For example, the Communications Alliance classifies codes dealing with matters such as the handling of life-threatening and unwelcome communications;[71] priority assistance for life-threatening medical conditions;[72] and the deployment of mobile phone network infrastructure,[73] as operations codes, not consumer codes. Arguably, consumer and public interest organisations also have an interest in network and operations codes.[74] The Communications Alliance has also formulated and registered many more operations and technical codes under Part 6 than consumer codes. Nevertheless, Communications Alliance consumer codes were selected as the focus of this book because it is undisputed within the telecommunications industry that the general public has a direct interest in their content. Moreover, their development has been the most contentious of the three types of codes. Further, it is accepted that Part 6 rule-making (and industry rule-making more generally) faces its greatest test in the consumer protection arena due to scepticism that industry actors have the capacity to act in anything but their own interests, such as profit maximisation.

[68] ACIF, *Guideline: Development of Telecommunications Industry Operations* Codes (March 1998) 6; ACIF, *Guideline: Development of Self-Regulatory Telecommunications Industry Consumer Codes of Practice* (January 1998) 1.

[69] ACIF, *Guideline: Development of Telecommunications Industry Operations Codes*, above n 68, 5–6.

[70] See, eg, Horrocks and Hill, above n 45, 529.

[71] See, eg, Communications Alliance, *Industry Code C625: Handling of Life Threatening and Unwelcome Communications* (2017).

[72] See, eg, ACIF, *Industry Code C609: Priority Assistance for Life Threatening Medical Conditions* (2007).

[73] See, eg, Communications Alliance, *Industry Code C564: Mobile Phone Base Station Deployment* (2011).

[74] See, eg, K Bowrey, *Law and Internet Cultures* (Cambridge, Cambridge University Press, 2005) 47–79.

C. Procedural and Institutional Legitimacy, Responsiveness and Their Criteria

The book evaluates the three case studies to determine if the Part 6 rule-making process was procedurally and institutionally legitimate. It does not assess, beyond the brief review that follows, whether the formal and substantive requirements of the rule of law have been met.

The formal aspect of the rule of law involves the idea that law should, among other things, be clearly prescribed prior to its application. Prospective prescription is seen as essential because it reduces the potential for arbitrariness.[75] It provides citizens and others with the opportunity to learn the rules that are recognised by the state as law and to alter their behaviour in order to comply with them.[76] It also limits the discretion of those tasked with applying the law.[77] It requires judges and officials to act 'within the powers' they have been given by the legislature.[78] In addition, the formal aspect of the rule of law encompasses the notion of non-discrimination, which dictates that no person is above the law.[79] Everyone, regardless of social status, is subject to the law. The law may differentiate between different groups and types of situations. However, 'like cases' must be 'treated alike'.[80]

The substantive aspect of the rule of law, on the other hand, focuses on the content of the law.[81] Its principal concern is whether the substance of the law conforms to wider notions of justice and morality. Dworkin's 'rights conception', for example, exemplifies a substantive rule of law approach; law is 'just' only to the extent it recognises and is consistent with the moral and political rights of the citizens who are subject to it.[82] However, for the reasons explained below, neither the codes of practice that Part 6 rule-making generates nor the process itself raises concerns that the formal and substantive facets of the rule of law are not satisfied.

Brief analysis of the three codes of practice that are the focus of the book and other consumer codes that have been registered under Part 6 reveals that they easily meet the rule of law's formal demands. They are, among other things, prescriptive. Indeed, a particular concern of Part 6 rule-making expressed by some within the telecommunications sector is that they are needlessly so. Whether codes contain superfluous and unnecessarily inflexible rules cannot be considered

[75] Kingsford Smith, 'Beyond the Rule of Law?', above n 28, 452.

[76] Craig, above n 27, 467; RH Fallon, Jr, '"The Rule of Law" as a Concept in Constitutional Discourse' (1997) 97 *Columbia Law Review* 1, 14.

[77] Jowell, above n 27, 18.

[78] ibid 18.

[79] ibid 19; Westerman, above n 30, 85; Kingsford Smith, 'Beyond the Rule of Law?', above n 28, 452.

[80] Jowell, above n 27, 19.

[81] See, Craig, above n 27, 477–85; Fallon, above n 76, 21–24.

[82] See, eg, R Dworkin, *Taking Rights Seriously* (London, Duckworth, 1977).

here but, as will be seen in the three case studies used to explore the question of procedural and institutional legitimacy, detailed rules were often used as a technique to resolve disputes between participants on the working committees that drafted them. Moreover, the codes of practice do not discriminate between industry participants. They impose various obligations on different industry players but they do not differentiate between similarly situated entities. The ethos of the 'level playing field', which pervades the regulation of the telecommunications sector, may explain the absence of any discrimination between industry participants. The precise cause of non-discrimination does not need to be determined here, however. The key point is that the rules the codes of practice contain fulfil the formal requirements of the rule of law.

Substantive rule of law concerns also do not arise. The Telecommunications Act 1997 (Cth) (the Act) specifies numerous public policy objectives that the process of Part 6 rule-making is designed to achieve. There are too many objectives to list all of them here. However, the three principal goals specified by the Act are the promotion of the long-term interests of end-users of 'carriage services' or of services provided by means of carriage services; the efficiency and international competitiveness of the Australian telecommunications industry; and the availability of accessible and affordable carriage services that enhance the welfare of Australians.[83] Consumer and public interest advocates involved in the process of Part 6 rule-making have repeatedly argued that industry involvement in rule-making has made promotion of the long-term interests of end-users and the enhancement of the welfare of Australians much harder to achieve. However, concerns about the effectiveness of Part 6 rule-making raise a series of questions that are different from the concerns that underpin the many substantive conceptions of the rule of law. The latter are directed to the issue of whether the broad (and rather nebulous) objectives of the Act are unfair. However, scholarly criticism of Part 6 rule-making has not been directed toward the fairness of the aims of the Act. Rather, criticism has been directed to the means by which those ends are to be achieved, ie whether the process of Part 6 rule-making conforms to the procedural and institutional values of law.

As Part 6 rule-making appears to satisfy the formal and substantive requirements of the rule of law, the issue which has generated controversy is the focus of this book: whether the process followed by the Communications Alliance to develop the three consumer codes of practice discussed in the case studies was procedurally and institutionally legitimate. This question is determined in the book by reference to the four principles of deliberation, impartiality, transparency and accountability. These are the principles, it is argued in chapter three, that give procedural and institutional legitimacy to rule-making by legislatures and

[83] Telecommunications Act 1997 (Cth) s 3(1).

administrative bodies. If they underpin the institutional design of legislative and administrative bodies that formulate what is readily recognised as law and the procedures by which it is made, so too should they ground rule-making by industry bodies. However, it is recognised that Part 6 rule-making challenges the traditional understanding of impartiality, transparency and accountability. As discussed in chapter three, many of the mechanisms that are thought to ensure that rule-making by legislatures and administrative bodies is procedurally and institutionally legitimate are absent from Part 6 rule-making. For example, the public cannot attend meetings of the working committees of the Communications Alliance, which are not transcribed or published. It has no rights to access minutes and other documentation exchanged between working committee members. No participant in the code development process is impartial. The courts do not review the codes of practice or the process by which they are made. Parliament does not scrutinise their content and the public is not given an opportunity to vote for or against them. It is therefore argued in chapter eight that Part 6 rule-making necessitates some adjustment to the formulation of these principles to accommodate the aims of proceduralized rule-making while also remaining compatible with the rationales supporting their use in traditional law-making processes. It is for that reason that transparency is adapted to mean the disclosure by industry to working committee members, including consumer and public interest representatives, and others of information necessary to hold industry to account. Impartiality is reframed as a question of whether industry genuinely considered the relevant concerns of others before it reached its decisions. It is suggested that accountability should be a search for 'real-time' mechanisms that achieve the same goal of accountability in traditional rule-making—ensuring that industry answers for its decisions or explains itself to others—rather than a quest for processes that operate retrospectively.[84] Along with deliberation, which retains its traditional definition—the exchange of 'information and opinions' and taking into account 'public regarding reasons',[85] these three principles (as modified) are applied to evaluate if Part 6 rule-making was procedurally and institutionally legitimate.

The four principles of deliberation, impartiality, transparency and accountability (as defined) are also used to evaluate the 'responsiveness' of the Part 6 rule-making process for reasons that are more complex. There are now many well-developed theories of responsive regulation.[86] However, the argument made here, which is developed in detail in chapter nine, is that what makes the process of industry rule-making responsive (and therefore more likely to be effective in

[84] Industry's compliance with code rules is an additional criterion of accountability but is outside the scope of this book.

[85] A Vermeule, *Mechanisms of Democracy: Institutional Design Writ Small* (Oxford, Oxford University Press, 2007) 5.

[86] See, eg, the sources cited in nn 12–17.

meeting public policy goals set by the state) is better understood (at least in a domestic, state-based context) as an alternative formulation of the question of procedural and institutional legitimacy. In other words, it is suggested that, in the 'decentred' state, the concept of responsiveness has subsumed the concerns that procedural and institutional legitimacy is intended to address. If that is correct, then the principles of deliberation, impartiality, transparency and accountability (as amended) illuminate the meaning of responsiveness, which has not yet been clearly defined in the regulatory literature. Applying these principles has merit for two reasons. First, it acknowledges the objectives and limitations of law, as it is conceived in this new regulatory state. Second, and more importantly, it binds the objectives of regulatory regimes set by the state—the desire to render disparate systems less insular to each other—and law's indirect methods of procedural regulation to certain normative principles in a way that permits decentred regulation to retain its moral frame. In developing this argument, no one theory of democracy is endorsed. Rather, it is suggested that the principles of deliberation, impartiality, transparency and accountability resonate in each of a number of theories that could provide a normative basis for law in the 'fragmented' state. If responsiveness is understood in this way, the principles of procedural and institutional legitimacy, often seen as barriers to the achievement of regulatory goals, are transformed into important regulatory tools that facilitate the overall effectiveness of regulatory systems.

D. The Wider Context of Industry Rule-making

Industry rule-making is, of course, not limited to the innovative means of rule-formulation envisaged by strategists of proceduralization. Industry actors also draft rules when they engage in purely voluntary self-regulation within the geographical boundaries of nation states. Moreover, industry actors formulate rules and other norms in the transnational sphere[87] where, for example, they set technical[88] and other[89] standards for global markets; and establish governance

[87] For an overview, see C Scott, F Cafaggi and L Senden, 'The Conceptual and Constitutional Challenge of Transnational Private Regulation' (2011) 38 *Journal of Law and Society* 1; F Cafaggi, 'New Foundations of Transnational Private Regulation' (2011) 38 *Journal of Law and Society* 20.

[88] See, eg, T Büthe and W Mattli, *The New Global Rulers: The Privatization of Regulation in the World* (Princeton, Princeton University Press, 2011); T Büthe, 'Engineering Uncontestedness? The Origins and Institutional Development of the International Electrotechnical Commission (IEC) (2010) 12 *Business and Politics* 1; H Schepel, *The Constitution of Private Governance: Product Standards in the Regulation of Integrating Markets* (Oxford, Hart Publishing, 2005).

[89] See, eg, KT Hallström, 'ISO Enters the Field of Social Responsibility: Construction and Tension of Global Governance' in GF Schuppert (ed), *Global Governance and the Role of Non-State Actors* (Baden-Baden, Nomos, 2006) 117.

frameworks designed to address worldwide regulatory problems related to matters as diverse as food,[90] financial products and services,[91] consumer protection[92] and the Internet.[93]

However, these forms of industry rule-making fall outside the scope of this book because the rules they generate ordinarily acquire authority in a way that is fundamentally different from the rules that are the product of the type of proceduralized rule-making that is of interest here. When the state authorises industry to assume responsibility for its rule-making functions, it incorporates the industry-drafted rules into its existing body of law—law which has authority because it can be enforced via the mechanisms of the state. Rules drafted by industry actors in purely self-regulatory and transnational contexts, on the other hand, typically acquire authority from 'sociological legitimacy'—their acceptance by members of society[94] or relevant 'legitimacy communities'.[95] Acceptance turns on a variety of factors, including, for example, reasons of pragmatism, morality, other normative values or cognition.[96] Unlike legal legitimacy, sociological legitimacy is a wholly 'empirical phenomenon'.[97]

Where the state actively incorporates purely voluntary self-regulatory and transnationally-made rules into its law, questions of their legal legitimacy and coherence with law also arise. In those situations, the criteria of deliberation, impartiality, transparency and accountability (as refined) may provide a useful way of thinking about whether voluntary self-regulatory and transnational rule-making processes satisfy those aspects of the rule of law. Decoupled from the mechanisms that are said to confer procedural and institutional legitimacy in traditional rule-making contexts, they make it at least theoretically possible for a wide range of mechanisms—mechanisms that may be present in the purely

[90] See, eg, N Hachez and J Wouters, 'A Glimpse at the Democratic Legitimacy of Private Standards: Assessing the Public Accountability of GlobalG.A.P' (2011) 14 *Journal of International Economic Law* 677.

[91] F Cafaggi, 'New Foundations of Transnational Private Regulation' (2011) 38 *Journal of Law and Society* 20, 33; GV Rauterberg and A Verstein, 'Assessing Transnational Private Regulation of the OTC Derivatives Market: ISDA, the BBA and the Future of Financial Reform (2013) 54 *Virginia Journal of International Law* 9; J Biggins and C Scott, 'Public-Private Relation in a Transnational Private Regulatory Regime: ISDA, the State and OTC Derivatives Market Reform' (2012) 13 *European Business Organisation Law Review* 309.

[92] C Scott, 'Beyond Taxonomies of Private Authority in Transnational Regulation' (2012) 13 *German Law Journal* 1329, 1332–33.

[93] See, eg, I Brown (ed), *Handbook on Governance of the Internet* (Cheltenham, Edward Elgar, 2013).

[94] A Peters, L Koechlin and GF Zinkernagel, 'Non-state Actors as Standard Setters: Framing the Issue in an Interdisciplinary Fashion' in A Peters, L Koechlin, T Föster and GF Zinkernagel, *Non-state Actors as Standard Setters* (Cambridge, Cambridge University Press, 2009) 1, 18.

[95] See J Black, 'Constructing and Contesting Legitimacy and Accountability in Polycentric Regulatory Regimes' (2008) 2 *Regulation & Governance* 137.

[96] See, eg, MC Suchman, 'Managing Legitimacy: Strategic and Institutional Approaches' (1995) 20 *Academy of Management Review* 571; Black, 'Constructing and Contesting Legitimacy and Accountability in Polycentric Regulatory Regimes', above n 95, 144; D Casey and C Scott, 'The Crystallization of Regulatory Norms' (2011) 38 *Journal of Law and Society* 76, 87–88; P Paiement, 'Paradox and Legitimacy in Transnational Legal Pluralism' (2013) 4 *Transnational Legal Theory* 197, 211–17.

[97] Casey and Scott, above n 96, 87.

voluntary self-regulatory and transnational spheres—to facilitate the achievement of procedural and institutional legitimacy. Detailed empirical study of those rule-making processes is also needed in order to begin to evaluate if they can be procedurally and institutionally legitimate as a matter of practice, but such a study awaits another day.

II. Terminology

A. Consumer and Public Interests

The concepts of consumer interest and public interest are referred to throughout the book and require some explanation. They are treated as two distinct concepts because they reflect more accurately what is at stake in Part 6 rule-making—the potential displacement of either or both consumer and public interests by telecommunications providers (thereby providing a more useful analytical tool). The accommodation of both interests also sets a high standard that must be satisfied if the codes of practice produced by the Part 6 process are to be recognised as 'law'. It is acknowledged that 'the consumer interest' is increasingly equated with 'the public interest' by governments in a number of areas of regulation[98] and there has been academic criticism that the distinction between 'the consumer interest' and 'the public interest' is not as stark as is frequently argued.[99] However, the view taken here is that industry rule-making must accommodate both the interests of consumers—buyers of goods and services offered by commercial providers participating in the market[100]—and the interests of citizens living in a wider political, social, and cultural community[101] if it is to be deemed legitimate.

The meaning of each term as used in the book is explained below.

i. Consumer Interest

A wide definition of consumer interest (any measure needed to preserve the purchasing autonomy of consumers) is adopted. Its breadth reflects the difficulty of

[98] See, eg, M Schudson, 'The Troubling Equivalence of Citizen and Consumer' (2006) 608 *The Annals of the American Academy of Political and Social Science* 193; S Livingston and P Lunt, 'Representing Citizens and Consumers in Media and Communications Regulation' (2007) 611 *The Annals of the American Academy of Political and Social Science* 51; S Livingston, P Lunt and L Miller, 'Citizens and Consumers: Discursive Debates During and After the Communications Act 2003' (2007) 29 *Media, Culture & Society* 613.

[99] See generally D Lewinsohn-Zamir, 'Consumer Preferences, Citizen Preferences and the Provision of Public Goods' (1998) 108 *Yale Law Journal* 377.

[100] C Scott and J Black, *Cranston's Consumers and the Law* 3rd edn (London, Butterworths, 2000) 8.

[101] C Graham, *Regulating Public Utilities: A Constitutional Approach* (Oxford, Hart Publishing, 2000) 87; G Born and T Prosser, 'Culture and Consumerism: Citizenship, Public Service Broadcasting and the BBC's Fair Trading Obligations' (2001) 64 *MLR* 657, 671.

identifying with a degree of accuracy the interests of all consumers in the market because of the assumptions of diversity and individuality inherent in the consumer interest paradigm. Consumers may be rational[102] and self-interested,[103] seeking to maximise utility in the short-term,[104] but they are not homogenous. They have different interests and demands, which are often in conflict with those of other consumers.[105] Whatever enables consumer A to enjoy a 'good'[106] product or service may be completely different to what consumer B wants or needs. However, the definition also underlines the fact that consumers share some interests;[107] interests that manifest themselves in competition and consumer protection law and policy. Competition law may seek to safeguard economic efficiency, a choice of suppliers and the avoidance of artificially high prices as a result of monopoly or price-fixing.[108] Consumer protection may aim to protect consumers from supplier fraud and require the disclosure of all relevant information prior to purchasing goods and services.[109] However, what they have in common is the preservation of consumer 'sovereignty', the capacity of consumers to freely exercise their preferences in the market.[110]

ii. Public Interest

The public interest is defined as the ability of citizens to access and utilise communications services in order to exercise what Marshall has termed their 'social rights of citizenship'—their rights 'to live the life of a civilised being according to the standards prevailing in the society.'[111] The concept is employed in this way because ensuring that all citizens, regardless of their location, income-levels and capacities to hear and speak, can communicate with each other via the telephone has been an underlying rationale for much state-based regulatory activity in the

[102] Scott and Black, above n 100, 2; Iain Ramsay, *Consumer Law and Policy: Text and Materials on Regulating Consumer Markets* 3rd edn (Oxford, Hart Publishing, 2012) 47.

[103] Lewinsohn-Zamir, above n 99, 378.

[104] Ramsay, *Consumer Law and Policy*, above n 102, 9.

[105] Graham, above n 101, 88; Ramsay, *Consumer Law and Policy*, above n 102, 14. See also Scott and Black, above n 100, 13.

[106] Graham, above n 101, 88.

[107] Scott and Black, above n 100, 14–15.

[108] See, eg, E Buttigieg, *Competition Law: Safeguarding the Consumer Interest: A Comparative Analysis of US Antitrust Law and EC Competition Law* (Alphen aan den Rijn, Kluwer Law International, 2009).

[109] On consumer protection law generally in the UK, see Ramsay, *Consumer Law and Policy*, above n 102, and Scott and Black, above n 100; in Australia, see, eg, S Corones and PH Clarke, *Australian Consumer Law: Commentary and Materials* 5th edn (Sydney, Thomson Reuters (Professional) Australia, 2011).

[110] I Ramsay, 'Consumer Law, Regulatory Capitalism and the "New Learning" in Regulation' (2006) 28 *Sydney Law Review* 9, 13.

[111] L Hitchens, 'Citizen Versus Consumer in the Digital World' in AT Kenyon (ed), *TV Futures: Digital Television Policy in Australia* (Melbourne, Melbourne University Publishing, 2007) 343, 351 (quoting Thomas H Marshall, *Sociology at the Crossroads and Other Essays* (London, Heinemann, 1963) 74).

telecommunications sphere, both in Australia and elsewhere.[112] For example, one of the express objectives of the Telecommunications (Consumer Protection and Service Standards) Act 1999 (Cth) is to 'ensure that standard telephone services and payphones are *reasonably accessible* to *all people* in Australia *on an equitable basis*, wherever they reside or carry on business'.[113] To achieve this end, the communications legislative framework empowers the Minister for Communications and the Arts to mandate that communications providers must supply telephony services and payphones to customers living in rural areas, for example, where it is often uneconomical to provide them.[114] It also empowers the Secretary of the Department of Communications and the Arts to enter into contracts with and make financial grants to private providers and state-owned operators, such as the government business enterprise building and operating the National Broadband Network (NBN) throughout Australia,[115] to ensure standard telephone services and payphones are provided throughout Australia.[116] Telstra, the largest network operator in Australia, is required under the terms of its licence to offer products to and make suitable arrangements for low-income customers,[117] so that they may be able to enjoy a basic level of communications service and remain in contact with others, even though they face financial hardship. Another aim of the Telecommunications (Consumer Protection and Service Standards) Act 1999 (Cth) is for the 'National Relay Service to be *reasonably accessible* to *all persons* in Australia who: (1) are *deaf*; or (ii) have a *hearing and/or speech impairment*; wherever they reside or carry on business.'[118] This objective is fulfilled by the Secretary of the Department of Communications and the Arts entering into contracts with private providers and state-owned operators for the provision of these services, notwithstanding their high costs.[119] The political and civil rights[120] also associated with the notion of citizenship, which is central to any conception of the public interest,[121] have not been a focus of Australian lawmakers when regulating telecommunications.

[112] For an overview of the position in Australia, see A Grant and H Raiche, 'Consumer Protection and Universal Service' in A Grant and D Howarth (eds), *Australian Telecommunications Regulation* 4th edn (Sydney, CCH Australia Ltd, 2012) 386–98. For the positions in the UK and US, see, respectively, MH Ryan and S Cloke, 'Significant Market Power (SMP) and Other Conditions' in M Conradi (ed), *Communications Law Handbook* (Haywards Heath, Bloomsbury Professional, 2009) 86–89; K Lee and J Prime, 'US Telecommunications Law' in I Walden (ed), *Telecommunications Law and Regulation* 4th edn (Oxford, Oxford University Press, 2012) 242–50.

[113] Telecommunications (Consumer Protection and Service Standards) Act 1999 (Cth) s 3 (emphasis added).

[114] ibid pt 2, div 2.

[115] The NBN is an open-access, wholesale-only broadband network.

[116] Telecommunications (Consumer Protection and Service Standards) Act 1999 (Cth) pt 2, div 3.

[117] Carrier Licence Conditions (Telstra Corporation Limited) Declaration 1997 (Cth) cl 22.

[118] Telecommunications (Consumer Protection and Service Standards) Act 1999 (Cth) s 13(d) (emphasis added).

[119] ibid pt 2 div 3.

[120] See, eg, Hitchens, 'Citizen Versus Consumer', above n 111, 351.

[121] See generally M Feintuck, 'Regulatory Rationales Beyond the Economic: In Search of the Public Interest' in R Baldwin, M Cave and M Lodge (eds), *The Oxford Handbook of Regulation* (Oxford, Oxford University Press, 2010) 39.

III. Structure of the Book

The book is divided into three parts.

Part 1 provides the background for the three empirical case studies of Part 6 rule-making that form the heart of the book. Chapter two explores why Part 6 was enacted and frames the regulatory problem that the Commonwealth legislature sought to address by permitting industry to formulate codes of practice. Chapter three explains the rule-making framework of the Communications Alliance. It identifies the principles used to determine if traditional rule-making—rule-making by legislatures and administrative bodies—is procedurally and institutionally legitimate. The chapter then sets out the theoretical challenges raised by industry's reliance on a confidential, consensus model of rule-making to formulate law. The findings of this chapter serve as the hypotheses that will be tested in the three case studies.

Part 2 comprises the empirical study of Part 6 rule-making. Chapter four explains the conceptual approach used to characterise Part 6 rule-making and sets out other background information to assist an understanding of the case studies. The following three chapters focus on the development of three consumer codes of practice prepared by working committees established under the auspices of the Communications Alliance and registered by the ACA or its successor ACMA. They are presented in the order in which they were completed by the relevant working committees. Chapter five concentrates on the Consumer Contracts code,[122] drafted between May and December 2004. Chapter six examines the Information on Accessibility Features for Telephone Equipment code,[123] prepared between April 2004 and November 2005. Chapter seven focuses on the Mobile Premium Services (MPS) code, developed between April 2008 and March 2009. Drawing on Schattschneider's theory of the scope of political conflict,[124] the approach used by Page in his study of the making of statutory instruments by ministers and related government departments in England and Wales,[125] each case study seeks to identify the 'politic'—the 'conflict and controversy'[126]—behind each code. Each looks at the roles and motivations of the various participants of the process, the strategies working committee participants from industry and elsewhere used in an attempt to advance their interests in the process, how conflicts were resolved and the biases (if any) that the rule-making process produced or permitted.

[122] ACIF, *Industry Code ACIF C620: Consumer Contracts* (2005).

[123] ACIF, *Industry Code ACIF C625: Information on Accessibility Features for Telephone Equipment Code* (2005).

[124] EE Schattschneider, *The Semisovereign People: A Realist's View of Democracy in America* (New York, Holt, Rinehart and Winston, 1960).

[125] EC Page, *Governing by Numbers* (Oxford, Hart Publishing, 2001).

[126] ibid 2.

Part 3 provides a substantive analysis of the case studies. Chapter eight evaluates if the process of Part 6 rule-making was procedurally and institutionally legitimate, ie if it satisfied the principles of impartiality, accountability, transparency and deliberation that characterise traditional rule-making. It revisits the meaning of the principles of transparency, impartiality and accountability and suggests that they need to be modified for the purpose of evaluating the procedural and institutional legitimacy of industry rule-making. It asserts that the definitions proposed for each of the three principles are compatible with the rationales supporting their requirements in traditional law-making and accommodate the aims of proceduralized rule-making, and explores why all four principles of procedural and institutional legitimacy were met. It is argued that the 'politic' that Part 6 rule-making generated, in conjunction with certain elements of the Communications Alliance's rule-making framework, ensured that consumer and public interests were at a minimum taken into account. Hence the codes it produced can be legitimately integrated into the wider system of case law, statutes and regulations that comprise the 'law.'

Chapter nine considers whether the process of Part 6 rule-making was responsive to the 'practices and norms'[127] of the various stakeholders. It is argued that questions of responsiveness should be determined by reference to the four principles of procedural and institutional legitimacy, as defined in chapter eight, to facilitate the achievement of the 'collective goals of the community'[128] set by the state. The means used to satisfy these principles will, of course, be different from the mechanisms that are used by the state to legitimate traditional legislative and administrative rule-making. However, responsiveness and legitimacy share in common the rationales that underpin the four principles of procedural and institutional legitimacy. Chapter nine concludes that the process of Part 6 rule-making was responsive to the needs of consumer, public interest and private sector stakeholders for the same reasons the process was procedurally and institutionally legitimate: the politic of Part 6 rule-making and certain elements of the rule-making framework of the Communications Alliance.

Chapter ten sets out the 'state of play' with respect to our knowledge of activating and sustaining legitimate and responsive industry rule-making. It discusses the mechanisms observed in the three case studies that contributed to the procedural and institutional legitimacy of the Part 6 rule-making process and its responsiveness to the public interest and the interests of all relevant stakeholders. It identifies a number of indicia that suggest when industry rule-making is more likely to be procedurally and institutionally legitimate and responsive. It also highlights a number of issues that require further empirical investigation.

[127] Parker and Braithwaite, above n 1, 128.
[128] Yeung, above n 5, 49.

Part I

Background to Case Studies

2

The Adoption of Part 6 of the Telecommunications Act 1997 (Cth)

I. Introduction

This chapter explores why Part 6 of the Telecommunications Act 1997 (Cth) (Part 6), which permits 'sections of the telecommunications industry' to draft and seek the registration of codes of practice dealing with a variety of matters relating to their 'telecommunications activities' with the Australian Communications and Media Authority (ACMA), was adopted. The history of Part 6 is traced for three reasons. First, it facilitates the identification of the regulatory problem that Australian policy-makers and legislators sought to address by enacting Part 6. Second, it enables an assessment of whether policy-makers and legislators were seeking to act 'responsively' when addressing the regulatory problem; and if so, for what reasons. Third, some of the events that led to the adoption of Part 6 also explain why consumer and public interest groups have always been directly involved in the development of industry codes by working committees of the Communications Alliance even though Part 6 does not require their direct participation. As discussed in chapter eight, the participation of consumer and public interest groups was one of several factors that contributed to the procedural and institutional legitimacy of the Part 6 process in the three case studies explored in chapters five, six and seven. Given their participation was a significant factor in the legitimacy of the process, and it is suggested in chapter ten that a history of some form of collaboration between industry, regulators and consumer and public interest groups is an indicator of when industry rule-making is more likely to be responsive, it is important to understand how consumer and public interest groups came to be involved in industry rule-making in the telecommunications sector.

Using publicly available materials,[1] the chapter explains the development of Part 6 by answering four of the questions that have become central to regulatory

[1] DCITA would not provide copies of key consultation papers and internal 'option papers' relating to Part 6 prepared by DOCA.

impact analysis[2] and to 'good' regulatory design in the regulatory literature:[3] (1) what was the problem which policy-makers and legislatures were seeking to address?; (2) what were the policy goals policy-makers and legislatures were trying to achieve?; (3) what were the regulatory options available to them to resolve the underlying regulatory problem?; and (4) what were the benefits and costs of these options?[4] Section II of the chapter provides the background information needed to answer these four questions. Section III of the chapter addresses each of them. It is argued that Part 6 was enacted because policy-makers and legislators believed it would encourage competition in a sector that was technically complex, undergoing rapid change and soon to be fully liberalised. They also believed that Part 6 would simultaneously protect residential and small business consumers from the types of abusive market practices manifest in the 'Casualties of Telecom' affair, which had left consumers distrustful of the customer complaints handling and privacy policies of Telecom,[5] the then government-owned, duopoly provider of fixed line telecommunications services in Australia. The chapter concludes by arguing that the reasoning behind the adoption of Part 6 shares much in common with arguments made in favour of industry rule-making by regulatory scholars. However, it also departs from the philosophy of responsiveness that underpins the arguments of these scholars in significant ways, and these differences have contributed to complaints about the Part 6 process made by consumer and public interest groups.

II. Background Information

Section II of this chapter begins by briefly describing the steps taken by the Australian government between 1989 and 1997 to liberalise the telecommunications sector and its rationale for introducing competition. It then discusses the recommendations of the Independent Committee of Inquiry on National Competition Policy,[6] and the response of the Commonwealth government and each of the Australian States and Territories to it. Finally, it explains the Casualties of Telecom (CoT) affair, which occurred between 1992 and 1994 and during the transition from a closed telecommunications market serviced by monopoly providers to a

[2] See, eg, R Deighton-Smith, 'Regulatory Impact Assessment in Australia: A Survey of 20 Years of RIA Implementation' in C Kirkpatrick and D Parker (eds), *Regulatory Impact Assessment: Towards Better Regulation?* (Cheltenham, Edward Elgar, 2007) 145.

[3] See, eg, N Gunningham and D Sinclair, 'Designing Environmental Policy' in N Gunningham and P Grabosky, *Smart Regulation: Designing Environmental Policy* (Oxford, Oxford University Press, 1998) ch 6; Arie Freiberg, *Regulation in Australia* (Sydney, The Federation Press, 2017) ch 5.

[4] Part 6 was promulgated before regulatory impact analysis became the norm at the Commonwealth level in Australia.

[5] Since 1 July 1995, Telecom has traded under the name Telstra.

[6] Independent Committee of Inquiry into Competition Policy in Australia, *National Competition Policy* (August 1993).

fully liberalised market with multiple competitors. Each of these events significantly influenced the decision to adopt Part 6 and will be referred to throughout the analysis in section III of the chapter. The decision of the Australian government to liberalise the telecommunications sector was not unique. Other countries such as the US and UK had liberalised their telecommunications markets well before Australia. However, Australia was one of the first countries to respond to the regulatory challenges of market liberalisation by permitting industry participants to engage in rule-making. An understanding of the particular political circumstances in Australia that led to the decision to adopt Part 6 is therefore important.

A. Market Liberalisation

i. Chronology

Liberalisation of the Australian telecommunications sector began in the late 1980s when the government introduced competition into the markets for value-added services, private network services, customer equipment and cable installation.[7] Until then, all telecommunications systems were installed, operated and provided by three government-owned monopoly providers: Telecom, the Overseas Telecommunications Commission (OTC) and AUSSAT Pty Limited (AUSSAT). Telecom provided all domestic telecommunications services via a fixed telecommunications network. OTC provided all international telecommunications services. AUSSAT owned and operated a satellite used to provide domestic satellite services.[8]

In November 1990, the government announced it would introduce competition in all other telecommunications markets.[9] However, because the task of moving from a monopoly market to a fully competitive market was so complex, competition was phased in over a six-year period between 1 July 1991 and 30 June 1997. During this period, the government permitted only two entities to install and operate fixed networks: the Australian and Overseas Telecommunications Corporation Limited (AOTC) and Optus (now SingTel Optus). The AOTC resulted from the merger of OTC and Telecom in 1992.[10] Initially, it traded under the name of Telecom, becoming known as Telstra in 1995.[11] Following a competitive tender process, a privately-owned company, Optus, was granted a licence, the award of

[7] See generally Minister for Transport and Communications, G Evans, *Australian Telecommunications Services: A New Framework: Summary* (25 May 1988).

[8] H Raiche, 'The Policy Context' in A Grant (ed), *Australian Telecommunications Regulation* 3rd edn (Sydney, University of New South Wales Press, 2004) 1, 2–4.

[9] Minister for Transport and Communications, K Beazley, *Micro-Economic Reform: Progress Telecommunications* (November 1990).

[10] Minister for Transport and Communications, G Richardson, 'New Era in Telecommunications Set to Begin on 1 Feb' (Media Release, 1/92, 31 January 1992) 1.

[11] R Joseph, 'Politics and Telecommunications Deregulation' (1996) 46(1) *Telecommunication Journal of Australia* 9, 9.

which was conditional on the purchase of AUSSAT, on 19 November 1991.[12] Notwithstanding the duopoly in fixed networks, other privately-owned companies were allowed to lease capacity from Telecom and Optus, and sell services to the general public in competition with them.[13] In addition, three entities were authorised by the government to install and operate terrestrial mobile networks: Telecom, Optus and Vodafone (now Vodafone Hutchison Australia). Vodafone was awarded its licence in December 1992 and commenced its operations in September 1993.

On 1 July 1997, the exclusive rights of Telstra, Optus and Vodafone came to an end. Subject to complying with the provisions of the Telecommunications Act 1997 (Cth), anyone is now permitted to enter the market, roll out telecommunications networks and provide telecommunications services and customer equipment.

ii. Rationale

The decision to liberalise all facets of the telecommunications market was driven by a number of factors. It is not necessary to detail all of them here.[14] However, chief among them was acceptance of the view that the communication needs of Australian citizens and businesses would be better served in the future by a competitive market. At the time, countries on whom Australia modelled itself, such as the US and the UK, had already rejected the premise that the provision of telecommunications infrastructure, services and related equipment was a 'natural monopoly', and had embraced market competition in the belief that it would deliver a greater diversity of services that were cheaper and of higher quality. Moreover, the liberalisation of the telecommunications sector formed part of a wider political agenda to make Australia more competitive internationally by deregulating core sectors of the economy.

B. The Hilmer Report

In August 1993, the Independent Committee of Inquiry on National Competition Policy, chaired by Frederick Hilmer, published a highly influential report (the Hilmer report) that made a series of recommendations about the steps the Commonwealth, State and Territory governments could take to fulfil the objective of formulating a new integrated national competition policy. The report broadly

[12] Minister for Transport and Communications, K Beazley, 'Government Selects Optus Communications as Second Carrier' (Media Release, 68/91, 19 November 1991) 1.

[13] See, eg, *Micro-Economic Reform: Progress Telecommunications*, above n 9, 12–13.

[14] For a comprehensive explanation, see Joseph, above n 11, 9; 'The Redefinition of Australian Telecommunications Policy: An Historical Overview' (1996) 46(2) *Telecommunication Journal of Australia* 51; 'Analysing the Telecommunications Deregulation Process in Australia' (1996) 46(3) *Telecommunication Journal of Australia* 49.

defined 'competition policy' to encompass 'all policy dealing with the extent and nature of competition in the economy'.[15] Competition policy encompassed the rules limiting the anti-competitive conduct of firms as well as all regulatory restrictions limiting competition in statutes and regulations. Regulatory restrictions included government-owned monopolies and mandatory licensing requirements restricting market entry. To ensure that regulatory restrictions were kept to a minimum, the report argued that government had to satisfy a 'public interest' test[16] before any regulatory restriction could be imposed. In other words, the government could overcome a presumption that a restriction was unnecessary only if the public interest test was satisfied. The report recognised that regulation may be necessary to protect consumer welfare, for example; however, any regulatory restriction imposed could be 'no more than necessary in the public interest'. The benefits of a restriction also had to outweigh the 'likely costs'. Although the Commonwealth, State and Territory governments did not embrace all of the suggested reforms of the Hilmer report,[17] they did accept that regulatory restrictions should meet a public interest test.[18]

The Hilmer report did not expressly mention or consider industry rule-making or other alternatives to traditional government regulation in its report. Nevertheless, the consideration and potential use of alternative regulatory mechanisms was a logical consequence of the Hilmer committee's recommendations.[19] Indeed, the use of alternative mechanisms of regulation was supported by the Commonwealth, and each of the Australian States and Territories in the agreements implementing the recommendations of the Hilmer report.[20] If the same or better results could be achieved by means less intrusive and costly to the marketplace, they were preferable. The logic of the Hilmer report dictated that alternative mechanisms had to be followed in those circumstances. Otherwise, any proposed government regulation would be more than necessary and would fall foul of the public interest test.

C. The Casualties of Telecom

The so-called 'Casualties of Telecom' (CoT) consisted of a group of small business enterprises that were customers of Telecom. They alleged that intermittent

[15] *National Competition Policy*, above n 6, 6.

[16] The Hilmer report does not define the term 'public interest.'

[17] Industry Commission to the Council of Australian Governments, *The Growth and Revenue Implications of Hilmer and Related Reforms: A Report of the Industry Commission to the Council of Australian Governments* (March 1995) 512–13.

[18] See COAG, Competition Principles Agreement (11 April 1995) cl 5(1).

[19] C Hardy, M McAuslan and J Madden, 'Competition Policy and Communications Convergence' (1994) 17 *University of New South Wales Law Journal* 156, 168 (citing the federal Minister for Consumer Affairs, J McHugh's address 'Consumers and the Reform of Australia's Utilities: Passing on the Benefits', 18 March 1994).

[20] See, eg, COAG, above n 18, cl 5(9)(e).

network faults made it difficult for their own customers to contact them. The types of faults experienced varied but included false busy signals, disconnection of calls when the small businesses answered and dropped calls during conversations. The small businesses also complained that their phones often would not ring even though their customers were trying to call them. Despite repeated complaints to Telecom, the network faults were not fixed. Concerns were not limited to network faults, however. Serious concerns emerged as to how Telecom dealt internally with customer complaints; one complainant had experienced problems with Telecom's network over a 10-year period.[21]

The Australian Telecommunications Authority (Austel), which was responsible for regulating the Australian telecommunications sector at the time, initially played the role of an 'honest broker' between Telecom and the CoT. However, after nearly 12 months had passed without success, it formally started to investigate whether Telecom had fundamental network problems and difficulties with its complaints handling procedures in June 1993.[22] Initial progress in Austel's investigation was slow due to a lack of cooperation from Telecom. However, following a Senate Estimates hearing[23] held in early September 1993 during which Telecom's behaviour was severely criticised and cries for a Senate inquiry into the CoT cases were made, Telecom started to address the problems.[24] Around that time, Telecom's fixed line customers were also being asked to pre-select either Telecom or Optus as their preferred long-distance carrier.[25] In an effort to fend off a Senate inquiry into the CoT cases[26] and to deflect bad publicity, Telecom belatedly announced a 'six-point plan', including the development of new complaints handling procedures, to address the concerns of CoT complainants.

When the 'six-point plan' was announced, the general manager of Telecom's consumer division publicly admitted that its complaints handling procedures no longer had the support of the public and stated that Telecom staff could not address the problems by themselves.[27] Telecom then sought the advice of the newly appointed Telecommunications Industry Ombudsman (TIO), who began work on 1 December 1993, on its complaints handling procedures.[28] Telecom also

[21] For further detail of the principal complaints made by the CoT and the duration of their difficulties, see Austel, *The CoT Cases: Austel's Findings and Recommendations* (April 1994) 27–48.

[22] ibid 49–56, 92.

[23] During estimates hearings, members of committees of the Australian Senate review proposed government expenditure.

[24] S Lewis, 'COT Cases Return to Haunt Telecom', *The Australian Financial Review* (Sydney), 10 September 1993, 4.

[25] See, eg, I Willox, 'Public Bludgeoned in Phone Ads War', *The Age* (Melbourne), 2 September 1993, 28; R Burbury, 'High Stakes, With Our Ears as Trophies', *Sydney Morning Herald* (Sydney), 30 July 1993, 8.

[26] B Potter, 'Telecom Acts to End Complaints', *The Age* (Melbourne), 17 September 1993, 19.

[27] B Potter, 'Telecom Says It Is Working Hard to Remedy Deficiencies', *The Age* (Melbourne), 22 September 1993, 23.

[28] ibid.

appointed accounting firm Coopers & Lybrand to review its existing procedures.[29] It produced a report in November 1993. Fundamentally, the report found that existing procedures did not meet basic requirements of adequacy, reasonableness and fairness.[30] Austel published its own damning report into the CoT cases on 13 April 1994 but elected not to take enforcement action. Instead, it relied on the revised and detailed customer complaints guidelines prepared by Telecom with input from Coopers & Lybrand, the TIO and itself, with a request to Telecom to update it regularly on the implementation of the additional measures called for in the Coopers & Lybrand report.

While it was investigating the underlying causes of the CoT complaints, Austel discovered evidence that Telecom had been recording phone calls of CoT customers without their consent. Despite denying claims early on, Telecom admitted the truth of the allegations to the newly appointed Minister for Communications, Michael Lee, in early January 1994.[31] Telecom's confession provoked a number of responses. First, the Privacy Commissioner, who was responsible for monitoring compliance with the Privacy Act 1988 (Cth),[32] and the TIO became involved.[33] Second, Telecom voluntarily sought input from two consumer organisations about its monitoring and recording guidelines.[34] Third, and perhaps most importantly, consumer privacy was placed firmly on the political agenda. Within days of Telecom's admission, Minister Lee asked the Attorney-General to determine whether Telecom had breached provisions of the then Telecommunications (Interception) Act 1979 (Cth), which prohibited the interception of communications carried over telecommunications networks. In addition, Lee requested Telecom review its internal procedures to avoid a recurrence of unauthorised recording and monitoring.[35] Lee was also concerned about the underlying weaknesses of the regulatory regime in respect of the privacy of telecommunications consumers and directed significant political energy to these issues. The Attorney-General was later asked to evaluate if the Telecommunications (Interception) Act 1979 (Cth) needed to be amended in light of the CoT cases.[36] Lee also pushed Optus and Vodafone to adopt monitoring and recording guidelines similar to the revised guidelines adopted by Telecom.[37]

[29] B Potter, 'Telecom Rapped Again on Disputes', *The Age* (Melbourne), 29 September 1993, 24; S Lewis, 'Telecom Draws More Fire From Austel', *The Australian Financial Review* (Sydney), 29 September 1993, 4.

[30] B Potter, 'Telecom under Fire over Complaints', *The Age* (Melbourne), 25 November 1993, 6.

[31] A Davies and M Riley, 'Police Asked to Rule on Telecom Phone Taps', *Sydney Morning Herald* (Sydney), 2 February 1994, 5.

[32] In 1994, the provisions of the Privacy Act 1988 (Cth) did not extend to Telecom.

[33] M Dwyer, 'Telecom Hit by Bugging Claims', *The Australian Financial Review* (Sydney), 6 January 1994, 1.

[34] 'Telecom Australia Tightens Up Privacy and Monitoring Rules', *Telecomworldwide M2 Communications*, 9 May 1994.

[35] Commonwealth, *Parliamentary Debates*, House of Representatives, 21 September 1994, 1263, 1264 (M Lee, Minister for Communications and the Arts).

[36] Davies and Riley, above n 31, 5; M Lee, 'Minister Promises Lower Prices and Better Service' (1994) 2 *Telecommunications Law and Policy Review* 103, 103.

[37] S Lewis, 'New Rules for Telecom', *The Australian Financial Review* (Sydney), 2 May 1994, 55.

Despite the active involvement of the Minister, privacy concerns did not abate. Consumer groups and the TIO were actively calling for additional privacy measures to deal with a number of consumer concerns, including calling number display,[38] nuisance calls and telemarketing,[39] brought about by the deployment of digital technology that used calling line identification (CLI) technology. The technology permitted the generation of significant call data[40] which in turn gave the industry scope to introduce new consumer services. Lee responded to the mounting political pressure by requesting Austel to establish a Privacy Advisory Committee (PAC) on 16 August 1994.[41] He identified protection of customer personal information, caller identification and telemarketing as top priorities.[42] The irony of the Minister's request was that Austel had called for the establishment of a Telecommunications Privacy Committee (TPC), which would play the role of central coordinator in a voluntary self-regulatory model, to deal with these issues nearly two years earlier when it published *Telecommunications Privacy: Final Report of Austel's Inquiry into the Privacy Implications of Telecommunications Services* in December 1992. Austel complied with Lee's request, and the terms of reference of PAC[43] prepared by Austel drew heavily on the rule-making framework Austel had recommended in its final report on the TPC, which was never established.

The work of PAC centred on consumer privacy issues, and it was given the task of developing general privacy principles applicable to the sector as a whole and preparing specific guidelines if needed. Moreover, it could offer specific advice on particular codes of conduct as well as give general advice to industry participants and community organisations on code preparation.[44] It was envisaged that the principles and guidelines it prepared would inform the development of any code of practice formulated by industry. The composition of PAC reflected the emphasis on the importance of consulting and discussing the relevant issues between all interested parties that Austel placed in its December 1992 report. PAC consisted of 12 members: four industry members; three consumer and public interest group members; three regulatory body members; and two government department members. In addition, the role of PAC was not to monitor or enforce codes.

[38] Calling number display allows called parties to identify the telephone number from which a call is made.

[39] H Meredith, 'Ombudsman Calls for Telecom Privacy Policy', *The Australian Financial Review* (Sydney), 10 June 1994, 14. See also W Smith, 'Ensuring a Consumer Voice Beyond 1997' (1994) 44(3) *Telecommunications Journal of Australia* 25.

[40] Examples included the phone numbers of the calling and called parties, the time of the call, its length and the path the call took through the relevant carrier's network. Austel, *Telecommunications Privacy: Final Report of Austel's Inquiry into the Privacy Implications of Telecommunications Services* (December 1992) 65.

[41] Minister for Communications and the Arts, M Lee, 'Minister Asks Austel to Set Up Telephone Privacy Body' (Press Release, 16 August 1994).

[42] ibid. See also Lee, 'Minister Promises Lower Prices and Better Service' above n 36, 104.

[43] See Attachment B in Austel Privacy Advisory Committee, *The Protection of Customer Personal Information: Silent Line Customers* (June 1995).

[44] ibid.

Whether Austel or another body would enforce and monitor any codes adopted by industry with input from PAC was not made clear in PAC's terms of reference.[45] Nevertheless, the creation of PAC and its three privacy-related reports[46] mark the end of the CoT affair.

III. The Regulatory Design of Part 6

On 1 August 1995, the then Labor government endorsed industry rule-making in the telecommunications sector and announced its intention to create a legislative framework that would support the development of industry codes.[47] The development of Part 6 took approximately 18 months and went through a number of iterations, some of which were prompted by a change of government on 2 March 1996, and the decision of the newly elected Coalition government to sell its ownership in Telecom's successor, Telstra, before the Telecommunications Act 1997 (Cth) was adopted on 26 March 1997. Throughout the policy-making and legislative process, no comprehensive explanation of the rationale behind Part 6 was ever given. However, with an understanding of the market liberalisation agenda, which enjoyed bi-partisan support; the Hilmer report; and the CoT affair, it is possible to shed some light on why Part 6 was conceived. The regulatory problem that policy-makers and legislatures were seeking to address is considered first, followed by the objectives they hoped to achieve, the regulatory options available to them, and the benefits and costs of each possible option.

A. The Regulatory Problem

Part 6 does not impose any regulatory obligations on the Australian telecommunications industry. Rather, it creates a framework that empowers sections of the industry to draft and register codes of practice to resolve regulatory problems as and when they arise. If industry fails to develop a code that addresses the underlying regulatory problem(s), then ACMA is permitted to intervene and establish an industry standard. Thus in theory, subject to a small number of limitations,[48] Part 6 can be used by industry and ACMA to address a wide array of regulatory

[45] H Raiche, 'A Telecomms Privacy Committee at Last' (1994) 1 *Privacy Law and Policy Reporter* 101.

[46] Austel Privacy Advisory Committee, *The Protection of Customer Personal Information: Silent Customers* (June 1995); Austel Privacy Advisory Committee, *Telemarketing and the Protection of the Privacy of Individuals* (October 1995) and Austel Privacy Advisory Committee, *Calling Number Display: Third Report of the Austel Privacy Advisory Committee* (December 1995).

[47] Minister for Communications and the Arts, M Lee, 'A New Era in Telecommunications' (Press Release, 1 August 1995).

[48] See Telecommunications Act 1997 (Cth) ss 115–16.

problems, including—but not limited to—consumer protection matters. Indeed, as discussed in chapter one, the Communications Alliance has used Part 6 to address network and operational issues on numerous occasions. However, when Part 6 was enacted, it was intended by the government to be used primarily as a mechanism for regulating industry behaviour that could adversely affect residential and small business consumers in a technologically complex and rapidly changing market.[49]

Market failures can, of course, take many forms. However, policy-makers and legislators expected the framework would be used to resolve the types of regulatory difficulties that were manifest in the CoT affair. They also expected the framework would be used to formulate other rules needed in order for consumers to reap the benefits of full competition in the newly liberalised telecommunications market. The CoT affair had highlighted that Telecom had stronger negotiating power than its customers. The imbalance resulted in the provision of poor service, failure to resolve customer complaints and infringements of privacy. Technological developments were also making it easier for Telecom and other carriers to obtain and use private customer information. Strong commercial incentives existed to exploit the new technologies. The possibility of new infrastructure providers entering the market and the anticipated growth of service providers meant problems for consumers would, in all likelihood, only increase in the future. Although not at issue in the CoT affair, the government was also concerned that consumers had the information they needed in order to make 'informed choices' about providers in the newly liberalised telecommunications market.[50] The expectation of policy-makers and legislators that industry would use Part 6 to address these issues explains why the Telecommunications Act 1997 (Cth) lists them[51] as examples of the matters that can be dealt with in an industry code and industry standard.

B. The Policy Goals

When Part 6 was formulated, policy-makers and legislators were confronted by numerous (and arguably) competing policy objectives. Chapter one referred to the three principal goals of the Telecommunications Act 1997 (Cth): promotion of the long-term interests of end-users of carriage services or of services provided by means of carriage services; the efficiency and international competitiveness of the Australian telecommunications industry; and the availability of accessible and affordable carriage services that enhance the welfare of Australians.

[49] See, eg, Commonwealth, *Parliamentary Debates*, House of Representatives, 5 December 1996, 7799, 7801 (W Smith, representing the Minister for Communications and the Arts, Senator Alston).

[50] Minister for Communications and the Arts, M Lee, *Beyond the Duopoly: Australian Telecommunications Policy and Regulation Issues Paper* (September 1994) 65; Minister for Communications and the Arts, M Lee, *Telecommunications Bill 1996, Trade Practices Amendment (Telecommunications) Bill 1996: Exposure Drafts and Commentary* (20 December 1995)19.

[51] Telecommunications Act 1997 (Cth) s 113(3)(a), (d), (f).

However, two other policy objectives, both of which were eventually codified in the Telecommunications Act 1997 (Cth), are particularly relevant to an analysis of the regulatory design of Part 6: the desire to stimulate rigorous competition in the Australian telecommunications market and the need to ensure that consumers were protected from the excesses of the market.[52] As we have seen, since November 1990, when the micro-economic reforms for the telecommunications sector were first announced, the government had been working toward the introduction of full services and infrastructure competition in the sector. The reforms were driven in the belief that competition would improve the quality and reduce the cost of telecommunications services available to Australian consumers. Ending the duopoly that Telecom and Optus enjoyed and permitting other suppliers to enter the market were the principal ways of achieving that goal. However, the government also wanted to protect consumers from the 'disadvantages' that competition may bring.[53] Again, the CoT affair had highlighted that there were significant 'disparities'[54] between consumers and telecommunications providers that could be exploited by market participants to the detriment of residential and small business subscribers, in particular.

C. The Possible Regulatory Options and Their Benefits and Costs

Without access to the internal documentation of the then Department of Communications and the Arts, it is not possible to state definitively which regulatory options policy-makers and legislators considered when Part 6 was drafted. However, without a doubt, their thinking was influenced significantly by the regulatory responses to the CoT affair and the recommendations of the Hilmer report. Evidence of the latter is seen especially in the government's October 1994 Issues Paper entitled *Beyond the Duopoly: Australian Telecommunications Policy and Regulation*, which set forth three 'guiding principles' that were to steer policy-makers when selecting the regulatory mechanisms best able to remedy the identified regulatory problems. All echoed the principles articulated in the Hilmer report. First, regulation was not to be an end in itself. It was a means to achieve a result. Second, reliance on general legal principles as opposed to industry-specific legislation was preferable. Third, if industry-specific legislation was necessary, it had to comply with the principle of 'least cost' to industry.[55] The Issues Paper did not refer expressly to the need to consider alternatives to traditional government regulation, such as industry rule-making. However, as suggested earlier, this principle was a logical consequence of the Hilmer committee's recommendations, and it clearly guided policy-makers and legislators. Consequently, policy-makers and legislators

[52] Telecommunications Act 1997 (Cth) ss 3(2)(d), (h).
[53] *Beyond the Duopoly*, above n 50, 63.
[54] ibid.
[55] ibid 21–24.

would have formulated and evaluated at least four regulatory options: reliance on general consumer protection and privacy legislation; adoption of ex ante industry specific rules; industry self-regulation; and development of the Part 6 framework. Each option is explained and considered below.

i. General Consumer Protection and Privacy Legislation

The first option involved relying on the then Trade Practices Act 1974 (Cth), the fair trading laws of the Australian States and Territories and the Privacy Act 1988 (Cth). Policy-makers and legislators had a strong preference for making use of the general law (wherever possible), and existing legislation would have been their starting point. If existing laws could adequately protect consumers from abuse by telecommunications providers, then the logic of Hilmer dictated that they should be relied upon. Additional regulatory measures would be superfluous. They would be 'more than necessary in the public interest'.

Nevertheless, it is quite clear that policy-makers and legislators believed that reliance on general consumer protection legislation would not serve as a sufficient safeguard for residential and small business users. Arguably, fair trading legislation may have afforded consumers some protection from industry failures to disclose relevant information about prices, and other terms and conditions. However, the general consumer protection legislation did not address many of the other issues listed in Part 6 as examples of the matters that can be dealt with in a Part 6 code.[56] At the time, the provisions of the Privacy Act 1988 (Cth) did not extend to private companies. Moreover, the absence of any applicable privacy law had forced Austel, at the request of the Minister, to establish PAC. There were also no rules that regulated, for example, security deposits given by customers, debt collection, consumer credit and the disconnection of customers. If policy-makers and legislators wanted to address these underlying issues, another regulatory mechanism would have to be relied upon.

ii. Ex Ante Industry Specific Rules

The second option most likely considered by policy-makers and legislators involved imposing industry-specific rules either by way of legislation, delegated legislation or another instrument such as a licence condition. However, while this option would lead to a certain and arguably robust framework for telecommunications consumers, it had a number of drawbacks. First, drafting such detailed rules was likely to be a costly exercise for government, and it was unlikely to have the expertise or knowledge needed to draft them. All of the issues Part 6 codes can address relate to the internal operational procedures of telecommunications providers about which government knows very little. Second, a consumer protection framework that was overly prescriptive could hinder the development of the very

[56] Telecommunications Act 1997 (Cth) s 113(3)(a), (d), (f).

market it was trying to create. Third, even if such a framework could address the specific regulatory problems that existed at the time, it would not allow industry and/or the regulator to respond to the practices of the market as it evolved and the problems that arose in the future. In a technologically driven market that was changing rapidly, it was inevitable that Parliament would not be able to keep pace with the industry.

iii. Industry Self-regulation

A third alternative was to permit industry to self-regulate. This option provided the flexibility that policy-makers and legislators sought. It also gave industry the opportunity to become involved in the regulatory process, which could (in theory) generate 'efficiency gains' and lead to 'better designed' regulatory arrangements.[57] However, because of the CoT affair, it was recognised from the outset[58] that industry may not have an incentive to stop abusive practices that adversely affect residential and small business customers. There was concern that the inequality of bargaining power would always force consumer and public interests to give way to the powerful economic interests of the industry. Permitting industry to self-regulate therefore carried significant risks. Residential and small business consumers were more likely than not to be exploited by the market and would not experience the promised benefits of market competition.

iv. The Part 6 Framework

The fourth and final option was the Part 6 rule-making framework, which shares many similarities with the TPC and PAC models of rule-making. It had many advantages over the other three options. Unlike reliance on general consumer protection and privacy legislation, it was a mechanism by which the current industry practices causing harm to residential and small business customers, such as the monitoring and recording of communications, could be addressed. It could also be used to formulate the rules governing the disclosure of information that government believed residential and small business customers needed to participate fully in the liberalised telecommunications sector. Further, it provided flexibility. Unlike imposing ex ante industry-specific rules, if circumstances changed, rules developed in accordance with Part 6 could be modified without the need for and delay caused by enacting primary legislation. The flexibility could benefit both industry and consumers alike. Inappropriate or ineffective rules would be revised and replaced with new provisions that attempted to tackle the underlying market failure. Moreover, like industry self-regulation, industry was responsible for drafting the rules in the first instance. With input from industry, which was obliged to

[57] Both factors were mentioned in the second reading speeches of the Telecommunications Bill 1996 in the House of Representatives and the Senate.
[58] *Beyond the Duopoly*, above n 50, 63.

consult with relevant regulators and at least one consumer body or association, rules could be better designed and targeted. Again, the industry as well as residential and small business consumers stood to gain. The direct costs of rule-making would also be borne by the industry rather than Australian taxpayers. However, if industry failed to formulate a code of practice that was needed to provide 'appropriate community safeguards' or otherwise adequately regulate the industry,[59] the Australian Communications Authority (ACA), ACMA's predecessor, could determine an industry standard. Thus, the Part 6 framework created a strong incentive for industry to self-regulate. If it failed to regulate when needed, the privilege of self-regulation would be lost. Further, a requirement that the ACA register Part 6 codes avoided the difficulty that delegating rule-making to industry would have posed. Under Australian constitutional law, Parliament cannot delegate rule-making authority to private bodies without some mechanism providing legislative oversight.[60] Some form of industry supervision was therefore necessary in order to satisfy constitutional requirements.

In addition, the handling of the CoT affair provided policy-makers and legislators with a credible empirical argument that Part 6 rule-making could deliver improvements for consumers. The process by which Telecom's guidelines for customer complaints were redrafted was not dissimilar from that codified in Part 6. No consumer groups directly participated in or were consulted during this exercise. However, the guidelines were revised collaboratively by industry, a large international accounting and consultancy firm and a number of regulatory bodies. PAC's detailed policy reports and recommendations were prepared by delegates representing all of the interested parties. At the time, there was some evidence that industry rule-making would not solve all regulatory problems. Austel and industry had, for example, struggled to develop a code of practice on the transfer of mobile service customers between market participants. However, the responses to the CoT affair provided a plausible alternative to traditional regulatory intervention by government that the Commonwealth was obliged to consider.

IV. Conclusion

As we know, policy-makers and legislators ultimately elected to proceed with the fourth option—the adoption of the Part 6 framework. However, the analysis has provided some insight into the factors that they most likely weighed before making their final decision. They wanted to encourage genuine competitive conduct while simultaneously protecting residential and small business consumers from abusive market practices. Some of the market failures that were likely to occur

[59] See, eg, ss 123(1)(c), 124(1)(e), 125(7) of the Telecommunications Act 1997 (Cth).

[60] See *Victorian Stevedoring and General Contracting Co Pty Ltd and Meakes v Dignan* (1931) 46 CLR 73, 119–21 (Evatt J).

were known when Part 6 was enacted. However, most were not. Policy-makers and legislators could not predict how the market would develop. Relying on general consumer protection and privacy legislation was not a realistic option. Had it been selected, it would have amounted to no more than a decision to do nothing. Such a decision would, most likely, have been highly unpopular politically, given the interest of the public and the media in the problems of the telecommunications sector. Existing provisions did not address the specific market failures the CoT affair had revealed. Ex ante industry specific rules had some attractions but concerns about 'ossification', harm to a fledging market and lack of knowledge about the internal operational procedures and telecommunications technology overrode them. In theory, industry self-regulation too offered some benefits. However, they were negated because of the absence of any obvious incentive for industry to address behaviour harming residential and small business consumers. Delegating rule-making authority to industry also raised constitutional difficulties. In the end, the Part 6 framework was selected because it gave industry an incentive to regulate and address current regulatory problems. Either industry regulated itself or the ACA could exercise its power to adopt an industry standard. In theory, the knowledge of industry could be harnessed in a way that would not lead to consumer neglect. Finally, Part 6 provided flexibility, thereby avoiding the pitfalls of ex ante industry-specific rules. Industry and the ACA, where necessary, could adapt the regulatory framework as regulatory problems arose.

There is no indication in the publicly available materials concerning Part 6 that policy-makers and legislators knew of or were attempting to apply what have become known as strategies of proceduralization when formulating the Part 6 rule-making framework. There are, for example, no references to Ayres and Braithwaite's *Responsive Regulation: Transcending the Deregulation Debate*,[61] published in 1992, three years before work on Part 6 began. Nevertheless, the reasoning behind the adoption of Part 6 suggests that policy-makers and legislators were thinking in a broadly 'responsive' way. Rather than automatically assume that prescriptive rules drafted by them would solve the regulatory problem they had identified, they considered other mechanisms that might better achieve the regulatory goals of protecting residential and small business consumers from market abuse while supporting market competition. Moreover, their decision to rely on Part 6 rule-making was influenced by many of the same factors that regulatory scholars cite as advantages of proceduralized rule-making: utilisation of industry expertise, better regulatory design, efficiency, flexibility and shifting the responsibility for and the cost of regulation to industry.

Drawing attention to these similarities, however, is not meant to imply that the regulatory design analysis in which Part 6 policy-makers and legislators engaged accords entirely with the philosophy of responsiveness or other strategies of

[61] I Ayres and J Braithwaite, *Responsive Regulation: Transcending the Deregulation Debate* (Oxford, Oxford University Press, 1992).

proceduralization. Part 6 mandates that at least one body or association representing the interests of consumers be consulted before ACMA registers an industry code of practice.[62] However, the degree of participation required falls significantly short of the level of consumer participation that Ayres and Braithwaite call for in their 'tripartism' model of regulation.[63] In particular, Part 6 does not require consumer or public interest groups to be present at the negotiating table when sections of industry formulate codes of practice. It does not impose an obligation that requires members of industry to provide consumer or public interest groups with the same information it provides to regulatory bodies. As will be argued in chapter eight, the direct involvement of consumer and public interest groups in code development has become an entrenched feature of Part 6 rule-making. However, their participation initially came about because of industry's response to the chaos of the CoT affair instead of a conscious decision by Part 6 policy-makers and legislators that direct participation by consumer or public interest groups was an integral feature of responsive regulation. Indeed, the requirement of consumer consultation was added at the last minute (three weeks before Parliament passed Part 6), following review of the Telecommunications Bill by the Senate Legislation Committee in March 1997.[64] The absence of a statutory framework mandating direct participation by consumer and public interest groups, and defining clearly the role of these groups has been an ongoing source of controversy. Consumer and public interest groups have complained repeatedly their voices are not adequately heard in the Part 6 process.[65] In 2008, the Communications Alliance tried to exclude consumer and public interest groups from the working committee it established to develop the Mobile Premium Services (MPS) code, on the basis that Part 6 did not require these groups to participate directly in the process.[66] The Communications Alliance was ultimately unsuccessful, most likely because ACMA and the Minister recognised the contributions consumer and public interest groups made to Part 6 rule-making and urged the Communications Alliance to appoint some such groups to the MPS code working committee. However, the Commonwealth Parliament has never amended the Part 6 framework to require direct participation by consumer and public interest groups or to set out their role.

[62] Telecommunications Act 1997 (Cth) s 117(1)(i).
[63] Ayres and Braithwaite, above n 61, ch 3.
[64] Opposition Senators' Report, Senate Environment, Recreation, Communications and the Arts Legislation Committee, *Telecommunications Bills Package 1996* (1997) 165.
[65] See, eg, the sources cited in n 61 of ch 1.
[66] See para 6 of s I of ch 7.

3

The Challenges of Industry Rule-making

I. Introduction

The Communications Alliance, the Australian communications sector's 'peak' self-regulatory body, defends the allegation that industry rule-making is 'like putting Dracula in charge of the blood bank'[1] by arguing that codes of practice registered under Part 6 of the Telecommunications Act 1997 (Cth) (Part 6) are made in accordance with a procedure that embodies elements of the 'internal administrative law'. Coined by Schepel, the term refers to five elements common to the rule-making procedures used by standard-setting bodies worldwide to formulate technical standards.[2] First, standards are formulated by 'technical committees with a balance of represented interests (manufacturers, consumers, social partners, public authorities)'. Second, the technical committees must draft standards by consensus. Third, there is 'a round of public notice and comment [on the draft standards], with the obligation on the committee to take received comments into account.' Fourth, the members of the technical committee ratify the draft standards by voting on them. Fifth, there is an obligation to periodically review the adopted standards.[3] It is true that the internal administrative law is increasingly being proposed as the solution to the problem of how to legitimise industry rule-making in a transnational context.[4] Moreover, many of the principles for code registration set out in Part 6 mirror elements of the internal administrative law. However, there remains scepticism that the process used by the Communications Alliance to formulate Part 6 codes is procedurally and institutionally legitimate.

This chapter explores why reliance on the internal administrative law to formulate rules in a domestic context is seen as so problematic. It begins by explaining the rule-making framework of the Communications Alliance, which contains

[1] This simile was used repeatedly by Johanna Plante, ACIF's first CEO, in discussions with the Australian press in the first year of ACIF's operations.

[2] H Schepel, *The Constitution of Private Governance: Product Standards in the Regulation of Integrating Markets* (Oxford, Hart Publishing, 2005) 6.

[3] ibid.

[4] ibid 403–14. See also GP Calliess and P Zumbansen, *Rough Consensus and Running Code: A Theory of Transnational Private Law* (Oxford, Hart Publishing, 2010).

all (bar one) of the core elements of internal administrative law.[5] It then seeks to identify the principles used to assess if 'traditional' rule-making—rule-making by legislatures and administrative bodies—is procedurally and institutionally legitimate. It is recognised that distinguishing between procedural and substantive limitations on rule-makers can be difficult. However, it is argued that in the Anglo-Australian context, the procedural and institutional frameworks used by legislatures and administrators to formulate rules have been influenced significantly by three theories of representative democracy—what Craig calls 'unitary, self-correcting democracy',[6] pluralism and republicanism. Important differences exist between each of these theories. However, they share four principles that are also consistent with the analysis of legitimacy undertaken by leading 'legisprudential' theorists—theorists who study the creation of law by legislators using the methods of jurisprudential reasoning.[7] The three theories of representative democracy require rules to be made using transparent procedures that promote deliberation and to be formulated by institutions that are impartial and held accountable for the rules they make, if they are to be recognised as law. How these principles manifest themselves in the rule-making frameworks used by legislatures and administrative bodies is then considered. Although not intended to be a comparative study, this section draws on literature from the US, Australia and the UK dealing with law-making by federal and Commonwealth bodies and Westminster. The political contexts of each of these countries clearly differ. The 'adversarial legalism'[8] of the US is a notable factor. However, they reveal a wide range of measures that are used to achieve and maintain a commitment to the four principles of procedural and institutional legitimacy. The focus is also on what Vermeule calls 'mechanisms of democracy'—the micro-processes of law-making—rather than 'large-scale institutional arrangements' dealing with separation of powers, federalism and participation in the electoral process.[9]

After delineating the principles and mechanisms that confer procedural and institutional legitimacy on traditional rule-making, the chapter identifies the features of the rule-making framework of the Communications Alliance that underpin the anxiety expressed by many of its critics. The analysis highlights that the rule-making framework incorporates few (if any) of the mechanisms used in legislative and administrative rule-making and/or their comparable equivalents to

[5] The Communications Alliance does not require codes of practice to be reviewed from time to time as does the internal administrative law. However, ACMA has mandated that codes be regularly reviewed.

[6] P Craig, *Public Law and Democracy in the United Kingdom and the United States of America* (Oxford, Clarendon Press, 1990) 12.

[7] LJ Wintgens (ed), 'Rationality in Legislation—Legal Theory as Legisprudence: An Introduction' in LJ Wintgens, *Legisprudence: A New Theoretical Approach to Legislation* (Oxford, Hart Publishing, 2002) 1.

[8] RA Kagan, *Adversarial Legalism: The American Way of Law* (Cambridge, MA, Harvard University Press, 2001).

[9] A Vermeule, *Mechanisms of Democracy: Institutional Design Writ Small* (Oxford, Oxford University Press, 2007) 4.

ensure that the principles of impartiality, transparency, deliberation and accountability are met. The chapter concludes by accepting the premise that the procedural and institutional legitimacy of industry rule-making should be evaluated by reference to the same principles used to determine the legitimacy of legislative and administrative rule-making. As a consequence, the question of whether rule-making by the Communications Alliance is procedurally and institutionally legitimate is accepted as a valid one. However, it is asserted that in the absence of empirical data which tests the assertion of its opponents, it is possible that industry rule-making may nevertheless satisfy the principles of impartiality, transparency, deliberation and accountability. The criticisms levelled against industry rule-making are often polemical, and it is the purpose of Part II of the book to determine if they are warranted.

II. The Rule-making Framework of the Communications Alliance

The procedures used by the Communications Alliance to formulate codes of practice are set out in its Operating Manual. There have been six versions of this document.[10] Earlier versions of the Operating Manual are very prescriptive and more detailed than the latest one.[11] However, in all iterations, the Communications Alliance's rule-making framework can be distilled into six core elements. First, all codes of practice are developed by a working committee 'representative' of interested parties—those 'who have a stake in or are affected by the subject matter of the proposed Code'.[12] Second, working committees develop codes by way of 'consensus'.[13] Third, the public is provided an opportunity to comment on the draft code and working committee members are obliged to consider any comments received. Fourth, once the period for public consultation has closed and the submitted comments (if any) have been considered, the working committee proceeds to a formal vote. Votes are cast by ballot. Fifth, assuming a code of practice is adopted by a working committee, it is submitted to the board of directors of the Communications Alliance, which determines if it should be published on the

[10] New versions were adopted in August 1997, April 2000, May 2000, October 2001, July 2002 and June 2007.

[11] Communications Alliance, *Operating Manual for the Development of Industry Codes, Standards and Supplementary Documents and the Establishment and Operation of Advisory Groups* (June 2007).

[12] ibid cl 2.1.

[13] The meaning of consensus is not defined in the current version of the Operating Manual. However, a 'backstop' definition of consensus arguably remains. When a working committee formally votes to adopt a code, it will be deemed to be adopted if (a) a minimum of two-thirds of those eligible to vote voted; (2) a minimum of 80 per cent of votes received was affirmative, and (3) no major interest maintained a negative vote. ibid cl 7.5.

Communications Alliance's website and submitted to the Australian Communications and Media Authority (ACMA) for registration. The board cannot amend the content of a code. Its principal function is to assess if 'due process', which the Communications Alliance understands to mean 'consensus', has been achieved and if the code does not have 'shortcomings'.[14] If any problem is found, the board must direct the working committee to address the underlying issues. Sixth, the code development process is 'confidential'.

Two other points about the Communications Alliance's rule-making process must also be made. The first concerns the forum where codes of practice are drafted; the second with the nature of the representatives who serve on the working committees of the Communications Alliance. The meetings of all working committees are held in the Communications Alliance's office in Milson's Point, Sydney, but certain representatives may 'attend' by audio or video conferencing. As is typical for many industry self-regulatory organisations,[15] the Communications Alliance is a company limited by guarantee. From its establishment in 1997, an object of the company has been to promote a 'co-operative environment' for self-regulation and developing codes of practice.[16] However, since July 2006, when the Australian Communications Industry Forum (ACIF) merged with the Service Providers Association (SPAN), additional purposes of the company have been 'to advance the interests of Members and the Industry'[17] and 'to make representations' to governments, agencies and other interested parties 'with a view to promoting the common interests'[18] of the industry and the members of the Communications Alliance. These amendments to its constitution are particularly significant as they mark the beginning of the Communications Alliance's transformation from a self-described 'facilitator'[19] of self-regulation to an industry advocate.

Second, the composition of working committees is now determined and/or approved by the CEO of the Communications Alliance. Prior to May 2005, the board made this determination. Despite this change, the principles that guide the selection of working committee members have remained the same. Voting members of working committees are chosen to reflect a balance of viewpoints among the various parties with an interest in the relevant code of practice, including consumer and public interest groups.[20] It also remains the case that the vast majority of voting members appointed to working committees consists of companies operating telecommunications networks or providing telecommunications and

[14] ibid cl 8.3.

[15] G Richardson and H Genn (eds), *Administrative Law and Government Action: The Courts and Alternative Mechanisms of Review* (Oxford, Clarendon Press, 1994) 196–97.

[16] See, eg, *Constitution of Communications Alliance Ltd CAN 078 026 507* (v12) (November 2007) cl 1.5(a).

[17] ibid cl 1.5(l).

[18] ibid cl 1.5(m).

[19] 'New ACIF CEO in the Driver's Seat', *ATUG Newsbrief*, August 1997, 3 (quoting Johanna Plante, ACIF, CEO).

[20] June 2007 Operating Manual, above n 11, cl 2.4(b).

related services, and which are also members of the Communications Alliance. The delegates of voting members, often employees of the voting members, are expressly required to 'maintain the integrity of the Working Committee process' and 'to adhere to good meeting principles',[21] but it is implicit in the Operating Manual that they are expected to act in the best interests of the organisations they represent.

III. The Procedural and Institutional Legitimacy of Traditional Rule-making

Identifying the procedural and institutional components that give legislative rule-making its legitimacy within case law and the legal literature is not an easy exercise. Both legal practitioners and academic lawyers have traditionally been fixated on the courts, leaving legislation and legislatures to the 'power game' of politics.[22] Many lawyers view the legislative branch of government with disdain or at least a strong sense of distrust.[23]

The lack of interest by legal practitioners can perhaps be explained by the conventional jurisprudence of the courts in the UK, Australia and the US. Because of separation of powers concerns, the courts have been largely deferential to legislatures, giving them significant freedom both to formulate their own rule-making procedures and to determine if they have complied with them. In each of the three jurisdictions, the courts have adopted and applied (albeit to varying degrees) the 'enrolled bill' or 'enrolled Act' rule, which serves to create a realm of legislative sovereignty. In the US[24] and the UK,[25] the rule stipulates that the courts must accept the attestation of the legislature that all relevant procedural requirements of the written or unwritten constitution and any internal rules it has adopted to regulate its rule-making function have been followed. In Australia, the situation is more complex, reflecting the historical influence of the UK and the fact that Australia has a written constitution.[26] In instances where a federal court determines a procedural provision of the Constitution to be, in the 'old' language of the High Court, 'mandatory',[27] in the sense that it sets out 'essential conditions for [the] exercise

[21] ibid cl 3.3.

[22] Wintgens, 'Rationality in Legislation', above n 7, 1.

[23] J Waldron, *Law and Disagreement* (Oxford, Oxford University Press, 1999) 30–32.

[24] *Marshall Field & Co v Clark*, 193 US 649 (1892).

[25] *Edinburgh and Dalkeith Railway v Wauchope* [1842] UKHL J12; *British Railways Board v Pickin* [1974] UKHL 1.

[26] R Keith, 'Judicial Intervention in Parliamentary Proceedings: The Implications of *Egan v Willis*' (2000) 28 *Federal Law Review* 549, 551; D Kinley, 'Constitutional Brokerage in Australia: Constitutions and the Doctrines of Parliamentary Sovereignty and the Rule of Law' (1994) 22 *Federal Law Review* 194, 197–99.

[27] E Campbell, *Parliamentary Privilege* (Sydney, Federation Press, 2003) 112 fn 1.

of … power',[28] it will look behind the parliamentary roll to evaluate if Parliament has complied with it.[29] However, the courts will invoke the enrolled bill rule when asked to review compliance with Parliament's rules of procedure and constitutional rules of legislative procedure deemed to be 'directory'.[30]

The lack of attention to the procedural and institutional aspects of rule-making by most legal academics and jurisprudential theorists is harder to explain, especially as it has long been argued by members of the legal positivist school that before any law-applying body can adjudicate, it must first be able to recognise 'law'.[31] Implicitly (if not explicitly), law-making procedure forms part of the criteria used to make that assessment. Moreover, as Raz stated, the rule of law necessitates 'the making of particular laws … by open, stable, clear and general rules',[32] even if he never elaborated on what those rules should be. Wintgens, a leading legisprudential scholar, attributes the neglect to the influence of 'strong legalism'.[33] For Wintgens,[34] strong legalism has four principal characteristics: representationalism (the idea that law represents reality, a view that is shared with positivism); timelessness (the view that the law is 'true'); 'concealed instrumentalism' (the hiding of the fact that law is a tool to achieve particular political ends); and etatism (the principle that the sovereignty of the state outweighs any other values). These characteristics are then supplemented by the view that the study of law is a science from which it is assumed that law is a 'closed set of logically connected propositions'.[35] All facets of strong legalism boil down to the belief that human behaviour is ethical provided it complies with all applicable rules, regardless of where or how those rules originated. It is this separation of politics from law that is the hallmark of strong legalism. It is therefore unsurprising that the lawyers who have considered the process of rule-making are judicial review sceptics;[36] advocates of judicial review of the legislative process;[37] or are supporters of the 'new view' of parliamentary sovereignty.[38]

[28] ibid 113.

[29] P Hanks, F Gordon and G Hill, *Constitutional Law in Australia* 3rd edn (Chatswood, NSW, LexisNexis, 2012) 121, 129–42, 150–59, 177–82.

[30] ibid; Campbell, above n 27.

[31] See, eg, HLA Hart, *The Concept of Law* 2nd edn (Oxford, Clarendon Press, 1994) 100–23.

[32] J Raz, *The Authority of Law: Essays on Law and Morality* 2nd edn (Oxford, Oxford University Press, 2009) 213.

[33] LJ Wintgens, 'Legisprudence as a New Theory of Legislation' in LJ Wintgens (ed), *The Theory and Practice of Legislation* (Abingdon, Ashgate, 2005) 3, 6.

[34] The following discussion is based on ibid 5–6.

[35] ibid 6.

[36] See, eg, Waldron, above n 23; Vermeule, above n 9.

[37] See, eg, WN Eskridge, Jr and PP Frickey (eds), *Henry M Hart, Jr and Albert M Sacks, The Legal Process: Basic Problems in the Making and Application of Law (tent ed 1958)* (New York, Foundation Press, 1994); HA Linde, 'Due Process of Lawmaking' (1976) 55 *Nebraska Law Review* 197; I Bar-Siman-Tov, 'The Puzzling Resistance to Judicial Review of the Legislative Process' (2011) 91 *Boston University Law Review* 1915.

[38] See, eg, RFV Heuston, *Essays in Constitutional Law* 2nd edn (London, Steven & Sons, 1964) 82–100, WI Jennings, *The Law and the Constitution* 5th edn (London, University of London Press, 1959) 137–92; G Marshall, *Constitutional Theory* (Oxford, Oxford University Press, 1971) 35–72.

Whatever may be the cause of the oversight, it is generally understood among lawyers in democratic countries that law-making is procedurally and institutionally valid if the process used is consistent with the principles of representative democracy embodied in the relevant constitution or what Michelman calls the 'law of law-making'.[39] As Adler and Dorf state, 'The whole test of legality [procedural and substantive] ... is *not* contained in the Constitution, but the function of much, if not all, of the Constitution is to contribute to that test.'[40] The link between democracy and rule-making is seen most clearly in the American constitutional law scholarship of Sunstein, Michelman and Vermeule (among others) but it is also present in the Commonwealth literature on the 'new view' of parliamentary sovereignty and the enforceability of 'manner and form' requirements—statutory obligations stipulating that the validity of future legislation turns on compliance with designated procedures or a prescribed form.[41] Writing in the Canadian context, Elliott argues that if the courts are called upon to evaluate manner and form requirements, they should be evaluated in light of the underlying principles of the 'legal and political culture' that manifest themselves in the relevant constitution ('entrenched' or otherwise) of the jurisdiction involved.[42]

Among the numerous democratic principles shared by the US, UK and Australia, four are fundamental to an understanding of the frameworks used to make statutory and administrative rules: deliberation, impartiality, transparency and accountability.[43] Interestingly, these principles complement or are at least consistent with the relatively new but most comprehensive legisprudential theories of rule-making: those developed by Waldron and Wintgens. Although Waldron and Wintgens are writing about rule-making in democratic countries, neither theory is based on a particular iteration of representative democracy. Given their importance to traditional rule-making frameworks, the principle of representative democracy and three of its most influential theories will be considered in some detail before turning to the commonalities they share with Waldron's 'principles of legislation' and Wintgens' 'duties of the legislator', the latter of which are underpinned by a rational theory of rule-making. How these principles manifest themselves in constitutional and administrative law will then be explored.

A. The Meaning of Representative Democracy

At the outset it must be recognised that the principle of representative democracy is an 'essentially contested concept.'[44] Disagreement over what representative

[39] F Michelman, *Brennan and Democracy* (Princeton, Princeton University Press, 1999) 6.

[40] MD Adler and MC Dorf, 'Constitutional Existence Conditions and Judicial Review' (2003) 89 *Virginia Law Review* 1105, 1130 (emphasis in original).

[41] J Goldsworthy, *Parliamentary Sovereignty: Contemporary Debates* (Cambridge, Cambridge University Press, 2010) 174.

[42] R Elliot, 'Rethinking Manner and Form: From Parliamentary Sovereignty to Constitutional Values' (1991) 29 *Osgoode Hall Law Journal* 215, 236, 238–39.

[43] Vermeule, above n 9, 4.

[44] DM Kahan, 'Democracy Schmemocracy' (1999) 20 *Cardozo Law Review* 795, 796–97.

democracy means and how best to achieve it continues to abound.[45] Nevertheless, three democratic theories, in particular, have influenced and continue to dominate legal discourse in the common law jurisdictions considered here. Moreover, their descriptive and normative components have had a profound effect on the procedural and institutional rule-making frameworks used by legislators and administrators.[46] In the UK, unitary, self-correcting democracy, a form of indirect representative democracy, underpins Dicey's classic principle of parliamentary sovereignty. This idea of democracy and parliamentary sovereignty continues to be influential in Australia despite its adoption of a written constitution. The theories of pluralism and republicanism (sometimes called 'neo-republicanism'[47] or 'civic republicanism'[48]) have gained the greatest traction in the US,[49] which strictly separates (at least in theory) legislative and executive powers. However, they (or versions of them) have also been important (albeit to a significantly lesser degree) in the UK and Australia. As it is thought in large part that these theories of democracy serve as the foundations of traditional rule-making frameworks, they and the roles of legislative representatives they imply merit some review.

i. Unitary, Self-correcting Democracy

Dicey himself never explicitly articulated a theory of democracy in support of his concept of parliamentary sovereignty. However, as Craig argues, the term 'parliamentary sovereignty' as used by Dicey has two different meanings from which a concept of democracy (albeit an incomplete one) that is both self-correcting and unitary can be implied.[50]

The first meaning commonly attributed to Dicey's 'orthodox' notion of parliamentary sovereignty is that the legislature holds 'legally unlimited'[51] legislative power. As Dicey explains, the legal 'omnicompetence' of Westminster[52] confers the right 'to make or unmake any law whatever; and further, that no person or body recognised by the law as having a right to override or set aside the legislation of Parliament'.[53] Importantly, for Dicey, legal sovereignty (which is conceptually distinct from political sovereignty) is subject to two limits: external and internal.[54]

[45] ibid.

[46] See generally Craig, above n 6.

[47] WN Eskridge, Jr and others, *Cases and Materials on Legislation: Statutes and the Creation of Public Policy* 5th edn (St Paul, MN, West Academic, 2014) 57.

[48] M Seidenfeld, 'A Civic Republican Justification for the Bureaucratic State (1992) 105 *Harvard Law Review* 1511, 1514.

[49] Kahan, above n 44, 796–97; CR Sunstein 'Beyond the Republican Revival' (1988) 97 *Yale Law Journal* 1539, 1558; CR Sunstein, 'Interest Groups in American Public Law' (1985) 38 *Stanford Law Review* 29, 31–35.

[50] Craig, above n 6, 13–29.

[51] Goldsworthy, above n 41, 106.

[52] Craig, above n 6, 13.

[53] AV Dicey, *Introduction to the Study of the Law of the Constitution* (London, Macmillan Press, first published 1885, 1960 edn) 38.

[54] Craig, above n 6, 15.

First, all lawmakers have to obtain some support from the populace—the political sovereign—and it is this need that gives rise to the external constraint. The wishes of the legal sovereign influenced by his or her 'social environment', on the other hand, impose the internal limit that shapes or 'conditions'[55] the substantive legislation the sovereign seeks to enact. According to Dicey, in a majoritarian democracy, the internal and external constraints on legislative sovereignty should coincide. At the very least, the views of the legal sovereign will concur with those of the majority. Otherwise, 'civil disobedience' on a large scale is likely to ensue.[56] To retain power, the legal sovereign must therefore act in accordance with the desires of the voters. Indeed, the purpose of representation is 'nothing else than a mode by which the will of the representative body or the House of Commons is made to coincide with the will of the nation.'[57] Because the views of the legislative sovereign must ultimately accord with the political sovereign, Dicey's notion of representative democracy is said to be 'self-correcting'.

The second, lesser known meaning of sovereignty is the idea of parliamentary monopoly, which holds that 'all significant governmental power [is] and should be directed through Parliament'.[58] The executive arm of government may exercise power but only on Parliament's order. Moreover, the exercise of power is overseen by, and in fact, derives its legitimacy from, the democratically elected Parliament.[59] It is the centralisation of legislative and executive power in Parliament that gives rise to the unitary state.[60]

ii. Pluralism

There are many variants of pluralist democracy reflecting the different political and jurisdictional contexts in which they originated. It is simply not feasible to consider all of them. Instead, the focus will be on what Eskridge, Frickey and Garrett have called the 'optimistic' vision of pluralism[61] (or what Craig terms the 'process model' of pluralism[62]), principally because of its influence on administrative rule-making frameworks, particularly in the US (as will be seen in section III.C below). The optimistic theory of pluralism draws on the work of early modern American pluralist theorists, such as Bentley, Latham, Truman and Dahl, who argued that there is no public interest ideal.[63] Instead, there are only interest groups who, acting out of the self-interest of their members, organise to

[55] ibid.
[56] C Saunders and K Le Roy, 'Perspectives on the Rule of Law' in C Saunders and K Le Roy (eds), *The Rule of Law* (Sydney, Federation Press, 2003) 1, 8.
[57] Craig, above n 6, 19 (quoting Dicey, above n 53, 43).
[58] ibid 21.
[59] ibid 20.
[60] ibid 21.
[61] WN Eskridge, Jr, PP Frickey and E Garrett, *Cases and Materials on Legislation: Statutes and the Creation of Public Policy* 3rd edn (St Paul, MN, West, 2001) 49.
[62] Craig, above n 6, 91.
[63] Eskridge, Jr, Frickey and Garrett, above n 61, 48–49.

advocate their specific positions, which often differ in substance from one another. The strength with which various interest groups hold their views varies. The rules that are encapsulated into legislation (often described as an 'equilibrium point') reflect the triumph of the views of one interest group over another following a period of intensive bargaining. The aim of the political process is to provide a forum where this interest group conflict can be resolved.[64]

However, unlike the public choice theorists who followed them, the early pluralists believed that political power was distributed among the various interest groups.[65] Critically, they assumed that all interests are in fact represented and have access to the political arena. The quality or degree of access may vary depending upon the particular economic strength of an interest group but, at the very minimum, all interest groups are allowed to 'make themselves heard' if they so wish.[66] It is for this reason that optimistic pluralists tend to see the legislative bargaining process as much more benign than public choice theorists who have observed distortions of the political market. For optimistic pluralists, politics is a 'marketplace of ideas ... [t]he best ideas succeed, while the worst are discarded'.[67] The function of representatives is therefore to oversee the market competition between interest groups and to respond accordingly by adopting the 'winning' idea.[68] As Latham has commented, 'The legislature referees the group struggle, ratifies the victories of the successful coalitions, and records the terms of their surrenders, compromises, and conquests in the form of statutes.'[69] This notion of the lawmaker as an umpire distinguishes optimistic pluralists from their more cynical counterparts who portray representatives as passive participants who do nothing more than 'aggregate' citizen preferences or simply adopt what voters want.[70] Under either view of pluralism, the elected representative is seen as an 'agent' of the electorate.[71]

iii. Republicanism

Like pluralism, republicanism has many variants.[72] Nonetheless, unlike pluralism, republicanism believes that there is such a thing as the 'public interest' or the 'common interest' (as distinct from 'the private good').[73] Indeed, the very role

[64] ibid 49.

[65] ibid 50.

[66] Craig, above n 6, 62 (describing the views of R Dahl).

[67] Eskridge, Jr, Frickey and Garrett, above n 61, 49.

[68] Sunstein, 'Beyond the Republican Revival', above n 49, 1543.

[69] RE Schiller, 'Enlarging the Administrative Polity: Administrative Law and the Changing Definition of Pluralism, 1945-1970' (2000) 53 *Vanderbilt Law Review* 1389, 1400 (quoting E Latham, *The Group Basis of Politics: A Study in Basing-Point Legislation* (Ithaca, NY, Cornell University Press for Amherst College (1952) 35).

[70] Sunstein, 'Beyond the Republican Revival', above n 49, 1542–43.

[71] Eskridge, Jr, Frickey and Garrett, above n 61, 121; HF Pitkin, *The Concept of Representation* (Berkeley, University of California Press, 1967) ch 9.

[72] Sunstein, 'Beyond the Republican Revival', above n 49, 1547–48, 1564–71; Craig, above n 6, 318–40.

[73] Sunstein, 'Beyond the Republican Revival', above n 49, 1550.

of elected representatives is to serve as 'trustees'[74] or 'guardians'[75] of the public interest.[76] They are expected to be above 'the fray'.[77] Similar to optimistic pluralism, republicanism emphasises debate.[78] However, for republicans, law is the product of consensus and agreement among representatives following intensive and 'reasoned'[79] deliberation rather than the result of a division of the 'political spoils'[80] or backroom deal-making that even the optimistic view of pluralism envisages.[81] It is the belief in 'universalism'[82] that makes republicanism less 'coercive'[83] and theoretically less arbitrary than pluralism. Individual interests nevertheless remain an important 'input' to the law-making process but are subject to 'critical scrutiny' by representatives. Ideas are tested, evaluated and modified.[84] As Sunstein remarks, deliberation has a 'transformative dimension. Its function is to select values … [and] to provide opportunities for preference formation rather than simply to implement existing desires.'[85] For republicans, deliberation is both an end—the enhancement of civic virtue—as well as the means of promoting better-informed decision-making to reach that end.[86]

Also central to the republican ideal is equality of access to the political process and participation by the citizenry.[87] Citizenship participation is essential to furthering civic virtue—community spirit—and the well-being of the self.[88] It is also the principal mechanism by which it can be assured that the conduct of political representatives is in the public interest ie, not corrupt.[89] Equality of access (which also mandates economic equality under some republican theories[90]) is said to improve the quality of deliberation as it enables all views to be taken into account.[91]

[74] JR Pennock, 'Political Representation: An Overview' in JR Pennock and JW Chapman (eds), *Representation: Nomos X* (New York, Atherton Press, 1968) 14.

[75] M Shapiro, *Who Guards the Guardians? Judicial Control of Administration* (Athens, University of Georgia Press, 1988).

[76] Eskridge, Jr and others, above n 47, 117.

[77] Sunstein, 'Interest Groups in American Public Law', above n 49, 42.

[78] Sunstein, 'Beyond the Republican Revival', above n 49, 1548; Eskridge, Jr and others, above n 47, 57.

[79] Sunstein, 'Interest Groups in American Public Law', above n 49, 32.

[80] Seidenfeld, above n 48, 1514.

[81] ibid 1528.

[82] Sunstein, 'Beyond the Republican Revival', above n 49, 1554.

[83] Seidenfeld, above n 48, 1514.

[84] Sunstein, 'Beyond the Republican Revival', above n 49, 1541.

[85] ibid 1545.

[86] ibid 1548; Eskridge, Jr and others, above n 47, 57.

[87] Sunstein, 'Beyond the Republican Revival', above n 49, 1552–53; 1555–58.

[88] ibid 1556; F Michelman, 'Law's Republic' (1988) 97 *Yale Law Journal* 1493, 1503.

[89] Sunstein, 'Beyond the Republican Revival', above n 49, 1556; Sunstein, 'Interest Groups in American Public Law', above n 49, 32.

[90] Craig, above n 6, 324–28; Michelman, above n 88, 1504.

[91] Sunstein, 'Beyond the Republican Revival', above n 49, 1552–53.

iv. The Common Principles of Representative Democracy

Differences between optimistic pluralism and republican theories of democracy clearly exist. For example, whereas optimistic pluralism envisages that a representative is the agent of the voter, republicanism emphasises the 'independence'[92] of the representative to engage in discussion and debate. As Michelman states, 'the normative character of [republican] politics depends on the independence of mind and judgment, the authenticity of voice.'[93] Despite this and other discrepancies, pluralism and republicanism nevertheless share a number of common principles (at least at a high level). As Vermeule emphasises, all democratic theories (not just pluralism and republicanism) extol the impartiality of rule-makers, deliberation, accountability and transparency.[94] The 'degree' of insularity that rule-makers must achieve from the voting populace in order to 'promote the performance of their deliberative tasks'[95] may be higher for a republican, but even a pluralist would argue that representatives have an obligation not to act in their own self-interest.[96] The image of lawmakers as umpires further suggests that pluralism requires some form of obligation not to be partial. Deliberation is a fundamental aspect of both republicanism and pluralism even though its purpose and character differ. Under either theory, deliberation requires decisions to be made after an exchange of relevant information and consideration of 'public-regarding reasons',[97] not self-interested ones. Accountability—the idea that rule-makers must answer for their decisions—is also a feature of these two theories. What a rule-maker must account for varies. For a republican, it is whether elected officials have acted in the public interest; for a pluralist, whether representatives did 'not stray too far from the desires of their constituents'.[98] Transparency (or what Luban calls the 'publicity' principle[99]) is important because voters must be able to 'observe official decision-making in some way'[100] in order to hold lawmakers to account. The incomplete portrait of unitary, self-correcting democracy that underpins Dicey's concept of parliamentary sovereignty makes it difficult to evaluate the 'thickness' of the notions of impartiality, deliberation, accountability and transparency that it adopts. Despite this, there is no reason to doubt that these principles are consistent with the nineteenth century version of British parliamentary practice that Dicey observed.

[92] ibid 1561.
[93] Michelman, above n 88, 1504.
[94] Vermeule, above n 9, 4.
[95] Sunstein, 'Beyond the Republican Revival', above n 49, 1561.
[96] Eskridge, Jr and others, above n 47, 262; Vermeule, above n 9, 4.
[97] Vermeule, above n 9, 5.
[98] Sunstein, 'Interest Groups in American Public Law', above n 49, 46–47.
[99] D Luban, 'The Publicity Principle' in RE Goodin (ed), *The Theory of Institutional Design* (Cambridge, Cambridge University Press, 1996) 154–98.
[100] Vermeule, above n 9, 4–5.

v. Overlaps with Legisprudential Theories

Vermeule adopts a 'thin' conception of each of the four principles that all theories of representative democracy share.[101] Nevertheless, the principles of impartiality, transparency, deliberation and accountability that he identifies are consistent with the 'thicker' analyses of the legitimacy of rule-making that have been undertaken by leading legisprudential theorists, Waldron and Wintgens. Admittedly, neither Waldron nor Wintgens bases his theory of the legitimacy of rule-making on a particular conception of representative democracy. For Waldron, the legitimacy of rule-making derives from the processes used to formulate it. For Wintgens, it is sourced from rationality. Nevertheless, Waldron's principles of legislation and Wintgens' duties of the legislator have much in common with the four principles of representative democracy that Vermeule identifies. Below, each of Waldron and Wintgens' theories of the legitimacy of rule-making is explained. The consistencies between the four principles of representative democracy and Waldron's principles of legislation, and Wintgens' 'duties of the legislator' are then explored.

For Waldron, legislation is 'authoritative' if the people who disagree with its substance will work within the system to overturn it, rather than ignore it. Legislation does not earn authority because voters 'consent' to it or merely because they have participated in the selection of representatives.[102] Rather, legislation has authority because of the way in which and the context from which it emerges. Waldron's positivist argument is grounded in what he identifies as the four structural elements of legislatures: their size (ie, they usually have a large number of representatives);[103] their diversity, which follows in part from their size; the presence or incorporation of disagreement; and the procedures, including party organisation, deliberative structure, formal debate, rules of order and majority voting, by which decisions are made.[104] Participation by voters is not trivial for Waldron. In *Law and Disagreement*, Waldron refers to participation as 'the right of rights'.[105] However, he believes the authority of legislation cannot be derived from its substance because of the 'circumstances of politics'.[106] Likened to a 'partial conflict coordination problem',[107] the circumstances of politics involve a 'felt need among the members of a certain group for a common framework or decision or course of action on some matter'.[108] They also involve disagreement about 'what that framework, decision or action should be'[109] because of the 'burdens of judgement'—the

[101] By 'thin', Vermeule means, 'least-common-denominator definitions that capture premises widely shared by different democratic views.' ibid 4.

[102] Waldron, above n 23, 54; J Waldron, 'Representative Lawmaking' (2009) 89 *Boston University Law* Review 335, 336.

[103] Waldron, above n 23, 49.

[104] ibid 24.

[105] ibid 254 (quoting W Cobbett, *Advice to Young Men and Women, Advice to a Citizen* (1829)).

[106] ibid 101–03.

[107] ibid 103–05.

[108] ibid 102.

[109] ibid.

differing values, the various 'positions, perspectives and experiences in life' which affect the judgement of citizens as well as the complexity of the issues faced.[110] In the absence of any ability to agree on the normative substance of law, a rule-making procedure informed by 'integrity'[111] or the principles of legislation[112] must be used to determine which of the many competing views wins.[113]

Wintgens, on the other hand, argues that law is legitimated when the restrictions it imposes on the freedom of individuals, who are assumed to be autonomous, moral and capable of self-regulation, can be rationally justified.[114] Rule-makers must satisfy four principles: the principles of 'alternativity', 'normative density', temporality and coherence.[115] The principle of 'alternativity' requires a showing that the promulgation of a statutory provision is 'preferable' to not adopting it or leaving individuals to govern themselves.[116] The principle of 'normative density' requires lawmakers who seek to impose some form of sanction if a particular rule is breached to identify if there are alternative tools that are less invasive of the freedom of individuals that achieve the same desired end. Any method that achieves the same effect but has less impact on freedom overall should prevail.[117] The principle of temporality makes two demands on legislators. The first claim is that rules and sanctions must be justified at the time they are adopted: in other words, rule-makers must take 'concrete circumstances' into account. The second claim obligates them to continuously review whether existing rules and sanctions satisfy the principles of alternativity, normative density and coherence. If those rules and sanctions cannot, they must be repealed or modified to address the present circumstances.[118] The principle of coherence forces rule-makers to look at the legal system as a whole—the extent to which particular rules and sanctions 'hang together' as a collective.[119] For Wintgens, these four principles are then translated into the six duties of the legislator: the duties of relevant fact finding, problem formulation, weighing and balancing alternatives, taking future circumstances into consideration, evaluating the effects (if any) rules have had, and correction.[120]

Of particular interest here is the fact that Waldron's principles of legislation and Wintgens's duties of the legislator, derived from different premises, are consistent with the four 'thin' principles of democracy identified by Vermeule. For example, Waldron's concept of the 'very idea of legislation'—the idea of making or changing

[110] ibid 112.

[111] J Waldron, 'Legislating with Integrity' (2003) 72 *Fordham Law Review* 373.

[112] J Waldron, 'Principles of Legislation' in RW Bauman and T Kahana (eds), *The Least Examined Branch: The Role of Legislatures in the Constitutional State* (Cambridge, Cambridge University Press, 2006).

[113] Waldron, *Law and Disagreement*, above n 23, 245.

[114] Wintgens, 'Legisprudence as a New Theory of Legislation', above n 33, 7–9, 11.

[115] ibid 11–22.

[116] ibid 12.

[117] ibid 13.

[118] ibid 15.

[119] ibid 15–22.

[120] LJ Wintgens, *Legisprudence: Practical Reason in Legislation* (Abingdon, Ashgate, 2012) 294–304.

law 'explicitly through a[n open] process and in an institution publicly dedicated to that task'[121]—embodies the value of transparency. His principle of 'responsive deliberation',[122] with its emphasis on 'openness to others' views and a willingness to be persuaded',[123] encapsulates deliberation and implies some form of an obligation of impartiality. The duty to 'take care'[124]—the 'responsibility to arrive at a sound view' taking into account the effects law may have on individuals and the legal system as a whole—so as to promote the 'general good'[125] echoes the importance of deliberation seen especially in the theory of republicanism, even though Waldron disagrees strongly that consensus can ever emerge from dialogue.[126] Other principles of legislation directly relevant to the democratic value of deliberation include the principles of representation; respecting disagreement; legislative formality; and political equality. The principle of representation emphasises diverse perspectives with the aim of ensuring that a wide variety of opinions is heard. The principle of political equality, which overlaps to some extent with representation, is the idea that each citizen is directly or indirectly entitled to participate in the law-making process.[127]

Similarly, the six 'concrete' duties of legislators identified by Wintgens are compatible with the democratic principles of deliberation, impartiality, accountability and impartiality. The duties to find relevant facts; to identify and formulate problems; to weigh and balance alternatives; and to take reasonably foreseeable effects of rule adoption into account,[128] in particular, embody the principle of deliberation. Collectively, they require rule-makers to gather relevant information about current practices and evaluate if they are undesirable. They insist that rule-makers consider multiple means of addressing identified problems and determine which option is best able to resolve them. All of these obligations are the hallmarks of deliberation. These four duties and the duties of retrospection and correction also imply a degree of impartiality on the part of legislators. The duty of retrospection is the obligation to reflect on and evaluate whether the actual effects of a rule accord with its original aim. The duty to correct is the requirement to repeal laws that are no longer justified.[129] To carry out each of these six duties requires some degree of objectivity. None of them could be adequately performed by legislators who are biased and/or act only in their self-interests. Wintgens does not explicitly impose duties of accountability and transparency on legislators. In spite of this, he clearly envisages that courts will hold legislators accountable. He states that a role

[121] Waldron, 'Principles of Legislation', above n 112, 22.
[122] ibid 27–28.
[123] ibid 27.
[124] ibid 23–24.
[125] ibid 23.
[126] Waldron, *Law and Disagreement*, above n 23, 91–93.
[127] Waldron, 'Principles of Legislation', above n 112, 24–27, 28–31.
[128] Wintgens, *Legisprudence: Practical Reason in Legislation*, above n 120, 294–302.
[129] ibid 302–04.

of the courts is to assess whether legislators have satisfied their duties.[130] By implication, rule-making must also be sufficiently transparent. Otherwise, the parties entitled to judicially review the legislative process would have no means by which to determine if judicial challenge were warranted.

B. Institutional and Procedural Manifestations of Democratic Principles in Legislative Rule-making

The high level principles of deliberation, impartiality, transparency and accountability manifest themselves in a number of ways in the institutional design of the bodies that formulate legislation and the procedures by which it is made (whether they be set out in a constitution (written or otherwise), legislation or internal parliamentary rules). Parliamentarians have to follow 'highly stylised'[131] rules of parliamentary and congressional procedure whose purpose is to structure and bring order to debate, enabling people who have 'very little else in common'[132] to communicate with each other. Moreover, there are rules designed to ensure that legislators are not corrupted or otherwise partial to their own or other particular interests when they should not be. Australia, the UK and the US have all adopted measures dealing with bribery, described as 'the classic threat to the integrity of government',[133] extortion and conflicts of interest. Australia and the US also created, respectively, a new territory and district so their Commonwealth and federal legislatures could be located on neutral terrain.[134] All such measures promote impartiality, which in turn is likely to affect the quality and nature of the underlying substantive debate, and to mitigate the risks of factionalism.[135] Allowing members of the general public to attend legislative deliberation; to watch and/or listen to legislative debate via television, radio and the Internet; and to access Hansard or the Congressional Record, introduces a degree of transparency to the process. Such steps are intended to foster accountability by giving the public some information with which to assess the performance of their representatives when they next vote at the ballot box.[136]

The strength of the principle of parliamentary sovereignty in the UK and (to a lesser extent) Australia has meant that their courts do not hold legislatures accountable. Moreover, they have not imposed a judicial overlay on the process of law-making or the institutional design of legislatures. However, the importance of the procedural principles of deliberation, rationality and accountability in

130 ibid 304–07.
131 Waldron, 'Principles of Legislation', above n 112, 28.
132 ibid 28–29.
133 Linde, above n 37, 240.
134 Australia established the Australian Capital Territory. The US created the District of Columbia.
135 Sunstein, 'Interest Groups in American Public Law', above n 49, 35–45.
136 Sunstein, 'Beyond the Republican Revival', above n 49, 1561.

law-making is clearly visible in some US case law even though the US has adopted the enrolled bill rule.[137] In the context of reviewing whether the content of legislation conforms to the substantive requirements of the constitution, the Supreme Court has considered if Congress has adequately complied with legislative process.[138] 'Defects' in the legislative process,[139] however, become relevant only if the underlying legislation somehow 'encroaches'[140] into the substantive sphere and a constitutional violation is alleged. The meaning of a procedural defect for these purposes is evolving although failures to establish an adequate 'legislative record' in the eyes of the court have rendered invalid statutes that interfere with states' rights. As Frickey and Smith argue, the requirements imposed by the Supreme Court represent a shift towards a 'due deliberation' model of judicial review[141] or impose what Sunstein would call a 'reasoned analysis'[142] requirement onto law-makers. Many of the procedures mandated in this line of cases are comparable to the requirements of the hard-look doctrine applied by the US courts when reviewing administrative rule-making (discussed further below). For example, legislators must demonstrate that they have gathered adequate factual evidence, made formal findings that legislative action is necessary and adequately deliberated relevant matters before passing laws affecting substantive rights.[143] Importantly, however, the use of these so-called 'structural rules' has not been limited to states' rights cases. Sunstein argues they, or their functional equivalents, have also been deployed in equal protection and due process cases.[144] Moreover, as Coenen identifies, the courts have deployed a variety of other 'participation-oriented, representation-reinforcing'[145] techniques, including 'proper-purpose' rules, that frame the deliberative responsibility of representatives.[146]

C. Institutional and Procedural Manifestations of Democratic Principles in Administrative Rule-making

Vermeule, Waldron and Wintgens are not directly concerned with rule-making by government administrators. However, the principles that they identify also manifest themselves in administrative law and the broader framework in which

137 See the text accompanying nn 24–29.

138 Bar-Siman-Tov, above n 37, 1924; DT Coenen, 'The Renquist Court, Structural Due Process, and Semisubstantive Constitutional Review' (2002) 75 *Southern California Law Review* 1281, 1282–83.

139 Bar-Siman-Tov, above n 37, 1924.

140 PP Frickey and SS Smith, 'Judicial Review, the Congressional Process and the Federalism Cases: An Interdisciplinary Critique' (2002) 111 *Yale Law Journal* 1707, 1716 (quoting T Sandalow, 'Judicial Protection of Minorities' (1977) 75 *Michigan Law Review* 1162, 1188).

141 ibid 1716–18.

142 Sunstein, 'Interest Groups in American Public Law', above n 49, 57.

143 Frickey and Smith, above n 140, 1710, 1718–27.

144 Sunstein, 'Interest Groups in American Public Law', above n 49, 49–50.

145 Craig, above n 6, 93 (quoting JH Ely, *Democracy and Distrust: A Theory of Judicial Review* (Cambridge, MA, Harvard University Press, 1980) 87).

146 Coenen, above n 138, 1755–73.

delegated legislation and administrative rules are made. In all of the jurisdictions considered, there was initially great resistance to administrative rule-making. In England, it was called 'the new despotism'[147] or a 'menace'[148] in some quarters because of its threat to the idea of parliamentary sovereignty and the rule of law ideal that Dicey developed around it. In the US, opposition to the delegation of law-making authority to administrators is seen, for example, in the strict application of the federal non-delegation doctrine by the Supreme Court, which required Congress to 'promulgate rules, standards, goals, or some "intelligible principle" to guide the exercise of administrative power' when the practice first emerged.[149] Similar concerns arose in Australia but delegation of Commonwealth rule-making authority was ultimately held to be constitutional by the High Court in 1931.[150] Rule-making authority in all three countries is now routinely granted to administrative agencies. Delegations of power and the rules administrators adopt have come to be accepted, in part, because the nature of the various rule-makers and the procedural requirements they must follow are consistent with the democratic values of deliberation, impartiality, transparency and accountability. The rule-making frameworks that have been developed are primarily the product of statute; but unlike in the constitutional context, the courts have also significantly shaped how administrators should formulate rules as a result of their willingness to judicially review administrative law-making. Again, the precise schemas adopted vary depending on the particular contexts in which they were developed, but they share the similar goal of ensuring the procedural and institutional principles of representative democracy are met.

i. Impartiality

A fundamental 'safeguard' in administrative rule-making is 'the disinterested and professional public official'.[151] Administrative rule-makers in the UK, Australia and the US must be (and seen to be) impartial and, in the case of the UK and Australia, are often described as being anonymous.[152] All administrators must comply with codes of conduct[153] dealing with conflicts of interest, gifts, benefits and outside employment. In Australia and the UK, administrative rule-making does not typically trigger the application of the no bias rule[154] but the US courts have stated that

[147] Lord Hewart of Bury, *The New Despotism* (London, Ernest Benn Limited, 1929).

[148] GW Keeton, *The Passing of Parliament* (London, Ernest Benn Limited, 1952) 64.

[149] RB Stewart, 'The Reformation of American Administrative Law' (1975) 88 *Harvard Law Review* 1667, 1672–73.

[150] *Victorian Stevedoring and General Contracting Co Pty Ltd and Meakes v Dignan* (1931) 46 CLR 73.

[151] LL Jaffe, 'Law Making by Private Groups' (1937) 51 *Harvard Law Review* 201, 248.

[152] Anonymity is a consequence of the principle of Ministerial responsibility. Craig, above n 6, 20.

[153] See, eg, US Office of Government Ethics, Standards of Ethical Conduct for Employees of the Executive Branch, 5 CFR pt 2635 (2017); *Australian Public Service Code of Conduct* (set out in s 13 of the Public Service Act 1999 (Cth)); *UK Civil Service Code* (16 March 2015).

[154] See, eg, GJ Craven, 'Legislative Action by Subordinate Authorities and the Requirements of a Fair Hearing' (1988) 16 *Melbourne University Law Review* 569.

rule-makers 'must be disqualified if there is clear and convincing evidence that [they have] "an unalterably closed mind on matters critical to the disposition of the proceedings"'.[155] The US courts have also gone so far as to prohibit informal ex parte communications between administrators, regulated entities and other parties during rule-making proceedings to facilitate impartiality.[156] They have since distanced themselves from this requirement but agencies must disclose when and with whom they have communicated informally for the rule-making record. Disclosure alone may be no guarantee of impartiality but, when it is combined with court-imposed obligations for administrative rule-makers to 'adequately consider' all interests and alternatives when formulating rules and statutory requirements to consult publicly prior to adopting rules, partiality is minimised.

ii. Transparency

Transparency is also an important component of administrative rule-making. In the UK, in the absence of an express or implied statutory intention to the contrary, before adopting rules targeted at particular individuals, rule-makers must consult with the individuals who are the object of those rules.[157] Similarly, in Australia, procedural fairness requires consultation if the legislative instrument affects the interests of an individual in a 'direct and immediate way' and there is no contrary statutory intention.[158] In both countries, rule-makers have no general duty to consult with the public prior to adopting rules of general application.[159] However, consultation is required in specific contexts. It is also increasingly the general norm as is publication of comments on draft rules submitted to the administrator.[160] In the US, public consultation is mandatory before any administrative rule is adopted, reflecting what Stewart has described as the central function of US administrative law today: 'the provision of a surrogate political process to ensure the fair representation of a wide range of affected interests in the process of administrative decision.'[161] The Administrative Procedure Act requires administrative agencies following the 'informal'[162] rule-making procedure—the one that is most commonly used—to comply with a 'notice and comment' obligation.[163]

[155] E Rubin, 'It's Time to Make the Administrative Procedure Act Administrative' (2003) 89 *Cornell Law Review* 95, 123 (quoting *Ass'n of Nat'l Advertisers v FTC*, 627 F 2d 1151, 1170 (DC Cir 1979)).

[156] *HBO v FCC*, 567 F 2d 9 (DC Cir 1977).

[157] See, eg, *Bank Mellat v HM Treasury (No 2)* [2013] UKSC 39.

[158] See, eg, *Kioa v West* (1985) 159 CLR 550, 584 (Mason J).

[159] For the position in Australia, see *Kioa v West* (1985) 159 CLR 550 and Legislation Act 2003 (Cth), ss 17–19; for the UK position, see P Craig, *Administrative Law* 8th edn (London, Sweet and Maxwell, 2016) 449.

[160] See, eg, Department of Prime Minister and Cabinet (Cth), *The Australian Government Guide to Regulation* (March 2014) 39–45; Craig, *Administrative Law*, above n 159, 449–56; UK Cabinet Office, *Consultation Principles* (14 January 2016).

[161] Stewart, above n 149, 1670.

[162] See, eg, L Blomgren Bingham, 'The Next Generation of Administrative Law: Building the Legal Infrastructure for Collaborative Governance' (2010) 297 *Wisconsin Law Review* 297, 306.

[163] 5 USC §§551-59 (2012 & Supp 2016).

Subject to some exceptions,[164] an agency must publish a notice in the Federal Register that sets out the terms or substance of the proposed rule and its proposed legal basis. 'Interested persons' must be given an opportunity to participate in the rule-making exercise by way of 'submission of written data, views, or arguments with or without opportunity for oral presentation.' The courts have interpreted these provisions to also impose obligations on rule-makers to accurately describe the substance of the rules they propose and to publish the methodology and underlying data used to formulate them.[165] Moreover, the US Government in the Sunshine Act[166] stipulates that administrative agencies must provide advanced public notice of their meetings during which, for example, decisions are taken on rules. Subject to certain exceptions, meetings must also be open to the public, enabling observation of the decision-making process.

Transparency in the rule-making process has been further enhanced by the adoption of freedom of information laws which enable citizens (at least in theory) to access documents concerning administrative decision-making, including rule-making. Australia, the US and the UK have all adopted legislation giving individuals the right to request and receive information held by administrators.[167]

iii. Deliberation

The principle of deliberation and the rationality it arguably implies are also manifest in the administrative law of the UK, Australia and the US, although it must be said that it has a much greater significance in the US. In the UK and Australian systems, the courts will, for example, overturn rules on the grounds that administrators have acted with an improper purpose when adopting particular rules and have taken into account irrelevant considerations. No doubt, these grounds of review are likely to affect how administrators formulate rules. However, their primary purpose has been to ensure the principle of parliamentary sovereignty is upheld. They serve to constrain the discretion of administrators granted in primary legislation.

On the other hand, in the US, the courts have interpreted the informal rule-making requirements and 'arbitrary and capricious' standard of judicial review in the Administrative Procedure Act widely, contributing to the 'interest representation model' of American administrative law that Stewart describes.[168] The so-called 'hard-look' or 'adequate consideration'[169] doctrine that has emerged from the case law imposes procedural requirements that go to the heart of how the rule-maker

[164] 5 USC §553(a) (2012 & Supp 2016).
[165] M Asimow, 'Delegated Legislation: United States and United Kingdom' (1983) 3 *OJLS* 253, 256.
[166] 5 USC §552b (2012 & Supp 2016).
[167] See, eg, Freedom of Information Act 1982 (Cth); Freedom of Information Act, 5 USC §552 (2012 & Supp 2016); Craig, *Public Law and Democracy*, above n 6, 200–04.
[168] Stewart, above n 149, 1760–90.
[169] ibid 1756 fn 426.

takes into account multiple interests and reaches a 'fair accommodation'.[170] These procedural requirements also enhance the transparency of the rule-making exercise. For example, US administrative rule-makers must clearly articulate their reasons for adopting rules, demonstrate that they have considered all other reasonable alternatives, explain why these options were rejected, examine all relevant considerations, take all views into account and (if applicable) justify why they have departed from current practice.[171] The US courts have also required rule-making decisions that turn on findings of fact to be supported by the record generated during a rule-making proceeding.[172] The Supreme Court's decision in *Vermont Yankee*[173] may have curtailed the ability of lower courts to impose procedural obligations more onerous than those in the Administrative Procedure Act but the hard-look doctrine is very much 'alive.'[174]

iv. Accountability

Finally, administrative rule-making incorporates a number of mechanisms to promote accountability in the process. In Australia and the UK, accountability in rule-making is said to be achieved primarily by two mechanisms: oversight by the Parliament, which is in turn held responsible by the electorate; and judicial review. Both mechanisms are consistent with the principle of parliamentary monopoly central to the unitary, self-correcting theory of representative democracy. The Parliament in both countries has the ability to override legislative instruments promulgated by administrators by adopting new, primary legislation. However, administrators may also have obligations to lay a legislative instrument before the Parliament to give elected representatives an opportunity to pass a motion disallowing or affirming the relevant instrument.[175] Delegated legislation is also routinely scrutinised by standing committees dedicated to that task.[176] Where the administrative rule-maker is also a Minister, ministerial accountability to Parliament contributes to legislative oversight of rule-making.[177] In Australia and the UK, judicial review of subordinate legislation by the courts further enhances

[170] ibid 1750.

[171] See, eg, MB Garland, 'Deregulation and Judicial Review' (1985) 98 *Harvard Law Review* 505, 526–27.

[172] See, eg, ibid 533–53.

[173] *Vermont Yankee Nuclear Power Corp v Natural Resources Defense Council, Inc* 435 US 519 (1978).

[174] Rubin, above n 155, 117–18.

[175] For the Commonwealth position in Australia, see ss 37–48 of the Legislation Act 2003 (Cth). For the UK position, see Craig, *Administrative Law*, above n 159, 440–42.

[176] On the current committees in the UK and Australia, see, respectively, Craig, *Administrative Law*, above n 159, 442–49; D Pearce and S Argument, *Delegated Legislation in Australia* 5th edn (Chatswood, NSW, LexisNexis Butterworths, 2017) 62–69.

[177] On Ministerial accountability in the UK, see, eg, C Graham, *Regulating Public Utilities: A Constitutional Approach* (Oxford, Hart Publishing, 2000) 7–11; in Australia, see R Creyke, J McMillan and M Smyth, *Control of Government Action: Text, Cases and Commentary* 4th edn (Chatswood, NSW, LexisNexis, 2015) 20–22.

accountability to Parliament by creating a procedure whereby the courts verify if the relevant delegate has complied procedurally and substantively with the intention of the legislature and acted within the boundaries imposed in primary legislation.[178]

In the US, accountability in administrative rule-making is fostered by the opportunity for interested parties to participate in rule-making proceedings and the rights of aggrieved parties to seek judicial review in the Administrative Procedure Act.[179] Unlike the UK and Australian Parliaments, Congress cannot veto or override executive rules without passing primary legislation.[180] However, Congress has used 'report and wait' requirements[181] and other measures, including submission of annual reports and the need to obtain budgetary approval, to exert a degree of indirect control over administrative rule-making. The statutory right to judicial review has been accompanied by a 'relaxation' of the rules of standing and ripeness by the courts. Consistent with the interest representation model of US administrative law, there is relative ease of access to the judiciary[182] when compared, for example, to the administrative law regimes of Australia and the UK. The 'arbitrary and capricious' standard of review applied by the US courts permits review on the basis of the ultra vires grounds used in the UK and Australia. However, as discussed above, the US courts have developed the hard-look doctrine to enlarge the scope of what they review.

D. Conclusion

This overview of traditional procedural and institutional rule-making frameworks and the theories of representative democracy and legisprudence that underpin them is in no way suggesting that the underlying theories are correct or that the mechanisms that have been adopted to implement their core principles of deliberation, impartiality, transparency and accountability fully work in practice or are somehow free of costs. On the contrary, the empirical legislative studies that underpin public choice theory[183] and the studies of sociologists, political scientists and lawyers of administrative capture[184] suggest that existing constitutional and

[178] See, eg, Craig, *Public Law and Democracy*, above n 6, 19–26; Pearce and Argument, above n 176, chs 12–24.

[179] Rubin, above n 155, 101.

[180] *Immigration and Naturalization Service v Chandra* (1983) 462 US 919.

[181] Rubin, above n 155, 133. Report and wait obligations require agencies to provide copies of administrative rules to Congress and then wait for a period of time before implementing them.

[182] Stewart, above n 149, 1670, 1716, 1723–47.

[183] For an overview of this literature, see Craig, *Public Law and Democracy*, above n 6, 63–67.

[184] See, eg, ME Levine and JL Forrence, 'Regulatory Capture, Public Interest, and the Public Agenda: Toward a Synthesis' (1990) 6 *Journal of Law, Economics, and Organization* 167; SA Talesh, 'The Privatization of Public Legal Rights: How Manufacturers Construct the Meaning of Consumer Law' (2009) 43 *Law and Society Review* 527, 528.

administrative law mechanisms do not work or may not work in all instances. Discussion of the legitimacy 'crisis' in the US administrative process, including rule-making, endures.[185] Scholars continue to query if the premise of participation on which informal rule-making is based is correct[186] and to make recommendations to improve transparency and public participation in the federal rule-making process.[187] In the UK, numerous critiques of the constitutional law system have been made throughout the years with Harden and Lewis going so far as to call it a 'noble lie'.[188] Even the relatively new legisprudential theories of rule-making offered by Waldron and Wintgens have been open to criticism. For example, Posner and Stone have criticised Waldron for not paying enough attention to the practical realities of the legislative process.[189] Eskridge has queried if legislatures are as diverse as Waldron assumes.[190]

Instead, the purpose of providing this overview has been much more modest. It has sought to highlight that the theories of unitary, self-correcting democracy; pluralism; and republicanism have significantly influenced the procedural and institutional frameworks by which legislation and administrative rules are made. There are differences between each of the three theories of representative democracy but they share a number of common principles—principles that are broadly consistent with Waldron's principles of legislation and Wintgens' duties of the legislator. Importantly, these theories dictate that before a rule can be recognised as law, it must be made using transparent procedures that promote deliberation and be formulated by institutions (and the individuals which comprise them) that are impartial and held accountable for the rules they make. The importance of these principles is seen in the various procedural mechanisms and institutional structures used to prepare legislation and formulate administrative rules. Depending on the context in which rules are made, the precise mechanisms used to meet the principles of impartiality, transparency, deliberation and accountability differ. However, legislative and administrative rule-making design addresses all four principles.

185 See, eg, JO Freedman, 'Crisis and Legitimacy in the Administrative State' (1975) 27 *Stanford Law Review* 1041; D Schoenbrod, *Power Without Responsibility: How Congress Abuses the People Through Delegation* (New Haven, Yale University, 1993).

186 See, eg Stewart, above n 149, 1760–90; Rubin, above n 155, 102; Seidenfeld, above n 48, 1560–61.

187 See, eg, C Coglianese, H Kilmartin, E Mendelson, 'Transparency and Public Participation in the Federal Rulemaking Process: Recommendations for the New Administration' (2009) 77 *George Washington Law Review* 924.

188 I Harden and N Lewis, *The Noble Lie: The British Constitution and the Rule of Law* (London, Hutchison Education, 1986).

189 RA Posner, 'Review of Jeremy Waldron, *Law and Disagreement* (2000) 100 *Columbia Law Review* 582, 590; A Stone, 'Disagreement and an Australian Bill of Rights' (2002) 26 *Melbourne University Law Review* 478, 494.

190 WN Eskridge, Jr, 'The Circumstances of Politics and the Application of Statutes' (2000) 100 *Columbia Law Review* 558, 579–80.

IV. The Difficulties and Threats Posed by Industry Rule-making

Having identified the principles and mechanisms that are thought to give procedural and institutional legitimacy to traditional legislative and administrative rule-making, it is possible to pinpoint the attributes of the rule-making framework of the Communications Alliance that cause so much uncertainty for the opponents of industry rule-making. The argument developed here is that the anxiety that industry rule-making will always trump consumer and public interest concerns is caused principally by the absence of 'small-scale rules'[191] that address the principles of impartiality, transparency and accountability. The absence of rules designed to foster transparency and impartiality is particularly problematic because, in traditional rule-making, they are seen as essential for robust debate. Without mechanisms designed to promote transparency and impartiality, proper deliberation is thwarted. The discussion that follows begins by identifying the lack of rules designed to promote transparency and impartiality. It then considers the impact the absence of such rules is thought to have on deliberation. It concludes by highlighting the absence of mechanisms that promote accountability in legislative and administrative rule-making: voting, parliamentary oversight and judicial review.

A. Partiality

There are no mechanisms in the code development framework that appear to ensure that rule-makers are disinterested and/or formulate rules in a neutral forum. The rule-making framework adopted by the Communications Alliance does not impose any requirements that members of working committees be disinterested. There are no conflict of interest rules, for example. On the contrary, it assumes that voting members will act in their best interests. This presumption may not trouble republican theorists who believe the common interest can emerge from rational debate. However, absent any degree of insulation between working committee representatives and their employers, it is doubtful if rational debate can occur. Moreover, the forum where consumer codes of practice are drafted is not neutral. As stated earlier, since July 2006, the Communications Alliance has been an advocate for industry. As a matter of practice, a chair is appointed to each working committee and his or her role is to 'ensure [its] fair and equitable operation'.[192] However, there is no requirement that the chair must be independent of industry or of the Communications Alliance.

[191] Vermeule, above n 9, 4.
[192] June 2007 Operating Manual, above n 11, cl 2.6.

B. Minimal Transparency

There are few mechanisms that promote transparency in the industry rule-making process. The Communications Alliance must publish codes in draft and consult on them. However, other than the opportunity to read and submit written comments upon draft codes, the general public has no oversight of code development. It cannot observe the rule-making process. The confidentiality of the code development process prevents private individuals from attending working committee meetings, the dates of which are also not disclosed. Moreover, members of and delegates to working committees are prohibited from discussing matters before them with third parties. Further, the discussions of working committee participants are not recorded or transcribed. As a matter of practice, minutes of meetings are prepared by project managers, employees of the Communications Alliance, and circulated to working committee participants.[193] However, they are not publicly disclosed. It is possible to identify the names of the companies and/or organisations appointed to working committees and their representatives. However, this information is only placed in the public domain when the Communications Alliance publishes a draft code for comment, often months after rule-making has commenced. Since 2014, subject to some exceptions, the Communications Alliance must publish the submissions it receives during the public comment phase of code development.[194] However, the public has no right to be provided with copies of working committee meeting papers or earlier versions of the draft code. Working committees also do not have to provide reasons for the codes they adopt. The lack of information about the process makes it difficult for the general public and others to scrutinise the rule-making process and enhances the appearance that the process is entirely partial to industry. It is also said to increase the likelihood that the process fosters opportunities for 'collusion' between interest groups appointed to code development committees and/or has become 'captured' by industry interests.[195]

C. Tainted Deliberation

The Communications Alliance's rule-making framework incorporates a limited number of mechanisms that are designed to ensure that working committee members properly evaluate consumer and public interest concerns or engage in some form of fact-finding and analysis before reaching their decisions. Members must 'consider' any comments received during public consultation and notify submitters in writing of their reasons for rejecting any comments.[196] In addition,

[193] See, eg, ibid cl 6.5(a).

[194] See Telecommunications Act 1997 (Cth) ss 117(1)(e)(iii), 117(1)(f)(iii), 119B.

[195] J Freeman, 'Collaborative Governance in the Administrative State' (1997) 45 *University of California at Los Angeles Law Review* 1, 83.

[196] June 2007 Operating Manual, above n 11, cl 6.5(a).

working committees must be 'representative' of all interested parties. However, there is no express requirement that consumer and/or public interest organisations must be appointed to them. Similarly, there are no provisions that structure debate between working committee members. There is no requirement that an equal number of representatives from industry, and consumer and public interest organisations serve on working committees. Arguably, the incorporation of such rules, along with rules making the process transparent and its rule-makers impartial, would promote consideration of public regarding reasons.

D. Accountability Deficits

Finally, the mechanisms used to ensure that legislators and administrative rule-makers must answer for their decisions—voting, parliamentary oversight and judicial review—are not part of the Communications Alliance's rule-making framework. The general public does not vote to accept or reject codes of practices adopted by working committees. Neither the Communications Alliance nor ACMA tables them before each House of Parliament. Therefore, these codes are not subject to review by elected representatives. The decisions of the Communications Alliance and/or the members of its working committees cannot be judicially reviewed. In order for them to be legally enforceable, the Communications Alliance must register codes of practice with ACMA. However, industry and ACMA are not, strictly speaking, in a 'relationship'[197] of accountability as the term is traditionally understood. There is no connection between a principal and an agent. ACMA does not entrust industry with any responsibility to formulate codes of practice. It could be argued that ACMA is an agent of Parliament because Parliament has delegated to ACMA a power to determine if the code development process and the codes themselves comply with the registration criteria specified in Part 6.[198] However, as discussed further in chapter eight, it is questionable if classifying ACMA in this manner is appropriate when the process of Part 6 rule-making is designed to be industry led. In any event, the key point made here is that industry is clearly not accountable to ACMA or Parliament in any formal or substantive sense. On its face, therefore, there is a significant accountability deficit that the rule-making framework does not address.

V. Conclusion

The concern that industry rule-making will ignore the interests of consumers and the public interest, expressed by its opponents, is based on the assumption that

[197] R Mulgan, *Holding Power to Account: Accountability in Modern Democracies* (Basingstoke, Palgrave Macmillan, 2003) 11.

[198] Telecommunications Act 1997 (Cth) s 117.

the procedural and institutional legitimacy of industry rule-making should be determined by reference to the same principles manifest in the theories of unitary, self-correcting democracy; pluralism; republicanism; and legisprudential scholarship, which confer procedural and institutional legitimacy upon traditional rule-making. This assumption is accepted. The principles of impartiality, transparency, deliberation and accountability should be used to evaluate the procedural and institutional legitimacy of industry rule-making. If, as argued, the procedural and institutional legitimacy of legislative and administrative rule-making turns on the satisfaction of the four principles of impartiality, transparency, deliberation and accountability, then it is appropriate that the same principles should anchor the procedural and institutional legitimacy of rule-making by industry bodies. It is also accepted that whether rule-making by the Communications Alliance is procedurally and institutionally legitimate is a valid question. On the face of it, industry rule-making contains few (if any) of the features found in traditional rule-making and/or comparable equivalents that promote the principles of impartiality, transparency and accountability. The absence of mechanisms that promote impartiality and transparency, in particular, raises doubt that the working committees of the Communications Alliance will take a hard look at the consumer and public-interest matters that come before them.

However, the extent to which the practice of Part 6 rule-making departs from the standards used to assess traditional legislative and administrative rule-making has not been tested empirically. Part 6 rule-making may satisfy the spirit of impartiality, transparency, deliberation and accountability despite the formal omissions in the framework that have been catalogued. Other elements of the rule-making framework of the Communications Alliance and/or the dynamic within the working committee may ensure that the process is procedurally and institutionally legitimate. The principle of representativeness may facilitate the achievement of the four principles of impartiality, transparency, deliberation and accountability. The requirement to reach consensus may perhaps be better understood as a 'veto-gate'[199] that gives weaker interest groups a degree of power in rule-making proceedings, and that ensures consumer and public interest concerns are voiced and adequately deliberated. As Jaffe suggests, the dynamic of rule-making may result in a 'fair' process as well as a fair outcome.[200] However, detailed empirical study is necessary to evaluate if these arguments have any more merit than the challenges that underpin the principal concern of the opponents of industry rule-making. Part II of the book takes up this challenge. The conceptual approach used to characterise Part 6 rule-making and the institutional context in which the three consumer codes that are the focus of the case studies were developed are explained in the following chapter.

[199] Eskridge, Jr and others, above n 47, 53.
[200] Jaffe, above n 151, 247–53.

Part II

Empirical Study of Part 6 Rule-making

4

The Conceptual Approach and Institutional Context

I. Introduction

The purpose of this chapter is to provide some background information needed to understand the three case studies in chapters five, six and seven.

Section II of this chapter explains the conceptual approach used to characterise the Part 6 rule-making process and why it was adopted. It defines the key terms used in chapters five, six, seven and eight to identify and analyse the politic of Part 6 rule-making. It also explains the common structure of the three case studies—a structure that reflects the conceptual approach used to characterise the Part 6 rule-making process—and the information used to prepare the case studies.

Section III of this chapter sets out the institutional context in which the three consumer codes that are the focus of the case studies were developed. It gives an overview of the Australian telecommunications industry; the bodies that regulate it; and the consumer and public interest organisations, and advisory bodies appointed to the working committees of the Communications Alliance that developed the three consumer codes. It explains the decline of consumer and public interest representation within the Communications Alliance. It discusses the travel assistance that the Communications Alliance provided to representatives of consumer and public interest organisations who served on working committees.

II. Conceptual Approach

A. Characterising the Rule-making Process

Each of the case studies focuses on identifying the nature of the 'politic'[1]—the 'conflict and controversy'[2]—of Part 6 rule-making. How best to 'characterise' the

[1] EC Page, *Governing By Numbers* (Oxford, Hart Publishing, 2001) 2.

[2] ibid 3. Page does not precisely delineate what he means by conflict but suggests that it involves '[a] person's battle won or lost.' ibid 2.

politic of a process is open to debate but the approach adopted in this book draws on Schattschneider's theory of the scope of political conflict.[3] For Schattschneider, the character and outcome of a conflict is determined by its scope—the number and type of people who participate in it.[4] Moreover, the scope of a conflict is 'partisan' in nature; it has a bias that reflects the particular groups and/or individuals who participate in the process.[5] Further, 'socializing' conflict by joining parties to a debate or 'privatizing' conflict by reducing those who can participate can be an important strategy to 'change the balance of power' between participants because it can and will alter the underlying dynamic of the conflict.[6] Indeed, Schattschneider states that altering the scope of conflict is 'the most important strategy of politics'.[7] However, by implication, increasing or decreasing the number and type of people who participate in a conflict may or may not be possible depending on the scope of the relevant conflict.[8]

Schattschneider's theory of the scope of political conflict was developed in order to explore the 'nationalization of politics' occurring in the US during the 1950s.[9] However, the core elements of the theory—participants, strategies and bias—informed this study of Part 6 rule-making for several reasons. First, the theory resonated with the changes that Part 6 rule-making (and other forms of proceduralized rule-making) have brought about. They fundamentally alter who is involved in rule-making. They 'democratize' regulation by including industry participants in the rule-making process in a way they never were before. On its face, the confidentiality of the Communications Alliance working committee process (described in chapter three) also excluded other participants, including, for example, the general public and elected officials, from it. With its emphasis on the effect that a change of participants can make, the theory provided a way to capture the dynamic of Part 6 rule-making. Second, there is nothing in Schattschneider's theory that confines it to US federal politics or the politics of the state. It is sufficiently broad to encompass all types of conflict, including conflict within the decentred state. The theory has also been used to inform Page's study of the politic of statutory instrument formation in the UK.[10] For similar reasons, Brown has suggested that the theory could be used to explain the 'politics of globalization'.[11]

[3] EE Schattschneider, *The Semisovereign People: A Realist's View of Democracy in America* (New York, Holt, Rinehart and Winston, 1960).

[4] ibid 2–3.

[5] ibid 4–5.

[6] Page, above n 1, 5.

[7] ibid 3.

[8] ibid 9–11.

[9] Schattschneider, above n 3, 11.

[10] Page, above n 1.

[11] R Brown, 'The Contagiousness of Conflict' (2010) 5 *Information, Communication & Society* 258, 265–66.

B. Clarifying Terminology

Before moving on, it is also necessary to define the precise meaning of the terms 'participant', 'strategy' and 'bias', as used in this book, because of their importance to the conceptual approach it adopts and the book as a whole.

A 'participant' is an actor who was able to 'influence the flow of events.' In other words, a participant is someone or something that affected the character and outcome of the code development process. The notion of 'influencing the flow of events' is used to describe the power of various participants in the process because it accords with a broad understanding of regulation that accommodates the presence of non-state actors.[12] Importantly, a participant is not necessarily someone who sat on a working committee of the Communications Alliance. All members of working committees (and their delegates) were participants. However, many actors involved in the process did not sit on a working committee. Nevertheless, they satisfied the definition of a participant.

A 'strategy' is a tactic deployed (with or without success) by a participant with the intention of 'secur[ing a] favourable outcome'[13] in the process.

'Bias' means 'a tendency for certain participants, or certain types of participants, to enjoy advantages'[14] that are different from those they have in other rule-making fora, as a result of the process of Part 6 rule-making, that other participants do not. Such advantages may include, but are not limited to, the ability to act 'unchecked' absent the 'normal constraints'[15] of legislative and administrative rule-making.

C. Common Structure of the Consumer Code Case Studies

The three case studies that follow in chapters five, six and seven share a common structure. It mirrors the core information needed to characterise the code development process according to Schattschneider's theory of the scope of political conflict. Section I of each case study provides some information about the specific context in which the relevant code of practice was developed. It explains the reasons why the Communications Alliance convened the working committee to develop the particular Part 6 code and describes the composition of the working committee. Section II explains the power of the voting members of the working committee to shape the development of each code and the source(s) of that power. Section III of the case studies discusses the roles played by the participants in the relevant code development process. Sections IV and V of the case studies describe, respectively, the strategies the various participants used in an

[12] C Parker and J Braithwaite, 'Regulation' in P Cane and M Tushnet (eds), *The Oxford Handbook of Legal Studies* (Oxford, Oxford University Press, 2003) 119, 119.

[13] Page, above n 1, 182.

[14] ibid 11.

[15] ibid.

attempt to advance their interests in the process and the means used to resolve conflict among working committee members.

D. Data Sources

The information used to prepare the case studies came primarily from two sources: the files held by the Communications Alliance for each of the three Part 6 codes; and interviews with individuals who had served on the three working committees that drafted the codes. Each file contained meeting agenda, details of working committee members, all drafts of the relevant code, committee meeting papers, including the minutes of meetings, the original project proposal and the working commitee's terms of reference. The Appendix explains in full the methodology used for the case studies and why it was chosen.

Information that helps contextualise the case studies is discussed below.

III. The Institutional Context

A. Industry Information

i. Terminology

The three case studies use a number of terms as defined in the Telecommunications Act 1997 (Cth) to describe, classify and distinguish between the various industry participants that served on the working committees of the Communications Alliance: carriers; carriage service providers; content service providers; and manufacturers and importers of customer equipment. The Information on Accessibility Features for Telephone Equipment code (the IAF code) case study also refers to 'standard telephone services' as defined in the Telecommunications Act 1997 (Cth). To appreciate the case studies, it is not essential to know in detail or master the complex wording of each term within the statute—each contains multiple references to other defined terms—but it is helpful to have some understanding of what they mean.

A 'carrier' is an entity that has obtained a carrier licence from the Australian Communications and Media Authority (ACMA) (formerly the Australian Communications Authority (ACA)). The licence permits the use of one or more 'network units'—in broad terms, any communications infrastructure, including wires, cables, fibres, base-stations and satellite-based facilities—owned by the licensee for the provision of carriage services to the public. Carriage services, generally speaking, consist of all telecommunication services, such as fixed-line telephony, mobile, Internet and data services, which transmit the underlying messages and data that users wish to convey to and/or receive from a third party. Provision of a carriage service to the public includes its supply to anyone beyond the 'immediate circle' of the owner.

A 'carriage service provider' does not own and operate communications infrastructure. Rather, it supplies 'listed carriage services'—carriage services provided within and/or to and from Australia—to the public using network units owned and operated by a carrier.

A 'content service provider' uses listed carriage services to provide content services, including, for example, broadcasting, video-on-demand and interactive computer game services, to the public.

Carriage and content service providers (collectively referred to as service providers) are not individually licensed by ACMA. They have a general authorisation to provide listed carriage and content services to the public, provided they comply with the service provider rules set out in the legislation. Subject to some exceptions,[16] carriers are free to act as either a carriage or content service provider; and in practice, the largest carriers within Australia are also the largest carriage service providers.

'Manufacturers and importers of customer equipment' are those entities that make and import customer equipment—the equipment, apparatus or systems used on the customer side of the termination point of a telecommunications network. In everyday parlance, telephone and mobile handsets are most commonly associated with the term 'customer equipment' but customer equipment can encompass any object or device communications users seek to connect to a telecommunications network.

Finally, a 'standard telephone service' is a voice telephony service and any of its equivalents that satisfy the 'any-to-any connectivity' test. The 'any-to-any connectivity' test is satisfied when an end-user of a voice telephony service and its equivalents is 'ordinarily able to communicate, by means of the service, with each other end-user who is supplied with the same service for the same purpose, whether or not the end-users are connected to the same telecommunications network.'

ii. Structure of the Relevant 'Sections of the Telecommunications Industry'

Each of the three codes of practice that are the focus of the case studies regulated different sections of the industry. The Consumer Contracts code, which forms the basis for chapter five, was addressed to carriage service providers offering telecommunications services, including related goods, such as handsets and other services to residential and small-business/non-profit organisation users. The IAF code, discussed in chapter six, was directed at manufacturers and importers of telephone and mobile handsets, and other customer equipment with in-built

[16] The government-owned enterprise building and operating the NBN, the open-access, wholesale-only broadband network that is being built throughout Australia, is subject to certain restrictions.

handsets for use with the standard telephone service, such as fax machines. The Mobile Premium Services (MPS) code, explored in chapter seven, imposed obligations on the commercial actors involved in the mobile premium services industry, including content providers, 'aggregators' and mobile carriage service providers. Below, the leading players of—and their market power within—each industry sector at the time the codes were developed are explained. However, it is important to recognise that the three sectors did not operate independently or in isolation from one another. As will be seen in the case studies, market players from the telecommunications services industry in particular were influential in shaping the rules adopted for the customer equipment manufacturing and mobile premium services industries because of their participation in various supply chains and their power in the telecommunications services market.

a. The Telecommunications Services Industry

The Consumer Contracts code was addressed to carriage service providers—the entities that provide telecommunications services to the public. However, the telecommunications services industry is composed of carriage service providers and licensed carriers whose infrastructure is used to provide the underlying services. When the Consumer Contracts code was drafted, the industry consisted of three markets. The first market was a fixed-line voice market dominated by Telstra, the formerly state-owned, 'vertically integrated incumbent'[17] with a 'near ubiquitous copper access network'.[18] The second market was the much more competitive market for mobile services. From 2003 until the merger of Vodafone and Hutchison in May 2009, the market for mobile services had four licensed mobile carriers. After the merger, there were three carriers: Telstra, Optus and Vodafone Hutchison Australia (VHA). The third market was the Internet access services market.

Fixed-line Voice

During April 2004 and November 2005, when the IAF and Consumer Contracts codes were drafted, approximately 87–88 per cent of Australian homes and businesses depended on Telstra's copper network to access telephony services.[19] Optus, which was granted fixed and mobile carrier licences in 1991, had a hybrid fibre coaxial cable (HFC) network but it passed only between 2.2 to 2.5 million homes.[20] Competition for fixed-line services, which consist of line rental, local

[17] Ovum, *Unfinished Business—20 Years of Competition in Australia's Telecommunications Sector: A Report for* Optus (November 2011) 2.

[18] ACCC, *Telecommunications Reports 2003–04* (2004) 12.

[19] ibid; ACCC, *Telecommunications Reports 2004–05* (2005) 17; ACCC, *Telecommunications Reports 2005–06* (2006) 14.

[20] *Telecommunications Reports 2003–04*, above n 18, 12; *Telecommunications Reports 2004–05*, above n 19, 17; *Telecommunications Reports 2005–06*, above n 19, 14.

calls, national and international long-distance services and fixed-to-mobile calls was also limited. As of 30 June 2004, in addition to Telstra and Optus, only seven other companies offered line rental services to residential customers (including AAPT), most of which were reliant on Telstra's copper network to provide the service.[21] In June 2005, the Australian Competition and Consumer Commission (ACCC) estimated that Telstra had a 63 per cent share of the national and international long-distance services market.[22] Optus had 12 per cent, while AAPT had nine per cent. All other providers shared nine per cent of the market.[23]

Mobile Services

By contrast, in 2004–05, each of Telstra, Optus and Vodafone's 2G mobile networks covered between 95–96 per cent of the Australian population.[24] Hutchison, which entered the market in 2003, had deployed a 3G network to Australia's major capital cities and the Gold Coast, and was deploying its network to other parts of Australia. Optus commenced the roll-out of its 3G mobile network in April 2005. Vodafone was trialling its 3G network in July 2005. Telstra's 3G network was already 'operational' in Australia's major capital cities by September 2005.[25] In addition to Telstra, Optus, Vodafone and Hutchison, there were a number of other mobile carriage service providers. They included Mobile Virtual Network Operators (MVNOs),[26] such as Virgin Mobile and AAPT, and approximately 90 resellers.[27] However, the retail market for mobile services was highly concentrated in the hands of Telstra, Optus and Vodafone. The three carriers controlled between 94–95 per cent of the market from 1 July 2004 until 30 June 2006.[28] In 2005–06, Telstra had 8.6 million subscribers (the most of any provider), followed by Optus with 6.5 million, Vodafone with 3.45 million and Hutchison with 1.13 million.[29] When work on the MPS code began in April 2008, the market share of each of the four carriers had not changed significantly.[30]

[21] *Telecommunications Reports 2003–04*, above n 18, 13.
[22] *Telecommunications Reports 2004–05*, above n 19, 30.
[23] ibid.
[24] ACMA, *Telecommunications Performance Report 2004–05* (2005) 73.
[25] The Allen Consulting Group, *Australian Mobile Telecommunications Industry Economic Significance: Report to the Australian Mobile Telecommunications Association* (September 2005) 4.
[26] MVNOs buy wholesale mobile network capacity from a carrier but 'provide a technical support layer that replicates the mobile network operator's mobile switching centre', which gives them some flexibility to differentiate their services from the mobile carriers. *Telecommunications Reports 2005–06*, above n 19, 23. All services are 'badged' under the name of the MVNO. ACMA, *Communications Report 2005–06* (2006) 58.
[27] Unlike MVNOs, resellers just purchase wholesale mobile network capacity from a carrier and retail it under their own names. *Telecommunications Report 2005–06*, above n 19, 23; *Communications Report 2005–06*, above n 26, 58; The Allen Consulting Group, above n 25, 9.
[28] *Telecommunications Reports 2004–05*, above n 19, 33; *Telecommunications Reports 2005–06*, above n 19, 26.
[29] *Communications Report 2005–06*, above n 26, 59–60.
[30] See ACCC, *Telecommunications Reports 2007–08* (2008) 32–34.

Internet Access Services

In March 2004, one month and two months, respectively, before the IAF and Consumer Contracts code working committees were formed, there were 694 Internet service providers (ISPs).[31] This number had fallen to 689 by March 2005.[32] However, the number of Internet service providers is not an accurate indicator of the degree of competition within the market for Internet access services. In June 2004, Telstra had 42 per cent of the retail market for fixed broadband access, then the most conventional form of broadband access.[33] One of the reasons, if not the principal reason, for Telstra's leading position in the fixed broadband access retail market was its ability to exploit its existing copper access network using xDSL technology.[34]

Other

Two other features of the Australian telecommunications services market should be noted. First, by global standards, the Australian market has been and continues to be small. To give but a flavour of the difference in scale, market analyst BuddeComm estimated that the total revenue for all telecommunications services in 2011 had surpassed AU$40 billion.[35] Although it is difficult to find exactly comparable figures, the Federal Communications Commission reported that the total revenue for the US services market in the same year was nearly US$2.6 trillion.[36] Second, Telstra was not fully privatised until 24 November 2006 (well after the completion of the IAF and Consumer Contracts codes) when the Australian government no longer had a controlling share in the company. Telstra was partially privatised in 1997 when the government sold one third of its shares. A further 16.6 per cent was sold in 1999 with the remaining 50.1 per cent sold in 2006.

b. The Customer Equipment (Handset) Manufacturing Industry

Publicly available data on fixed and mobile telephone handset manufacturers and importers supplying the Australian market, when work on the IAF code, discussed in chapter six, began in April 2004, were difficult to locate. Data on fixed telephones and their manufacturers and importers, in particular, are lacking. However, in a report prepared for the Australian government in December 2002, McKinsey & Company highlighted that the Australian market for mobile handsets

[31] ACA, *Telecommunications Performance Report 2003–04* (2004) 85.

[32] *Telecommunications Reports 2005–06*, above n 19, 31.

[33] *Telecommunications Reports 2003–04*, above n 18, 30.

[34] ibid 23–24.

[35] BuddeComm, 'Executive Summary: Australia—Analysis Telecom Market—mid 2012' (Media Release, 2012).

[36] FCC, *Universal Service Monitoring Report 2013 (Data Received Through October 2013)* Table 1.1.

was concentrated in the hands of three players: Nokia, Motorola and Ericsson. Nokia had approximately 52 per cent share of the market, Ericsson 14 per cent and Motorola nine per cent.[37] In addition, while the number of mobile handsets sold in Australia was not insignificant, the size of the Australian market was relatively tiny. For example, in 2001, it was estimated that sales in Australia accounted for only 0.6 per cent of the global revenue for mobile handsets.[38]

c. Mobile Premium Services Industry

MPS are premium rate Short Message Services (SMS), Multimedia Messaging Services (MMS)[39] and proprietary network services[40] provided via mobile phones and similar devices. There are two principal participants in the industry: content service providers and aggregators. Content service providers generate or package the content that is eventually delivered to mobile phone users. Aggregators facilitate the delivery of the content by operating an IT platform that interfaces with the terrestrial networks of the three licensed mobile carriers: Telstra, Optus and VHA. There is little publicly available information about the number of content service providers and aggregators operating in the Australian industry when work on the MPS code began in April 2008. As will be seen in chapter seven, ACMA and the Telecommunications Industry Ombudsman (TIO) had no real way to track these entities before the MPS code was registered. Indeed, one of the code's key requirements was for content service providers and aggregators to register with the Communications Alliance prior to supplying MPS and to keep their contact details up-to-date so the regulators could find out who they were.[41] However, in October 2009, five months after the code was registered, 237 content service providers and 16 aggregators were listed in the Communications Alliance's register.[42] According to ACMA, 23 per cent of the content service providers were based overseas in 16 countries. Of those 59 content service providers, 40 per cent were located in the UK.[43] As will be explained in detail in chapter seven, mobile carriers and carriage service providers are involved with the industry: they are responsible for the physical delivery of the content and they bill subscribers for MPS. However, they are not generally seen as industry members.[44]

[37] McKinsey & Company, *Australia: Winning in the Global ICT Industry: Final Report* (December 2002) 201.

[38] ibid 199, 201.

[39] Customers typically access these services from their mobile phones by dialing/sending a text to a number with a 19X prefix.

[40] These are services provided by mobile carriage service providers that enable customers to access content services not otherwise generally available via their mobile handsets for a fee. They are commonly referred to as 'walled-garden' or 'portal' services.

[41] Communications Alliance, *Industry Code C637: Mobile Premium Services* (2009) cls 4.1.1, 4.1.2.

[42] ACMA, *Communications Report 2009–10* (2010) 111.

[43] ibid.

[44] ibid.

B. Regulatory Bodies

The case studies refer to three regulatory bodies: ACMA, the ACCC and the TIO. It is necessary to describe ACMA's role in the regulation of the telecommunications sector; the functions of the ACCC and the TIO in the Part 6 process; and their role in the regulation of the telecommunications sector. It should already be clear that ACMA registers codes of practice in accordance with Part 6 and is responsible for enforcing them. In addition, the case studies distinguish between the staff of ACMA and the members of the 'Authority' itself. In order to appreciate the distinction, it is necessary to have some understanding of the composition of ACMA and its power to make decisions.

i. Roles and Functions of the ACMA, ACCC and TIO

Like its predecessor, the ACA, ACMA's functions in the telecommunications sector extend primarily to administering Commonwealth legislation dealing with matters such as the licensing of telecommunications carriers, technical standards and telecommunications-specific consumer protection provisions, including universal service. Responsibility for all competition-related aspects of the sector rests with the ACCC. For example, it administers Parts XIB and XIC of the Competition and Consumer Act 2010 (Cth), which pertain, respectively, to anti-competitive conduct by carriers and carriage service providers, and the ability of service providers to access the facilities owned by carriers or services provided by carriage service providers. In addition, the ACCC has a number of other powers to protect all consumers from other unlawful activity, such as misleading, deceptive and unconscionable conduct. The division of responsibility for the regulation of telecommunications between ACMA and the ACCC is unlike the UK, which created a single 'super' regulator overseeing all aspects of the communications sector in 2003, and inconsistent with a wider global trend to confer all sector-specific regulatory functions on a single regulator.[45] While not a decision-maker in the code registration process, the ACCC must be 'consulted' about the development of a code of practice before ACMA can register it.[46]

The TIO is the individual appointed by the Board of TIO Ltd whose principal responsibility is to investigate, make determinations and give directions concerning end-user complaints about 'eligible carriage service providers'—carriage service providers supplying standard telephone services to residential and small business customers, public mobile telecommunications services and Internet access—and their services.[47] TIO Ltd is the company responsible for operating the TIO scheme mandated by the Telecommunications (Consumer Protection

[45] See generally Y Okamoto, Directorate for Science, Technology and Industry, OECD, *Telecommunication Regulatory Institutional Structures and Responsibilities* (11 January 2006).

[46] Telecommunications Act 1997 (Cth) s 117(1)(g).

[47] See *TIO Terms of Reference* (26 February 2014).

and Service Standards) Act 1999 (Cth). Along with complaints handling, the ombudsman is tasked with investigating systemic problems and liaising with ACMA, the ACCC and other industry bodies to whom it may refer unresolved problems (where appropriate).[48] The ombudsman must also exercise the functions and powers conferred, with his or her consent, in a Part 6 code.[49] For example, the Consumer Contracts and MPS codes gave the ombudsman the authority to investigate end-user complaints about code-related matters, including non-compliance.[50] In addition, the TIO shares complaints and code compliance data with ACMA.[51] The Telecommunications Act 1997 (Cth) mandates that industry must consult with the TIO before a Part 6 code applicable to a section of the telecommunications industry can be registered by ACMA.[52]

ii. Composition of and Decision-making by ACMA

ACMA consists of a chair, a deputy chair and at least one and not more than seven other members. All members, including the chair and deputy chair, are appointed by the Governor-General of Australia, on the recommendation of the relevant Minister for Communications. The chair and deputy chair are appointed as full-time members. ACMA may also have associate members who are appointed by the Minister. Unless it has delegated a function or power, all decisions of ACMA must be determined by a majority of its members. Associate members may vote on matters in limited circumstances. ACMA's predecessor, the ACA, was similarly constituted. However, in addition to the chair and deputy chair, it could not have more than three other members. When the Consumer Contracts and the IAF codes were drafted, Dr Bob Horton was acting chair of the ACA. When the MPS code was drafted, Chris Chapman was the chair of ACMA.

C. Consumer and Public Interest Organisations, Communications Alliance Advisory Bodies and Related Matters

A number of different consumer and public interest organisations and internal advisory bodies of the Communications Alliance were members of the working committees that developed the three codes considered in the case studies. Only four consumer and public interest organisations—CTN, the Small Enterprise Telecommunications Centre Limited (SETEL), the Telecommunications and Disability Consumer Representation (Tedicore) and the Communications Law Centre (CLC)—will be introduced here. While they were not the only consumer

48 ibid ss 5, 6.

49 ibid s 6.1.

50 ACIF, *Industry Code ACIF C620: Consumer Contracts* (2005) s 3.2; *Industry Code C637: Mobile Premium Services*, above n 41, s 8.2. No such grant was made in the IAF code.

51 See, eg, *Memorandum of Understanding between ACMA and TIO 2013* cl 23.

52 Telecommunications Act 1997 (Cth) s 117(1)(h).

and public interest organisations involved with the development of either the Consumer Contracts code, considered in chapter five, or the IAF code, discussed in chapter six, they were recognised as the leading consumer and public interest organisations in the telecommunications sector. Moreover, CTN, SETEL and Tedicore were active within the two internal bodies the Communications Alliance established to provide advice on consumer and disability matters. An overview of these bodies and a summary of the decline in consumer and public interest representation within the Communications Alliance then follow. The former is provided because one or more of the internal bodies were appointed as members of the working committees that developed the IAF and the MPS codes. The latter is provided because it accounts, in part, for the tension and distrust that existed between consumer and public interest representatives, and staff of the Communications Alliance when the MPS code, discussed in chapter seven, was developed. This sub-section concludes by explaining briefly the funding the Communications Alliance gave to consumer and public interest organisations to support their participation in working committees.

i. Telecommunications Consumer and Public Interest Organisations

Until the establishment of the Australian Communications Consumer Action Network (ACCAN) in July 2009, there were three 'peak' organisations representing the interests of residential, small business and disabled telecommunications users in Australia: CTN, SETEL and Tedicore. Created in 1989, CTN represented residential consumer and community interests in the field of telecommunications policy. Its members included national and state organisations representing consumers from non-English speaking backgrounds, Indigenous Australians, young people, the elderly, individuals with disabilities, including the deaf, and end-users residing in rural and remote parts of Australia.[53] The role of SETEL, founded in 1992, was to promote the interests of 'small, micro and home business'[54] users to government departments, regulators and the telecommunications industry. Tedicore was established in 1998 to represent the interests of people with disabilities; its principal objective was to increase the accessibility and affordability of telecommunications services and equipment for people with disabilities.[55] Like ACCAN, each organisation was funded by a telecommunications consumer representation grant from the Commonwealth. However, relative to what ACCAN has received,[56] the total amount of money allocated to each body was small.

[53] See, eg, CTN, Submission to DBCDE, *Independent Disability Equipment Program Feasibility Study*, April 2009, 1.

[54] SETEL, Submission to Productivity Commission, *Consumer Policy Framework*, 6 February 2008, 1.

[55] Tedicore, Submission to Productivity Commission, *Inquiry into the Disability Discrimination Act 1992*, May 2003, 1.

[56] ACCAN received AU$2 million (indexed for inflation) annually between 2009 and 2013. ACCAN, *Annual Report 2009* (2010) 12.

From 2002 to 2009, AU$850,000 per year were allocated by the government to all consumer representation grant recipients[57] with a 'large proportion' of that sum distributed to CTN, SETEL and Tedicore.[58] At most, each organisation had only a handful of full-time staff members.

In Australia, only one public interest organisation has been active in the telecommunications policy sphere: the CLC. Established in 1988, the CLC was an 'independent, not-for-profit research, teaching and public education organisation specialising in media and communications law and policy.'[59] It was affiliated with the University of New South Wales from 1988 until June 2005 and Victoria University from 1996 until 2008. It was based at University of Technology, Sydney from 2009 until it closed in December 2015. When the three codes discussed in chapters five, six and seven were drafted, it had only a small number of full-time staff members and relied on volunteers.

ii. Communications Alliance Advisory Bodies

When the IAF code was developed, the two internal bodies the Communications Alliance established to provide advice on consumer and disability matters were known as the 'Disability Advisory Body' (DAB) and the 'Consumer Advisory Council' (CAC). When the MPS code was developed, they were known as the 'Disability Council' and the 'Consumer Council'. The name changes were the consequence of the adoption of a common framework for consumer participation and a 'consumer interests register'.[60] Both the framework and register were motivated by a desire to 'professionalise' consumer involvement in the organisation. However, the practical effect they had on the development of the MPS code of practice was minimal. They did not fundamentally alter the role of either body. They did not change to any significant extent the consumer and public interest organisations that were participating in the Communications Alliance. They did not affect the rule-making framework used by the Communications Alliance to develop Part 6 codes.

The function, composition and selection process of the members of each body are briefly explained below.

a. The Disability Advisory Body/the Disability Council

DAB, which was a member of the IAF code working committee, was established in 1998. Like the Disability Council, its role was to advise on the likely impact of

[57] DBCDE (Cth), *Mid-term Review of the Australian Communications Consumer Action Network (ACCAN)* (April 2012) 5.

[58] DCITA (Cth), *Review of Telecommunications Consumer Representation and Telecommunications Research Grants Programs: Discussion Paper* (September 2005) 3.

[59] CLC, Submission to ABA, *Commercial Radio Inquiry* (September 2000) 2.

[60] ACIF, *Consumer Participation Framework* (July 2006); ACIF, *Principles for Registration on ACIF's Consumer Interests Register and Application Form* (July 2006).

proposed rules on disabled end-users and the appropriate methods of consultation with these individuals and those organisations representing their interests.[61] It was comprised of nine members, including a chair.[62] Organisations such as the Australian Association of the Deaf and Blind Citizens Australia[63] served as DAB and Disability Council members.

The selection process of DAB members was never documented. Members of the Disability Council were chosen from the consumer interests register by a selection committee appointed by the Communications Alliance.[64] To be added to the register, an organisation had to be able to demonstrate, among other things, its ability to represent consumer or public interest perspectives.[65]

b. The Consumer Advisory Council/the Consumer Council

CAC was established in 2002 in response to the decision of CTN, SETEL, the CLC and other consumer bodies to cease participation in the ACIF in December 2001 citing (among other things) failure by ACIF to consider sufficiently the needs of consumers.[66] Modelled on DAB, CAC was responsible for providing consumer 'input' into the work of ACIF.[67] It was comprised of up to 15 members, which consisted of the chair of DAB and organisations representing a variety of consumers.[68] Inaugural CAC members were appointed by the ACIF board; subsequent CAC members by CAC.[69] Applicants for membership had to meet the same selection criteria that organisations had to satisfy in order to be added to the consumer interests register (discussed above). When CAC was renamed the Consumer Council, its membership was reduced to 12 members, and included ACIF's CEO and the chair of the Disability Council.[70] Its members were also chosen from the consumer interests register by a selection committee appointed by the Communications Alliance.[71] However, its function remained the same as CAC's.

iii. The Decline of Consumer and Public Interest Representation within the Communications Alliance

Consumer and public interest organisations have always been represented on consumer code working committees of the Communications Alliance. Indeed,

[61] ACIF, *1999 Annual Report* (1999) 39; ACIF, *Industry Guideline: Consumer Participation in ACIF and ACIF Processes* (2002) 7.

[62] DAB, Terms of Reference (28 October 2002).

[63] See, eg, ACIF, *Annual Report 2003* (2003) 82; ACIF, *Annual Report 2004* (2004) 76.

[64] *Consumer Participation Framework*, above n 60, s 3.4

[65] *Principles for Registration on ACIF's Consumer Interests Register*, above n 60, 2–3.

[66] See, eg, Letter from P Marsh, Chair, CTN, to J Plante, CEO, ACIF (30 November 2001); Letter from H Campbell, CEO, CTN, to J Plante, CEO, ACIF (11 February 2002). Following ACIF's decision to create CAC and to develop guidelines for payment of travel expenses incurred by consumer groups, CTN, SETEL and CLC resumed participation in ACIF processes, but not all consumer groups did.

[67] ACIF, *Industry Guideline: Consumer Participation in ACIF and ACIF* Processes (2002) 11.

[68] ibid 8.

[69] ibid 9.

[70] *Consumer Participation Framework*, above n 60, s 3.1(b).

[71] ibid 2.

it will be argued in chapter eight that participation by consumer and public interest organisations is an entrenched feature of Part 6 rule-making. However, the degree to which they are permitted to become involved with the industry organisation itself has diminished significantly, particularly since the Communications Alliance reviewed consumer involvement within the organisation in 2008–09 and the establishment of ACCAN. For example, CTN was an initial subscriber to ACIF in 1997. In addition, consumer and public interest organisations could be (and often were) members of the Communications Alliance until 2008–09.[72] In fact, consumer and public interest organisations were guaranteed some representation on the Communications Alliance board until 2006. Moreover, until 2008, consumer and public interest organisations could (and did) serve on Communications Alliance Reference Panels,[73] which are responsible for 'professional oversight of particular areas of Industry activity'.[74] When the MPS code was being developed, the Communications Alliance was also reviewing whether it should continue to have the Disability and Consumer Councils. Both councils were disbanded shortly after the completion of the MPS code.

iv. Funding of Working Committee Participation

Finally, the Communications Alliance provided travel assistance, including hotel accommodation for the representatives of consumer and public interest organisations.[75] As will become clear in the case studies, there were significant imbalances in terms of resources between the consumer and public interest organisations, and the members of industry appointed to the three working committees. However, it must be acknowledged that the limited funding industry provided facilitated and improved the quality of participation by consumer and public interest organisations in the code development process.

[72] CTN and SETEL were ACIF members when they served on the working committees for the Consumer Contracts and IAF codes. *ACIF Annual Report 2004*, above n 63, 68.

[73] CTN and SETEL were members of ACIF's Consumer Codes Reference Panel when the Consumer Contracts code was drafted. The CEO of SETEL was its deputy chair. ibid 72; Interview with former CTN employee (Name Withheld) (Sydney, 4 April 2012).

[74] See, eg, ACIF, *Operating Manual for the Development of Codes, Standards, Specifications, Guidelines and Other Supporting Arrangements* (April 2000) s 3.1.

[75] See, eg, ACIF, *Provision of Travel Assistance to Consumer Representatives on ACIF Panels, Committees and* Groups (2002).

5

The Consumer Contracts Code

I. Working Committee Composition and Context

The Consumer Contracts code was written by a working committee consisting of an independent chair, eight voting members and three non-voting members. The eight voting members included four consumer and public interest organisations (Communications Law Centre (CLC), Consumers Telecommunications Network (CTN), Country Women's Association of Australia and the Small Enterprise Telecommunications Centre Limited (SETEL)), and four industry bodies (Telstra, Optus, Vodafone and Hutchison). The non-voting members were the Australian Communications Authority (ACA), the Australian Competition and Consumer Commission (ACCC) and the office of the Telecommunications Industry Ombudsman (TIO). The Australian Communications Industry Forum (ACIF) invited the three regulatory bodies to sit on the working committee so they could provide their comments (if any) as work progressed. Voting and non-voting members often fielded more than one representative during working committee meetings and occasionally replaced representatives during the development process, for example, due to maternity leave and/or employee departures from their organisations. Consumer Contracts code representatives attended 24 all-day face-to-face meetings from May–December 2004 plus a full day mediation session and scrutinised more than 17 drafts of the code. In its final form, the code prohibited the use of 'unfair' contract terms by carriage service providers in contracts with residential consumers and small-businesses; required carriage service providers to employ contracts that used plain language and followed a specified format and structure (eg one that was written and legible); and imposed certain obligations relating to information accessibility.

ACIF convened the working committee following a formal request of the ACA dated 26 November 2003 made under Part 6 of the Telecommunications Act 1997 (Cth) (Part 6) to prepare a code.[1] The request was prompted after the CLC

[1] Letter from B Horton, Acting Chair, ACA to J Plante, CEO, ACIF (26 November 2003).

found, on two occasions,[2] that the leading industry players were not complying with a non-binding ACIF industry guideline adopted in 2002 (the 2002 industry guideline).[3] The industry guideline dealt with 'unfair' terms, and the intelligibility and clarity of consumer contracts. Instances of non-compliance discovered by the CLC included, for example, terms requiring mobile subscribers to pay a fee for the reconnection of certain services even though disconnection was the fault of the provider; terms permitting Internet dial-up and broadband providers to terminate subscriber contracts without reasonable notice; and clauses allowing for the automatic renewal of fixed term contracts.[4] In its request, the ACA also cited its analysis of TIO complaints statistics for the 12 months to 30 September 2003 as further justification for the code.[5] Despite having reservations about the need for a code, due in part to its view that the TIO's statistics did not provide sufficient evidence of the need for a code,[6] industry acquiesced to the ACA's request for a number of reasons.

Under Part 6, failure to adopt a code after receipt of a formal request enabled the ACA to determine a standard for the industry.[7] In other words, if industry did not adopt a code, rule-making power would shift from industry to the ACA: the ACA would be permitted to intervene directly in the sector by adopting an industry standard. This threat of regulatory intervention was perceived to be real by at least two committee industry representatives interviewed, both of whom said they and their employers were conscious of the possible loss of control. The ACA's formal request had followed two earlier informal requests to industry to prepare a code: when ACIF established the working committee to develop the 2002 industry guideline and while the 2002 industry guideline was being developed.[8] Furthermore, it was made at a time when there had been years of sustained criticism of Part 6 rule-making by consumer and public interest advocates. Problems identified included the length of time taken to adopt consumer codes; the ability of ACIF's code development process to develop adequate consumer protection measures; and industry's commitment to complying with the 2002 industry guideline and registered consumer codes dealing with matters such as credit management, billing, customer transfer and complaints-handling.[9]

[2] CLC, *Report on Fair Terms in Telecommunications Consumer Contracts* (May 2003); ACA, *Telecommunications Consumer Contracts: Compliance with the ACIF Consumer Contracts Industry Guideline: Prepared for the Australian Communications Authority by the Communications Law Centre Ltd* (October 2003).

[3] ACIF, *Industry Guideline ACIF G601: Consumer Contracts* (December 2002).

[4] CLC, above n 2, 3–21; ACA, *Telecommunications Consumer Contracts*, above n 2, 8–56.

[5] Letter dated 26 November 2003 from B Horton, above n 1, 1.

[6] See, eg, Letter from J Plante, CEO, ACIF to B Horton, Acting Chair, ACA (9 December 2003).

[7] Telecommunications Act 1997 (Cth) s 123.

[8] Letter dated 26 November 2003 from B Horton, above n 1, 2.

[9] See, eg, Louise Sylvan, 'Self-Regulation—Who's in Charge Here?' (Australian Institute of Criminology's 'Current Issues in Regulation: Enforcement and Compliance' Conference, Melbourne, 2 September 2002).

The situation had also attracted the attention of the then Minister for Communications and staff of the Department of Communications, Information Technology and the Arts. They had indicated that self-regulation had to be seen to deliver benefits for consumers or other regulatory alternatives would have to be explored. The development of the Consumer Contracts code was therefore seen as a significant test of the viability of ACIF as an organisation and industry self-regulation more generally. As one industry representative stated, 'If ACIF was seen to fail on this one, then ACIF would fail altogether and, thereafter, there would be no self-regulation, whether that works or not.'[10]

Against this backdrop there were also legal and regulatory developments occurring at the state level. When the 2002 industry guideline was prepared, unlike the UK and EU with whom they had been compared,[11] the Commonwealth, States and Territories had not enacted statutory provisions regulating unfair terms in consumer contracts.[12] However, when the ACA's formal request to draft a code was received, the Victorian Parliament had just adopted the Fair Trading (Amendment) Act 2003 (Vic), which rendered void 'consumer contracts' deemed to be 'unfair'. Along with Queensland, Victoria had also chaired a Working Party on Unfair Contract Terms, established at the request of the Ministerial Council on Consumer Affairs, which had recommended the Commonwealth, States and Territories adopt uniform legislation dealing with unfair contract terms.[13] Although one industry representative interviewed believed there was no real prospect of Commonwealth legislation at the time, the Working Party's recommendation was made when consumer groups were lobbying for new state and territory laws based on the Victorian legislation. Of greatest concern to industry, however, was the fact that Consumer Affairs Victoria (CAV), a division of the Victorian Department of Justice charged with administering the new provisions in the Victorian legislation, began investigating the standard form mobile contracts of Telstra, Optus, Hutchison, Vodafone, Virgin Mobile and AAPT for possible unfair terms in 2003.[14] Collectively, these developments generated fear of legal action and other possible regulatory intervention. Adoption of a prescriptive code of practice jointly developed and agreed to by consumer and public interest groups was therefore seen as a way to reduce the ambiguity of the 'unfairness' principle and the lack of certainty in its application by CAV. One industry representative described this strategy as naïve in hindsight. Towards the end of the Consumer Contracts code process, CAV

[10] All statements attributed to working committee participants involved in the development of this code were made to the author during interviews held in March and April 2011. The names of interviewees are not provided to preserve the anonymity of the individuals concerned. For information about the research methodology used for the case studies, see the Appendix.

[11] CLC, *Unfair Practices and Telecommunications Consumers* (January 2001).

[12] The relevant UK and EU provisions were The Unfair Terms in Consumer Contracts Regulations 1999 SI 1999/2083 and Council Directive 93/13/EEC of 5 April 1993 on unfair terms in consumer contracts [1993] OJ L95/29.

[13] Unfair Contract Terms Working Party, COAG Standing Committee of Officials of Consumer Affairs, *Unfair Contract Terms: A Discussion Paper* (January 2004) 5.

[14] Consumer Affairs Victoria, *Annual Report 2004–05* (2005) 110.

made it quite clear the code would not influence its enforcement of the legislation. However, at the time it was a motivating factor for industry to draft the code.

II. Power

By virtue of the composition of the voting members of the working committee and the principle of equal representation for consumer and public interest organisations and industry suppliers adopted by ACIF for this code, rule-making power lay between consumer and public interest organisations, and industry. Representatives from all regulators contributed to the discussion that took place between consumer, public interest and industry representatives, and it was reported they often sided with consumer and public interest delegates on a variety of issues.[15] However, the debate centred on obtaining agreement between industry representatives and consumer and public interest delegates who often (but not always) fell into their respective camps—the 'us and them'. As one regulatory representative stated, he gave his views during working committee meetings and his organisation submitted comments during the public comment phase. However, as a non-voting member and one which had no power to register the code, he 'couldn't really do more than that'. Even the presence of the ACA (which had code registration authority) in the working committee room did not alter the landscape because its representatives were less willing to become actively involved in the detail of working committee discussions. The reasons for the ACA's reluctance to become directly involved in this code are not known. As discussed in chapter six, at the time, the ACA generally saw its role in the Part 6 process as a mere observer. However, as argued below, the ACA used the satisfaction of consumer and public interest representatives as a proxy for its regulatory approval, thereby giving the latter a significant amount of authority during the code development process.

A. Inside the Blocs

From the outset, the bargaining strategy of consumer and public interest representatives was to negotiate as a bloc in an effort to avoid what one consumer and public interest delegate described as the 'divide and conquer process' deployed by industry representatives in previous code working committees. Industry representatives did not initially adopt this approach, notwithstanding the broad alignment of their commercial interests. However, once debate began to stall, they did. Within their respective groups, power was evenly distributed amongst voting

[15] These included, for example, unilateral variation and the period of notice suppliers had to provide their customers before terminating a contract.

members although disagreement within the two was resolved differently. All consumer and public interest representatives stressed the importance of educating and learning from each other about the particular perspectives of their constituents and drawing on the particular strengths and talents each individual brought. Inevitably, however, a single leader who '[kept] people together' and '[kept] people going when they wanted to give up on a particular issue either because agreement could not be reached [with industry] or for other reasons' emerged. Despite imbalances in terms of market power in the industry, it was reported that the largest player did not have a disproportionate influence on the positions ultimately adopted by industry delegates or the working committee as a whole. Disagreement between consumer and public interest representatives was resolved by decision of the majority.[16] If industry delegates could not reach agreement among themselves, the dissenters were left to 'fend for themselves'. They were required to argue their case before the working committee.

B. David versus Goliath?

With respect to expertise, access to information and resources, there were imbalances between consumer and public interest organisations, and industry members on this working committee. With one exception, all individuals who represented industry were lawyers based in either the commercial or regulatory divisions of their employers. Amongst consumer and public interest organisations, only one, the CLC, was represented by an individual with legal training. Admittedly, the CLC had been heavily involved in drawing attention to the issue of unfairness in consumer contracts in Australia[17] and had been engaged by the ACA to assess industry compliance with the 2002 industry guideline.[18] However, one consumer and public interest representative reported feeling overwhelmed by the complexity of the legal issues discussed. Equally, other consumer and public interest representatives interviewed reported the presence of information asymmetries. Their lack of knowledge of economics and general business practice made it difficult for them to assess often-cited industry arguments that consumer and public interest proposals were too costly. However, one industry representative pointed out that its ability to calculate the impact of proposals was also limited. With some exceptions, costing was just 'guess work' and a 'finger in the air sort of thing'. There was some disparity in the amount of information consumer and public interest delegates could access. Industry's own resources were not unlimited—one company was represented by someone on secondment from a law firm because it was short of staff—but industry had greater resources at its disposal than consumer

[16] Some issues more relevant to small businesses were not pursued as a result.

[17] See, eg, CLC, *Unfair Practices*, above n 11.

[18] See CLC, *Report on Fair Terms*, above n 2; ACA, *Telecommunications Consumer Contracts*, above n 2.

and public interest representatives. Unlike consumer and public interest organisations, several industry organisations instructed external legal counsel to assist in code development. To inform their thinking, industry representatives also drew on large 'reference groups', the size of which varied depending on the company involved. In one case, up to five people from each commercial division of the business and individuals from the regulatory department, along with lawyers from each of those divisions and general counsel, were involved. By contrast, two consumer and public interest representatives suggested the duty of confidentiality imposed by ACIF prevented them from soliciting information and specific comment about the substance of working committee discussion from the members of their organisations. However, they could seek their views on the draft of the code released by ACIF for public consultation.[19] There was no significant imbalance in the time each representative spent preparing for and attending working committee meetings. Most delegates from both sides spent about two and one-half days per week on the project although one consumer and public interest representative worked full-time on it and another less than two days per week.

Whatever skills, resources and other advantages industry had, consumer and public interest representatives nevertheless wielded a significant amount of power in this working committee or were at least perceived to have equivalent bargaining strength by both industry representatives and others involved in the process. Consumer and public interest representatives, and others involved in the process, mentioned three contributing factors: the equal representation of consumer and public interest organisations, and industry suppliers on the working committee; the presence of a lawyer on the 'side' of consumer and public interest organisations; and ACIF's appointment of a truly independent chair for the very first time.[20] Equal representation was believed to be important because it enabled consumer and public interest representatives to negotiate as a bloc.[21] Industry representatives cited other factors, including the 'fantastic' organisation, planning and preparation of consumer and public interest delegates: 'They just seemed so much more prepared than we were most of the time. So when we would raise something, they would have five arguments as to why it was an issue or not an issue.' Industry representatives also saw the ability of consumer and public interest delegates to bundle issues together as crucial. As one industry representative stated:

> They took a lot of time to essentially bundle up issues and they would say, well, we're prepared to give you this, if you're prepared to give us this and this and this and this. We'd go, well, that's a big one for us, and we really need it, and we kind of lost all the rest

[19] Whether this was because of their interpretation of the obligation or ACIF's understanding of the obligation at the time is unclear.

[20] Historically, chairpersons had been elected from among and by the voting members of the working committee. Prior to April 2000, chairpersons could also vote.

[21] One industry representative interviewed believed the bloc-style of negotiation had the effect of moderating the more extreme views of the consumer advocates, allowing the stronger arguments to emerge in the debate.

> of it, so that we could get that bit which was important to us. They were very, very, very good at that.

Another factor cited by one industry representative was the ability of consumer and public interest representatives, all of whom were senior within their organisations, to bind their employers on the spot without the need to consult further internally and to obtain permission. By contrast, industry representatives often had no authority to deviate beyond an 'authorised' position, which necessitated 'time outs' so they could seek instructions, thus hindering the flow of working committee discussion, and giving consumer and public interest representatives more time to develop and strengthen their own position.[22] Finally, there were no 'wall flowers': 'People [consumer and public interest representatives] were prepared to articulate their position and articulate it strongly and forcefully and with reasoned argument.'

No doubt these factors contributed to the ability of consumer and public interest representatives to extract concessions from industry. However, the wider context was a significant (if not the most important) influence. One industry representative indicated his employer committed fully to the code development process only after obtaining legal advice that there were reasonable arguments that circumstances specified in the code would have to be taken into account in assessing unfairness under Victorian law. Industry also knew if it did not develop a code, the ACA could adopt an industry standard with possibly more stringent obligations. For example, during working committee discussions, both the ACA and the ACCC advocated that industry should not be permitted to make any detrimental variations during the term of a consumer contract, a position described as 'untenable' for his employer by one industry representative. As a result, industry knew it had a fine line to tread and 'couldn't push [its position] too hard'. As one industry representative said, industry 'felt a lot like we were being pulled over a barrel and one way or another we were going to get it [the code] done and it was how much and how long it took really'.

III. Roles

A. Corporate, Consumer and Public Interest Representatives

Corporate, consumer and public interest delegates each performed a number of functions within the organisations they represented and outside of those entities. The working committee was the locus of rule-making but a significant amount

[22] Only one consumer and public interest interviewee believed the discrepancy in authority weakened the bargaining power of consumer and public interest representatives.

(if not the majority of rule-making activity as one industry representative claimed) was performed outside of it. At a broad level, corporate, consumer and public interest delegates had similar internal and external roles and responsibilities. For example, all were responsible for soliciting the views of their stakeholders,[23] formulating a position on the underlying issues and presenting that stance to either the other representatives in their class outside of working committee meetings or the working committee as a whole. However, until working committee debate on unilateral variation became polarised and formulating an 'industry' position became important (discussed further below), the principal focus for corporate representatives was their internal responsibilities. Discharging these internal responsibilities was difficult as a result of the size and varying commercial operations of their employers and the divisions found within them. By contrast, consumer and public interest representatives placed greater emphasis on the liaison work needed to develop a unified 'consumer' policy position, with other consumer and public interest representatives, and working committee meetings themselves. In addition, all representatives identified and performed other responsibilities, which affected the working committee process and arguably tempered the final positions they reached. Perhaps surprisingly, neither the salaries nor the bonuses (if any) of industry, consumer and public interest representatives were dependent on achieving a particular outcome in the code. In fact, participation took time away from work that could earn corporate employees a bonus. However, one industry representative reported that involving 'the right people' and 'taking the right views' were some of the criteria used by corporate employers to assess the performance of their delegates on ACIF working committees.

i. *Internal Corporate Responsibilities*

Identification of internal stakeholders affected and/or potentially affected by a code rule throughout the rule-making process was described by one individual as a significant 'networking' exercise, requiring knowledge of and contacts within the organisation as well as an ability to correctly assess whether representatives should 'try and take up people's time with the set of issues raised [by the code and working committee]'. Solicitation of information from internal stakeholders—the need to 'ask the right questions, get answers'—was also emphasised by all industry representatives so that they could educate themselves about existing corporate practice.[24] While that information may have been forthcoming in many instances, it was implied by some individuals interviewed that it was not in all cases. As one representative stated, 'We were relying on our ability to

[23] Note, however, that some consumer and public interest representatives reported the obligation of confidentiality hindered their ability to solicit stakeholder views. In addition, the extent to which consumer and public interest representatives were provided with feedback from internal stakeholders varied depending on the organisation involved.

[24] Education took the form of determining the historical rationales for particular contract terms and evaluating if they remained relevant.

influence and extract information from our colleagues and take time out from their day-to-day functions to allow us to collect information to take into the working committee.' As a consequence, internal information gathering was not a foolproof exercise. The same representative commented, 'we [working committee representatives] are not pretending to be the source of all wisdom in [consumer] areas; [customer-facing staff] may have information working committee representatives do not receive'. Importantly, the flow of information was not one-way. Conveying the views expressed and information provided by other working committee delegates to internal stakeholders was seen as equally important to the discharge of internal functions.

The most difficult responsibility was developing an internal position, where one did not exist, on issues raised by the working committee. Differences of opinion existed between commercial divisions, each of which had different business models, goals and most likely performance indicators. For example, the issue of whether and in which circumstances the unilateral variation of a contract by a provider should be 'unfair'—one of the most contentious issues considered by the working committee—was equally fraught for at least one of the companies represented because of the differences between its business divisions. As one representative described it, developing internal positions involved a 'dynamic and interactive' process of synthesising information received. It involved comparing and contrasting information gathered from different corporate divisions; adding and/or combining the commercial perspective with the views of their legal and/or regulatory staff; and developing a 'reasoned' position that could either be advocated or defended. For all industry representatives, the process of internal consultation and internal policy formation was continuous for the duration of the working committee; working committee discussion prompted further internal debate.

The positions that industry representatives adopted were obviously consistent with what were thought to be in the best interests of their employers. However, two of the representatives stressed that the broader interests of consumers and others were factored into the views they adopted. One stated that he always bore in mind 'what is good for the customer is good for business'. Another indicated that legal and regulatory staff are often required to 'wear several hats' in this area and assess positions from public policy, public interest and consumer interest perspectives. In addition, the position eventually adopted by industry on unilateral variation aligned with consumer and public interests. That is not to say that the conclusions reached accorded entirely with either the views of consumer and public interest advocates at the negotiating table or with the personal views of the representatives themselves. One industry representative said that industry's argument to justify the right to unilaterally vary a contract was weak. On the one hand, it was saying to customers, if you can commit to us for a period of time, we can give you a fixed price. On the other hand, it was saying that it wanted to be able to vary that fixed price during the term of the contract. This particular representative described no unilateral variation as 'how it should be' and the consumer and public interest advocates 'on the side of right'.

ii. The Diversity of Working Committee Roles and Duties

Consumer, public interest and industry representatives emphasised educating each other, a responsibility closely related to their advocacy roles. Consumer and public interest representatives sought to educate industry about the position and expectations of consumers ('how the real world works out there'). Industry delegates hoped to teach consumer and public interest groups, and regulators about the dynamic of the sector, sharing information with them about the technical characteristics of the supply chain, the way providers contracted with each other and areas where industry had no discretion to act. Similarly, one industry representative stressed the importance of gathering information from working committee members. Other industry delegates highlighted their roles as drafting experts, 'problem solvers' and 'resolution finders'. Some industry representatives were tasked by their employers to 'get an outcome' for the reasons explored earlier.[25] As one representative stated, 'I was being sent to that table, being told make a code, whatever happens in the end. We may have to walk away but we will not walk away until all of our teeth are pulled by their roots and they're bleeding.' There was no explicit obligation imposed by ACIF for industry delegates to represent the wider industry (as there was when the Mobile Premium Services code was developed)[26] and no attempt by industry to do so. However, all industry representatives were cognisant of the effect that rule-making would have on the broader industry. One delegate stated the purpose of his participation was to 'get the reputation of the telecommunication industry onto a much better foot'. A consumer representative highlighted that the desire to improve consumer welfare was subject to the belief that industry should not be forced to make bad business decisions. She emphasised that she brought a certain degree of impartiality and willingness to hear the views of industry, 'I didn't have a point in saying let's get Telstra or let's get Vodafone or let's get Optus on whatever.' Finally, two consumer and public interest representatives were members of ACIF's board while also serving as working committee members. Although giving rise to the appearance of a conflict of interest, one consumer and public interest representative stated board membership did not affect his approach to code development. However, it was suggested by another who did not serve on the ACIF board that ACIF membership made it difficult for those representatives with a 'stake' in the preservation of the Part 6 process to be overly critical of industry.

B. Regulators

The ACCC, TIO and ACA were non-voting committee members and strictly speaking only observers; although consistent with ACIF's practice, a rigid

[25] See the text accompanying nn 7–14 of this chapter.

[26] See para 5 of s I of ch 7.

distinction between voting and non-voting members was not made by the independent chair of this working committee.[27] All regulatory representatives were given 'pretty substantial latitude to jump in' and offer their views during the working committee process and were seen as participants in the process. The ACCC and TIO representatives interviewed believed that their primary roles were to respect the participants and their particular views, and to be independent and objective. However, both wanted to 'make their voice heard' and were keen to get something that was 'actually going to improve the situation for consumers'. As one representative stated, 'it's not an equal industry in terms of consumer powers and provider powers.' As a result of the imbalance, it often meant 'having to provide more help and support to the consumer side of things in order to get a reasonable resolution'. Another said 'we were on the side of consumer groups, trying to push industry as hard as we could.' Guiding industry by reviewing complaints statistics, identifying case law and providing relevant examples from different industry sectors were cited by the regulatory representatives interviewed as the ways in which they could influence industry behaviour. They discussed some matters with each other during working committee meetings and breaks. However, unlike the representatives of consumer and public interest organisations and industry, they did not work together outside of working committee meetings to articulate a unified 'regulatory' position because they were (or felt) constrained by statute and other limitations.

Delegates of the ACA were not interviewed, because the chair of its successor, the Australian Communications and Media Authority (ACMA), declined to assist with the research for the book, citing the organisation's obligations of confidentiality under the Australian Communications and Media Authority Act 2005 (Cth). However, consumer, public interest and industry representatives who were interviewed reported that the ACA's principal representative was supportive of the positions advocated by consumer and public interest representatives. He articulated his views, even if he was not as forthright as the other regulatory representatives.

C. Independent Chair and Project Manager

It is also important to explain the roles of the independent chair and the ACIF project manager, as each sought in their own way to create a neutral environment where debate between all representatives (voting and non-voting) could take place. Moreover, the appointment of an independent chair was a departure from past ACIF practice, and all interviewees saw the chair's independence as a central component of the validity of the process.

[27] Apart from ratification of the final version of the code, nothing was put to a formal vote.

The independent chair was a well-respected figure. He had been a director of planning and review at the Department of Communications and the Arts, and a chair of the ACA. ACIF's brief for him was to 'get an outcome' that industry, and consumer and public interest groups could agree to—something that was practical and sensible, and could be registered. Payment for his services was not contingent on an outcome and, although he reported to the ACIF CEO throughout the working committee process, he was never formally directed in his role. The chair's responsibilities, as he defined them, included giving 'everyone a chance to contribute' and encouraging the parties to formulate and express their views. Once 'on the table', the objective was to make these views operational and, where agreement could not be reached, to identify the problems and explore solutions to them. Although he largely perceived his role to be procedural in nature, the independent chair also aimed to make the code 'sensible' to the extent he could influence it. In addition, many representatives interviewed described him as a 'referee' who kept order and remained neutral but was more than a mere facilitator. He was someone who could hold the parties to their positions and identify critical points.

The role of the project manager, who was legally trained, was primarily administrative. She stressed that her function was to help create an atmosphere of trust between working committee representatives. She tried to ensure that she and ACIF were seen by working committee delegates to be 'independent and neutral'. She emphasised listening carefully to both sides; never adopting a position; and taking detailed, accurate notes of what was discussed and agreed to in working committee meetings to which the parties could later refer. In addition, there was never any substantive discussion between working committee representatives and ACIF staff outside of meetings.

D. Other

Again, in a departure from past practice, ACIF hired a solicitor from Baker & McKenzie to assist with drafting the code. The solicitor was not (or at least seen not to be) a central player and did not participate in the negotiations. As one individual interviewed stated, 'He did in large measure what he was asked to do.'

IV. Strategy

For this particular code development process, it is difficult in many respects to distinguish between the strategies used by the representatives of voting members to advance their interests and the techniques the parties used to resolve disputes. Some tactics, such as ceasing discussion on or 'parking' issues at particular junctures (taking 'time outs'); seeking highly prescriptive rules to minimise industry's discretion; and pursuing detailed exceptions to the principle of 'unfairness' ('carve outs') to mitigate its scope, arguably served a dual purpose of advancing their employer's interest and contributing in some way to the settlement ultimately reached among the delegates.

Certainly, consumer, public interest and industry representatives adopted strategies in an effort to ensure their preferred positions were adopted. Consumer and public interest organisations negotiated as a group, always adopted positions unacceptable to suppliers as their starting point, bundled issues, and threatened to walk out of the code development process and rely instead on a standard made by the ACA and/or the Fair Trading Act 1999 (Vic) (as amended). Personal anecdotes were used to counter the frequently cited industry arguments of cost. As one consumer and public interest representative explained, these narratives proved to be powerful because industry's only retort to them was to accuse the representative of lying, which was never done. At least one consumer and public interest organisation also engaged in some 'moaning and groaning' with industry in the press.[28] Like consumer and public interest organisations, industry negotiated as a block and bundled issues when it worked to its advantage. It also, as one regulatory representative described it, 'catastrophised' the impact improvements in consumer protection rules would have on industry: 'If we have to do that, we'll have to go out of business and that will mean we'll have to double our prices and ultimately we'll have to destroy the industry. Do you want that on your head?' Repeated use of the 'cost card' was 'tried and played'. Appeals to the black letter of the law were made with industry highlighting the interrelationship (and possible conflict) between the draft code, existing regulatory rules, and state and federal legislation. Similarly, the time needed to implement new rules was emphasised. One industry representative also reported using a strategy of 'good cop, bad cop', which the company was able to do because two representatives regularly attended working committee meetings.

However, representatives do not appear to have used a significant amount of gamesmanship. Many representatives from both consumer and public interest groups, and industry described a process of fairly open and, in some cases, frank discussion about provider behaviour, industry practice, the meaning of legislative provisions and broader public policy considerations. One industry representative stressed that industry's arguments were made genuinely with no attempt to be 'bloody minded' or score points. This individual explained he engaged in 'straight forward advocacy—[an] information, understanding and articulating positions sort of approach'. To the extent 'playing' the process was possible, the strategies adopted were relatively unsophisticated and there was nothing which one regulatory representative characterised as 'inappropriate'. The reason why that was the

[28] See, eg, D Wilding, Director, CLC, University of New South Wales, Letter to the Editor, *The Australian Financial Review* (Sydney), 3 November 2004, 59; E Beal, CLC, Victoria University, Letter to the Editor, *The Australian Financial Review* (Sydney), 15 November 2004, 60.

case is not clear, although the relative equality of bargaining power, the broader context in which working committee debate occurred and the relative neutrality in which rule-making took place may have been factors.[29]

V. Dispute Resolution

Given the obvious tension between commercial, consumer and public interests, many disputes arose during working committee meetings with various participants describing the process, which became quite personal at times,[30] as 'horse trading', 'full-on negotiation', 'bargaining', 'water torture', 'contentious', 'excruciating' and 'intense'. As a result, many techniques were and had to be deployed within and outside of the working committee room to facilitate their resolution. Some have already been referred to: robust (and repeated) discussion, sharing of information, educating the other side, 'parking' issues and rehearing them at a later date and developing carve outs from general principles.[31] Others used included the breaking up of big issues into a number of sub-parts that were then discussed. The chair often cajoled the parties by emphasising the risk to both sides if the ACA intervened directly. At times, consumer and public interest delegates and industry representatives broke into their respective camps (or 'group huddles' as several individuals described them). They also broke into smaller groups with one industry and one consumer and/or public interest representative. In some cases, a regulatory representative joined them. These sub-committees would formulate a position that would be reported to the working committee as a whole for further discussion and possible agreement. At the request of the chair, position papers suggesting alternative ways of addressing a particular problem were developed by participants.

Although these various methods were used to achieve 'consensus' in several instances, genuine agreement, particularly on those issues which one regulatory representative described as 'fundamental', was not achievable on all. Even if it could be reached it was often because representatives from industry and consumer and public interest organisations bundled issues together such that agreement was reached on a suite of issues rather than the specific elements of the bundle. Moreover, agreement was reached for reasons of pure pragmatism as well as exhaustion. As one representative expressed it, 'Sometimes it was just wearing people down and it went both ways for consumers and industry and regulators. In the end, you

[29] See the text accompanying nn 7–14 of this chapter.

[30] The working committee minutes note on several occasions reminders from the chair of the importance of respecting the views of others.

[31] Subject to a significant number of caveats, the Consumer Contracts code exempted 20 types of terms from its general principle that contract terms must not be unfair.

just couldn't be bothered arguing about it anymore.' On one occasion, consumer and public interest representatives had argued vehemently that the code should stipulate that assignment clauses enabling a telecommunications provider to unilaterally assign a contract to a different provider without permitting the subscriber to terminate the contract were unfair. In the end, the debate was resolved not by making any real policy decision but by an 'agreement to disagree'. The code made no reference to assignment clauses. Consumers were left to argue the point citing the code's general principle of unfairness and any protections in relevant state and federal legislation and the common law. Similarly, an industry member agreed to continue negotiations, provided its opposition to certain issues was officially noted in the minutes. Importantly, compromises were also struck on the issue of unilateral variation—an issue of fundamental importance for all voting members of the working committee throughout the process.

As it illustrates the dynamic between voting members of the working committee, the resolution of two aspects of the unilateral variation dispute will be explored below. The first aspect is the extent to which 'standard forms of agreement' (SFOAs)[32] subject to Part 23 of the Telecommunications Act 1997 (Cth) and regulated at the time by the Telecommunications (Standard Form of Agreement Information) Determination 2003 (Cth) (referred to below as the 2003 determination or the ACA determination) should be excluded from any code provision rendering unilateral variation clauses unfair. The second aspect is the level and type of detriment a customer had to suffer before the code provision applied (eg, did detriment have to be 'material', 'significant' or otherwise?).

A. Unilateral Variation

From the beginning, the ACCC expressed the view (supported and advocated by consumer and public interest representatives) that any unilateral variation clause adopted had to apply to SFOAs.[33] It also expressed the view that the ACA determination, which permitted unilateral variation of contract terms causing 'detriment', provided suppliers gave their customers three working days' prior notice of the modification,[34] was inadequate to protect consumers. The ACCC argued that unilateral variation in those circumstances risked contravening Part IV of the then Trade Practices Act 1974 (Cth), which prohibited unconscionable conduct. The ACA adopted the position that the 2003 determination did

[32] SFOAs are contracts whose terms are not individually negotiated with customers. Most telecommunications contracts are SFOAs.

[33] SFOAs were excluded from the unilateral variation provision in the 2002 ACIF industry guideline. See ACIF, *Industry Guideline ACIF G601: Consumer Contracts* (December 2002) s 5.1(h).

[34] See Telecommunications (Standard Form of Agreement Information) Determination 2003 (Cth) s 11(2).

not preclude a code imposing additional (and more rigorous) rules, and it would amend the 2003 determination to ensure consistency with the final version of the Consumer Contracts code. However, industry argued throughout the process that Part 23 of the Telecommunications Act 1997 (Cth) gave it a right to unilaterally vary SFOAs. In addition, it maintained that customers had to suffer 'material detriment' (a higher threshold than that advocated by the ACCC) before any unilateral provision should be deemed unfair. As a compromise, midway through the process, consumer and public interest representatives proposed two unilateral variation provisions—one dealing with changes to price which would apply where a subscriber suffered 'detriment' and another dealing with changes (other than price) in which case a 'material detriment' standard applied. Several exceptions to the price variation rule were also granted. When industry rejected the 'detriment' standard for price variations, a mediator was called in.

When no agreement could be reached and under time pressure to release the code in draft for public comment,[35] the working committee made two decisions, both of which departed from established ACIF practice. First, it agreed to publish a draft that sought comment on which of the two different standards of detriment for price variation was preferable and, if the lower threshold were adopted, whether additional exceptions permitting industry to vary contract terms were necessary. Second, with the support of the independent chair, it asked for the view of the ACA on which standard of detriment should be adopted. Although the ACA expressed support for the consumer and public interest representatives' position and public comments on the matter were received, a second (and more formal) mediation session with Tony Fitzgerald, a former member of the NSW Court of Appeal, was scheduled for 8 December 2004. This all-day meeting also did not produce agreement. However, during the working committee's twenty-third meeting, the impasse was broken. Industry capitulated. It agreed that, subject to a number of exceptions, unilateral variation of terms dealing with the characteristics of goods and services, including price, in a contract with a fixed contract period (other than month to month),[36] without notifying the customer in advance and offering them the right to terminate the contract, was 'unfair'.

Why did industry depart from its entrenched position and adopt the stronger consumer protection measure? One possible explanation is that, as one industry representative stated, industry thought it could live with the provision. Industry did not receive all of the exceptions it wanted. However, the carve outs permitting variation for special offers and services over which it did not have complete control went some way towards addressing the commercial risks industry faced

[35] The Telecommunications Act 1997 (Cth) requires that members of industry and the general public must have a minimum of 30 days to submit comments on the draft code. If ACIF were to finalise a code by the end of the year, it had to publish a draft by the end of September 2004.

[36] Prepaid customers were excluded from the code's provision. Unilateral variation terms in their contracts remained subject to the provisions of the Telecommunications (Standard Form of Agreement Information) Determination 2003 (Cth).

if it could not pass on price increases or make other modifications as a result of changes made by its own suppliers. That account may be correct. However, given that industry pushed its unilateral variation arguments for so long, so strenuously and in some situations where it did have control over costs, it is difficult to discount the importance of the context in which the code was drafted and the particular importance code development had for industry in its final decision. It wanted (and needed) to make a code for reasons explored earlier.[37] In addition, both mediation sessions had failed. Agreement with consumer and public interest representatives could not be reached. They were holding firm in the face of forceful argument from industry, and time to submit a code for registration was running out. Unless it was prepared to walk away from the process, which it was reluctant to do, it was not going to achieve exactly what it wanted. Even if it did walk away, the ACA was likely to impose the same standard consumer and public interest representatives had advocated. In its response to the working committee's request for its opinion, the ACA affirmed the view of its working committee representatives, expressed during numerous meetings, that the 'detriment' standard was preferable. The ACA's opinion was by no means determinative—one could argue its stance was ignored by industry until the end—but it was ultimately influential. What is also notable is that the unilateral variation issue was not resolved by public consultation. Submissions made to the working committee were duly considered, but approximately one-third of written comments were made by representatives already at the negotiating table with the remaining commentators split along consumer and industry lines.

VI. Conclusion

Notwithstanding the appointments of a truly independent chair and an equal number of consumer and public interest organisations, and industry suppliers to the working committee, there are facets of this case study that raise concerns about the procedural and institutional legitimacy of the Part 6 process. In particular, working committee members engaged in some bargaining. Agreement could not be achieved on all issues. When it was reached, it was often because delegates were too tired to discuss the underlying matters any further. On occasion, delegates compromised for purely pragmatic reasons. Some consumer and public interest representatives reported the obligation of confidentiality hindered their ability to solicit the views of their stakeholders.

[37] See the text accompanying nn 7–14 of this chapter.

6

The Information on Accessibility Features for Telephone Equipment Code

I. Working Committee Composition and Context

The Information on Accessibility Features for Telephone Equipment code (the IAF code) was prepared by a working committee established by the Australian Communications Industry Forum (ACIF) in response to a formal request of the Australian Communications Authority (ACA) to develop a code and guideline 'to improve telecommunications access for consumers with communications impairments'.[1] The ACA's request, dated 22 October 2003, was issued in an attempt to resolve a long-running dispute, between consumer and disability advocates and manufacturers and importers of telephone handsets and other customer equipment (collectively referred to as 'equipment suppliers' below), about the nature and number of features equipment suppliers had to include in their products destined for the Australian market so persons with disabilities could access communications services. The dispute began in 1998 when ACIF convened a working committee to prepare a new 'disability standard' for fixed, cordless and mobile handsets used in connection with standard telephone services. The disability standard, which would prescribe the accessibility features for all customer equipment supplied to the Australian mass market (ie, apparatus used primarily by persons without a disability),[2] was to be submitted to the ACA for adoption in accordance with Part 21 of the Telecommunications Act 1997 (Cth). Consumer and disability representatives on the disability standard working committee called for the number of accessibility features to be increased from two to 37.[3] However, the disability standard ACIF submitted to the ACA in 2001 maintained the status quo: fixed handsets had to include induction loops to assist people using hearing

[1] Letter from B Horton, Acting Chair, ACA to J Plante, CEO, ACIF (22 October 2003).

[2] Specialist equipment for people with disabilities such as teletypewriters (TTY) and teleBraille fell outside the scope of this particular debate.

[3] See, eg, T Corbin and H Campbell, Consumers' Telecommunications Network, *Technical Standards for Disability Needs* (1998).

aids, and all customer equipment with a keypad was required to have a raised pip on the key associated with the number 5.[4]

Although the ACA was disappointed with the limited content of ACIF's disability standard, particularly in light of regulatory developments in Europe[5] and the US,[6] and the amount of time ACIF took to develop it,[7] the ACA adopted the standard in 2002. The ACA did, however, ask its Communications Technical Regulation Advisory Committee (CTRAC)[8] to establish a Disability Standards Working Group (DSWG) to advise on the accessibility features that should be included in future disability standards and appropriate compliance arrangements. The DSWG made up of representatives from the ACA, industry, and consumer and disability groups recommended the adoption of a new disability standard requiring equipment suppliers to comply with certain 'overarching' design principles centred around the concept of 'inclusive design'. It also suggested customer equipment had to include a greatly expanded number of accessibility features for those with mobility, vision and hearing impairments.

CTRAC rejected the DSWG's February 2003 report. Instead, it recommended to the ACA that industry adopt a non-binding, voluntary guideline incorporating the features and principles outlined by the DSWG. CTRAC rejected the report for two principal reasons. The first was the limited size of the Australian market for handsets and other customer equipment relative to other geographic markets. The second was the belief that onerous technical obligations would discourage the supply of handsets to Australia thus reducing the availability of and increasing the price of equipment to consumers. As one industry representative who served on the IAF code working committee explained, equipment suppliers wanted to

[4] ACIF, AS/ACIF SO40: 2001, Australian Standard: Requirements for Customer Equipment for Use with the Standard Telephone Service—Features for Special Needs of Persons with Disabilities, cl 5.

[5] The Open Network Provision Directive required Member States to 'take specific measures to ensure equal access to and affordability of fixed public telephone services' for disabled users. Directive 98/10/EC of the European Parliament and of the Council of 26 February 1998 on the application of open network provision (ONP) to voice telephony and on universal service for telecommunications in a competitive environment [1998] OJ L101/24, art 8. The Terminal Equipment Directive empowered the European Commission to decide that telecommunications apparatus had to be manufactured with specific features to facilitate its use by users with a disability. Directive 1999/5/EC of the European Parliament and of the Council of 9 March 1999 on radio equipment and telecommunications terminal equipment and the mutual recognition of their conformity [1999] OJ L91/10, art 3(3)(f).

[6] The Telecommunications Act of 1996 imposed an obligation on manufacturers of telecommunications equipment to ensure their products are 'designed, developed, and fabricated to be accessible to and usable' by people with disabilities, if 'readily achievable.' Telecommunications Act of 1996 §255; 47 USC §255 (2012 & Supp 2016).

[7] W Jolley, Jolley William and Associates, *When the Tide Comes In: Towards Accessible Telecommunications for People with Disabilities in Australia: A Discussion Paper Commissioned by the Human Rights and Equal Opportunity Commission* (June 2003) 74. See also Communications Technical Regulation Advisory Committee-Disability Standards Working Group (CTRAC-DSWG), *Report on Features for Inclusion in Future Disability Standards* (24 February 2003) 4.

[8] CTRAC was established to provide strategic policy advice and recommendations dealing with the compliance framework for the technical regulation of communications. It was chaired by the ACA but some of its members were from industry.

be able to differentiate themselves in the market. Regulation prescribing that all customer equipment had to have every accessibility feature would have had the effect of rendering the cost base identical for all customer equipment, hindering the capacity of equipment suppliers to distinguish themselves, on the basis of price, in the market.

To break the impasse between industry, and consumer and disability advocates, the ACA brokered a compromise by shifting the focus from a prescriptive disability standard to addressing the difficulty that had been noted during the various proceedings: acquiring information about the accessibility features of telephone equipment supplied to the Australian market.[9] It requested ACIF to develop a code of practice under Part 6 of the Telecommunications Act 1997 (Cth) (Part 6) for registration and a non-binding industry guideline to accompany the code. The ACA envisaged that, under the code, equipment suppliers would be required to provide helpful information about their products to carriage service providers offering standard telephone services. They, in turn, would be required to give that information to their customers. Information was to be provided to carriage service providers because, in addition to offering standard telephone services, they, as a matter of practice, retailed telephones and mobile handsets. The proposed guideline was to implement CTRAC's recommendation.[10]

As one representative on the IAF code working committee commented,[11] the settlement made everyone unhappy. Consumer and disability advocates were disappointed. They wanted to see an improved disability standard. Equally, equipment suppliers wanted a different outcome. Although a code would preserve the ability of equipment suppliers to differentiate themselves in the market with regards to accessibility features, they saw an obligation to provide information as an imposition. They were also fearful that any information they provided would serve as the basis for imposing more onerous regulation in the future. Despite the uneasiness of equipment suppliers, and consumer and disability advocates, ACIF agreed to the ACA's request. However, it decided with the ACA's approval that the duties imposed on carriage service providers would be incorporated into the Customer Information on Prices, Terms and Conditions code[12] being reviewed by another working committee. The sole focus of the IAF code working committee was to delineate the obligations imposed on equipment suppliers, which were for the first time since Part 6 was enacted to be made subject to a code.

[9] R Garrett and G Astbrink, 'Are We There Yet? The Struggle for Phone Accessibility Information' (2010) 60(2) *Telecommunications Journal of Australia* 22.1, 22.3.

[10] The proposed guideline implementing CTRAC's recommendation was started but never completed by the ACIF working committee.

[11] All statements attributed to working committee participants involved in the development of this code were made to the author during interviews held in February, March and April 2012. The names of interviewees are not provided and only feminine pronouns are used in this chapter to preserve the anonymity of the individuals concerned. For information about the research methodology used for the case studies, see the Appendix.

[12] ACIF, *Industry Code C521: Customer Information on Prices, Terms and Conditions* (2004).

Initially, the working committee was made up of nine voting members: four equipment suppliers, two carriage service providers, and three consumer and disability organisations. The four equipment suppliers were the now defunct Australian Electrical and Electronic Manufacturers Association (AEEMA), Cisco Systems, NEC Business Solutions and Trillium Communications. The two carriage service providers were Telstra and Vodafone. The three consumer and disability organisations were Australian Rehabilitation and Assistive Technology Association (ARATA),[13] Telecommunication and Disability Consumer Representation (Tedicore represented ACIF's Disability Advisory Body (DAB)[14]) and the Consumers' Telecommunications Network (CTN). There was no independent chair. In accordance with ACIF's practice at the time, the voting members of the working committee elected the chair from among the individuals representing them. They selected the representative from CTN.[15] However, as will be explored later, she was replaced towards the end of the process, in July 2005, by the CEO of ACIF, Anne Hurley. The ACA was appointed as a non-voting member, and its representatives were present for all 21 meetings of the working committee held during April 2004 and November 2005. Following the release of the draft code for public comment in November 2004, Nokia joined the working committee as a non-voting member.

Working committee representatives were geographically disbursed, so all meetings were held via video and audio conference. Some working committee members met face to face. With some exceptions, all meetings were convened every two weeks for half a day until a formal subcommittee was created in July 2005. Debate centred on four areas: the type of information equipment suppliers had to supply; the quantity of information equipment suppliers had to supply; how frequently they had to provide it; and to whom.

II. Power

Working committee negotiations involved three distinct groups: equipment suppliers, carriage service providers, and consumer and disability representatives. Each group brought different perspectives on the issues to the negotiating table. Interviewees reported that each group contributed to the discussion. However, negotiation largely occurred between equipment suppliers, and consumer and disability representatives. This result was largely due to the way the working

[13] Incorporated in 1994, ARATA is an information-sharing forum for those with an interest in 'assistive technology', including but not limited to users and manufacturers of devices that improve the functional capacities of people with disabilities. It had not previously sat on an ACIF working committee but was and had been a member of DAB when it served on this working committee.

[14] For information on DAB, see s III.C.ii.a of ch 4.

[15] On four occasions, the Tedicore representative stood in for the CTN representative as chair.

committee's task was framed and the 'hands-off' approach to code formation the ACA adopted for most of the process. Carriage service providers were an important link in the distribution chain of information about accessibility features; but ultimately, they were only the channel through which information would be passed to consumers. They did not have the information sought by the consumer and disability representatives. Equipment manufacturers were the gatekeepers of that information.

To better understand the power dynamic that existed between the various parties, it is important to look at the two fora in which the IAF code was developed: the working committee and the formal subcommittee (reluctantly agreed to by the members of the working committee when negotiations stalled in May 2005). The subcommittee met four times between August and November 2005 and was chaired by the CEO. It resolved most of the significant issues in dispute between the parties. After the subcommittee was established, the working committee met only once more to approve the code, as revised by the subcommittee, and to determine outstanding matters. In both arenas, consumer and disability representatives were, on balance, at a disadvantage but arguably more so in the formal subcommittee. The amount and form of the information given ultimately turned on the willingness of equipment suppliers to provide it. On the whole, the outcome of the debate did not depend on expertise (legal, technical or otherwise), access to specialist information and other resources. Whatever power consumer and disability representatives had was greatest in the working committee prior to public consultation. Arguably, it eroded as industry and the members of the ACA engaged more fully with the code's substance during and after public consultation.

A. The Working Committee

i. Composition

The initial composition of the working committee (and hence the balance of interests within it) was criticised from a number of quarters. For example, one consumer and disability representative interviewed stated there was a 'total imbalance' among the members of the working committee in favour of equipment suppliers. In absolute terms, the number of equipment suppliers outweighed the number of consumer and disability representatives by four to two. Three consumer and disability organisations were appointed to the working committee. However, by virtue of being appointed the chair of the working committee, the CTN representative was expected to be 'independent'. CTN was entitled to send another representative but did not have enough staff to send an alternate.

However, the effect the numerical imbalance between consumer and disability representatives, and equipment suppliers may have had on working committee deliberations was curtailed by two factors. First, the chair was allowed to express views on behalf of CTN, provided she 'clearly identified' when she was speaking on behalf of the organisation. Although some interviewees from each of the three groups of participants indicated the chair listened to all participants and was willing to allow members to discuss every point, an equipment supplier representative stated that the chair (intentionally or otherwise) 'push[ed]' the discussion towards certain outcomes in favour of consumers. Even if this recollection is incorrect, it is true that the version of the code released for public comment was 'friendlier' to the consumer and disability sectors than the final version of the code submitted for registration to ACMA.[16] The former required equipment suppliers to provide 21 more pieces of information about the accessibility features of their products than the latter. The draft code released for public comment was prepared under the supervision of the chair from CTN. The version submitted for registration was prepared by the formal subcommittee chaired by ACIF's CEO.[17] Second, the presence on the working committee of two carriage service providers, who were supplying and/or retailing equipment to their own customers, served as a counterbalance to the power of equipment suppliers. The carriage service providers did not drive the discussion concerning the information equipment suppliers ought to provide. Moreover, they queried the value of certain information consumer and disability representatives requested. However, equipment suppliers, and consumer and disability representatives reported that carriage service providers wanted information about accessibility features for their customers. As one carriage service provider representative stated, 'I was basically on the consumer side in most cases …' She sought to ensure that 'the information that was going to come out of this work … was actually going to be of use to us for our customers.' Her company did not want to provide 'totally useless information' to its customers. Moreover, she saw the information as essential to her ability to perform her job. One equipment supplier said carriage service provider representatives were 'quite willing to do everything that [could] help the customer'.

Consumer and disability representatives were not, however, the only parties to have concerns about the composition of this working committee. One equipment supplier representative believed that the representation of equipment suppliers was inadequate because two of the three organisations appointed to the working committee were more involved with the provision of telephony services than the manufacture of telephone equipment. Conversely, carriage service providers felt that manufacturers of fixed handset equipment were adequately represented. However, mobile manufacturers and/or their industry associations were conspicuously absent. One of the carriage service provider representatives was 'uncomfortable' with the arrangement and expressed her concerns to ACIF on a number of occasions that the working committee did not have 'the right mix of people'. She believed that at least one mobile manufacturer had to be on the working

[16] When ACIF submitted the IAF code for registration, the ACA had been merged with the ABA and had become the ACMA.

[17] See s II.B of this chapter (below).

committee because mobile manufacturers continuously upgrade their mobile handsets and release new models; they would have to provide information much more regularly pursuant to the code compared to fixed handset manufacturers. After a draft of the code was released for public comment, mobile manufacturers themselves raised concerns about the inadequate representation of their interests on the working committee. For example, in its written submission to the working committee, Motorola asserted that the Australian Mobile Telecommunications Association (AMTA), which represents global mobile manufacturers in Australia, had been invited to join the code working committee as an observer. However, the invitation was received after the deliberations of the working committee began. In addition, Motorola alleged that after AMTA received the invitation, a mobile manufacturer had asked to join the working committee as a voting member but ACIF never responded to the request.

It is unlikely, however, that the absence of some of the key players on the working committee was an oversight by ACIF. For example, Nokia, which later became a non-voting member of the working committee and a member of the formal subcommittee, was a member of ACIF's Customer Equipment and Cabling Reference Panel (CECRP), which formulated ACIF's response to the ACA's request to develop the IAF code. It would have been aware that the code was being formulated, and it was given an opportunity to participate in the process. ACIF solicited expressions of interest for membership of the IAF code working committee from all CECRP members. An ACIF staff member also individually invited mobile equipment manufacturers to serve as working committee members. The project manager asked AMTA to attend some working committee meetings.

A more likely explanation for the absence of mobile equipment manufacturers was their disengagement with the code development process. Industry disengagement may have been strategic. At least one interviewee from a fixed customer equipment manufacturer expressed surprise that mobile manufacturers raised the composition of the working committee as an issue because some mobile manufacturers were members of AEEMA, and she was providing code development information to another industry group. Similarly, it is noted in the minutes that Nokia and Ericsson were to be kept informed of the working committee's progress and that AMTA would be given working committee documentation on a confidential basis.[18] Other representatives interviewed attributed the disengagement of mobile manufacturers to their lack of experience with the Part 6 process. They were familiar with the process by which technical standards were made but had no prior exposure to Part 6. As a carriage service provider representative stated:

> A lot of manufacturers didn't see themselves as being part of the ... telecommunications industry, even though they'd develop and sell equipment that's used on networks ... one of the things that I think we had the biggest issue with [was] the [lack of] recognition

[18] Whether ACIF provided Nokia, Ericsson and AMTA with information is unclear.

or the acknowledgment by various manufacturers, and even manufacturer groups, that they were actually part of the telecommunications industry for the purposes of this code.

Whatever may have been the reasons for the absence of a representative from the mobile manufacturing industry on the working committee, the alleged deficiency was rectified when ACIF's CEO decided to appoint Nokia as a non-voting member of the working committee and a member of the formal subcommittee, where most substantive policy decisions were taken. The appointment of a non-voting member to the formal subcommittee, which had not been a member of the working committee from the beginning was described as 'very unusual' by one equipment supplier interviewed. She was personally opposed to it. Yet, for most working committee representatives interviewed, including consumer and disability representatives, the appointment of Nokia to the working committee played an integral role in the adoption of the code. The procedural anomaly was therefore overlooked and/or justified by interviewees on that basis. As one consumer and disability representative stated 'the reality was that we realised that the representation on the working committee wasn't broad enough.' Nokia's omission from the working committee was 'wrong'. In addition, Nokia could provide 'some leadership' to the rest of the equipment supplier industry. It already had a website to help people with disabilities determine which of its products were helpful to them.

ii. The Dynamic within the Groups

Consumer and disability representatives clearly worked towards the same goal and supported one another. However, they did not negotiate as a bloc. There was no designated leader as each representative could contribute different perspectives to the discussion. As one stated, she did not 'hide behind the consumer caucus'. She also did not believe that strict solidarity could strengthen the position of consumer and disability representatives on this working committee. Equally, the equipment suppliers interviewed did not negotiate as a group although there was regular communication between certain representatives outside of meetings. One equipment supplier reported liaising periodically with an industry association not represented on the working committee. Carriage service providers also conferred on matters outside of the working committee but addressed matters individually during meetings.

iii. The Dynamic within the Working Committee

Consumer and disability representatives reported, prior to the publication of the draft code, varying levels of engagement by equipment suppliers on the working committee. The variance can perhaps be explained by a number of factors. First, one equipment supplier had competing interests, which could have affected the positions its representative was able to adopt publicly during working committee meetings. The equipment supplier was an equipment manufacturer and a consultant to two other members of the working committee. Second, another equipment supplier representative indicated that the amount of information consumer and disability representatives were asking equipment providers to supply was not a significant concern for the company. However, she did not want to 'obviously oppose ... other industry members'. A chair seen as partisan, and industry scepticism that the information being requested would reach end customers, may also have contributed to disengagement. As one equipment supplier interviewee stated, 'no one was really sure that the carriage service providers out there would actually be that good at [getting the information out to or available to the people who needed it].'

Although disengaged and, as some asserted, disenfranchised prior to public consultation, equipment suppliers engaged vigorously with code development during and after public consultation. It was at this point the negotiating power of consumer and disability representatives began to wane. Seven equipment suppliers and industry associations, including two members of the working committee, made written submissions in response to the call for public comments. In addition, a number of industry observers, at the invitation of the working committee, attended meetings 16 (3 March 2005) and 17 (15 April 2005). The minutes of meeting 16, the first working committee meeting held following receipt of comments submitted during public consultation, do not record the contributions (if any) the observers made. However, seven individuals attended. An additional employee of NEC Business Solutions and an employee of ICT Australia, which did not submit written comments in response to the public consultation, attended meeting 17. Both represented AEEMA. The individual from NEC Business Solutions actively contributed. She argued that working committee members should take into account the amount of time equipment suppliers would need to provide the information requested in the code. Also, she wanted it acknowledged that importers may not have easy access to the requested information and may have to incur substantial costs testing the equipment to obtain it.[19] Industry's preference was to answer 'yes/no' questions rather than questions that necessitated some form of qualitative measurement in order to answer them. Following this meeting, along with ACIF's CEO, representatives from AMTA, AEEMA and the Australian Information Industry Association (AIIA) met with the deputy chair of the ACA on 17 June 2005. During that meeting, the 'high-level principles' that would govern the working committee's review of the draft code were agreed. An employee of Nokia, representing AMTA, was also appointed as a non-voting member of the working committee and joined the formal subcommittee.

Observers who broadly supported the positions adopted by consumer and disability representatives on the working committee also attended and contributed to meetings before and after public consultation. For example, prior to public consultation, the working committee held two meetings with members of ACIF's

[19] It is not clear why importers were unable to include in their contracts with equipment manufacturers obligations to provide the accessibility features information.

DAB to discuss a draft of the code. A representative of the Human Rights and Equal Opportunity Commission (HREOC), which was concerned about the interrelationship of the code and the Disability Discrimination Act 1992 (Cth) (DDA), also attended six meetings after the draft code was released for public comment.[20] The working committee minutes record the HREOC's 'growing sense of frustration on the slowness of the development of the code'. They also record its belief that it had the power to address a number of complaints placed on hold through a process of 'conciliation' under the DDA, with agreements reached enforceable by the courts. However, the involvement of the HREOC did not affect the decisions of equipment suppliers, because as one representative stated, the development of the code lay in the hands of the working committee members.

iv. Expertise, Access to Specialist Information and Resources

Consumer and disability representatives may have been outnumbered in the working committee but they were more than capable of speaking to the issues. The central issue involved the information equipment suppliers had to provide. Its resolution turned to a significant degree on the information people with disabilities needed to assess if phone equipment was appropriate for their particular circumstances. All consumer and disability representatives were knowledgeable about those issues and could draw on developments in the UK and elsewhere. One had involvement with Cost 219, a European Community-funded project which among other things, considered accessibility features and telephone equipment. Another was a trained electronics engineer with over 10 years' work experience modifying electronics equipment for individuals with physical disabilities. The third representative co-wrote an extensive report on accessibility features in 1998. As one consumer and disability representative stated, with some exceptions, equipment manufacturers were the ones lacking knowledge of the issues surrounding disability. The ability of consumers to easily access and comprehend information provided by equipment suppliers at the point of sale was another significant issue. However, one consumer and disability representative stressed that no one on the working committee, including industry representatives, was an expert in how people process information. Equipment suppliers also emphasised throughout the process that any features specified in the IAF code had to be objectively assessable ie, capable of measurement from a technical viewpoint. Further, they highlighted operational difficulties information provision would cause. However, the consumer and disability representative with the engineering background was able to critically assess these arguments. The carriage service provider interviewed reported she could address many business operations matters.[21]

[20] It was hoped that the HREOC would become a non-voting member of this code committee. However, it could not attend all meetings due to a lack of resource.

[21] Whether her views were trusted by the consumer and disability representatives is another matter.

Equipment suppliers and carriage service providers spent approximately the same amount of time participating in the working committee, including preparation for and attendance at meetings. Consumer and disability representatives devoted more time to preparation. They also emphasised that working committee participation had 'stretched' the resources of their organisations. Their costs of participation could not be recouped elsewhere as one equipment supplier suggested. Moreover, they had to forego other projects in order to participate in the working committee. However, the quality of their participation in the actual working committee was not diminished as a consequence.

ACIF did not appoint specialist legal drafters to prepare the IAF code. It was drafted by representatives of voting members with the assistance of ACIF's project manager who had legal qualifications and on some occasions, the ACA's delegate. The draft code released for public consultation was poorly drafted and did not always accurately reflect that which had been agreed by the working committee. For example, it did not limit its scope to equipment used in connection with the standard telephone service, an issue that mobile manufacturers, especially, exploited to their advantage during public consultation. Undoubtedly, drafting errors created confusion and exacerbated tensions between voting members of the working committee and interested parties not at the negotiating table. Some delegates reported they became bogged down in 'wordsmithing'. However, the absence of specialist drafters did not significantly influence the substance of the underlying working committee debate.

B. Formal Subcommittee

The composition and function of the formal subcommittee (and ultimately the decision it reached) are integrally related to the efforts of ACIF's CEO to break the apparent deadlock between consumer and disability representatives, and equipment suppliers about all aspects of the code.[22] Before these aspects can be reviewed, however, it is important to understand why it came into existence.

i. Formation

On 26 April 2005 (meeting 18), the working committee discussed the issue of when the code should be implemented for the first time. Equipment suppliers were asked to provide, at the next meeting, information about the systems and processes they needed to put in place in order to comply with the code and the amount of time they would need to implement them. During the May meeting, equipment suppliers adopted the position that the code should be voluntary for and reviewed after 12 months, before it should be registered. That stance angered

[22] See further s V of this chapter (below).

consumer and disability representatives. First, it was inconsistent with the ACA's earlier request for a code. Second, it did not take into account the important concessions consumer and disability representatives had already made to equipment suppliers. For example, they had accepted that equipment suppliers should not be required to provide information about certain attributes categorised as 'extra features' in the public comment version of the draft code. They had accepted that equipment suppliers should not be required to 'negatively report'.[23] Equipment suppliers would not have to tell carriage service providers if their products did not have features specified in the code. They would only be required to inform carriage service providers about the features their customer equipment had. Third, consumer and disability representatives were under enormous pressure to reduce obligations on suppliers to provide information that had to be measured, such as audio output seen as critical for the hard of hearing, and the size of keys and fonts because of alleged cost implications.

Following the 17 June 2005 meeting between ACIF's CEO; the five individuals representing AMTA, AEEMA and AIIA; and a member of the ACA, the CEO and the ACIF project manager suggested a way for the working committee to 'move forward'. However, before their proposal could be discussed by the working committee in meeting 20 (21 July 2005), consumer and disability representatives, in conjunction with ACIF's DAB, issued a 'consumer statement' urging equipment suppliers to produce 'a clear proposal … that meets the needs of those who have a disability' and for the version of the code discussed at the May meeting (meeting 19) to be registered. During meeting 20, ACIF's CEO argued that the consumers' position statement made it clear that the working committee would not be able to reach an outcome. In an attempt to salvage the work of the working committee and no doubt the reputation of ACIF, she suggested that a subcommittee should be formed.

The minutes of that July meeting note that working committee members queried the value of the subcommittee and whether it would be better placed to produce a code. One equipment supplier representative, in particular, was 'unhappy' with the formation of the subcommittee. She believed ACIF's CEO had a right to make certain decisions, including the creation of the subcommittee, but she queried if the rationale for its creation—that the working committee was unable to reach a decision—was justified. She would have preferred for the working committee to hold a vote on the adoption of the code. Despite several interviewees indicating that the decision to create the formal subcommittee was the CEO's, the minutes note that the working committee agreed to the formation of the subcommittee. Exhaustion was a factor in the decision-making of some representatives.

[23] Industry believed negative reporting put industry in a bad light. As one industry representative interviewed said, in practice, a lot of suppliers would provide only 10 per cent or less of the listed features: 'they thought that was really bad for them … to have a … list [that] … shows basically that their products have got very limited use.'

Although one consumer and disability representative interviewed believed that creation of the subcommittee was outside the remit of ACIF, she did not oppose it. It was a way of retrieving the whole 'horror' process. An equipment supplier delegate supported the decision for similar reasons. When the CEO intervened, everyone was 'getting pretty tired'. She stated:

> People took very strong stands … I was of the view … let's get something out there and then we can review how it's going and tweak it and fix it up. We don't have to have it perfect because we don't know how it's going to work first off.

ii. Composition

The formal subcommittee consisted of five members: an equipment supplier representative (Nokia), a carriage service provider representative (Vodafone), a representative of consumer and disability groups (ARATA), a project manager and a chair. The ACIF CEO served as the chair. However, she was absent from two of the four meetings of the subcommittee. The working committee's project manager acted as the project manager for the formal subcommittee. The members of the formal subcommittee were designated by the CEO, and it was implied by certain individuals interviewed that its members were selected on the basis of their amenability to negotiation. Members of the working committee had no say as to whom was selected. Nokia, the equipment supplier representative, was newly appointed as a non-voting member of the working committee. The designated representatives of the carriage service providers, and consumer and disability representatives sat on the working committee from the beginning. Apart from the first meeting of the formal subcommittee, which took place in ACIF's offices in Sydney, meetings of the subcommittee were held via video and audio conferencing. A significant amount of its work was also done by email.

iii. Function

The remit of the formal subcommittee was heavily influenced by the meeting between ACIF's CEO, the five individuals representing AMTA, AEEMA and AIIA, including the delegate from Nokia who joined the formal subcommittee, and a senior member of the ACA on 17 June 2005. Its remit was also influenced by a follow-up email dated 20 July 2005 from the ACA's manager of communications engineering[24] (commenting on an attendance note of the June meeting); and an ACIF options paper prepared after that meeting. During the June meeting, the ACA expressed support for phased implementation and early review of the code once it had been registered.[25] More importantly, it was agreed with equipment

[24] The individual had attended working committee meetings from April 2005.

[25] Carriage service providers and consumer and disability representatives had already accepted that industry would need some time to implement the code after it was registered prior to the ACA meeting.

suppliers that the code had to be based on six 'high level principles', including, for example, the code's requirements should not be overly prescriptive or restrictive and the code should not mandate any measurements that required special tests.[26] The ACA's email of 20 July 2005 also encouraged stakeholders to adopt 'a pragmatic approach' when identifying the information about accessibility features equipment suppliers had to provide and to make use of information that manufacturers already had to hand. In addition, it wanted equipment suppliers to give the same information in a uniform format to facilitate the ability of consumers to compare information about different handsets.[27] Furthermore, it reiterated that it wanted the working committee to produce a code for registration to the ACA. Other factors to be considered by the formal subcommittee when accessibility features were reviewed were later added to the ACA's list by the CEO of ACIF.[28] They included: information that was of the most importance for people with disabilities; information people with disabilities most frequently requested; and information that equipment suppliers could more easily provide. All of these principles were later set out in the subcommittee's terms of reference and were emphasised during its first meeting on 9 August 2005.

C. Analysis and Conclusion

It may be that consumer and disability representatives had been asking industry to provide too much information. As one individual stated, consumer and disability representatives really wanted the ACA to adopt a more onerous disability standard rather than a code that required industry to provide information about accessibility features. The code was seen as a 'default' mechanism. Thus, when the list of accessibility features against which equipment suppliers had to report was generated, consumer and disability representatives wanted everything in it. ACIF's brief attendance note of the 17 June 2005 meeting with the ACA also remarks that equipment supplier representatives provided the ACA with examples of why it was practically difficult for suppliers to comply with the draft code. An options document for the subcommittee prepared by the Nokia representative pointed out that information that had to be generated by laboratory testing could cost up to $5,000 per product per day and would be uneconomic to obtain. For equipment suppliers with a large number of products, the costs could rise considerably.

[26] The formal subcommittee eventually rejected the principle that the code should require the provision of accessibility features information only for those products with special features for those with disabilities.

[27] Industry had demanded each equipment supplier should have the freedom to provide what ACIF called 'effective equivalent information' about the accessibility features included in the code.

[28] The working committee minutes suggest these changes were made with the agreement of the working committee, although interviewed delegates suggested they were presented to the formal subcommittee as a *fait accompli* without consulting working committee members.

Moreover, arguably they had a limited sales market against which to defray those costs, making it difficult to keep the retail cost of handsets at a price that many consumers were willing to pay. For those reasons, the terms of reference of the formal subcommittee, which were in essence stipulating that suppliers would not have to provide as much information as they did in the draft of the code released for public consultation, may have been appropriate from an economic perspective.

However, it is difficult to believe that the way in which the function of the formal subcommittee was defined in the terms of reference did not put the consumer and disability representative, and the members of her constituency, at some form of disadvantage. First and foremost, the terms of reference are underpinned by a belief that industry's assertions about the adverse effects of the code on the market were correct. However, many claims do not appear to have been substantiated with concrete costing data (at least on the face of the minutes and documentation reviewed). Second, many of the review principles seemingly endorsed by the ACA at the June meeting were formulated in the absence of carriage service providers and consumer and disability representatives. Neither group had the opportunity to put their case before the member of the ACA.

Nevertheless, it could be argued that the absence of either consumer and disability representatives or carriage service providers had no real effect on the final outcome reached by the subcommittee. Its terms of reference certainly note the principal concern of consumer and disability representatives that reducing the amount of information equipment suppliers had to provide would have the effect of excluding certain groups of people with particular disabilities. In exchange for consumer and disability representatives dropping their demands for an exhaustive list of accessibility features, industry also agreed to a code rule requiring equipment suppliers to respond to 'all reasonable requests' from consumers wanting more information about the features of their customer equipment. Moreover, it was agreed that the code would permit equipment suppliers to provide information about accessibility features not otherwise specified if they believed it useful to potential consumers. However, it is debatable if the requirement did enough for individual consumers who were left to argue with equipment suppliers that their requests were reasonable. As a consumer and disability representative pointed out, the hearing community lost out as a result of industry's lack of willingness to carry out any measurements. For example, in the final version of the code, industry was not required to provide information about acoustic coupling and the volume of sound, as it had been in the draft code issued for public comment. In any event, what is noticeable from a review of the minutes for the subcommittee is that the feedback the Nokia representative solicited from industry dominated the agenda of the subcommittee. The opinions of consumer and disability groups are not noted. The draft code the subcommittee gave to the main working committee also contained 21 less accessibility features than the working committee had included in the public comment version of the code.

III. Roles

A. Working Committee

i. Equipment Suppliers

The two equipment suppliers interviewed saw their roles in relatively simple and procedural terms. Their function was to represent the interests of their employers by participating in all working committee meetings, providing assistance to the working committee, where possible, and voting. Prior to public consultation, their input (like that of consumer and disability representatives, and carriage service providers) centred on defining the accessibility features against which equipment suppliers had to report. Both representatives brought technical expertise to the working committee. One had an engineering degree and significant professional experience; the other some formal training, and extensive professional experience testing and maintaining customer equipment. The two emphasised the importance of adopting descriptions of features that were objective and measurable to facilitate accurate reporting by staff. For one individual, an important aspect of participation was 'teaching' the consumer and disability representatives about the industry:

> I think, in a lot of cases, some of the stuff … they didn't realise was pretty hard or not practical to implement and they wouldn't have necessarily had a good knowledge of what was available or where the technology was going or where things were happening, like those buffs in the industry might have.

Similarly, one representative identified explaining his position to other working committee members as a core responsibility. In practice, certain representatives may have performed other functions. For example, a consumer and disability representative reported that an equipment supplier delegate also provided clarification about disability matters to other equipment suppliers.

In sharp contrast to the Consumer Contracts code,[29] the narrative of engagement with internal stakeholders (eg, corporate divisions within the company) was weaker. The lack of emphasis by those interviewed can perhaps be explained by the fact that most equipment suppliers represented on the working committee were relatively small businesses. One interviewee specifically responsible for corporate compliance also declined to elaborate, in any detail, about the internal corporate consultation process, so it is difficult to assess its depth. At a minimum, it involved circulation of the public comment version of the code for comment and obtaining internal clearance prior to voting to adopt the final version of the code. Permission was sought to verify that the company could comply with the code.

[29] See s III.A.i of ch 5.

There was also some form of engagement with industry stakeholders external to the process. One equipment supplier conveyed information about the development of the code to an industry association that was not a member of the working committee, of which it was a member. However, the extensiveness of this form of engagement prior to public consultation is unclear. The relevant industry association became directly involved in the process as an observer to the working committee after public consultation, and a representative attended ACIF's June meeting with the ACA.

ii. Carriage Service Providers

The carriage service provider interviewed reported her role on the working committee was to ensure her employer's interests were 'factored into the process' and that her employer could 'deliver' whatever outcome the working committee reached even though the IAF code did not strictly apply to it. She also sought to ensure that the information equipment suppliers had to provide would be of use to her employer's customers because her company was routinely asked for information about accessibility features. For that reason, both carriage service provider delegates saw themselves as 'trying to broker good outcomes' between the fixed equipment suppliers around the table, and consumer and disability representatives. As the carriage service provider interviewed stated, 'I knew what our customers actually wanted, which was information about accessible features, but I could also understand what the manufacturers were saying "Well, how are we going to do this?"'. The 'outcomes broker' role was confirmed by a consumer and disability representative interviewed who reported that carriage service providers became an intermediary between manufacturers, and consumer and disability representatives at times. For example, they had a good understanding of business processes, which they explained to consumer and disability representatives. Another important motivator for this particular carriage service provider was the fact her employer was 'a big participant' in ACIF. As a result, she did not want any of its 'processes or initiatives [to] ... drop into a hole somewhere' and therefore sought to keep the process moving and to ensure a code was developed.

The carriage service provider interviewed also performed a number of functions internal to the company she represented. She was primarily responsible for matters of disability within the company, but she briefed and sought feedback from staff with an interest in the area. Staff contacted included relevant operational areas; regulatory and legal groups; and the individual responsible for managing her employer's relationship with ACIF. Drafts of the code and the submission her employer made during the public comment phase were circulated and discussed with these colleagues. However, because of her 'intimate involvement' with disability matters, decisions were 'her lead' with 'okay' from other staff.

iii. Consumer and Disability Representatives

Consumer and disability representatives wanted to improve the ability of people with disabilities to access telecommunications products and services. One sought the 'best outcome' for those with disability, which involved generating a comprehensive flow of information by way of the code; the other, who believed it was 'totally unrealistic' to expect industry to meet all of the needs of people with disability by way of a disability standard, still wanted a 'significant change' for end users who were not in a position to demand regulation. Their additional responsibilities included working with other consumer and disability representatives on the working committee; presenting their case to industry; and educating other working committee members about disability and the importance of the information on accessibility features sought. Liaison with the members of ACIF's DAB, which involved listening to their concerns and taking them into account when formulating the case of consumer and disability representatives before the working committee, was a responsibility of Tedicore's delegate. Another consumer and disability representative believed she had a duty to be frank, open and honest with other working committee members although she did not believe that other members of the working committee met that standard.

iv. ACA

The ACA, which merged with the Australian Broadcasting Authority (ABA) to become the Australian Communications and Media Authority (ACMA) while the code was being negotiated, was represented by three different individuals at different stages of the process. The role of the ACA was outlined clearly during the first meeting of the working committee: slides prepared by an ACA staff member were shown by ACIF's project manager to working committee members. The ACA was merely an observer of the process. It was not willing to facilitate, coordinate, mediate, draft or vote but it would advise on the consistency of the proposed code with its regulatory and policy decisions as well as those of government. Advice could come from either ACA employees or the ACA.[30] Written advice was to be provided on the draft of the code released for public comment and would consist of registration- and non-registration-dependent comments. Registration-dependent comments were comments that industry had to address or the ACA would not register the code. A rationale for the ACA's limited involvement in the development of the IAF code is not given in the slides. All interviewed individuals who represented voting members described the role played by the ACA played in broadly similar terms. However, a consumer and disability representative emphasised that, when this code was developed, the ACA did not know what its role in industry rule-making was. Many interviewees recalled ACA representatives

[30] See s III.B.ii of ch 4 for the distinction between the ACA and its staff.

contributing to discussion and having a more significant role in some meetings. However, they confined their input to reminding the working committee of its task—to produce a code and a guideline. When negotiations became difficult after public consultation, they referred to the formal request of the ACA and its ability to adopt an industry standard if a code were not developed.[31] Surprisingly, the ACA made only one registration-dependent comment on the public comment draft of the code. It did not comment on the remit of the code—an issue hotly contested by equipment suppliers, and consumer and disability representatives—and/or evaluate if the code was consistent with its original request. In addition, the ACA expressed its 'commitment' to developing a portal containing the information equipment suppliers had to supply to carriage service providers so members of the public could access it from a central location—a mechanism which arguably would have overcome some of industry's inertia to providing the information because of its concern that it would never reach end customers. However, the implementation of other projects, including the ACA's merger with the ABA, was given higher priority.

It is possible that the ACA was more active in and influential on the working committee than some delegates may have recalled. The working committee minutes record that certain representatives assisted with some (albeit limited) drafting of the code. One equipment supplier also reported that an ACA representative rang him after a working committee meeting when voting delegates had disagreed with each other in an attempt to 'close the gap'. The ACA staff member, who did not agree with the equipment supplier, explained the ACA's view and attempted to resolve the 'grievance'. Towards the end of the process, one of two ACA representatives to the working committee objected to the position of equipment suppliers that compliance with the code should be voluntary for 12 months, expressing 'difficulty' in seeing why they would need that length of time to provide the information sought. Equally, the involvement of members of the ACA was influential at the later stages of the process. The meeting of 17 June 2005 between the ACA, AMTA, AEEMA and AIIA shaped, or at least sanctioned, some of the core terms of reference of the formal subcommittee. In his email of 20 July 2005, the ACA's manager of communications engineering encouraged working committee representatives to compromise and strike a deal 'recognising the difficulty in obtaining the "ideal" outcome (from each stakeholder's perspective) through the WC [Working Committee] process in the first round'. Finally, when equipment suppliers called for a mechanism that permitted the list of accessibility features against which they had to report to be updated regularly, without the need for

[31] It is doubtful that the threat of regulatory intervention was taken seriously. By the time the formal request was first made, nearly 16 months had passed since the date of the ACA's original request that had stipulated that the code be developed in six months.

continual re-registration of the code,[32] the 'highest levels' of the ACA expressed their views on how that goal could be achieved within the legislative framework of Part 6. The ACA also departed from its established practice that codes should stand alone and not reference other documents.[33] Admittedly, greater ACA involvement appears to have come about because of the decision of ACIF's CEO to elevate matters to members of the ACA: she initiated the meeting on 17 June 2005 and wrote to the ACA for feedback on three proposed options to address the updating issue. However, when it did engage, it would appear that the ACA had some effect on the process. The effect it had was arguably deleterious for consumer and disability representatives but it influenced the process.

v. Chair and Project Manager

The individual who represented CTN explained that one of her responsibilities when acting as chair was 'to try and create an environment where people are going to share their views in a respectful way [to] ... each other'. In addition to facilitating conversation, she had to keep the working committee 'on task' and the project 'moving forward', which involved making sure that people were 'supported [when they] needed to be' and following up different action items. Outside of working committee meetings, she spoke with the ACIF project manager to frame the working committee's agenda and updated ACIF's CEO about the work of the working committee. She was also involved in drafting certain code rules for the consideration of the working committee, as specialist legal drafters were not hired by ACIF to prepare the code.

However, she called into question her ability to be 'independent'—a responsibility she identified as central to the role of chair—when the members of the working committee began to disagree after the code was released for public comment. As she explained, 'it was fine for me as a consumer to be the chair while ... we were working through a process and the negotiations were functioning well ...' However, as soon as she needed to start taking positions when CTN adopted the Consumer Position Statement, she had to step down because she was not capable of being independent. She had 'an immediate conflict of interest' that prevented her from 'driving the process forward' because she recognised she 'didn't have the trust of all the people' on the working committee. She raised the issue with ACIF's CEO to whom she was expected to report working committee 'blockages',[34] and together they made the decision that she should step down as chair.

[32] When the IAF code was developed, it was not possible to vary a Part 6 code. All changes had to be 'achieved by replacing the code instead of varying the code.' Telecommunications Act 1997 (Cth) s 120.

[33] See ACA, *Developing Telecommunications Codes for Registration—A Guide* (October 2003) 7.

[34] The obligation to report difficulties formed part of the project management plan processes the ACIF CEO had implemented in an effort to overcome criticisms from a number of quarters that ACIF code development took too long.

Whether the CTN representative had the support of all members prior to the issuance of the Consumer Position Statement is less than clear. At least one equipment supplier delegate said the chair wanted certain outcomes for the consumer and disability sector. As she stated, 'I think we all used to dread the meetings with her because ... she was pretty attacking with ... the equipment suppliers.' For example, the chair asserted that industry was not doing enough to help the consumer and disability sector or that 'it wasn't like industry said it was'. Her replacement, the ACIF CEO, was perceived as 'much more independent'. Equally, it has to be questioned if genuine agreement between consumer and disability representatives and equipment suppliers had been reached at any stage prior to the final meeting of the working committee in November 2005. Consumer and disability representatives may have believed that the working committee's decision to release the draft code for public consultation signalled some form of consensus had been reached. Certainly, all working committee members agreed it could be published. However, the backlash from industry that followed and the reports of disagreement and frustration, and failure to resolve disputes by many of the representatives interviewed, suggest otherwise.

The same individual served as the project manager for the Consumer Contracts code and IAF code working committees. As for the Consumer Contracts code, her role involved a significant amount of administration and secretarial work. However, as ACIF did not hire specialist legal drafters for this code, she was also involved in drafting and/or editing provisions of the code as agreed to by the working committee and/or preparing particular sections of the code, which were then reviewed and discussed by the working committee. For example, she proactively rewrote the code's explanatory statement to address issues that arose during the public comment phase and put specific proposals to the working committee. She also appears to have been involved in drafting several options papers for the working committee at crucial junctures in the process as well as the working committee's response to the CECRP's request for comments on allegations made during public comment that it had exceeded its terms of reference.[35] The project manager believed an important aspect of her role was to be 'absolutely, unbelievably independent and neutral' and all of her work was carried out with the objective of creating an atmosphere of trust from which consensus could emerge.

vi. CEO

The role ACIF's CEO played in this process needs to be mentioned. Even though she was absent from two of the four formal subcommittee meetings and served as chair for only one meeting of the working committee, she was instrumental in bringing about an outcome. She tried to find mechanisms to resolve the underlying disputes and pushed the parties to reach some form of agreement.

[35] See s IV of this chapter (below).

The CEO was updated periodically throughout the process about the progress of the working committee by its chair. However, she did not become an active player until the chair asked her to after meeting 16 (3 March 2005), when the gulf between consumer and disability representatives, and equipment suppliers was made abundantly clear. The CEO attended the following meeting in April 2005, during which she emphasised the benefits of self-regulation, while raising the spectre of the ACA becoming the decision-maker. She presented the voting members of the working committee with two options. Either they agree to continue discussions in an effort to 'close the remaining gaps' or they agree that consensus could not be reached and the matter would be referred to the ACA for determination. All members agreed to continue. The CEO imposed a deadline:[36] agreement had to be reached within six weeks. She stipulated that there could be no more than two additional working committee meetings and offered the use of a professional facilitator, if necessary. Importantly, the CEO was also present for discussion of an options paper that identified a very high level 'compromise' position on which all parties agreed. All equipment suppliers would be required to report against a mandatory subset of accessibility features drawn from those included in the version of the draft code published by ACIF for public comment. However, they were free to provide additional information if they so wished. All information had to be given in the same format as that stipulated by the working committee to facilitate correlation and distribution of information by carriage service providers. The CEO again became directly involved at the conclusion of meeting 19 in May 2005, during which equipment suppliers adopted the position that the code should be voluntary. She actively sought a meeting with a member of the ACA to seek guidance and established the formal subcommittee, appointing herself as chair, in an attempt to produce a code. Her actions would appear to have been motivated by a desire to retain the organisational integrity and reputation of ACIF. According to one consumer and disability representative, ACIF (along with industry and the ACA) was 'embarrassed' by industry's apparent 'about face' to the code during and after public consultation.

B. Formal Subcommittee

The creation of the formal subcommittee did not fundamentally alter the objectives of the individuals designated by the CEO to serve on it. All delegates continued to advance the respective interests of their employers, even if their precise goals had altered in some way. For example, the consumer and disability representative who served on the formal subcommittee went from wanting to see a significant change for end users to a desire to negotiate an outcome that had as much value as possible.

[36] Neither the working committee nor the formal subcommittee met the deadline set by the CEO.

However, the subcommittee's terms of reference imposed additional obligations on its members that changed their roles and responsibilities quite significantly. Delegates acted on behalf of their 'constituencies', not themselves. They were required to consult with their constituencies and formulate 'agreed positions', which were to be brought back to the subcommittee for discussion. In practice, the consumer and disability representatives, and AEEMA's representative to the working committee, were already representing multiple interests prior to its creation. However, the subcommittee's terms of reference extended that practice to all delegates, stressing that whatever form of consultation were adopted, it must give subcommittee representatives sufficient time to consult with their constituencies. The obligation to consult was taken seriously and industry engaged actively with the process. In advance of the second subcommittee meeting, the Nokia representative solicited feedback from 'various'[37] mobile and fixed-line phone equipment suppliers, which was summarised and circulated to subcommittee members. A revised list of accessibility features and amended code rules were then circulated again to industry for comment. A third round of industry consultation also took place. Moreover, the consumer and disability representative met with ACIF's DAB to discuss the changes made to the code. In addition to a duty to consult, subcommittee representatives were charged with informing the working committee of its progress. Working committee members were sent emails updating them of the subcommittee's work and were afforded an opportunity to comment on revised drafts of the code. Interestingly, during the first subcommittee meeting, it was also stressed that subcommittee representatives were required to ensure that if they could reach agreement, the full working committee did not undermine it.

IV. Strategy

The consumer and disability representatives may not have strictly negotiated as a bloc but they did adopt common negotiating strategies, which relative to those deployed during the Consumer Contracts code[38] were straightforward. Their simplicity reflected in large measure the underlying nature of the exercise—justifying why equipment suppliers ought to provide information about accessibility features. In addition to appealing to the 'rational humanitarian side' of equipment suppliers, they adopted the argument that the provision of information about accessibility features was a marketing opportunity that had the potential to increase sales and possibly their market share (a point highlighted by ACIF's CEO later in the process). They cited the ever-increasing aged population,

[37] The companies consulted are not known. In the working committee documentation reviewed, comments from individual suppliers were anonymised.

[38] See s IV of ch 5.

noting there would be increased demand for customer equipment with particular types of features to address its needs. Similarly, they introduced the notion of a 'temporary disability', arguing that anyone could be disabled for a short time. They challenged the notion that disability was out of the ordinary. There were not two groups of individuals—those with and without disability. Rather, disability was a continuum and anyone could acquire and lose a disability in their day-to-day lives. As one would have anticipated, educating the other members of the working committee (either during meetings or during breaks (where possible)) about disabilities and how particular features could assist became a central plank in their discussions with equipment suppliers. For example, a consumer and disability representative described a 'light bulb' moment for equipment suppliers during the formal subcommittee when its representative pulled out a 'lipstick' mobile phone activated by voice. It was pointed out that the phone could be valuable for quadriplegics who had no use of their limbs.

Equipment suppliers interviewed, on the other hand, reported using a few different strategies. One reported adopting a 'win-win' strategy, while stating that her employer did not always win. They sought to avoid the adoption of prescriptive rules. For example, consumer and disability representatives wanted to require equipment suppliers to provide a free phone number so consumers seeking additional information about accessibility features could contact relevant suppliers at no cost. For one equipment supplier, the expense of a free phone number was significant. She sought to water down the requirement by including more general language in the code so compliance could be met in a multiplicity of ways. Equipment suppliers also sought to educate working committee members about what they wanted and why. Finally, the working committee minutes and related documentation record that ACIF staff, including the project manager, believed that some equipment suppliers used perceived procedural irregularities on which to hang their concerns about the amount of information required and the format of the information they had to provide under the code. For example, AEEMA's written submission on the public comment version of the draft code to the working committee noted that several members did not believe the working committee had adequately complied with its terms of reference as set by the CECRP and the ACA's code development guidelines.[39] In a subsequent working committee meeting, AEEMA representatives criticised the working committee for failing to seek clarification from the reference panel about whether equipment suppliers were required to provide information to general retailers, such as Kmart and Big W. In addition, AEEMA representatives chastised the working committee for neglecting to 'undertake a progress report half way through the project'; to educate importers, not previously subject to a code, about the draft

[39] See generally, ACA, above n 33.

code; and to publish the draft industry guideline[40] that the ACA requested in conjunction with the draft code.

Given the length of time it took to develop the code, it is also difficult to resist the conclusion that at least some organisations representing equipment suppliers on the working committee adopted delay on occasions as a strategy. It is true that the duration of code development cannot be attributed solely to deliberate industry behaviour. For example, the working committee extensively discussed the issue of whether equipment suppliers should have to provide information on accessibility features to general retailers who supplied customer equipment even though the ACA's request confined the obligation of supply to carriage service providers. However, both consumer and disability representatives interviewed reported 'blocking' and stalling by industry in various forms, such as failing to identify and articulate obstacles. Withholding information from the debate was seen as a particularly powerful tool. In addition, the contrast between the level of contribution of AEEMA made before and after the draft code went to public consultation is particularly noteworthy. Opposition from AEEMA and other equipment supplier representatives to the lengthy list of accessibility features is not noted in the minutes prior to public consultation even though it was agreed that NEC Business Solutions and AEEMA would 'test' their ability to complete the matrices of features prior to public consultation. However, AEEMA submitted a relatively lengthy list of comments critical of the draft code during public consultation. Additional (and presumably more senior) representatives from AEEMA and NEC Business Solutions also attended post-public consultation working committee meetings technically as 'observers' but were very active participants in some of those sessions. AEEMA representatives also attended ACIF's meeting with the ACA on 17 June 2005. At least one consumer and disability representative believed that, until public consultation, the higher echelons of industry had treated the process as a 'joke' by failing to communicate with the staff members who attended working committee meetings. Committee participation was ritualistic: industry wanted to be seen to be participating but in substance it did not. Similarly, the proposal that the code should be voluntary rather than binding, made by the representatives of AEEMA and Cisco in meeting 19, suggests a last-ditch attempt to postpone the application of the code.[41] Both organisations had been members of the CECRP, which had stipulated that an industry code was its 'preferred option'.

For carriage service providers, the strategy was to 'broker' a settlement between the equipment suppliers and consumer and disability representatives.

[40] See above n 10.

[41] Industry may have been lobbying ACMA not to register the code and/or to delay registration of the code. The code was not registered until 12 October 2006, which was nearly a year after the working committee finished it. See, eg, Galexia, *Consumer Protection in the Communications Industry: Moving to Best Practice* (October 2008) 32.

V. Dispute Resolution

As one equipment supplier representative explained, 'the context [was] everybody want[ed] to have more or less in the code.' For that reason, it is no surprise that several working committee representatives characterised negotiations as 'fraught', 'tough going', 'contentious' and 'robust.' Prior to the establishment of the formal sub-committee, some techniques were deployed to try to resolve the underlying tensions between the parties on the working committee. They included discussing issues 'backwards and forwards'; creating numerous (informal) subcommittees tasked with solving particular problems outside of working committee meetings and reporting back to the main committee; addressing non-contentious issues first; and postponing the discussion of difficult issues for later. In a departure from her usual approach, an outburst of anger from a delegate was used with some success on one occasion. However, none of the main issues in dispute was, as one consumer and disability representative stated, ever really resolved in the main committee. In sharp contrast to the Consumer Contracts code, the narrative of practical measures to 'produce agreement out of dissent' (as the project manager described consensus building)[42] is notably absent. Issuance of the draft code for public comment may have given rise to a reasonable belief on the part of consumer and disability representatives that the working committee had reached some form of agreement. However, as has already been demonstrated, not all equipment suppliers on the working committee believed they had, and public consultation only highlighted disagreement among a subsection of industry arguably inadequately represented on the working committee. As one equipment supplier interviewed said, 'I think we got very locked into a certain way of thinking and we didn't really think out of the square which I think happened ... towards the end.'

How and why then did the IAF code emerge? One equipment supplier interviewed said the determining factor in the process was that each party emerged satisfied. However, that explanation is overly simplistic. Undoubtedly, the decision of the chair to escalate the matters in dispute to ACIF's CEO, their mutual agreement that she should stand down as chair and the creation of the formal subcommittee were pivotal turning points. Equally, the CEO's decision to meet with a member of the ACA was influential. During that meeting, the ACA finally provided ACIF and working committee members with some guidance about the content of the code. Addressing the alleged inadequacy of representation for mobile manufacturers played a role too even though not everyone believed that it was appropriate or necessary. The emphasis in the formal subcommittee's terms of reference on consultation with constituencies was also important and arguably kept industry actively engaged with the process; although by the time the subcommittee was

[42] See s V of ch 5.

created, industry was involved. In addition, the roles of fatigue, annoyance and frustration on all sides and the CEO's desire to preserve ACIF's reputation cannot be underestimated. Importantly, too, consumer and disability representatives capitulated on a number of issues in the face of fierce industry opposition rather than abandon the process, which ACIF's CEO gave them the option of doing in meeting 16. As one consumer and disability representative said, 'it had got to the point where you sort of knew that you were getting the scraps of the scraps off the table …' and ultimately they would be better off with something rather than nothing. They dropped demands for information about measurable features, including the size of keys, fonts and audio output (with one exception); mechanisms to ensure that information provided by equipment suppliers would be understood by consumers; and information about the accessibility features of equipment used predominantly in the workplace. These concessions, coupled with the willingness of consumer and disability representatives to shift from particularity to generality (ie, by requiring equipment suppliers to respond to 'all reasonable requests' for additional information) and to allow industry to report information positively rather than negatively so its marketing concerns could be addressed, allowed a code to materialise.

Interestingly, although ACIF's Operating Manual permitted the CECRP to resolve any disputes referred to it unanimously by the working committee (and committee members were informed of that), no reference was ever made. The CTN representative who served as chair reported that panel members were periodically kept informed of 'challenges but it was never really considered that the CECRP would solve an impasse'. Keeping disputes within the working committee may have been due to the fact that the CECRP met quarterly. However, the composition of the CECRP may have been a factor. Some representatives on the working committee were also delegates to the CECRP. Most CECRP members were from industry. This may have created the perception that the concerns of consumer and disability representatives would not have received an impartial hearing. In addition, the working committee did not pursue the use of professional mediators—an idea suggested by ACIF's CEO and supported by some individual delegates. An equipment supplier interviewed believed that mediation would have been inappropriate because of its cost and the fact that the decision(s) being made by the working committee did not involve legal questions. As she stated, 'This is not like a court case, leave it to a judge to determine you are right …' There was also no voting on any matter until the code was finalised.

VI. Conclusion

There are a number of aspects of the IAF code process that raise procedural and institutional legitimacy concerns. There was a partial chair for most of the process. Consumer and disability representatives reported several incidents of blocking and stalling by equipment suppliers during working committee meetings. They also reported that equipment suppliers were not always forthcoming with relevant information and that equipment suppliers' assertions about the cost of providing accessibility features information and/or implementing the IAF code were often not substantiated. Consumer and disability representatives did not attend ACIF's and industry's June 2005 meeting with a member of the ACA. Therefore, they had no opportunity to put their case directly to the ACA. The establishment of a formal subcommittee was unusual. Fatigue played a role in its creation. Exhaustion also led consumer and disability representatives to make several significant concessions to equipment suppliers. They no longer had the energy or resources to continue to argue.

Perhaps the most troublesome aspects of this case study are the under-representation of mobile phone manufacturers and the appointment of Nokia to the working committee so late in the process to address the problem. On the one hand, if mobile phone manufacturers were genuinely under-represented, the modification the ACIF CEO made to the composition of the working committee should be welcomed. Public consultation highlighted a deficiency in the working committee; and ACIF rectified the situation when the difficulty was identified, aided by a rule-making procedure that was sufficiently flexible to allow for correction of errors while the process was on-going. On the other hand, there would appear to be some doubt that the problem of under-representation was not caused by mobile phone manufacturers themselves. If they disengaged deliberately, then the ACIF rule-making process is open to a form of gaming. In the end, the gaming may not have affected the substance of the rules ultimately adopted. One could argue that although the process was slow, had the parties actively engaged with the process from the beginning, the rules adopted would have been the same. However, disengagement clearly worked to the advantage of all equipment suppliers. They wanted to postpone the application of the code for as long as possible. Development of the code took 20 months.

7

The Mobile Premium Services Code

I. Working Committee Composition and Context

First introduced in Australia on a trial basis in 2003, mobile premium services (MPS)[1] were not regulated either by the state or industry until 29 June 2005 when the Australian Communications Authority (ACA) adopted the Telecommunications Service Provider (Mobile Premium Services) Determination 2005 (No 1) (Cth) (the Determination). The Determination provided that neither content service providers nor mobile carriage service providers (MCSPs) could supply MPS unless they complied with a self-regulatory scheme approved by the ACA or a designated 'default scheme'. To be approved by the ACA, a self-regulatory scheme had to impose a number of consumer-protection measures on providers, in addition to certain obligations relating to the content of MPS. Obligations included requirements to give accurate information about fees and contractual terms in their promotional material; to inform customers about the costs of mobile premium services before or at the time they used them; to adopt complaints handling procedures that met specified criteria; and, in the case of premium rate Short Message Services (SMS) and Multimedia Messaging Services (MMS), to have a facility that enabled a customer to cancel without charge the services by issuing a keypad command from a mobile handset. Originally, it was intended that a code of practice being developed by the Telephone Information Services Standards Council, members of the Australian Mobile Telecommunications Association (AMTA) and the Australian Direct Marketing Association (ADMA), when the Determination was adopted, would serve as the 'default scheme'. However, the Mobile Premium Services Self-Regulatory (MPSI) Scheme[2] and guideline[3] (hereafter referred to as the MPSI guideline) subsequently developed by ADMA's Mobile Marketing Council and AMTA and approved by the Australian Communications and Media Authority (ACMA) on 5 October 2006, became the default scheme. The MPSI Scheme and guideline sought to regulate the industry in two distinct but

[1] For an explanation of these services, see s III.A.ii.c of ch 4.

[2] *Mobile Premium Services Self-Regulatory Scheme Pursuant to the Telecommunications Service Provider (Mobile Premium Services) Determination 2005 No 1* (Cth) (22 August 2006) ('MPSI Scheme).

[3] *Guideline to the Mobile Premium Services Self-Regulatory Scheme* (22 August 2006).

complementary ways. The MPSI Scheme placed a number of substantive obligations on both content and mobile carriage service providers that were enforceable by ACMA. The rules of the MPSI Scheme were supplemented by other measures applicable solely to content service providers set out in the MPSI guideline. Under the MPSI Scheme, mobile carriage service providers had to 'refer to, be consistent with and not contradict' the MPSI guideline, as amended from time to time, in their contracts with content providers for the delivery of MPS.[4] It was also envisaged MCSPs would enforce the terms of the MPSI guideline by way of contract law mechanisms.[5] In the absence of any other self-regulatory scheme for MPS, the MPSI Scheme and guideline emerged as the de facto regulatory standard for the industry.

ACMA, however, had to revisit its Determination following the passage of the Communications Legislation Amendment (Content Services) Act 2007 (Cth) on 20 June 2007. The Act amended the Broadcasting Services Act 1992 (Cth) by, among other things, setting out a new framework regulating the content of services delivered over mobile phones and other communication devices. On 26 October 2007, ACMA published a consultation paper[6] soliciting comments on proposed amendments to the Determination to reflect the legislative changes and on whether the remaining consumer-protection provisions of the Determination and the MPSI Scheme should be retained or set out in a code of practice developed in accordance with Part 6 of the Telecommunications Act 1997 (Cth) (Part 6).[7] The CEO of the Communications Alliance, which had been designated as the 'custodian'[8] of the MPSI Scheme, expressed support for the latter option.[9] She argued that a Part 6 code would reduce the regulatory burden on industry because it would eliminate the need for bespoke provisions in the MPSI Scheme dealing with registration and variation of the scheme, and an escalated complaints handling body. Comparable rules were already set out in Part 6. Importantly, a Part 6 code would achieve the same level of consumer protection provided in the Determination and the MPSI Scheme. ACMA agreed, 'verbally inform[ing]' the Communications Alliance that it was 'comfortable' with its proposal to convert the MPSI Scheme into a Part 6 code.

[4] MPSI Scheme, above n 2, s 15.1.3.

[5] ibid s 15.1.1.

[6] ACMA, *Changes to the Restrictions on Access to Mobile Premium Services: An ACMA Consultation Paper Relating to the Amendment of the Telecommunications Service Provider (Mobile Premium Services) Determination 2005 (No 1) and a Variation to the Telecommunications Numbering Plan 1997* (2007).

[7] ACMA was prevented from registering the MPSI Scheme under Part 6 because of a statutory prohibition on Part 6 codes regulating the content of content services.

[8] On the meaning of custodianship, see Communications Alliance, *Mobile Premium Services Self-Regulatory Scheme: Information for Industry Members* (25 October 2006); MPSI Scheme, above n 2, s 14.1.2.

[9] Letter from A Hurley, CEO, Communications Alliance to Manager, Education and Telephone Content Section, ACMA (29 November 2007).

The Communications Alliance established the MPS working committee in early 2008. Consistent with the CEO's proposal to ACMA, its original focus was to transform the MPSI Scheme into a code capable of being registered under Part 6. The working committee's terms of reference stated expressly that the creation of new code rules and/or the revision of existing rules (other than in accordance with a list of amendments formulated by the Communication Alliance's 'MPSI Scheme Management Group')[10] were prohibited. However, as the MPS code was being developed, the remit of the working committee quickly changed from the relatively simple exercise of converting the MPSI Scheme and guideline to the task of overhauling the regulatory framework to address growing public dissatisfaction about the unscrupulous and misleading behaviour of some within the MPS industry. Consumers, many of whom were young children, were being billed for services they did not knowingly subscribe to. Their requests to cease the provision of services were not honoured. There were difficulties contacting content service providers, particularly those based overseas, to make complaints. If contact was made, consumers were referred to their MCSPs. Often complaints were never resolved.[11] ACMA's ability to take enforcement action was limited because many content service providers were not physically within Australia and ACMA did not know who was providing the services. It had no way to keep track of them.

Pressure was brought to bear on the working committee (as rule-maker) and ACMA (as code registrar) from a number of different entities. They included the Minister for Broadband, Communications and the Digital Economy, Stephen Conroy (the Minister), known for his strong personality and willingness to intervene in the telecommunications market,[12] the Australian Competition and Consumer Commission (ACCC), the Telecommunications Industry Ombudsman (TIO)[13] and the media. Two months after the working committee first met in May 2008, the Minister twice wrote to the Communications Alliance asking for modifications to the draft MPS code. In an address before the 'ACMA and Communications Alliance Consumer Dialogue' in July 2008, he welcomed development of the MPS code but stated that 'industry need[ed] to do more' with respect to ensuring compliance with codes and dealing promptly with consumer complaints to avoid undermining confidence in self-regulation.[14] If it failed,

[10] The MPSI Scheme Management Group carried out a year-long review of the MPSI Scheme and guideline.

[11] TIO, *Mobile Premium Services Complaint Drivers: Complaint Data Analysis* (17 September 2008) 5.

[12] See, eg, R LeMay, 'End of An Era: Stephen Conroy Quits as Comms Minister' (*Delimiter*, 26 June 2013) <https://delimiter.com.au/2013/06/26/end-of-an-era-stephen-conroy-quits-as-comms-minister>.

[13] The TIO was the designated 'escalated complaints handling body' for the purposes of the MPSI Scheme.

[14] Minister for Broadband, Communications and the Digital Economy, S Conroy, 'Address to the Australian Communications and Media Authority & Communications Alliance Consumer Dialogue 2008' (Speech delivered at the ACMA & Communications Alliance Consumer Dialogue 2008, Sydney, 22 July 2008).

'[t]he Government would then have little choice to consider a more interventionist approach'. In August 2008, the ACCC brought legal proceedings against TMG Asia Pacific Pty Ltd for alleged misleading and deceptive conduct in breach of the then Trade Practices Act 1974 (Cth) for its premium rate mobile subscription quiz services advertising,[15] subsequently securing an undertaking from the company.[16] Complaints data on MPS gathered by the TIO were also increasing. In September 2008, the TIO reported that from 1 December 2006 to 30 June 2007, the number of MPS complaints it received averaged 1,012 per month. By the fourth quarter of the 2007/2008 financial year, the figure had risen to 1,708.[17] Newspapers and television programs, such as *A Current Affair*, were also drawing attention to the difficulties many consumers experienced with the MPS industry,[18] with some running what some representatives interviewed described as 'campaigns' against the industry.[19] Some of these entities were more influential than others. For example, it will be argued later that the Minister's interest in the MPS code caused ACMA to adopt a 'hands-on' approach for this code, which had an important effect on the eventual shape of the MPS code.[20] However, collectively they contributed to what some industry representatives described as the 'pressure' to do something about MPS.

The composition of the working committee, which developed the code over 37 meetings[21] between 4 April 2008 and 11 March 2009, reflected the business model for MPS.[22] The supply chain consists of three different parties: mobile carriage service providers, 'aggregators' and content providers. Each has a unique role in the creation and delivery of the content mobile phone users receive if they buy a mobile premium service. A content provider generates the actual content that a mobile phone user requests. However, in order to supply the content, a content provider typically has to have a contract with an aggregator. Often described as an intermediary between a content provider and a mobile carriage service provider

[15] ACCC, 'ACCC Alleges Misleading and Deceptive Conduct by TMG Asia Pacific Pty Ltd in Advertising Mobile Premium Services' (Media Release, NR 236/08, 20 August 2008).

[16] *Undertaking to the Australian Competition and Consumer Commission Given for the Purposes of Section 87B of the Trade Practice Act 1974 by TMG Asia Pacific Pty Ltd (ACN 119 828 698) and The Mobile Generation I BV Accepted September 2008.*

[17] TIO, above n 11, 4.

[18] See, eg, R Viellaris, 'Threat to Put Brake on Mobile Marketing Ploys', *The Courier-Mail* (Brisbane), 23 August 2008, 25; J Rolfe, 'Snaring Children Is Morally Wrong', *The Daily Telegraph* (Sydney), 27 February 2009, 21.

[19] All statements attributed to working committee participants involved in the development of this code were made to the author during interviews held in February, March and April 2012. The names of interviewees are not provided to preserve the anonymity of the individuals concerned. For information about the research methodology used for the case studies, see the Appendix.

[20] See s II.B.iii of this chapter (below).

[21] For some meetings, all representatives met face-to-face or held a teleconference. In other instances, some participants met face-to-face while others joined the conversation via teleconferencing.

[22] See also s III.A.ii.c of ch 4.

(MCSP), an aggregator operates an IT platform that permits the requested content to be delivered to subscribers of mobile carriage services. An aggregator, in turn, must have an agreement with the relevant MCSP for the physical delivery of that content to its subscribers. It is the MCSP that is responsible for the actual delivery of the content to its subscribers. The MCSP bills its subscribers for the mobile premium services used. All revenue is collected by the MCSP, which retains a fee for the carriage of content and billing service it performs. The difference is passed on to the aggregator, which keeps a sum for providing the aggregation service. Content providers retain the balance. On a typical premium SMS/MMS transaction, one MCSP representative interviewed stated that most of the retail price paid is ultimately received by the content provider. On this working committee, MCSPs were represented by Telstra and Optus; the aggregators by Sybase 365; and content providers by MobileActive.[23] However, in a departure from the previous two case studies, working committee delegates were responsible for representing the interests of their respective constituencies (ie, MCSPs, aggregators and content providers) from the beginning of the rule-making process. In addition, not unlike the second case study, many overseas-based content service providers (believed to be the underlying cause for many of the complaints made to the TIO) did not engage in the rule-making process.[24]

Despite the MCSP representatives interviewed reporting that they 'saw [consumer involvement] as absolutely critical' to 'the overall success of the code and perception of the success of the Code', consumer and public interest groups were not members of the working committee for its first 15 meetings. Their initial absence was the result of the decision of the CEO of the Communications Alliance to adopt a 'formal' consultation approach, which was to involve members of the working committee meeting periodically with key stakeholders, such as the Department of Broadband, Communications and the Digital Economy (DBCDE), the ACCC, the TIO and the Office of the Privacy Commissioner (OPC),[25] in addition to a round of public consultation. Her rationale was that the MPS code was an adaptation of the MPSI Scheme, and the working committee was not starting from a 'blank page'.[26] However, it must be said that, at the time, the Communications Alliance was reviewing the level of involvement consumer and public interest groups were to have in the organisation more generally, and the manner in which it would satisfy its statutory obligation to 'consult' with all stakeholders, including consumer and public interest organisations, when formulating Part 6 codes. Although missing from the working committee,

[23] The company has since been renamed MobileEmbrace.

[24] See s III.A.ii.c of ch 4.

[25] Part 6 required the Communications Alliance to consult the OPC if a code related to certain privacy matters before it could be registered.

[26] Letter from A Hurley, CEO, Communications Alliance, to T Corbin, CEO, CTN and Chair, Communications Alliance Consumer Council (31 July 2008).

the Communications Alliance took steps to solicit the feedback of consumer and public interest groups about the development of the MPS code. For example, representatives from consumer organisations Choice[27] and CTN attended the Communications Alliance's first and second stakeholder consultation sessions held on 19 March 2008[28] and 15 July 2008. A copy of the draft MPS code and guideline prepared by the working committee was provided to CTN, and the Consumer and Disability Councils[29] for comment on 16 June 2008. The CEO also offered consumer and public interest specific consultation sessions, and again solicited substantive comments on the draft code and guideline on 18 July 2008.[30]

Consumer and public interest groups, which had been appointed to all other consumer code working committees of the Communications Alliance, were not placated by these initiatives. Perhaps emboldened by the announcement of the Minister that the government would fund the establishment of the Australian Communications Consumer Action Network (ACCAN) to 'give consumers a more powerful and effective voice in the development of telecommunications policy',[31] they pushed the CEO of the Communications Alliance for direct and equal representation of consumer and public interest groups on the working committee. They argued that, absent their participation, 'critical' issues such as inadvertent subscription to MPS would not be addressed. They asked for the working committee to be dissolved and another created with an equal number of representatives from industry, and consumer and public interest organisations.[32] On 31 July 2008, citing the 'timeframes and expectations of the Minister and ACMA',[33] the CEO refused to disband the working committee. However, she offered the CEO of CTN (who was also chair of the Communications Alliance's Consumer Council) a place on the working committee and an all-day joint working meeting on the draft MPS code with the Communications Alliance's Consumer and Disability Councils after the code had been released for public consultation.[34] In the end, the Communications Alliance's Consumer and Disability Councils were added as voting members and, with some exceptions,[35]

[27] Choice, previously known as the Australian Consumers Association, had ceased participating in all ACIF processes in December 2001. It had no further involvement with ACIF or the Communications Alliance until the MPS code was developed.

[28] One consumer and public interest representative interviewed alleged that consumer and public interest organisations were invited to the March meeting only because they learned in advance that the meeting was happening and 'demanded to come along.'

[29] See s III.C.ii of ch 4 for information on the Consumer and Disability Councils.

[30] Letter dated 31 July 2008 from A Hurley, above n 26, 2.

[31] Minister for Broadband, Communications and the Digital Economy, S Conroy, 'Grant to Strengthen Consumer Voice in Telecommunications' (Media Release, 84797, 23 June 2008).

[32] Letter from T Corbin, CEO, CTN and Chair, Communications Alliance Consumer Council; G Renouf, Choice; S Salthouse, Chair, Communications Alliance Disability Council; L Kreet, Communications Alliance Disability Council, to A Hurley, CEO, Communications Alliance (24 July 2008).

[33] Letter dated 31 July 2008 from A Hurley, above n 26, 2.

[34] ibid 3.

[35] See s V.A of this chapter (below).

their delegates attended all meetings of the working committee from meeting 16 (10 September 2008). Precisely why the Communications Alliance departed from its initial consultation approach and agreed to include consumer and public interest representatives is unclear. Consumer groups were lobbying ACMA and the Minister for greater involvement on the working committee. There was also some concern that CTN would withhold its 'mandatory consultation certificate'—a document that ACMA had previously required the Communications Alliance to submit when registering a Part 6 code. The certificate, signed by CTN as a matter of convention, demonstrated to ACMA that the Communications Alliance satisfied the statutory requirement of consultation with a consumer body. CTN had written to ACMA threatening that it would not sign the document if consultation was limited to the Communications Alliance's initial proposal.[36]

The voting members of the working committee were assisted by a chair and a project manager.[37] Both were employees of the Communications Alliance. Lawyers from Baker & McKenzie were hired by the Communications Alliance to draft the MPS code. More will be said about each of these parties later. However, for now, it is important to note that when the MPS code was developed, one of the objects of the Communications Alliance was 'to advance the interests of Members and the Industry',[38] and it had started to advocate industry views by submitting comments on government consultation documents, for example.[39] In the other two case studies, it did not take positions on policy developments and as was noted in the case study on the Consumer Contracts code,[40] was seen as a relatively neutral forum. What (if any) effect the change to the purpose of the Communications Alliance had on the substance of the MPS code is difficult to assess. However, it is clear that this additional function contributed to a strong sense of distrust of the chair, the project manager and the lawyers they instructed throughout the process among the consumer and public interest representatives interviewed. All were perceived to have a conflict of interest because they worked for the Communications Alliance. Moreover, the apparent bias—consumer and public interest representatives interviewed either could not identify any concrete evidence of any actual bias or declined to provide specific details—served only to intensify what were already strained relationships between consumer and public interest representatives, the Communications Alliance and the MPS industry when the consumer and public interest delegates arrived at the negotiating table.

[36] In the end, CTN withheld the certificate but for unrelated reasons. See s V of this chapter (below). ACMA registered the code in any event taking the view that Part 6 does not require consumer 'sign off.'

[37] Two individuals acted as project manager during the development of the MPS code. The first individual attended only the first three meetings of the working committee.

[38] *Constitution of Communications Alliance Ltd ACN 078 026 507* (v9) (August 2006) cl 1.5(l).

[39] See also s II of ch 3.

[40] See s III.C of ch 5.

II. Power

Explaining where rule-making power lay in the development of the MPS code is not a straightforward exercise. There were multiple sites of rule-making and different dynamics within each site. One set of negotiations was taking place within the respective constituencies of working committee members; another in the working committee itself. Important negotiations were also occurring between ACMA, the Communications Alliance and select members of the working committee outside of scheduled meetings of the working committee; and between the Minister, the Communications Alliance and the working committee. The end result was that there was no central node of power. The influence of any particular actor was distributed across various sites and discussions occurring at different times. The ability of any one actor or 'bloc' of actors to influence the process was also affected by the complex matrix of political and inter-personal dynamics operating across the sites. The dynamic within each negotiation site and the power of its participants are explored in more detail below.

A. The Voting Constituencies

i. Mobile Carriage Service Providers

The MCSP constituency consisted of Vodafone, Hutchison, Telstra and Optus because, in addition to providing mobile carriage services, they owned and operated the terrestrial mobile networks used by all other MCSPs to provide MPS. Neither Vodafone nor Hutchison had the resources to send a delegate to the working committee so it was agreed that Telstra and Optus would serve as the MCSP working committee representatives. However, when the working committee was established, employees and heads of the regulatory groups of all four companies attended a half-day workshop to discuss the MPS code. Vodafone and Hutchison employees also regularly met face-to-face, emailed and/or teleconferenced with the delegates from Telstra and Optus before or after committee meetings to discuss their views on proposed amendments to the MPSI Scheme and the perspectives of aggregators, content providers, and consumer and public interest representatives. One MCSP representative interviewed reported that meetings could 'get quite fiery', notwithstanding the perception that industry was 'homogenous'. He stated, '… there's a whole range of views within the different parties and different priorities within the organisations and different capacities.' Despite these differences, the other MCSP representative reported, with some exceptions, broad agreement among MCSPs was reached on a variety of issues: 'We all had pretty standard views in terms of wanting to ensure that those rogue operators were kicked out of the industry and that what was seen as a legitimate information provision service was achieved.' On many occasions, the position the MCSP representatives adopted was dictated by Vodafone and Hutchison even though the larger providers 'would have had no problem with' accepting a particular and more onerous obligation. As one MCSP representative stated:

> [the code has] got to be something that everyone can do because once the code's registered, you have to comply with the code ... there's no point in agreeing something that as soon as it's registered you're going to get hit for non-compliance.

In instances where Vodafone and Hutchison could not comply, discussion turned to 'what are we actually trying to achieve here?' and the identification of alternative means to achieve similar 'outcomes'.

An area of dispute between the MCSPs was 'double opt-in' but in that instance, the position industry ultimately adopted was driven by Telstra, the largest MCSP. As early as 29 September 2008 and during subsequent meetings with individuals from the working committee, ACMA requested that the MPS code should impose an obligation that, in effect, required subscribers who wanted to purchase MPS from their mobile handsets to send two text messages to a content provider in order to receive them. The first text message sent from subscribers had to 'clearly and positively' request the service. The second text message had to be made in response to a confirmation message sent by the relevant content provider, which among things instructed the customer to send a text message to the 'short code'[41] for that content provider in order to receive the service. However, MCSP representatives strongly opposed a double opt-in requirement. They believed that it would 'hinder the customer experience' and would impose additional costs without 'addressing [the problem of] illegitimate services'. Despite a letter dated 5 January 2009 formally requesting the imposition of double opt-in from the Minister, the MPS code submitted by the Communications Alliance to ACMA for registration did not contain this requirement. However, after the code was sent to ACMA for registration and following a request from the regulator to include a double opt-in requirement, Telstra changed its mind. It agreed to adopt double opt-in.[42] The decision was taken by a senior figure within the company without consulting the individual who represented Telstra on the working committee. It was motivated by several factors, including the desire to 'eliminate' complaints about MPS. However, similar to the first case study, the political climate was a very strong motivator. Telstra was under 'a lot of pressure from the Minister' to address MPS. Although no one interviewed made reference to it, at that stage, Telstra had also been excluded from the Government's original tender process for the National Broadband Network.[43] Further, the Minister had launched a wide-ranging consultation of the regulation of the Australian telecommunications

[41] A short code is the telephone number beginning with 19XX that the subscriber must dial to communicate with a particular content provider.

[42] See also s V.A of this chapter (below).

[43] See n 115 in s II of ch 1 and accompanying text.

sector, which, among other things, solicited comments on whether Telstra should be structurally separated. Regardless of the reasons for the 'canny political move', as one MCSP representative described it, Telstra's decision to adopt double opt-in forced the other MCSPs to rethink their positions. In the end, they agreed to implement double opt-in; in part because they thought they might be conceding competitive advantage to Telstra if they did not. Consumer and public interest representatives, for example, had been advising members of their constituencies to use Telstra because its mobile network permitted subscribers to bar access to MPS.

ii. Aggregators and Content Providers

The two individuals who represented aggregators and content providers on the working committee regularly consulted the Mobile Content and Services Group (MCASG), a standing group of the Communication Alliance consisting of aggregators and content providers that are members of the organisation. On occasion, the MCASG also met with the MCSPs. However, as none of the aggregator and content provider delegates on the working committee agreed to be interviewed, it is difficult to assess the dynamic within those constituencies.

iii. Consumer and Public Interest Representatives

After they joined the working committee, the two consumer and public interest representatives solicited and received feedback from the members of the Consumer and Disability Councils.[44] The Disability Council representative reported the council placed a lot of 'faith' in her legal expertise and she 'went back' only on a 'few issues', including, in particular, the decision of consumer and public interest delegates to walk out of the process after meeting 37 (11 March 2009).[45] The Consumer Council representative kept the members of her employer's consumer organisation informed about the development of the code. She explained to them the reasons for walking out of the process.

From time to time, the consumer and public interest delegates also consulted and discussed issues—including, in particular, proposed obligations on the MPS industry to monitor its compliance with the MPS code—with consumer and public interest groups that were not members of the Consumer and Disability Councils.

Consumer and public interest representatives worked together to develop agreed positions that they presented to the working committee as a bloc. Often one individual took the lead in formulating a particular position, reflecting respective areas of expertise and the limited time they had available to prepare for scheduled meetings.

[44] See s III.C.ii of ch 4.

[45] The walkout is discussed below. See ss III.B and V of this chapter.

B. Working Committee

i. Mobile Carriage Service Providers and Aggregators/Content Providers

Before consumer and public interest representatives became working committee members, the dynamic of the working committee reflected the tensions between the MCSPs, on the one hand, and aggregators and content providers, on the other. Until ACMA began to provide feedback on the draft MPS code to the working committee beginning on 14 July 2008,[46] the parties concentrated on converting the MPSI Scheme and guideline into the MPS code. However, throughout the entire process, delineating and allocating responsibilities between industry participants were central issues. The MCSPs did not control all aspects of the supply chain. For example, they had no contractual relationship with content providers. Nevertheless, throughout all stages of the working committee, the MCSPs had greater negotiating power vis-à-vis aggregators and content providers because the decision to grant access to the underlying communications networks was entirely within their discretion. As one MCSP representative stated, 'if the pain got to the extent that the carriers thought this [participating in the MPS industry] is not even worth doing, we'll just … turn it off.' For aggregators and content providers, many of whose businesses were built entirely around MPS, access to mobile carriage services was essential. Whether a MCSP would have prevented access to all MPS is debatable. There were (and are) strong commercial incentives for MCSPs to offer innovative new services. However, one MCSP representative interviewed reported that the percentage of his employer's customer base using MPS was small (less than 10 per cent) and, as the MPS code progressed, one of the smaller players informed him, it was 'quite seriously thinking of just getting out [of MPS] because it's just … the compliance burden is just not worth it. It's not actually core business. It's just a little thing we're doing on the side.' While the code was being developed, Telstra also terminated its contract with Oxygen 8, an aggregator, for breaches of the MPSI guideline.[47]

ii. Mobile Carriage Service Providers, Aggregators/Content Providers and Consumer and Public Interest Representatives

After the two consumer and public interest delegates joined working committee meetings, the dynamic of the working committee changed. It was reported, at that point, the focus of negotiations shifted from MCSPs and aggregators/content providers to MCSPs/aggregators/content providers, and consumer and

[46] See s II.B.iii of this chapter (below).

[47] See, eg, A Colley, 'Court Battle over SMS Allegations against Telstra' *The Australian* (Sydney, 14 April 2009) www.theaustralian.com.au/australian-it-old/telstra-accused-over-sms/story-e6frgalo-1225700546356.

public interest groups. However, in the opinion of at least one MCSP representative, MCSPs, aggregators and content providers never negotiated collectively with the consumer and public interest representatives. Most often, MCSPs negotiated with the consumer and public interest representatives due to their perception that MCSPs had more direct involvement with the provision of MPS than they in fact had. Aggregators and content providers became involved in only specific issues. The involvement of ACMA and the Minister in this process makes it difficult to identify the areas where changes to the code were made because of the involvement of consumer and public interest representatives, and to assess their actual bargaining power. For example, ACMA, the Minister and consumer and public interest representatives supported double opt-in. However, as argued above,[48] the MPS code was most likely modified in that regard because of Ministerial pressure. Similarly, some of the concerns of consumer and public interest representatives identified, such as the inability of mobile customers to identify the content providers whose charges appeared on their phone bills, had already been addressed or were in the process of being addressed by the time they joined the working committee either as a result of ACMA's involvement or industry's own initiative. Moreover, even if consumer and public interest delegates thought the provisions should have been more robust,[49] with assistance from ACMA, they were successful in enhancing the rules designed to protect minors. Content providers had to develop a process for handling complaints involving minors that took into account a number of factors, including whether advertisements for the relevant mobile premium service 'advised its potential audience to seek the permission of the relevant account holder.'[50]

However, on the issue that they viewed as their 'bottom line'—the need for rules imposing robust monitoring and compliance obligations on industry—the consumer and public interest representatives were arguably unsuccessful. In the end, the MPS code required mobile carriage and content service providers to 'cooperate' with 'MPS Code Monitoring'. However, even though the code envisaged that the Communications Alliance would appoint a 'code monitor', it did not and could not impose a legally binding obligation to select a code monitor on the Communications Alliance. The industry body was not a 'section of the telecommunications industry' as defined in Part 6. Similarly, consumer and government representatives could advise the Communications Alliance as to whom it should appoint. However, the final decision rested with the Communications Alliance. The obligation of content and mobile carriage service providers with respect to monitoring was also limited to answering 'reasonable requests for information' from the code monitor. Consumer and public interest representatives had demanded, for

[48] See s II.A.i of this chapter.

[49] See CTN, 'Mobile Premium Service Code Provides No Safety Net' (Media Release, 20 March 2009).

[50] Communications Alliance, *Industry Code C637: Mobile Premium Services* (2009) s 6.1.1 (m)(iv).

example, that they comply with any remedial action proposed by the code monitor and ensure sufficient resources were made available for code monitoring. Further, the code did not specify the functions and powers of the code monitor, including its capability to direct remedial action.

More will be said later[51] about how and why the final MPS code monitoring rule took this form; but for now, it should be noted that several factors undermined the strength of this particular argument and the ability of consumer and public interest representatives to secure agreement from industry committee members. First and foremost, their late arrival prevented them from tying their key issues to all other matters negotiated by the working committee, as they had done in the first case study.[52] While it is clear that consumer and public interest delegates tied matters together as they negotiated, some issues had been decided before they joined the working committee and could not be linked to 'live' matters. Second, the consumer and public interest representative who was primarily responsible for developing the arguments in support of monitoring and compliance reported that her thinking was not 'very well developed'. She was a practising lawyer in the area of consumer protection in the financial services sector and drew on personal contacts at and previous work of the ACCC. However, she did not have a 'good understanding' of how Part 6 codes fitted into ACMA's enforcement mechanisms under the Telecommunications Act 1997 (Cth), an understanding which became crucial when industry working committee members began to argue that consumer and public interest proposals duplicated the statutory scheme. Third, inadequate time to prepare for meetings must also be cited as a contributing factor. The Disability Council representative was forced to juggle work commitments around her involvement with the code. The Consumer Council representative was devoting significant energy and resources to the creation of ACCAN. Both representatives also attributed their 'compromised position' to the numerical imbalance between consumer and public interest organisations and industry members on the working committee and the inability of consumer and public interest organisations to participate in the decision concerning the scope of the MPS code.[53] More fundamental to the decision concerning code monitoring and compliance was the fact that neither ACMA nor the Minister had any real appetite at that stage to pursue the issue.[54] While the Minister agreed that the code should contain some form of monitoring obligation, it is noted in the working committee minutes that he wanted ACMA and the TIO involved in enforcement as they already had powers to take action against non-compliant members of industry.

[51] See s V of this chapter (below).

[52] See s IV of ch 5.

[53] Consumer and public interest representatives had been involved with scoping the remit of the Consumer Contracts and IAF codes discussed, respectively, in chs 5 and 6.

[54] ACMA has since pursued this issue vigorously. See, eg, ACMA, *Reconnecting the Customer: Final Public Inquiry Report* (September 2011) 12–13, 25–31, 130–31.

iii. ACMA and the Communications Alliance/Working Committee

ACMA did not have a representative on the working committee. Nevertheless, members of the working committee representing the MPS industry negotiated directly with ACMA about the MPS code via an exchange of written correspondence and a series of face-to-face meetings over the duration of the working committee.[55] ACMA engaged fully with the code's development from the outset; it stipulated that the Communications Alliance could release a draft of the MPS code for public consultation only if ACMA authorised it. This departure from ACMA's standard convention occurred because of the high profile MPS were receiving at the time in the media and the Minister's interest in the matter. As the MCSP representatives commented, ACMA was 'exposed'. It had been 'asleep at the wheel for quite a significant period of time' and was consequently feeling 'pressure from the Minister ... to get an outcome that provided ... customer service benefits across the board ...' After receiving extensive written comments from ACMA on the 'pre-public consultation' drafts of the MPS code and guideline on 14 July 2008, the Communications Alliance suggested that members of ACMA's staff meet regularly with working committee delegates. ACMA agreed. These meetings were attended by the chair and project manager of the working committee, at least one industry representative and a solicitor from Baker & McKenzie. A 'senior line-area representative' and legal counsel attended on behalf of ACMA. Initially, meetings were held every two weeks. However, they became weekly before the draft MPS code and guideline were released for public comment but after ACMA gave permission for publication, subject to a list of additional issues for consideration. Meetings discussed working committee progress and the latest draft of the code, with ACMA staff providing 'top of mind' feedback. According to one MCSP representative, during meetings, the MCSPs were clearly within ACMA's 'scope'. Content providers and aggregators 'relaxed to a certain extent' because ACMA wanted 'to put all responsibility on the carriers'. Written comments were often provided by ACMA staff members after those meetings. This process of meetings followed by written comments from ACMA continued well after the period for public consultation had finished. ACMA also requested to see a draft of the MPS code and guideline for 'informal evaluation' prior to their submission for registration. Throughout the process, letters between the chair of ACMA and the CEO of the Communications Alliance were occasionally exchanged. In addition—and, again in a departure from established practice and

[55] On occasion, a consumer and public interest representative attended these meetings with ACMA. However, due to concern that the meetings were 'directed' by the Communications Alliance and it did not fully represent the consumer and public interests, a consumer and public interest representative on the working committee regularly spoke to ACMA staff over the phone while the MPS code was being developed. During that time, she also had 'two to three' meetings with ACMA to discuss a number of topics, including MPS.

the other two case studies—MCSP representatives met with members of ACMA and some of ACMA's senior managers after the code was submitted for registration to explain the benefits of the code.

Regardless of the impetus behind ACMA's engagement, its participation altered the shape of the MPS code. On the whole, the MPS industry representatives on the working committee were largely receptive to the amendments ACMA wanted made. By no means did ACMA have everything its own way. For example, ACMA requested in July 2008 that mobile carriage and content service providers should provide it with regular reports providing certain information about each complaint they received. Industry resisted what was described as 'an extremely large logistical exercise'. In the end, in addition to amendments made to the code and elsewhere, ACMA accepted a lesser obligation with suppliers agreeing to provide copies of their complaints records for particular short codes within a reasonable period of time following a request from ACMA.[56] However, ACMA did effect change in a number of important areas. It required all substantive obligations set out in the MPSI guideline to be included in the MPS code, thus increasing the number of provisions it could enforce directly. It gave industry the choice of including the names, helpline details and email addresses of relevant content service providers in a subscriber's mobile phone bill or creating an online register whereby consumers could find details about a content service provider by entering that provider's short code. Industry agreed to the latter.[57] It also agreed to impose an obligation on content providers to provide and keep up-to-date specified information to their aggregators which were required to update the 'short code look-up database.' If a content provider did not have an aggregator, the information had to be provided to the Communications Alliance. Similarly, ACMA asked the working committee, which acceded to its request, to impose a requirement on content providers and aggregators to register their details, including the name of the principal or at least one director (if the relevant entity were a company), prior to providing a mobile premium service (if a content provider) or contracting with a content provider for the supply of a mobile premium service (if an aggregator). Why ACMA was able to secure these amendments is less clear. No doubt its powers of registration under Part 6 were significant factors, as one MCSP representative stated. The code had to 'survive some consumer protection tests'. However, the pressure placed on the MPS industry and the MCSPs, in particular, by the Minister who was under pressure from members of Parliament, consumer advocates and the general public cannot be underestimated. As one MCSP representative stated, ACMA and industry had a 'common interest in seeing a code that was registered'.

[56] *Industry Code C637: Mobile Premium Services* (2009), above n 50, s 6.1.17.
[57] ibid s 4.2.

iv. The Minister and the Communications Alliance/Working Committee

When the MPS code was developed, only ACMA had the authority to register a code and, in a limited set of circumstances listed in Part 6, adopt an industry standard. The Minister personally had no statutory power to intervene. The influence he was able to exert on this process derived from his ability to introduce legislation regulating the MPS industry in Parliament. One MCSP representative, who believed that industry handled the issue of MPS 'very poorly' from a political perspective, commented that the Minister did not assist the process in any way, other than 'putting pressure on the industry to do something'. Yet, in his view, there was 'no reticence [within industry] to do something'. Another representative stated, absent Ministerial involvement, the MPS industry would have addressed the issues but it did so more quickly 'because of the scrutiny from the politicians'. However, the Minister contributed to the process beyond increasing its speed. Certainly, his concerns were at a higher level than ACMA's and he never went to the level of granularity that ACMA did. Nevertheless, he acted independently of ACMA. He directly and indirectly shaped the content of the code and the wider regulatory environment in which MPS were provided, even though he was never present at the negotiating table of the working committee.

The Minister became directly involved in the process by sending two letters to the CEO of the Communications Alliance, both of which appear to have been followed up by the Communications Alliance's Regulatory and Public Policy Manager and/or its CEO in meetings with the DBCDE and the Minister's office in May/June 2008, and on 3 February 2009. On 20 May 2008, the Minister sent the CEO of the Communications Alliance a letter raising three principal concerns: (1) the amount of time it took for content service providers to act on a customer request to 'stop' a mobile premium subscription service; (2) the opt-out mechanism adopted by content service providers for mobile premium service-related marketing messages; and (3) the absence of and inconsistency in the level of detail about MPS supplied on mobile phone subscribers' bills. He again wrote to the Communications Alliance's CEO on 5 January 2009 and called for the MPS industry to adopt double opt-in and 'call barring'. The latter permits subscribers of mobile carriage services to block access to all MPS from their handsets. However, it is on the latter area where the Minister arguably had the most impact. Although the minutes record that the carriers had no opposition to call barring 'in principle', the MCSP interviewees recalled most delegates did not support it because of the 'investment' required to implement it and doubt that call barring would reduce the number of customer complaints about unknowingly subscribing to MPS. One MCSP representative stated that even though Telstra was not the largest player in the MPS market and had call barring in place, it had a 'hugely disproportionate number of complaints'. However, the Minister held firm. Citing overseas precedent and Telstra's decision to bar calls, he refused to accept 'anything other than a formal commitment from the carriers that call barring would be implemented'. With the Minister's agreement, call barring was not imposed as a requirement in the MPS code. However, its accompanying explanatory statement notes the intention of Optus, Vodafone and Hutchison to adopt call barring.

Several instances of the Minister's indirect involvement in this process and their effects have already been noted in sections II.A.i and II.B.iv of this chapter (above). It should also be mentioned that the Minister's public stance on MPS strengthened the resolve of the consumer and public interest representatives on the working committee, even though they reported they had no formal discussions about the MPS code with him. His speech on 31 March 2009 at the CommsDay Summit, in which he announced a review of the Part 6 code development process and ACMA's powers to enforce Part 6 codes,[58] provided 'strong ground to make a statement about the failure of self-regulation'. In addition, the announcement was a factor in the decision of the consumer and public interest delegates to walk out of the MPS working committee. A MCSP representative also reported that the 'consumer movement would harden their positions' every time the Minister threatened to regulate the industry. He stated, 'the implicit view across the table would be if you guys don't roll over on everything we want, the Minister is going to basically regulate you, and we like that outcome ...'

III. Roles

A. Mobile Carriage Service Providers, Aggregators and Content Service Providers

All individuals representing the MCSPs, aggregators and content service providers served four principal functions. They were responsible for formulating 'internal' positions on issues for their employers; advocating that agreed position to their respective constituencies; soliciting and synthesising the positions of others into a collective constituency stance; and then wearing their 'industry hats', advocating those views to the members of the working committee with whom they negotiated. As one MCSP representative stated, in the working committee 'our own companies are irrelevant, you're not wearing an [employer] hat into the room'. It was also emphasised that 'you absolutely were in the room basically holding a position or arguing your case that your own organisation didn't agree with ...'

Developing internal positions on code matters was a substantial exercise for the two MCSP representatives interviewed. They primarily consulted commercial and operational members of staff. In-house lawyers also provided input to the process although the employer of one representative relied heavily on the ability of

[58] Minister for Broadband, Communications and the Digital Economy, S Conroy, 'Reforms to Improve Consumer Protection in Telecommunications' (Media Release, 111642, 31 March 2009).

Baker & McKenzie to draft the code accurately. One MCSP representative said he developed 'extremely close working relationships' with 'three or four key people' responsible for the mobile premium services business within the company. In addition to phone conversations and emails, they had formal 'ops meetings' before working committee meetings. Code work was seen as a 'distraction' in the sense that it took away from the time operational staff had to work on the business. Although the regulatory team was perceived to be 'a cost centre in a profit-making enterprise', this individual reported it was not difficult to get internal business staff to focus on the issues. They recognised they had an incentive to participate—the interest in 'their business functioning sustainably'. Much of the discussion centred on reviewing the effect implementing proposed modifications to the code would have on the 'customer experience' and, where necessary, trying to come up with alternatives so that the customer base that wanted to use MPS did not complain, adversely affecting the bottom line. Over time, however, the discussion became 'less about the issues' and more about 'this thing's [the code] got to get wrapped up … you get to a point where it's got to be done'.

As the description of internal corporate consultation highlights, the 'mandate' and responsibilities of both MCSP representatives on the working committee were more nuanced than simply carrying out their four key functions described above. One individual said that the MCSPs had the objective of 'want[ing] to make sure that the revenues … that we were getting as carriers weren't tainted by customers not being aware of what the service was and what they were signing up to'. They also wanted to 'drive out those rogue operators'. For both individuals, how those objectives were to be achieved was coloured by their performance indicators set with their immediate supervisors as well as the commercial and other imperatives of the colleagues they consulted. For one representative, it was expected that he would produce a code that was 'workable', as agreed with operational staff, and had 'reasonable consumer protections in place which allocates responsibilities in a manner that is reasonable and can be enforced in a timely manner.'[59] For the other delegate, performance was evaluated by reference to ensuring an agreed industry solution emerged and there was no additional state regulation.

B. Consumer and Public Interest Representatives

Both consumer and public interest representatives were on the working committee to 'put the consumer view' although the individual with the least experience with the Communication Alliance's code development process stated that the expectations the organisation had of them were not clearly explained to her. In that

[59] Note, however, that a consumer and public interest representative interviewed stated that no one from industry had 'a clear picture that developing a code was about providing greater consumer protection.'

vacuum, she saw her main responsibility being to review the code draft already produced by the working committee and 'see if it met the consumer protection standards that we were looking for'.

Industry's view of the function of consumer and public interest representatives differed from the view of consumer and public interest representatives. Disagreement between the two sides is perhaps demonstrated most clearly in this case study because of the decision of consumer and public interest representatives to walk out of the process. The Consumer Council representative commented that industry believed consumer and public interest representatives were obliged to reach consensus with industry about the code because industry allowed them to participate in the process. She said, 'the assumption is that, if you go into a code process from the start, you're going to vote yes ... and that if you [do] not, what is the point of having consumer representatives in the process?' That industry viewpoint was consistent with the statements of one of the MCSP representatives interviewed. He said that he 'honestly struggled to work out whether the consumer objective in this whole process was for it not to work' with the consequence that it was 'very hard to have the conversation [about code formation]'. He added, 'I really think they just generally aren't looking for an outcome, they're looking for a reason to break the process up so they can basically go to the regulator and say "See, we told you it doesn't work."' It is true that when the MPS code was being developed, the consumer movement had concluded that 12 years after the adoption of the Telecommunications Act 1997 (Cth), the telecommunications industry was inadequately regulated and the cause of the problem was reliance on Part 6 rule-making. Whether a wider reform agenda was the 'real' reason for the walkout will never be determined. Certainly, the consumer and public interest representatives interviewed said their decision turned on other factors: their inability to participate on the working committee from the beginning, industry's refusal to accept their 'absolute compromise' on code monitoring and the level of complaints about the industry. However, if the expectation is that consumer and public interest representatives must agree with industry, they are placed in a very difficult position for the reason identified by a MCSP representative, 'they don't want to be ... tainted with having ... put their names on the piece of paper'. However, the industry saw some form of accountability mechanism on consumer and public interest representatives as critical. As one MCSP representative stated:

> [T]hey don't feel any pain if it [the code process] doesn't work. They don't have any skin in the game ... the ACMA has skin in the game; the industry has skin in the game; the Minister has skin in the game to a certain extent.

C. Project Manager, Chair and Baker & McKenzie

The two employees of the Communications Alliance—the project manager and the chair—worked hand-in-hand with members of the working committee to develop the code. However, as the project manager was new to the Communications Alliance (he joined shortly after MPS code development began), he primarily assisted the chair—who was also his immediate supervisor—playing what he described as a 'fairly low-key role' during working committee discussions. The chair, on the other hand, was a significant player both inside and outside of the working committee. She described her role as one of 'support management', 'not subject matter expertise'. Her responsibilities included ensuring the project was kept 'on track'. She managed the MPS code development project against the timelines and terms of reference approved by the Communications Alliance's CEO and made sure the working committee kept to its agenda. With the project manager's assistance, she produced the minutes of the working committee meetings, prepared meeting papers and coordinated interaction with other stakeholders, such as the MCAS and Standing Mobile Carrier Services Groups. In conjunction with the CEO of the Communications Alliance, who had principal responsibility for overseeing the relationship with the Minister, the chair looked after the interaction with ACMA. Other important aspects of the chair's position included facilitating discussion during meetings, to 'ensur[e] that all voices are heard, all issues are discussed appropriately'. Related to this function, she sought to give everyone the opportunity to 'understand the implications of suggestions' and to be 'fully informed' of the reasons why a proposal was rejected. Where disputes such as the protracted debate concerning code monitoring and enforcement arose, she escalated them where appropriate, to the CEO.

Another important duty of the chair, according to the Operating Manual of the Communications Alliance, was the requirement to take 'an independent role in relation to Working Committee debate to ensure the fair and equitable operation of the Working Committee'.[60] As already mentioned, the consumer and public representatives did not perceive the chair to be independent even though she retained the 'full support' of the CEO throughout the process. However, the MCSP representatives interviewed did not see her as 'being aligned to any particular group' or 'pro-industry'. Regardless of whether the chair was in fact 'independent', the perception of bias made it more difficult for the chair to effectively perform her facilitator and dispute resolution roles. A MCSP representative interviewed, who believed that general 'relationship building' was not managed particularly well on this working committee, said in hindsight it would have been better if the Communications Alliance had funded an independent contractor to facilitate working committee discussion if only so consumer and public interest representatives could not use the chair as an 'excuse for ... animosity'. He believed the chair was placed in an 'invidious' position when consumer and public interest representatives joined the working committee; and without doubt, the questions consumer

[60] Communications Alliance, *Operating Manual for the Development of Industry Codes, Standards and Supplementary Documents and the Establishment and Operation of Advisory Groups* (June 2007) s 2.6.

and public interest representatives raised of the chair's independence and integrity were taken 'personally'. The reasons for the decision of the CEO of the Communications Alliance not to revisit who served as the chair after consumer and public interest representatives joined the working committee are not documented. However, some of the factors cited by the CEO not to disband the working committee at the request of consumer representatives in July 2008 are likely to have been considered. The Communications Alliance was keen to meet the expectations of the Minister and ACMA. Minimising the cost of code development may also have been a consideration, as it was when the chair was initially selected. It was reported that independent chairs can be expensive. However, when the chair was appointed, the remit of the project was limited to converting the MPSI Scheme and guideline into a code, and the direct involvement of consumer and public interest representatives on the working committee was not envisaged.

According to the members of the working committee interviewed, Baker & McKenzie's role was straightforward. It served a 'legal drafting type function'. Its solicitors were instructed in the working committee meetings they attended or via a 'Drafting Requirements Log' prepared with agreement of working committee members and emailed to them by the chair. Based on the documentation reviewed, the law firm's role also extended to providing legal advice on certain issues related to code development, including whether a Part 6 code can grant the TIO enforcement power over entities who are not members of the TIO scheme, and liaising with the ACCC on whether the code could prohibit content and mobile carriage service providers from contracting with parties who had not registered with the Communications Alliance. In addition, their lawyers attended meetings with ACMA. On the face of the documentation reviewed, it was often difficult to determine the law firm's client—the working committee or the Communications Alliance. However, the chair confirmed that the Communications Alliance was the firm's client, which for the consumer and public interest representatives, contributed to their perception of bias in favour of industry.

D. ACMA and the Minister

As discussed in section II.B.iii (above), ACMA actively negotiated with members of the working committee and the Communications Alliance, and contributed in significant ways to the substance of the code. Whatever employees and members of ACMA may have believed their role to be, ACMA was limited to working within the confines of the Telecommunications Act 1997 (Cth). That said, unlike the previous two case studies, throughout this process ACMA was, as the chair of the working committee said, 'very much directing' in its role as code registrar. Areas of particular concern to ACMA have already been described.[61] However, ACMA had

[61] See s II.B.iii of this chapter (above).

many others. The minutes note numerous ACMA comments about which parties in the MPS supply chain should comply with particular code obligations. At one stage, it wanted mobile carriage and content service providers to share responsibility for many obligations over which MCSPs had no direct control. ACMA had no ability to take enforcement action against content service providers based offshore, and it wanted to be able to hold MCSPs vicariously liable for the actions of overseas content providers. Other points it raised included: the need to specify particular obligations dealing with matters such as advertising font size; avoidance of ambiguous terms such as 'scam', 'appropriate', 'good customer experience', 'matters beyond its reasonable control'; and aspects of the complaints handling obligations imposed on content and mobile carriage service providers. ACMA's chair also specifically requested the industry adopt a 'case management approach' to customer complaints. For the working committee chair, ACMA's 'stronger overview role' amounted to co-regulation of the sector rather than industry self-regulation. For that reason, one MCSP representative interviewed concluded that the code development process bore 'very little resemblance' to the procedure outlined in Part 6.

Like ACMA, the Minister played an important role. His intervention had a direct effect. Absent the involvement of the Minister, his office and the DBCDE, it is doubtful if call barring would have been introduced and/or agreed to by the MCSPs. Certainly, ACMA did not advocate call barring during its negotiations with the working committee, and the Minister's letter of 5 January 2009 requesting call barring came as a surprise to ACMA. The minutes of meeting 28 (20 January 2009) note that ACMA confirmed to the Communications Alliance that it had not been consulted by the Minister's office about it. The consumer and public interest representatives supported call barring but whether they would have been able to secure industry agreement absent ministerial support for the requirement is far from certain. The Minister's interest in MPS also influenced the process in a number of other ways. The political climate was a motivating factor in Telstra's decision to adopt double opt-in. It spurred ACMA, including its chair, to engage actively with code development, and encouraged consumer and public interest representatives to drive a hard bargain in working committee negotiations.

E. Other

The OPC, the ACCC and the TIO were consulted during the formal stakeholder consultation sessions organised by the Communications Alliance and all three submitted written comments on the draft MPS code released for public consultation. Of the three, the TIO and the ACCC had a greater impact on the code. The TIO's complaints data about MPS in its September 2008 report was seen by industry as an 'objective indicator of performance' at the time even though it had and continues to have more general concerns about how the TIO prepares and records complaints. The data added to the pressure the industry was under to identify and address the underlying causes for complaint. The ACCC, which also had 'extensive experience in handling MPS consumer complaints', strongly supported double opt-in, call barring and modifications to the advertising requirements in the MPSI Scheme and guideline. Whether, and the extent to which, the ACCC's views were influential on ACMA and the Minister is not documented. However, on 13 March 2009, the then chair of the ACCC, Graeme Samuel, who was also an observer on ACMA's board, reiterated his support for double opt-in and call barring in a speech delivered at the Australian Telecommunications User Group (ATUG)'s Annual Conference.[62] The ACCC may also have been applying pressure to industry by way of its powers under the then Trade Practices Act 1974 (Cth). In his March speech, the chair states the ACCC had 'recently written to local mobile carriers regarding mobile premium services' and was in the 'process of carefully examining the responses'. Consumer and public interest representatives were also keeping the ACCC abreast of their concerns about the code.

IV. Strategy

In the absence of interviews with staff of ACMA, the Minister's Office, the DBCDE, the ACCC and the TIO, it was not possible to identify all of the strategies used to negotiate with and/or apply pressure to the Communications Alliance as well as working committee and individual industry participants.[63] Clearly, the Minister was publicly using the rhetoric of legislative intervention if the MPS industry failed to deliver improvements for consumers,[64] a point which he reiterated in his letter of 5 January 2009 to the Communication Alliance. Similarly, the ACCC was warning MCSPs to 'exhibit a responsible attitude to closing down rogue operators [content providers]' or 'they must expect the ACCC to pursue remedies available to it under the TPA [Trade Practices Act 1974 (Cth)]'.[65] ACMA, as registrar, did not comment publicly about the substance of the code while it was being developed. In the correspondence between ACMA and the Communications Alliance and/or the working committee,[66] there is only one reference to the concerns of the DBCDE involving customer consent. In all other instances, ACMA's comments were made with the implicit understanding (sometimes made explicit) that the MPS code would not be registered if ACMA did not believe it satisfied the appropriate

[62] G Samuel, Chair, ACCC, 'Making Phones Fair-Australian Telecommunications and Poor Consumer Practice' (Speech delivered at ATUG Annual Conference, Sydney, 13 March 2009) 4.

[63] For information about the research methodology used for the case studies, see the Appendix.

[64] Conroy, 'Address to the Australian Communications and Media Authority & Communications Alliance Consumer Dialogue 2008', above n 14.

[65] Samuel, above n 62, 4.

[66] Not all of the correspondence, including emails, exchanged between them was seen.

community safeguards test set out in Part 6.[67] There is no evidence to indicate ACMA threatened to adopt an industry standard if industry could not develop a code of practice.

Within the working committee, the consumer and public interest representatives adopted a number of strategies to advance their interests. They worked together and negotiated as a bloc. They bundled issues together, where possible, and traded certain wishes against others. For example, it was recorded in the minutes for meeting 29 (28 January 2009) that consumer and public interest representatives had stated that resolution of the compliance and monitoring issue could result in a 'positive flow on to the issue of consent [ie, double opt-in]' for industry. Consumer and public interest delegates also informed the working committee about the other groups they had consulted, reminded working committee members about whom they represented and reiterated that MPS had become a political issue. Additional techniques used included raising issues ACMA, ACCC and the TIO 'might put on the record'; pointing out 'how far we [consumer representatives] had come, the things that we have accepted are off-the-table even though we'd like them to be there'; continually identifying and articulating their bottom line; and keeping ACMA and ACCC informed of their concerns. Likewise, the decision to walk out of the MPS code working committee and the subsequent press release[68] were made to gain strategic advantage. The decision led, in the opinion of one of the representatives, to the two determinations dealing with MPS[69] that ACMA adopted in 2010 after it registered the MPS code.[70] She stated, we had to make a

> political statement in order to push the ACMA to take a stronger position, and we couldn't have done that if we had stayed in the code, voted yes for the code, and then told the ACMA 'you know what, we'd like a service provider rule as well.'

In negotiations with aggregators and content providers, a MCSP representative reported that MCSPs used the 'card' that if particular consumer protection obligations were not placed on content providers and aggregators in the MPS code, they would impose them in their commercial agreements with the aggregators. Further, if they failed to comply with the requirements, the MCSPs would deny aggregators access to their networks. The other MCSP representative said he did not formulate any specific strategies as such. He was under 'phenomenal' time pressure and was 'just ... trying to crunch through the issues to keep it [the project] moving'.

[67] See, eg, Letter from C Chapman, Chair, ACMA to A Hurley, CEO, Communications Alliance (10 November 2008).

[68] See CTN, above n 49.

[69] See Telecommunications Service Provider (Mobile Premium Services Determination 2010 (No 1) (Cth); Telecommunications Service Provider (Mobile Premium Services Determination 2010 (No 2) (Cth).

[70] It is doubtful if that assertion is entirely correct. ACMA and the Communications Alliance were already looking for ways enforcement of the MPS code could be bolstered. In addition, industry commitment to call barring, which ACMA mandated on 5 March 2010, appears to have been made in response to requests from the Minister made during the development of the MPS code.

He stated, 'I certainly didn't have ... sufficient time to ... come up with ... a timeline or a strategy or something ... that formal.' However, he added that when responding to consumer and public interest proposals, the MCSPs tried to 'work through what is it they [consumer and public interest representatives] actually want[ed] to achieve [to see] ... if ... [the MCSPs could] come up with a proposal ... that met their needs ...' He said the MCSP representatives went back to the working committee 'factually ... saying, well, the reasons we can't do this is not because we're bad people but because these are the reasons we can't do it. But what we could do is this. We think this meets the outcome.' Attempting to shift the orientation of the debate from 'process' to 'outcomes' was a conscious strategy on the part of this MCSP representative, but it was also a source of tension between industry and consumer and public interest representatives who reported that industry representatives often reframed issues as technical matters, which could not be resolved or for which no technical solution could be found. In addition, they referred frequently to the costs of system modifications without quantifying them. It should also be added that after the MPS code was submitted for registration, the MCSP representatives initiated a meeting with members of ACMA, including its chair and deputy chair, and some of ACMA's senior managers, to explain the benefits of the code and to ensure that ACMA understood the structure of the MPS industry and the measures in the code designed to make it more transparent. The MCSPs feared ACMA's 'the carriers could make it happen' approach but also recognised that, because of delays and 'pressures coming back', it was in their interests to solve the underlying problems.

Neither of the two MCSP delegates were selected by their employers to participate in the rule-making exercise for any strategic reason. One was chosen because MPS fell within his area of responsibility. The other believed he was designated because of his regulatory and operational experience, and his understanding of the 'political nuances' of the situation. However, he said any 'strategic' decision-making as to who was selected would have been done 'subconsciously'. The 'reality' was the in-house regulatory team did not have the 'time' to strategise, given its small number of staff, and the range of regulatory and compliance issues that the company needed to address.

V. Dispute Resolution

Disputes arose in four contexts: within the respective constituencies of working committee members; the working committee itself; ACMA and the Communications Alliance/working committee; and the Minister and the Communications Alliance/working committee. However, dispute resolution within the respective constituencies of working committee members and the working committee itself is of the greatest interest. With some exceptions, the MPS industry was responsive to changes proposed by ACMA and the Minister to the draft code. Its receptiveness can most likely be explained by ACMA's statutory power of registration and the Minister's control over the relevant legislative portfolio. The minutes of working committee meetings where ACMA's concerns were discussed show that the committee on many occasions accepted the requested changes and/or developed 'packages' of measures. The latter may not have been precisely what ACMA wanted but they went some way to addressing the underlying problem it had identified.

Disagreements within the MCSP constituency arose about what was 'operationally doable' because, as one MCSP representative stated, 'what's operationally doable for one organisation is not the same for the others'. Most disputes were resolved by way of a 'lot of discussion and correspondence between the groups'. As one MCSP delegate described it, 'it's like any negotiation I guess, [at] what point do you … want to agree here …?' However, as discussed in section II.A.i above, with the exception of double opt-in where Telstra bowed to political pressure, which forced the remaining MCSPs to follow its lead, the smaller players had arguably greater influence on the end result than may have been anticipated. In many instances though, discussion often shifted to finding alternative operational means to reach identified and agreed outcomes. As a MCSP representative explained:

> often another company would sort of come up with an idea saying 'Well we can't give an alert like that, we just can't do it, but what we could do is on our website, we could put up something on our website that would basically say click on the link and basically you can do this.'

Within the working committee, there were three pressure points: strain between the MCSP and aggregator/content provider representatives; stress between all industry delegates and consumer and public interest representatives; and distrust between the consumer and public interest representatives, and Communications Alliance staff. The latter was described by one MCSP representative as a 'very awkward' dynamic. Intra-industry disputes often arose over technical issues, such as liability for failure to send MPS messages or delay in sending time-sensitive messages, including sporting results and horoscopes. They were primarily resolved by the technical staff of the delegates' constituencies. Another area of concern, mentioned earlier in section II.B.i, was determining the party in the supply chain that should have the burden of complying with particular measures. One MCSP representative reported if content providers and/or aggregators would not agree to particular obligations in the code, the MCSPs would announce they would put them in their commercial agreements and withhold access to the underlying networks. He stated, 'in some ways there was a lot of pressure on the suppliers to agree to those things. They argued and pushed back … but I think at the end of the day that [the] carriers probably … [won].' However, 'that wasn't to say that we just railroaded things through; there was a lot of discussion going on'. A consumer and public interest representative also reported that intra-industry matters tended to be discussed first with examination of the more difficult issues that arose between industry and consumer, and public interest delegates deferred until subsequent meetings.

Industry delegates, and consumer and public interest representatives could reach agreement on some issues. For example, some of the consumer protection standards added by the working committee to the MPS code were described as 'non-controversial' in the sense that they repeated what was already set out in statute. Other topics involving complaints handling and the ease with which MPS subscribers could unsubscribe from services raised what one consumer and public interest representative described as 'some conflict and differences of opinion'. However, these disputes were resolved by way of discussion and exploring what was technically possible. That said, there was an enormous lack of trust between industry, and consumer and public interest representatives, making it difficult for any form of agreement to be reached. One consumer and public interest representative stated:

> See what often happens in telecommunications is that they then say 'oh it's technically not possible.' But there's no advice about, no independent advice that actually supports that ... Well, there is a technical fix, they just don't put any money; if it's not in their interest to do it, they won't do it ... So you're very suspicious straight away when industry says they can't do it, because six months later you always find that they can.

Equally, a MCSP representative reported that consumer and public interest representatives saw 'the worst continuously' and had a 'skewed' perception of the industry. He stated, 'I'd go home and say [to my wife,] "I'm sitting there and they're looking at me and I'm thinking all they can see is this blood sucking capitalist ... it's very unproductive."' This individual also attributed the tension between industry delegates and consumer and public interest representatives to two different ways of thinking. The consumer and public interest representatives were procedurally orientated 'essentially trying to write operational[ly] prescriptive requirements onto something they just don't fundamentally understand', whereas industry was outcomes focused.

Agreement on some issues emerged despite the hostilities. However, consensus between industry and consumer representatives did not emerge on all issues even though the chair and project manager reported using some of the same dispute resolution techniques used in the Consumer Contracts code case study—encouraging participants to put their proposals in writing; reviewing them in detail; and returning to particularly contentious points once other code provisions had been agreed, thus giving working committee members time to reconsider their positions and/or formulate alternatives. In March 2009, consumer and public interest delegates took the decision to walk out of the code development process and subsequently called on ACMA not to register the MPS code as submitted by industry. Many reasons were given by consumer and public interest representatives publicly for the walkout[71] but the principal factor was the industry's refusal to agree to their requests for improved monitoring and compliance obligations—their 'bottom line'. Why consensus was not reached is worth detailed

[71] See CTN, above n 49.

consideration because it illustrates aspects of the working committee dynamic; the tensions between consumer and public interest representatives and Communications Alliance staff; and the fact that the battle for the content of the MPS code was played out publicly in the media.

A. Code Monitoring and Compliance

Even before the consumer and public interest representatives joined the working committee, the Communications Alliance had contemplated establishing an industry MPS Compliance Group. In the short-term, the MPS Compliance Group's task was to identify and discuss potential breaches of the MPS code and notify the relevant parties involved. In the long-term, it was envisaged that an independent, industry-funded board would examine alleged code breaches and impose sanctions. However, the Communications Alliance subsequently decided to abandon the idea. First, its lawyers had (correctly) advised that it would need to seek an exemption from the ACCC under the Trade Practices Act 1974 (Cth) to implement both proposals, which one MCSP representative interviewed said would have taken 'something like 10 months'. Second, there was a belief that establishment of an MPS Compliance Group 'may result in a perception that the MPS Code does not satisfactorily provide sufficient community safeguards'.[72] Finally, there were concerns about its cost, the 'uncertainty' of its terms of reference and constitution and its 'viability' in the long term.[73] Instead, the Communications Alliance sought to ensure that ACMA had sufficient ability to enforce the MPS code and to create a 'Co-Regulatory Liaison Group'. Comprised of the Communications Alliance, ACMA, the ACCC and the TIO, the Co-Regulatory Liaison Group was intended to be a forum where the four regulators could exchange information about trends in complaints and identify systemic breaches.

In October 2008, shortly after joining the working committee, the consumer and public interest representatives expressed reservations about the Co-Regulatory Liaison Group because it could not accept complaints about code breaches, investigate alleged breaches, require relevant parties to address systemic issues and/or impose sanctions on infringers. Moreover, although the TIO had the authority to investigate systemic complaints, subject to some important limitations, its primary purpose was to investigate individual complaints and it lacked the power to mandate modifications to industry practices. The solution for the consumer and public interest representatives was to create an industry-funded Code Monitoring Committee (CMC) similar to the Code Compliance and Monitoring Committee established pursuant to the *Code of Banking Practice*.[74] The CMC's primary

[72] MPS Code Working Group, Meeting 11 Minutes, 6 August 2008, 2.

[73] MPS Code Working Group, Meeting 20 Minutes, 8 October 2008, 2.

[74] For its latest iteration, see Australian Bankers' Association Inc, *Code of Banking Practice and Code Compliance Monitoring Committee Mandate* (January 2013).

function was to ensure industry's compliance with the MPS code and monitor its effectiveness. The desire for the CMC, however, also appears to have been motivated by concerns that ACMA was not investigating and/or enforcing breaches of the MPSI Scheme. Certainly, industry perceived the efforts of consumer and public interest representatives as an attempt to recreate the regulator. As one carrier representative stated:

> And I remember actually literally saying in one meeting 'There's already a body that does that … which is the ACMA.' And the view was, 'But they're not doing it.' And the view was, 'But that's a separate issue. You can't sort of recreate an entire new body just because the body you've got doesn't do the job. The issue is to make that body do what they were supposed to do in the first place.'

Industry rejected the CMC proposal outright. It argued that the industry register, the existence of a short-code look up tool and the decision to ask the TIO to record short codes in its complaint records would make the MPSI industry more transparent and consequently improve ACMA's ability to monitor and enforce compliance with the MPS code. The Co-Regulatory Liaison Group, an initiative ACMA supported, and a recently signed memorandum of understanding between the TIO and ACMA to share information about content providers further demonstrated the regulator's commitment to enforce the MPS code. Similarly, ACMA's 'aggressive enforcement of the Spam Act [2003 (Cth)]'[75] was evidence of its 'intent to sanction non-compliant parties'. In addition, the MCSPs reported they were revising and enforcing their own 'code of conduct' policies incorporated into their commercial agreements with aggregators—measures that were credited for the decline in customer complaints while the MPS code was being developed.

The issue of code monitoring and compliance was revisited during meeting 27 (22 December 2008) and meeting 29 (28 January 2009). During the latter, consumer and public interest representatives dropped the CMC proposal. Instead, they asked if industry would agree to a provision requiring mobile carriage and content service providers to arrange for an independent monitor to review their compliance with the MPS code. Benchmarks that industry had to meet would be set out in a guideline. In addition, any information generated by the code monitor would have to be provided to the Co-Regulatory Liaison Group, membership of which would be extended to ACCAN. Consumer and public interest representatives tabled a more developed proposal during meeting 31 (13 February 2009). However, discussion was deferred until meeting 32 (17 February 2009), a working committee meeting attended by the CEO of the Communications Alliance. During that meeting, she reported her discussions with the Minister's office about the Minister's letter of 5 January 2009, and its view that the TIO and ACMA had to be involved with code monitoring and enforcement because

[75] MPS Code Working Group, Meeting 20 Minutes, above n 73, 2.

they already had the power to take appropriate action. The CEO's involvement was not well-received by the consumer and public interest representatives. One representative stated:

> We felt bullied in relation to monitoring and compliance, that they [the Communications Alliance] really wanted us to fold and agree to what they were proposing, and we weren't happy about it ... it was more about getting the consumers to agree to what they wanted to put forward than any genuine engagement about trying to get the industry to move along and say 'you need to make a greater commitment to monitoring and your own code'.

Despite this, the consumer and public interest representatives did not back down. During the meeting, they insisted on greater clarity of the Co-Regulatory Liaison Group's mandate; public dissemination of its achievements; and a code obligation requiring providers to cooperate with any monitoring and compliance activity. Industry did not agree to address the first two concerns because amendments to the enabling legislation or other forms of charter of each member of the proposed group were necessary to address them. However, Baker & McKenzie was instructed to draft a code monitoring provision that was reviewed by the working committee during meeting 33 (20 February 2009) and again during meeting 36 (5 March 2009). During meeting 36, the consumer and public interest representatives sought five amendments to the code monitoring obligation that was a substantially weaker provision than the one they tabled during meeting 31 (13 February 2009). Modifications requested included express requirements for suppliers to provide sufficient resources for code monitoring and to comply with any remedial action proposed by a code monitor. The code monitor was to be appointed by an industry representative appointed by the Communications Alliance; a consumer representative appointed by ACCAN; and an independent chair appointed by the Communications Alliance and ACCAN. In response, industry repeated many of its earlier arguments: the inability of the monitor to take any remedial action absent an exemption from the ACCC, the potential overlap of the jurisdictions of the monitor, ACMA, the ACCC and the TIO, and the Minister's instruction that ACMA be involved in code enforcement.

Whatever reservations the MCSPs, aggregators and content service providers may have had about some of the consumer and public interest representatives' proposed modifications, it was agreed by the members of the working committee that Baker & McKenzie would be instructed to redraft aspects of the draft code monitoring and enforcement provision to deal with two concerns raised by the consumer representatives: the appointment of an independent chair and industry resourcing of the monitoring and enforcement initiative. However, in meeting 37 (11 March 2009), the chair reported that the drafting changes agreed to during the previous meeting had not been made and the Communications Alliance would not be seeking any additional legal advice on the code monitoring provision. The decision was taken by the chair (in consultation with the CEO) without speaking to members of the working committee. A MCSP representative interviewed reported that the Communications Alliance made the decision to 'close off' the issue of code monitoring in an effort to 'crunch this thing through'. He was not a party to it. Arguments recorded in the minutes made by the chair to cease discussion about code monitoring included: the numerous attempts to reach agreement between the members of the working committee; industry's belief that the code contained all that could be included; the duration of the code development process; ACMA's power to monitor and enforce the MPS code; the ACCC's power to take action against misleading and deceptive practices; and the involvement of the TIO and the Co-Regulatory Liaison Group. Concern was also expressed about the appropriateness of the code requiring suppliers to 'resource' code monitoring and the possible jurisdictional overlap between ACMA and the code monitor. It was argued that the latter might stop ACMA from registering the code.

After asking the working committee to 'consider whether it was possible to agree that it was preferable to submit a Code containing 90% of the desired provisions',[76] the chair then called for a 'readiness vote'—an informal vote to determine whether there was consensus among the members of the working committee that the MPS code was completed and ready for the 'content vote'. The latter involves a formal ballot to assess if the working committee members have reached consensus on the content of the code. Both consumer and public interest representatives refused to vote in favour of the code's 'readiness'. For one representative, 'there was no point in having a code which wasn't going to have sufficient monitoring and compliance'. For the other, there was significant concern that, if they put their names to the MPS code after making numerous statements in the media and submissions to the Senate over the years about compliance-related problems in the telecommunications services industry,[77] then 'we can't call ourselves a consumer group because we're not standing up for what we believe is right'. However, during the meeting, the consumer and public interest representatives also gave industry an ultimatum. It had to either reconsider its position and resume negotiations about code monitoring by Friday, 13 March 2009 or consumer and public interest representatives would issue a press release explaining its position. The chair referred the dispute to the CEO who decided to present the MPS code 'as is' to the board of the Communications Alliance for approval to 'publish' the MPS code and submit it to ACMA for registration. The board agreed. Acting in accordance with the Operating Manual of the Communications Alliance, it concluded that 'due process' was followed. The Communications Alliance submitted the code to ACMA shortly thereafter. It was registered on 14 May 2009.

In this instance, failure to reach consensus and the reaction of the Communications Alliance put the decision-making authority concerning code monitoring and compliance in ACMA's hands. However, it is clear that ACMA had no appetite

[76] MPS Code Working Group, Meeting 37 Minutes, 11 March 2009, 3.

[77] See s III.A.ii.a of ch 4 for information about the telecommunications services industry.

at the time to pursue the broader policy questions that the dispute raised.[78] Ministerial preference for ACMA and TIO involvement and pressure to quickly address the problems of MPS must have been key considerations. The need for industry to secure an exemption from the ACCC, the delay it would cause to code registration and maintaining its reputation would also have been important factors in ACMA's deliberation. However, the appeal by the consumer and public interest representatives to the general media—a press release was eventually issued on 20 March 2009[79]—had an important effect on the content of the MPS code. During code negotiations, the Minister dropped, and ACMA employees ceased to pursue, the issue of double opt-in. In February 2009, the Minister accepted representations made by the Communications Alliance that other measures incorporated into the code, including account management tools and expenditure caps, negated the need for it. However, after the consumer and public interest representatives walked out of the process, the matter of double opt-in was revived. As discussed earlier,[80] ACMA requested code amendments introducing double opt-in before the code was registered. Why ACMA made its decision is not clear. However, consumer group Choice had released the results of a survey about MPS of its members and called for double opt-in in a press release issued on 20 February 2009.[81] The ACCC chair, in his speech to ATUG on 13 March 2009, reiterated the commission's support for double-opt in.[82] The Minister announced a review of the Part 6 framework on 31 March 2009.[83] MCSP representatives also suggested that the Minister was applying pressure behind the scenes, and consumer and public interest representatives had fully briefed all government regulators about the decision to cease participating in the MPS working committee. Arguably, imposing double opt-in gave ACMA a way of 'saving face' to its own constituencies.

VI. Conclusion

There are many elements of the MPS code development process that could lead one to conclude that Part 6 rule-making was procedurally and institutionally illegitimate. Consumer and public interest organisations were appointed to the

[78] See n 54.

[79] Consumer and public interest representatives called on ACMA not to register the code, citing inadequate consumer safeguards, their initial exclusion from the code development process and the failure to reach consensus among working committee members. See CTN, above n 49, 3.

[80] See s II.A.i of this chapter (above).

[81] Choice, 'Premium Mobile Phone Services Rip Off Continues: New Survey Uncovers Serious Problems' (Media Release, 20 February 2009).

[82] Samuel, above n 62, 5.

[83] Conroy, 'Reforms to Improve Consumer Protection in Telecommunications', above n 58.

working committee well after the rule-making process started. Their delegates attended only 60 per cent of working committee meetings. Consensus among industry players and consumer and public interest organisations was never achieved. Representatives from consumer and public interest organisations walked out of the process. The Communications Alliance submitted the code to ACMA for registration, despite protest from these groups and the absence of consensus as required by its Operating Manual. Neither the chair nor the rule-making venue was perceived to be neutral by consumer and public interest representatives. The Communications Alliance overruled the working committee's decision to instruct lawyers to redraft the code monitoring and enforcement provision, a decision taken in light of concerns expressed by consumer and public interest representatives. Whether the Part 6 process was procedurally and institutionally legitimate or illegitimate is discussed in detail in Part 3 of the book.

Part III

Substantive Analysis of Case Studies

8

The Procedural and Institutional Legitimacy of Part 6 Rule-making

I. Introduction

Many (if not most) of the mechanisms that are thought to ensure that law-making is procedurally and institutionally legitimate are absent from the Part 6 rule-making process. The public cannot attend meetings of the working committees, which are not transcribed or published. It has no rights to access minutes and other documentation exchanged between working committee members. No participant in the code development process was impartial. The courts never reviewed the codes of practice or the process by which they were made. Parliament did not scrutinise their content and the public was not given an opportunity to vote for or against them. Nevertheless, it is argued in these concluding chapters that, on the evidence provided in the three case studies, Part 6 rule-making was procedurally and institutionally legitimate. Moreover, the reason why Part 6 rule-making was procedurally and institutionally legitimate can be explained by its 'politic'. The politic was the result of the interplay between and among the different actors involved in the process, the wider context in which rule-making occurred, and the principles of representativeness and consensus embodied in the rule-making framework of the Communications Alliance. It created a dynamic that channelled industry self-interest and ensured that Part 6 rule-making was consistent with the principles suggested in chapter three that underpin procedural and institutional legitimacy.

However, Part 6 rule-making challenges more than the many well-trodden assumptions as to how the principles of transparency, impartiality, deliberation and accountability can be fulfilled. It also pushes the limits of a traditional understanding of many of the principles themselves. Indeed, as will be argued in the analysis below, Part 6 rule-making forces us to revisit the underlying premises and purposes of transparency, impartiality and accountability. It requires us to adjust their precise meanings so that they remain relevant in the context of industry rule-making yet are consistent with their objectives in traditional law-making. It is for that reason that it is suggested that, in the context of the decentred state, transparency should be adapted to mean the disclosure by industry to working committee members, including consumer and public interest representatives, and others of information necessary to hold industry to account. Impartiality should be reframed as a question of whether industry genuinely considered the relevant concerns of others before it reached its decisions, and accountability should be a search for 'real time' mechanisms that achieve the same goal of accountability in traditional rule-making—ensuring that industry answers for its decisions or explains itself to others—rather than a quest for processes that operate retrospectively. Interpreting the principles in this way makes it possible for mechanisms other than those that have become synonymous with legislative and administrative rule-making—mechanisms present in the politic of Part 6 rule-making—to facilitate the achievement of procedural and institutional legitimacy.

Section II of this chapter characterises the politic of Part 6 rule-making. Section III revisits the meaning of each of the principles of transparency, impartiality, deliberation and accountability. It argues that the traditional understandings of transparency, impartiality and accountability need to be modified for the purposes of evaluating the procedural and institutional legitimacy of industry rule-making. It maintains further that the definitions proposed for each of the three principles are compatible with their goals in traditional law-making and accommodate the aims of proceduralized rule-making. It concludes with a discussion of why all four principles of procedural and institutional legitimacy (as amended) were satisfied in the context of the politic of Part 6 rule-making.

II. The Politic of Part 6 Rule-making

Part 6 rule-making is an inherently 'political' process. Although there is not and will most likely never be agreement among political scientists about what makes something 'political',[1] it displays what Schattschneider calls the 'root'[2] or what Page describes as the 'defining feature'[3] of politics: conflict and controversy. However, despite the conflict surrounding the process and the oft-asserted claims that industry rule-making is inherently biased toward private actors, it does not display a bias that favoured industry over consumer and public interest participants. No one, including industry, was able to consistently implement a strategy that allowed it to gain an advantage different from what it may otherwise enjoy in other rule-making fora.[4] Rather, the controversy that Part 6 rule-making generated was the result of the inevitable tensions among and interactions between

[1] For an overview, see C Hay, *Political Analysis: A Critical Introduction* (Basingstoke, Palgrave, 2002) 69–75.

[2] EE Schattschneider, *The Semisovereign People: A Realist's View of Democracy in America* (New York, Holt, Rinehart and Winston, 1960) 2.

[3] EC Page, *Governing by Numbers* (Oxford, Hart Publishing, 2001) 2.

[4] ibid 11.

the number and different types of actors who participated at any one time in a protracted and iterative process. The apparent inability of industry actors to monopolise the process, notwithstanding the imbalances of expertise, access to information and resources that existed between consumer and industry representatives, can be explained by several factors. No doubt, the threatened deployment of what Ayres and Braithwaite have termed the 'big stick'[5] or what Sabel and Zeitlin have called 'penalty defaults'[6] by the Australian Communications Authority (ACA), the Australian Communications Media Authority (ACMA), the Australian Competition and Consumer Commission (ACCC) and the Minister contributed to the willingness of industry to join (and remain at) the negotiating table. Along with 'reputation capital',[7] the presence of penalty defaults and the big stick gave industry a strong incentive to participate in the process when market failures arose. However, it was not the only reason. The principles of consensus and representativeness embodied in the Communications Alliance's rule-making framework were also influential. Representativeness (as understood by the Communications Alliance) brought together the different types of parties with an interest in the outcome of the process, including consumer and public interest groups, and industry actors operating at different layers in the supply chain, some of whom were instrumental in the eventual adoption of rules more favourable to consumers and citizens. The principle of consensus gave consumer and public interest delegates an important right of veto. However, the peculiar characteristics of the market for telecommunications services in Australia and the industry's response to the chaos of the Casualties of Telecom affair, discussed in chapter two, also played a role in shaping the parameters of debate and mitigating the possibility and/or presence of bias in favour of industry that opponents of industry rule-making have identified as a likely consequence of delegating law-making power to industry.

The analysis of the three case studies that follows is structured into three sub-sections; each centres on one of the three core aspects of Schattschneider's theory of political conflict discussed in chapter four: participants, strategies and bias. It begins by identifying the different actors that participated in Part 6 rule-making. It seeks to pinpoint the 'influence' that each actor brought to bear on the process—their capacity to affect 'the flow of events'[8]—and to explain how

[5] I Ayres and J Braithwaite, *Responsive Regulation: Transcending the Deregulation Debate* (Oxford, Oxford University Press, 1992) 19.

[6] CF Sabel and J Zeitlin, 'Learning from Difference: The New Architecture of Experimentalist Governance in the EU' (2008) 14 *European Law Journal* 271, 308.

[7] N Gunningham, RA Kagan and D Thornton, 'Social License and Environmental Protection: Why Businesses Go Beyond Compliance' (2004) 29 *Law and Social Inquiry* 307, 320 (citing S Joyce and I Thomson, 'Earning a Social License to Operate: Social Acceptability and Resource Development in Latin America' (11 June 1999) *Mining Journal* 441).

[8] C Parker and J Braithwaite, 'Regulation' in P Cane and M Tushnet (eds), *The Oxford Handbook of Legal Studies* (Oxford, Oxford University Press, 2003) 119, 119.

each could influence the content of the codes eventually registered by the ACA or ACMA. To facilitate the analysis, the various influences the actors could exert on the process are shown operating independently of each other. However, as will become clear throughout the discussion, it was largely the interaction between and among these actors that determined the degree to which individual actors, including industry players, could influence the process. The analysis then considers the tactics used by participants in Part 6 rule-making in an attempt to 'secure outcomes favourable to themselves'.[9] Focusing on the strategies used by consumer, public interest and industry organisations, it argues that representation on the working committee was essential to improving the likelihood of success. However, once appointed to working committees, there was no obvious way for them to advance their interests other than by discussing and addressing the issues raised by working committee members. The discussion concludes by arguing that, even though Part 6 rule-making was clearly an industry-driven process, it was not 'partisan'[10] to industry.

A. Participants

The main participants involved in Part 6 rule-making fall into four broad categories: industry actors, consumer and public interest actors (what Gunningham, Kagan and Thornton, writing in a compliance context, would call 'social licensors'[11]), regulatory bodies and other. The latter category encompasses a variety of players, including the press, the CEO of the Communications Alliance and the Minister for Communications. Neither Part 6 of the Telecommunications Act 1997 (Cth) nor the rule-making framework of the Communications Alliance prescribes their involvement in code development. Nevertheless, each contributed significantly to the exercise of rule-making and the positions industry delegates eventually adopted in working committees. The ability of each participant to affect code development and why it could influence the process are considered below.

i. Industry Actors

Depending on the particular code, there were up to five different types of industry actors involved in the process. Among these, the individual companies appointed as working committee members (including, in particular, their corporate divisions and working committee delegates); the different industry constituencies; and participants in supply chains were the most prominent and influential. Members of

9 Page, above n 3, 182.
10 Schattschneider, above n 2, 4.
11 Gunningham, Kagan and Thornton, above n 7, 308. They are the individuals and organisations from 'the surrounding civil society' which place 'demands on' and set 'expectations for a business enterprise.'

industry who were not represented (directly or indirectly) on working committees could submit written feedback to the working committee on the code published by the Communications Alliance in draft but, for the reasons given below, they were not significant players and the least likely of the five industry actors to affect the direction of Part 6 rule-making.

a. Industry Members, Their Corporate Divisions and Their Delegates

The individual companies that had a casting vote on the working committee were unsurprisingly influential. With some exceptions, most of the companies who represented themselves were the largest fixed and mobile carriers, and carriage service providers in the Australian telecommunications sector. They brought 'clout' and industry expertise to the table. However, these large corporations were not monolithic; they consisted of multiple operating divisions—often with different and competing business models, each of which should be seen as an actor in its own right. The presence of these players in Part 6 rule-making is seen most clearly in the Consumer Contracts code where interviewees who had served as industry delegates stressed that formulating an internal 'corporate position' was not a straightforward exercise. Continuous discussion about all aspects of the debate, including business, consumer and public interests, with every relevant division during the life of the working committee, was essential to reach what one representative described as a 'reasoned' position. In this instance, the internal debate was particularly intense because sharply divided commercial divisions offering different services were involved. Even though they represented the collective interests of mobile carriers and carriage service providers, the two representatives from the two mobile carriers interviewed in the Mobile Premium Services (MPS) code case study reported discussion of a similar nature taking place across their operational business units. However, there was no disagreement between them. The involvement of internal business divisions was not as prominent in the development of the Information on Accessibility Features for Telephone Equipment code (the IAF code), which can be explained by the fact that several equipment suppliers represented on the working committee were relatively small companies. However, some discussion did appear to take place.

Often (but not exclusively) time-poor 'middle managers' from regulatory affairs divisions, the industry working committee delegates were also important actors in the process. In addition to negotiating with consumer and public interest representatives, and others on working committees, these individuals were responsible for triggering the discussion within and between the different corporate divisions of their employers. Their ability to influence working committee discussion derived from the individual companies they represented. Their ability to stimulate internal discussion arose for three reasons. First, they were employed by the companies they represented. Only one delegate was not an employee. Second, industry delegates had sufficient knowledge of their relevant organisations to be able to identify the key individuals from the different corporate divisions with an interest in the outcomes of the three codes. Third, they had enough influence to be able to bring these individuals together, and to facilitate and conclude internal discussion. Their backgrounds were diverse. Some were lawyers. Others had training and/or experience in economics, engineering and government affairs. However, they all had enough authority to guide internal discussion, and it was this authority that enabled them to serve as effective conduits between working committees and their employers.

b. Industry Constituencies

In an effort to address the absence of participation by and under-representation of smaller market participants in working committees, the Communications Alliance formally required industry delegates to represent the collective interests of all similarly situated industry members in the MPS code case study in working committee meetings. In that instance, there were three different types of industry constituencies: mobile carriage service providers (MCSPs), aggregators and content providers. Each actively contributed to the process and was influential to the overall direction of the codes that emerged. Requiring industry representatives to consult with their respective sub-groups and identify a collective position was not mandated in the other two case studies. However, it occurred informally in response to the bargaining strategy of consumer and public interest representatives in the Consumer Contracts code working committee,[12] even if dissenters were permitted to 'fend for themselves'. Moreover, equipment suppliers who were members of the IAF code working committee conversed with each other outside of meetings. They also periodically spoke to an industry association of equipment suppliers that was not represented on the committee. However, the discussion between these groups does not appear to have been as robust as it was in the other two case studies. It was not until the formal subcommittee was established that the sole industry representative was expressly tasked to consult with industry constituents and define 'agreed positions' that could be taken to meetings of the formal sub-committee for discussion.

c. Supply Chains

The case studies also demonstrate that participants in the supply chains in the Australian communications market are important actors in the Part 6 process. The MPS and IAF code case studies provide the best examples of the ability of supply chain actors to influence code development. In the MPS code case study, content providers had to justify their position and/or behaviour to aggregators who, in turn, were required to explain themselves to MCSPs who also owned and operated the mobile networks used to deliver MPS services. These MCSPs were in

[12] Informal consultation may have occurred because the Australian telecommunications market is small and individuals working within the industry know each other relatively well.

a position to deny aggregators access to their networks (essential to the provision of MPS services) if they did not adopt their preferred approach in the code, giving them significant influence over the direction of the entire MPS industry. It is true that these MCSPs had a commercial incentive to enable their subscribers to access MPS services—the desire to keep their networks and services looking 'fresh'. However, the ability of aggregators and content providers to exert significant influence on these MCSPs was limited primarily because the number of mobile subscribers who actually used MPS services was relatively small. In the main working committee of the IAF code, the two carriage service providers were also supplying and/or retailing phone handsets and thus were in a position to scrutinise to a certain degree the information (or lack thereof) that equipment suppliers were prepared to provide to their end customers. They may have been motivated by the need to protect their reputation capital but nevertheless were able to exert some pressure on equipment suppliers to demand an explanation of their behaviour. The emphasis one carriage service provider representative placed on ensuring any information suppliers provided would be useful and not 'useless' is evidence of this phenomenon at work.[13] The power of supply chain actors was not as strong as it was in the MPS code case study but it arguably countered perceived imbalances in the composition of the working committee and it worked to the benefit of consumer and public interest representatives.

However, three important points must be made about participants in supply chains and their ability to influence the rule-making process. First, the importance of supply chain actors was understood by the Communications Alliance, which explains why it appointed players from each layer of the relevant supply chains to the working committees in the first place. They were 'representative' of the parties with a 'stake' in the proceedings. However, neither the regulator nor consumer and public interest organisations knew about or necessarily appreciated the impact the supply chain participants had (or could have). In the MPS code case study, in particular, the MCSPs reported they had to spend a lot of time explaining about the actors in the supply chain to ACMA and consumer representatives. Second, the influence the supply chain participants exerted on the process did not arise spontaneously. As the IAF and MPS code case studies reveal, it was stimulated because of pressure from a number of different entities but principally actors outside of the commercial arrangements. For example, ACMA misunderstood the structure of the MPS supply chain. As a consequence, it initially believed that MCSPs should be held responsible for all code breaches (whether committed by an aggregator, content provider or otherwise). It was this misunderstanding that was the catalyst for operators to begin inquiries into the behaviour of their counterparts. Finally, supply chain participants can also impose significant limitations that cannot necessarily be worked around. The Consumer Contracts code nicely illustrates this

[13] See s II.A.i of ch 6.

point. In that case, carriage service providers were prevented from agreeing to a broad definition of 'detriment' in the code's unilateral variation provision, in part because of contractual restrictions in its supply agreements over which it had no (or limited) control.

d. Industry Members Not Otherwise Represented on Working Committees

Industry members not otherwise represented (directly or indirectly) on working committees were able to submit written comments to members of the working committee (albeit relatively late in the process) because Part 6 requires the Communications Alliance to publish codes in draft and solicit feedback from all industry participants.[14] Based on the evidence reviewed, it appears that all written comments from industry were duly considered (as Part 6 also requires).[15] In addition, commentators were sent a letter, either noting that their suggestions had been accommodated and how; or explaining why the committee agreed not to amend the draft code. However, as one industry representative on the Consumer Contracts code working committee commenting on public consultation more generally stated, comments were considered to a greater or lesser degree, depending on whether they raised new arguments not previously considered by the working committee. Arguments that the working committee had already evaluated, it would appear, had significantly less influence. This practice occurred because there was concern consultation would 'reignite all of these things that we had reached … tenuous agreement on. All sides I think got this don't mess with the baby [feeling]. We've just put it to sleep, please don't wake it up again now'.[16]

ii. Consumer and Public Interest Actors

Private individuals were permitted to submit written comments to members of the working committee. Part 6 requires the Communications Alliance to publish codes in draft and solicit feedback about them from members of the public.[17] It also mandates any submissions must be considered.[18] However, private individuals were not significant players in any of the three codes studied. Very few (if any) comments were received from private individuals and, even if some were submitted, they were taken into account relatively late in the process. Moreover, unless the comments raised new issues not previously discussed by the working committee, they were unlikely to carry much weight for the same reason considered earlier in the context of consultation with members of industry not otherwise represented (directly or indirectly) on working committees. No one wanted to reopen matters on which members of the working committee had already reached consensus.

[14] Telecommunications Act 1997 (Cth) s 117(1)(e)(i).
[15] ibid s 117(1)(e)(ii).
[16] Interview with Name Withheld (Melbourne, 5 April 2011).
[17] Telecommunications Act 1997 (Cth) s 117(1)(f)(i).
[18] ibid s 117(1)(f)(ii).

Consumer and public interest organisations, on the other hand, were important actors in the process. They were appointed as voting members on all three working committees and could collectively influence the process. The influence of these bodies, which were predominantly represented by senior executives, was at its strongest in the Consumer Contracts code case study, where the debate was framed by ACIF as one between consumers and industry. However, the ability to influence is also seen in the IAF code working committee where achieving agreement between consumer and disability representatives, and equipment suppliers was paramount, notwithstanding the membership of carriage service providers. Despite the Communications Alliance's initial decision to alter the way in which the working committee was structured in the MPS code case study, consumers were eventually granted a seat at the negotiating table. They may have elected to walk out at a later stage but they did influence the process.

a. Reasons for Participation and Sources of Influence

The questions why consumer and public interest organisations were involved in each of the three case studies and why they could influence the direction of the working committees merit detailed consideration for two reasons. First, the involvement of consumer and public interest organisations on Communications Alliance working committees is unique. Not all industry associations or bodies that have registered Part 6 codes with ACMA permit consumer and public interest organisations to participate in industry working committees to prepare codes.[19] Second, the degree to which consumer and public interest organisations appear to have been able to influence the direction of the working committees in two of the three case studies is perhaps surprising, given the genuine imbalances in terms of resources and information between consumer and public interest representatives, and industry. However, as will be argued below, the direct involvement of consumer and public interest organisations on working committees of the Communications Alliance can be explained by industry's reaction to the Casualties of Telecom (CoT) affair. The influence such groups had on the process once appointed to working committees can be attributed, in part, to the principle of consensus enshrined in the Communications Alliance's rule-making framework. However, the interplay between participants in the rule-making process contributed significantly to the ability of consumer and public interest representatives to influence the process; the way they influenced code development; and which parties they sought to influence.

[19] For example, the Internet Industry Association, which operated from 1995 until March 2014 when it transferred its responsibilities, including code development, to the Communications Alliance, did not permit representatives of consumer and public interest groups to sit on their working committees. Email from P Coroneos, CEO, IIA to author (29 February 2008).

An Entrenched Feature of Part 6 Rule-making

The appointment of consumer and public interest organisations as voting members of Communications Alliance working committees can be traced directly to industry's response to the chaos of the Casualties of Telecom affair. As we saw in chapter two, Telecom voluntarily decided to seek input from consumer groups in order to strengthen the perception that its rule-making exercise had legitimacy. This occurred when its privacy monitoring guidelines were under review by the Telecommunications Industry Ombudsman (TIO), the Privacy Commissioner and the Australian Telecommunications Authority (Austel), following revelations that it had been recording phone calls of CoT customers without their consent. Further, the work of the Privacy Advisory Committee (PAC)—established at the request of the Minister as a result of growing privacy concerns raised by consumer groups and the TIO about the deployment of digital technology that used calling line identification—drew heavily on the operating principles of Austel's proposed (but never implemented) Telecommunications Privacy Committee (TPC). The TPC's framework had emphasised consultation and discussion among all interested parties, including consumer and public interest organisations. Each of the three reports on privacy-related matters produced by PAC was the output of 12 representatives drawn from industry, consumer groups and regulators. These experiences created an expectation that consumer and public interest representatives would serve on ACIF working committees, the importance of which was explicitly recognised by industry and senior ACIF executives in public statements made within the first year of ACIF's establishment.[20] When the Communications Alliance tried 10 years later, after becoming an industry advocate, to exclude consumer and public interest participants from serving on the MPS working committee, there was resistance from consumer and public interest groups, and most likely ACMA and the Minister. The resistance that the Communications Alliance experienced reflects the fact that direct consumer involvement had become an entrenched (or 'path dependent'[21]) feature of Part 6 rule-making (at least when undertaken by the Communications Alliance). The practice of the Communications Alliance of including consumer and public interest representatives on all consumer code working committees established after completion of the MPS code only strengthens this argument.

[20] See, eg, A Bedogni, Manager-Regulatory Affairs, Optus, 'The New Regime's Three Pillars' (July 1997) Issue 134 *Communications Update* 7; G Long, 'ACIF Tackles Regulatory Role', *The Australian* (Sydney), 12 August 1997, 63 (quoting Greg Crew, ACIF, Chair of Board); G Long, 'The World According to Johanna Plante', *The Australian* (Sydney), 4 November 1997, 56 (quoting Johanna Plante, ACIF, CEO).

[21] See, eg, A Kay, 'A Critique of the Use of Path Dependency in Policy Studies' (2005) 83 *Public Administration* 553; BG Peters, J Pierre and DS King, 'The Politics of Path Dependency: Political Conflict in Historical Institutionalism' (2005) 67 *The Journal of Politics* 1275, 1287.

The Principle of Consensus

However consensus may be defined—and there are several possible meanings[22]—it appears to have contributed to the ability of consumer and public organisations to influence the process in each of the case studies. Nevertheless, the precise effect that consensus had on their capacity was seemingly context-dependent. In the Consumer Contracts and IAF code case studies, consensus served as what Eskridge, Frickey and Garrett call a 'veto-gate'.[23] For a code to be adopted, achieving some form of agreement among all working committee members was a 'hurdle' that had to be 'overcome'.[24] Consensus therefore gave the consumer and public interest representatives appointed as voting members some control over whether that barrier was reached (even if they never felt like it), notwithstanding the imbalances in resources that may have existed between them. The influence the principle of consensus can give consumer and public interest representatives is perhaps best evidenced in the Consumer Contracts code case study where they made threats to walk out of the rule-making process. Industry took these threats very seriously because of the pressure from a number of quarters to deliver a code. Similarly, in the IAF code case study, consumer and disability representatives managed to secure provisions requiring equipment suppliers to provide information relating to 25 features for fixed handsets and 27 features for mobile handsets, even though consumer and disability representatives on the main working committee were outnumbered by equipment suppliers.

In the MPS code case study, consensus arguably gave consumer and public interest representatives much less (if any) real control over the direction of the code because the rule-making process was driven by entities external to the working committee. At a minimum, it enabled the contributions of individual consumer and public interest representatives to be seriously considered by the other members of the MPS working committee. However, unlike the other two case studies, their views carried less weight. The different treatment they received can be explained by three factors. First, consumer and public interest representatives became involved in the process very late. Many of their concerns about the MPS industry had already been raised by ACMA, the Minister and the TIO, and addressed by industry before they joined the working committee. Second, the two

[22] For an overview, see Cary Coglianese, 'Is Consensus an Appropriate Basis for Regulatory Policy?' in EW Orts and K Deketalaere (eds), *Environmental Contracts: Comparative Approaches to Regulatory Innovation in the United States and Europe* (London, Kluwer Law International, 2001) 93, 95–96. For the definition of consensus in effect when the Consumer Contracts and Information Accessibility codes were drafted, see ACIF, *Operating Manuals for the Development of Codes, Standards, Specifications, Guidelines and Other Supporting Arrangements* (July 2002) 5. It had been removed by the time the MPS code was developed. Interview participants who commented on the meaning of consensus also had different views. Many suggested it simply meant 'agreement'.

[23] WN Eskridge, Jr, PP Frickey and E Garrett, *Legislation and Statutory Interpretation* 2nd edn (New York, Foundation Press, 2006) 70.

[24] ibid.

consumer and public interest representatives were directing some of their energy to lobbying the Minister and ACMA, both of whom were heavily involved in the process. Industry representatives were aware of their activity, and consumer and public interest representatives arguably inadvertently undermined their ability to influence industry working committee members because of it. Third, neither the Minister nor ACMA had any real interest in requiring industry to establish and fund an independent code monitor—the two most important issues for consumer and public interest representatives.

Interplay between Participants

The amount and type of influence consumer and public interest organisations could exert was clearly affected by the actions of the other participants in the rule-making process. The Consumer Contracts and IAF code case studies provide two examples of actions of other participants enhancing the direct influence consumer and public interest organisations had on industry. The MPS code case study, on the other hand, illustrates that the involvement of different actors can also diminish the capacity of consumer and public interest representatives to directly influence industry participants. Further, it shows that the way consumer and public interest representatives influenced code development and who they sought to influence were affected by which actors participated in the process.

In the Consumer Contracts code, consumer and public interest organisations could be particularly forceful because regulatory and political actors were prepared to wield the big gun and penalty default of 'command and control' regulation.[25] As already mentioned, the Communications Alliance framed the development of the code as a dispute between consumers and carriage service providers. The ACA formally requested the code be developed, the failure of which could have led it to adopt an industry standard. Rather than attempt to exercise any control over the process, the ACA elected to rely on consumer and public representatives to make the case to industry and used their satisfaction with the process as a proxy for regulatory approval. Industry knew it had to secure the agreement of consumer and public interest representatives to obtain regulatory approval. The Minister had indicated to industry that self-regulation had to deliver improvements for consumers or other, more prescriptive regulation would have to be considered. In addition, Consumer Affairs Victoria (CAV) was investigating the standard form mobile contracts of a number of providers for possible unfair terms, fear of which brought industry to and kept it at the negotiating table. As argued in chapter five, the decision of industry to accept the position of consumer and public interest representatives on the vexed issue of unilateral variation was made after the views of the Minister for Communications, the ACA and the CAV were taken into account. In their capacities as non-voting committee members, the ACCC

[25] See Ayres and Braithwaite, above n 5, ch 2; Sabel and Zeitlin, above n 6, 308.

and TIO also offered support to consumer and public interest delegates during working committee meetings. Equally important for consumer and public interest representatives were the internal divisions within commercial suppliers. They were partially responsible for forcing industry participants to consider issues from alternative angles because industry often did not know what it wanted. It certainly never had all of the answers.

In the IAF code case study, consumer and public interest representatives could influence the process (albeit much less forcefully). As occurred in the Consumer Contracts case study, the ACA formally requested industry to develop a code but its request was an act of political compromise, which neutralised its power. Members of the ACA were also disengaged with the process, which made the process particularly messy. The capacity of consumer and public interest representatives to influence the process therefore arose for reasons other than the willingness of regulatory actors to wield big sticks or penalty defaults. Perhaps counter-intuitively, the initial disengagement of mobile equipment manufacturers (or their refusal to participate or give account) in the working committee room was the most significant factor. In their absence, consumer and disability representatives were able to negotiate a rigorous draft code (ie, one that required equipment suppliers to provide 21 more pieces of information than were eventually agreed to in the final version). The initial strength of the consumer and public interest bargaining position prior to publication of the draft code is evidenced by the response of mobile manufacturers and other equipment suppliers after it was published. They began to participate actively in the rule-making process and a Nokia representative was appointed to the formal subcommittee. Initial industry apathy created other problems for consumer and disability representatives (eg, wasted time, resources and delay in adoption of the code) but it allowed them to set the agenda of the main working committee. As intermediaries in the supply chain, carriage service providers were also broadly supportive of consumer and disability representatives, trying to ensure that the information that equipment suppliers provided was helpful to handset buyers. There were also conflicts of interest among the representatives of the fixed handset manufacturers who served on the main working committee. One representative was both a manufacturer and a consultant to one of the carriage service providers. All of these factors gave consumer and disability representatives some scope to affect the direction of the working committee.

In the MPS code case study, the process was driven by ACMA and the Minister who again brandished penalty defaults and big sticks. Under significant pressure to act proactively from the Minister to whom ACMA was accountable, ACMA adopted a 'hands-on' approach to code development, meeting regularly (weekly in certain periods) with representatives from the Communications Alliance and the working committee to discuss concerns. It reviewed and provided specific comments on numerous code drafts. It insisted that it had to approve the content of the draft MPS code before it could be published for public comment. ACMA's chair was directly involved. The Minister was threatening to regulate the MPS industry if it failed to regulate itself effectively. Consequently, delegates from consumer and public interest organisations had less ability to influence industry directly even though they were members of the working committee—industry saw ACMA (and the Minister) as the parties with whom it had to negotiate. The involvement of ACMA and the Minister did not render consumer and public interest delegates incapable of influencing the process. Rather, they switched the focus of their influence from industry members of the working committee to ACMA and the Minister. They also altered the way they influenced the process. While they still attended working committee meetings until the walkout, they were in constant contact with staff of ACMA and kept the Minister informed of progress on and their views of the code.

iii. Regulatory Actors

Unsurprisingly, the three regulatory bodies collectively responsible for the regulation of the Australian telecommunications sector were the chief regulatory actors involved in the development of the three codes. They were not necessarily the most important participants in the emergence of the underlying code in each of the three case studies but they were influential (in varying ways and degrees) in all of them. However, as the Consumer Contracts code illustrates, other regulatory bodies did (and can) emerge as powerful operators in the process even if they do not directly participate in it. CAV was not physically present on the consumer code working committee, did not submit written comments to ACIF during the public consultation phase of code development and was not formally consulted by industry about the code. Nevertheless, industry was fearful of CAV because it could enforce the rather ambiguous principle of unfairness codified in the Fair Trading (Amendment) Act 2003 (Vic). Industry was motivated to develop a prescriptive Part 6 code of practice in conjunction with consumer and public interest representatives because it believed it would reduce the lack of certainty in the application of the unfairness principle by CAV.

Part 6 specifies that the ACCC and the TIO are only 'consultees' in the code development process. ACMA must be satisfied that the TIO and the ACCC have been consulted by industry before it can register a code of practice.[26] However, the ACCC and the TIO were both able to influence the code development process significantly in two of the three case studies. In the Consumer Contracts code case study, they were appointed by ACIF to the working committee as non-voting members because they had knowledge and expertise that was valued by the industry. The TIO had knowledge about industry behaviours that generated consumer complaints and the ACCC had experience in applying generic consumer protection legislation to a number of different industries. The capacity of the ACCC to influence the process was enhanced by its ability to take formal legal action against carriage service providers for unconscionable conduct under provisions

[26] Telecommunications Act 1997 (Cth) ss 117(1)(g), 117(1)(h).

of the then Trade Practices Act 1974 (Cth). In addition, the TIO and the ACCC submitted written comments. In the MPS code case study, neither the ACCC nor the TIO was directly represented. However, both were influential players behind the scenes. The TIO had influence because it recorded MPS complaints, the number of which was rising rapidly. The ACCC could influence the process because it could enforce provisions in the Trade Practices Act 1974 (Cth) to stop misleading and deceptive conduct by MPS providers, conduct which was at the heart of most of the complaints filed with the TIO.

By contrast, the TIO and ACCC appear to have had minimal influence in the IAF code case study. Neither regulator actively participated in the process. The TIO had no knowledge about customer equipment suppliers, none of whom was or is required to join the TIO scheme mandated by legislation. Similarly, the ACCC had no relevant expertise in the subject matter of the code. Disability issues fall outside of the broad statutory remit of the ACCC.[27] The TIO submitted written comments to the IAF code working committee, but what effect his comments had precisely on the process is difficult to assess on the face of the documentation reviewed. The Communications Alliance must have consulted with the ACCC about the IAF code because such consultation is mandatory under Part 6. However, the documentation reviewed does not reveal what form it took or the influence (if any) the ACCC may have had.

The most obvious source of the ACA and ACMA's ability to influence code development in each of the three case studies was their ability to register codes under Part 6. In the Consumer Contracts and IAF code case studies, another source was their power to formally request the development of the underlying code under the Act. If industry failed to adopt a code to its satisfaction, they could determine a standard that would regulate the industry. Perhaps the most important source of their influence was their willingness (or otherwise) to become and remain actively engaged in the process. The mere existence of a statutory power was not sufficient to affect the process as illustrated below.

In the Consumer Contracts code case study, the ACA formally requested ACIF to develop a code. Thus, it had the power to make an industry standard if industry failed to adopt a code. The ACA also had the power to reject a code if it believed industry had not adequately addressed all relevant issues. However, it was the fact that the risk of losing regulatory control was perceived to be real by industry that was so significant. Had the ACA not been prepared to adopt an industry standard (if necessary), it is doubtful if industry would have decided in the end to accept a unilateral variation provision that was more advantageous to consumers. In this instance, the ACA did not negotiate directly with industry even though it sat on the working committee. In that sense, it was 'hands off'. However, the ACA engaged in the process. It threw its weight behind consumer and public interest

[27] See s III.B.i of ch 4.

representatives whose positions were (implicitly if not explicitly) endorsed by the ACA and commanded greater authority than they otherwise may have had. The ACA signalled to industry that it agreed with the consumer position and would take action if industry did not.

In the IAF code case study, the ACA had much less influence even though the ACA formally requested a code and sat as a non-voting member on the working committee. As explained in chapter six, the request was used as a tool to settle a dispute concerning disability standards between consumer and disability advocates, on the one hand, and manufacturers and importers of telephone handsets, on the other. Moreover, the ACA was disengaged generally with the development of the code, and its failure to threaten to or make use of the weapons in its regulatory arsenal contributed to the delay in its adoption. It was only after ACIF's CEO escalated matters to a member of the ACA (over a year after code development began) that the ACA exercised any real influence. At that stage, it agreed with industry that consumer and public interest representatives were demanding too much information from equipment suppliers, a view that profoundly affected the work of the formal subcommittee. The possible loss of regulatory control became an influential lever used by ACIF's CEO (rather than the ACA) in order to keep existing industry members of the working committee at the negotiating table. It was also used to bring mobile handset manufacturers into the process, following the furore that followed public consultation. However, the ACA's lack of engagement for most of the process neutralised its powers to influence the process in this instance.

In the MPS code case study, ACMA's source of influence derived from its power of registration and its active involvement in the process even though it was not appointed as a member of the working committee. As explored in chapter seven, at the behest of the Minister, it met regularly with working committee members from industry and sent numerous letters from the office of the chair requesting modifications to the code to facilitate its enforcement.

iv. Other

The involvement of the media, the CEO of the Communications Alliance and the Minister for Communications is not envisaged or prescribed by Part 6 or the rule-making framework of the Communications Alliance. Yet each was influential in the development of certain codes.

a. The Media

The media were not participants in the Consumer Contracts and IAF code case studies but they were participants in the MPS code case study. They were applying pressure to industry to address the underlying causes of the complaints about mobile premium services they were reporting. As seen in chapter seven, MCSPs never responded directly to allegations made by the media but they were acutely conscious of an adverse media 'campaign' against the MPS industry. Equally, the media targeted the Minister who consequently became involved in the process. He then pushed ACMA to negotiate the code directly with industry. Moreover, consumer and public interest representatives appealed to and used the media to air their grievances after they walked out of the process. The precise effect the media coverage of the walkout had is difficult to determine. ACMA and the Minister were already aware of the reservations consumer and public interest representatives had about the development of the MPS code.

b. The CEO of the Communications Alliance

Even though the rule-making framework of the Communications Alliance did not designate a role for the CEO, Anne Hurley (as CEO) had the capacity to intervene in the code development process and often became intimately involved in the resolution of working committee disputes. It is clear that she never acted (or had the power to act) as a decision-maker as to the actual content of codes. However, interested in preserving the reputation of the Communications Alliance, she was capable of influencing the direction of working committees in a number of ways. Her involvement was most prominent in the IAF code case study. She attended several meetings of the working committee when an impasse between equipment suppliers and consumer and public interest representatives was reached. She eventually became chair of the formal sub-committee and the working committee. In that case study, she also proactively contacted members of the ACA for their guidance and appointed mobile equipment manufacturer Nokia to the formal sub-committee. Although less involved in the MPS and Consumer Contracts code case studies, the CEO nevertheless played an important role. In the MPS code case study, she was responsible for the decisions to initially exclude consumer and public interest representatives from the working committee and to subsequently include them. She met periodically with the Minister and routinely corresponded with the chair of ACMA. Further, the CEO endorsed the decision of the chair not to seek additional legal advice on the contentious issue of the code monitoring provision. In the Consumer Contracts code case study, she authorised expenditure for arbitrators and a truly independent working committee chair, the latter of which was seen as a critical component of that process by all interviewees. In all three case studies, she suggested ways in which agreement could be reached to the committee chairs.

c. Minister for Communications

The Minister for Communications was an actor in two of the three case studies. Only in the IAF code case study was there no general political presence. The Minister, Stephen Conroy, as well as his political and departmental staff, were most active in the development of the MPS code case study. He made numerous public threats of legislative intervention if industry failed to regulate effectively. He and/or members of his staff also raised specific concerns either in writing or in face-to-face meetings with representatives of the Communications Alliance, including the CEO. Although not as 'hands-on' or publicly vocal as Minister Conroy, Helen Coonan, who was Minister when the Consumer Contracts code was developed, made it clear that if industry failed to address the problem of unfair terms in consumer contracts, then the government would have to consider other forms of regulatory intervention. Admittedly, the position she took was influenced by a prolonged period of criticism about Part 6 rule-making from consumer and public interest advocates. Nevertheless, the Minister's oversight of the process contributed to the perception there was a crisis in self-regulation that industry had to address. The difference in the way the Ministers exercised their influence can perhaps be explained by the individual personalities involved and also by their underlying approaches to market regulation. Senator Conroy was a member of the Australian Labor party; Coonan was a member of the conservative Coalition government elected in March 1996. Clearly, Conroy was more prepared to intervene early on and to become directly involved in the process, perhaps due to pressure from the media. Coonan was never directly or publicly involved in code development. She observed what industry did, but she was contemplating some form of intervention in the market if industry did not deliver. Despite their different styles, both were influential and altered the rule-making dynamic by flexing their political muscle. As explored earlier, Conroy's involvement caused ACMA to negotiate with industry, with the result that consumer and public interest representatives became less influential than they had been in the Consumer Contracts and IAF code case studies. In conjunction with other factors, Coonan's 'wait and see' approach served to enhance the influence of consumer and public interest delegates, and heightened the need for industry to secure their agreement.

It could not be determined why there was no political interest in the underlying subject matter of the IAF code. It may have been due to the fact that there was a change of Ministers while the code was being developed. Coonan replaced Darryl Williams, also a member of the Coalition government elected in March 1996, as Minister for Communications in July 2004, three months after work on the code commenced. Alternatively, issues of disability may not have been seen as important to the Coalition's voting constituencies. Regardless of the precise reason, the absence of any Ministerial involvement (in conjunction with the ACA's disengagement) contributed to the amount of time needed by the working committee to complete the code and the way the code development process unfolded. Had either Minister been more involved, mobile manufacturers may have been more willing to become involved with the process from its inception.

B. Strategies

It is not possible to comment on the strategies used by all of the different participants in each of the case studies to advance their particular interests. ACMA did not agree to be interviewed in relation to its involvement in any of the three codes. The individuals who were interviewed were delegates of either voting or non-voting members of code working committees. If participants in code development processes did not serve on working committees, they were not interviewed. Interview questions about the use of strategies also focused on tactics deployed by working committee members. Hence no specific data about strategies were gathered from or about those players who worked behind the scenes, such as the Minister for Communications, the office of the Minister, the Department of Broadband, Communications and the Digital Economy (DBCDE) and the individuals from the operating divisions of telecommunications providers consulted by their working committee representatives. Similarly, the ACCC was not interviewed about its involvement in the IAF and MPS codes; the TIO was not contacted about the MPS code.[28] However, some observations can be made about the strategies used by industry, and consumer and public interest representatives who served on the working committees.

For consumer and public interest organisations with an interest in the outcome of the process, it was seen as essential to be appointed as a voting member of the working committees. The strong reaction of consumer and public interest organisations to the Communications Alliance's attempt to deny them membership of the MPS working committee was a reflection of the influence appointments to the Consumer Contracts and IAF code working committees brought. Although it is doubtful for the reasons explored earlier that the influence consumer and public interest organisations enjoyed arose simply because of working committee membership, their physical presence at the negotiating table was an advantage. Several industry representatives interviewed for the Consumer Contracts code case study commented on the importance of interpersonal contact during negotiations. The need to look delegates from consumer and public interest organisations in the eye could be a daunting exercise; face-to-face meetings created additional incentives to solidly ground their positions.

Like consumer and public interest organisations, members of industry also valued involvement on working committees because it enabled them to exert influence early on and continuously throughout the process. As we have seen, while written submissions made during public consultation were duly considered, they were not taken into account until relatively late in the process and/or had limited impact if they raised issues previously discussed by the working committee. It would appear that mobile phone manufacturers initially believed non-participation would work to their advantage but, when confronted with a draft code they felt was too onerous, Nokia willingly joined the working committee. Participation by a mobile phone manufacturer was essential if the concerns of that sub-section of the customer equipment manufacturing industry were to be addressed.

However, the role of industry working committee members, once appointed, evolved throughout the three case studies. When the Consumer Contracts code

[28] See the Appendix for a full explanation of the research methodology used for the case studies.

was developed, all of the leading fixed and mobile carriage service providers—Telstra, Optus, Vodafone and Hutchison—were appointed to the working committee. Their delegates, in turn, triggered internal discussion among their relevant corporate divisions, which it would appear, had often decided matters individually rather than collectively. This internal debate eventually led to the adoption of a unified corporate position that could be brought back to the working committee. In the IAF code case study, industry members also represented themselves. Internal debate was not as prominent, but discussion led to the formulation of an agreed position by each industry member. In the MPS code case study, only some of the members of the relevant industry constituencies were appointed to the working committee; but their delegates were responsible for acting for other similarly situated entities. Industry representatives provoked the same internal discussion observed in the Consumer Contracts code case study (at least within their employers). In addition, they sparked a wider conversation across the industry that led to the adoption of a consolidated position that was put to the other members of the working committee. This change in the role of industry delegates appears to have occurred for two reasons. Serving on working committees is not an inexpensive exercise. Even the largest carriers and carriage service providers are under continuous pressure to minimise costs and maximise efficiency. Moreover and perhaps because of cost drivers, industry players overcame what one staff member of the Communications Alliance described as the initial distrust of their market rivals. Previously, they were sceptical that their competitors could adequately represent their interests.[29]

Similarly, the role of consumer and public interest organisations changed. With one exception, in the Consumer Contracts and IAF case studies, each consumer and public interest organisation represented its own interests. In the MPS working committee, there were two delegates from the Consumer and Disability Councils, but collectively they represented 17 different organisations. Unlike industry, the change of role was the result of the Communication Alliance's decision to restructure consumer participation in the organisation in 2006.

Once they were appointed to and/or had secured representation on working committees, consumer and public interest organisations and members of industry adopted different strategies to advance their interests. In both the Consumer Contracts and MPS codes, consumer and public interest organisations used a 'bloc style' negotiating strategy to counteract the 'divide and conquer' approach allegedly used by industry in previous code working committees. In addition, they tied issues of importance to consumers and others with matters commercially significant to the industry. They threatened to walk out of the process. In the IAF code, they reframed what was primarily a public interest issue—the ability of disabled consumers to obtain information useful to them about telephone handsets—as a marketing opportunity for equipment suppliers. In the MPS code, they 'socialised'[30] the conflict to some extent by consulting with the Minister, ACMA

[29] Interview with Name Withheld (Sydney, 30 July 2007).

[30] On the 'socialisation' of conflict, see Page, above n 3, 5 (discussing Schattschneider, above n 2).

and others outside of working committee meetings, and by informing industry delegates of their discussions. On the other hand, industry delegates appealed to the black letter of the law, played the 'cost card' or reframed policy issues as technical matters. In the IAF code, it was also alleged that industry delegates sought to delay the process by withholding information from the debate.

However, the distinguishing characteristic of the working committee process was the absence, in most instances, of any obvious way to advance one's interests other than by discussing and addressing the issues raised by working committee members. Most (if not all) delegates from industry, consumer and public interest organisations described extensive discussion between working committee members. Representatives from both sides emphasised information sharing and the education of others about constraints and expectations. Developing coherent and credible arguments in support of negotiating positions they adopted was also stressed. By no means was that discussion easy. Many interviewees described the process as 'water torture', 'excruciating' and 'contentious'. Because of the protracted and often repetitive nature of negotiations, most industry representatives said they never wanted to serve again on a working committee. However, the need for discussion was a central element of the process.

C. Bias

By design, Part 6 rule-making is an industry-led process. The Telecommunications Act 1997 (Cth) enshrines the right of 'sections of the telecommunications industry' to formulate and submit codes for registration to ACMA. Consumer and public interest organisations have no entitlement under Part 6 to draft codes and seek their registration with ACMA. Even ACMA's power to initiate rule-making in areas that can be the subject of Part 6 codes is limited.[31] With some exceptions,[32] the Communications Alliance has the power to determine if code development begins. It decides if a working committee is established and who its voting and non-voting members are. It also determines if observers may attend working committee meetings. It dictates if draftspersons, independent chairs and arbitrators are hired to assist working committees. Its board decides if a code is submitted to ACMA for registration.

Whether Part 6 rule-making favours larger corporate telecommunications providers over smaller businesses or benefits members of the Communications Alliance over non-members have not been the principal foci of inquiry in the case studies. Rather, the analysis has concentrated on the presence of any structural bias in the process that favours industry (as a whole) over consumer and public interest participants. However, as the case studies show, several aspects of code development appear to mitigate (even if they do not entirely eliminate) the advantages

[31] See Telecommunications Act 1997 (Cth) ss 123–25.
[32] See ibid s 118.

that Part 6 gives industry. As we have seen, the process brought about rule changes that were for the benefit of consumers. For example, in the Consumer Contracts code case study, industry representatives eventually agreed that, subject to some exceptions, unilateral variation of fixed term contracts without prior notification to individual consumers and an opportunity to terminate the contract was unfair. In the IAF code case study, equipment suppliers decided to provide various pieces of information that consumer and disability representatives had identified as useful for people with mobility, vision and hearing impairments. In the MPS code case study, content providers, aggregators and mobile carriage service providers acceded to a code with prescriptive rules designed to protect consumers that could be more readily enforced by ACMA. Not all representations made by consumer and public interest delegates and/or regulatory bodies were taken on board by industry. However, if the Part 6 process were completely dominated by industry, it is doubtful if the content of any of the three codes would have been the same. Why industry was prepared to consider and, in many cases, address consumer and public interest concerns can be explained by three principal factors: the dynamic that was generated between the participants in the process; the context in which Part 6 rule-making occurred; and aspects of the Communications Alliance's rule-making framework.

i. The Dynamic

Not all of the participants identified in section II.A were involved, played the same role and/or exercised the same degree of influence in each of the case studies. Delegates from industry, and consumer and public interest organisations featured in all three case studies but, for the reasons considered above, consumer and public interest organisations were not as influential in the MPS code case study as they had been in the development of the Consumer Contracts and IAF codes. The Minister, the ACCC and the TIO were not involved in the IAF code case study. In their absence, the CEO of the Communications Alliance emerged as a central figure. By contrast, in the Consumer Contracts and MPS code case studies, the Minister, ACCC and the TIO were significant players. The two relevant Ministers may have elected to influence the process in different ways but their impact on the process was felt. As code registrar, ACMA had some involvement in each of the three codes; but again, the influence it had on code development varied enormously. The media were a factor only in the MPS code case study. However, in each case study, whatever power and influence industry may have had was constrained (or at least redirected to addressing the underlying issues) as a result of the particular dynamic that was generated by and among the relevant actors in the process, each of whom, including industry, consumer and public interest organisations and regulators, had to explain and justify their positions to all other parties.

Consumer and public interest representatives were particularly influential in shaping the positions industry adopted in the Consumer Contracts and IAF code case studies. However, their capacity to influence (and the reception industry gave their ideas) was the result of other participants. In the Consumer Contracts code case study, they benefited from the dissension between corporate divisions with different business models, some of which were sympathetic to the arguments of consumer and public interest delegates. The position of consumer and public interest delegates was further strengthened as a result of the attitudes of the three regulatory bodies responsible for regulation of the Australian telecommunications sector. All were in agreement that industry had to address the issue of unfair terms in consumer contracts and along the lines consumer and public interest representatives suggested. The ACCC and TIO actively supported consumer and public interest representatives during working committee meetings. The ACA made it clear to industry that the approval of consumer and public interest representatives would serve as a proxy for regulatory approval or it would exercise a big stick or a penalty default. The Minister and CAV may not have been at the negotiating table, but their views motivated industry to seriously consider the issues consumer and public interest delegates raised. If they did not, they would face consequences.

On the other hand, in the IAF code case study, there was no involvement from regulatory bodies and the Minister, other than the ACA. In this scenario, consumer and public interest delegates were influential because of the initial disengagement of mobile handset manufacturers and the conflicts of interest that existed among suppliers represented in the working committee. They also received support from carriage service providers who retailed fixed and mobile handsets. However, the reason a code emerged at all from the process was the involvement of ACIF's CEO. When negotiations were on the verge of collapse following publication of the draft code, she kept manufacturing representatives at the table and forced senior ACA staff to become involved. Failure to adopt a code, as the ACA had requested, would have been a significant embarrassment for ACIF and the industry. It also carried the risk that the ACA could adopt a more prescriptive code, if it were so inclined. Preserving the organisational integrity and reputation of ACIF in the eyes of the regulator therefore became an important factor in motivating the adoption of something that could meet (or at least start to address) some of the concerns of consumers.

In the MPS code case study, influence was brought to bear on industry by the media, the Minister and multiple regulatory bodies. All contributed to industry's serious evaluation of proposals to improve the provision of MPS services. As already noted, unlike in the past, ACMA adopted a 'hands-on' approach to code development. However, ACMA was under pressure to act from the Minister. Responding to media reports, the Minister imposed pressure on industry by threatening it with legislation if it did not address the problems consumers were experiencing with mobile premium services. Ministerial pressure was also being applied to Telstra as a result of the Labor government's National Broadband Network initiative and wider sector regulatory reform, with the effect that Telstra departed from the collectively agreed position of MCSPs on double opt-in. In addition, the structure of the MPS supply chain enabled the MCSPs to force aggregators and, in turn, content providers to review the issues raised by regulators, and consumer and public interest representatives. However, the behaviour of the MCSPs was primarily in response to the demands made by the Minister and ACMA. Moreover, it must be remembered that consumer and public interest representatives continued to demand that the Minister and ACMA hold industry to a high standard, even after they walked out of the process. Of less importance, but nevertheless of significance, was the involvement of the ACCC and the TIO. Both were calling for industry to seriously assess the underlying causes of consumer complaints.

ii. The Context of Rule-making

The context in which code development occurred also contributed to the dynamic of Part 6 rule-making and hence moderated any actual bias that existed in favour of industry. Four aspects of the rule-making context, in particular, should be noted.

First, the delegates who represented industry came primarily from the regulatory affairs departments of their employers although in the Consumer Contracts code case study many were commercial lawyers. Regardless of their particular skills and expertise, all had high workloads and were time poor. Further, the individuals from the commercial divisions they consulted were under pressure to generate revenue. All three factors limited, even if they did not entirely eliminate, time for game playing. Industry delegates had to address the substance of the issues raised by code development participants.

Second, all industry representatives were unable to bind their employers and/or constituents on the 'spot' during working committee meetings. Although a source of much annoyance for consumer and public interest representatives who were often senior executives who could bind their employers, the inability of corporate employees to commit their employers and/or their constituents during working committee meetings generated an iterative process that forced their employers and constituents to internally discuss and actively evaluate their behaviour. It also forced them to formulate and coordinate rules for the market. Until the code development process began, corporate practice was the result of ad hoc internal decision-making by individual market players.

For example, in the Consumer Contracts code case study, industry delegates returned from each working committee meeting asking their co-workers, located within different internal divisions of their respective employers, the same questions posed by consumer and public interest representatives. These questions prompted internal discussion. Moreover, existing corporate practice was scrutinised and assessed by fellow employees who often had very different perspectives and supported the position of consumer and public interest working committee delegates. From this debate, agreed positions on existing practices and potential responses to identified problems emerged.

A similar iterative dynamic unfolded in the MPS code case study where each of the three industry delegates represented a different industry constituency.

Following working committee meetings, the MCSP delegates, employees of Telstra and Optus, reported to their employers and the individual employees designated by each of their other constituents: Vodafone and Hutchison. These four individuals in turn asked questions of, solicited information from, and discussed matters with their co-workers. These individuals then conveyed the agreed position of their employers to each other. Additional discussion between them ensued and eventually led to an MCSP position that was relayed by the MCSP delegates to the working committee for discussion. The representatives of aggregators and content providers were not interviewed,[33] but a similar process within their employers and constituencies was most likely triggered because they could not bind them in working committee meetings without obtaining their prior permission.

In the IAF code case study, it appears that the Nokia representative on the formal sub-committee was eventually able to trigger a dialogue similar to the one in the MPS code case study among mobile phone manufacturers. Internal discussion within and among fixed handset manufacturers may not have been as robust as it was in the Consumer Contracts and MPS code case studies, but to the extent it occurred, it occurred because their delegates could not bind them in working committee meetings.

Third, as chapter four highlighted, despite market liberalisation, there were only a few major carriers and carriage service providers in the Australian telecommunications industry. Collectively, they held the vast share of what is in global terms a small market. Most of these had offices and/or their headquarters in Melbourne, where the ACA administered and the ACMA administers the Telecommunications Act 1997 (Cth) and related legislation, or Sydney, where the Communications Alliance and representatives from many of the consumer and public interest groups that participated in code development were located. Key players from the telecommunications industry were actively involved in each of the three cases. They were not as influential in the IAF code case study but they were actively involved.

Fourth, the use of self-regulation by the incumbent and new market entrants, and the involvement of consumer groups in that process before Part 6 was adopted, were particularly significant. Consumer participation on working committees became a norm (or path-dependent feature) that did (and continues to) constrain the Part 6 process, as the CEO of the Communications Alliance found out in the MPS code case study.

iii. The Rule-making Framework

In addition, the rule-making framework of the Communications Alliance had some effect on the Part 6 process even though the activity taking place in working committee meeting rooms was not necessarily the most important to code development; and actors who were not working committee members could

33 See n 28.

influence the process. The principle of consensus and its contribution to the ability of consumer and public organisations to influence the Part 6 process have already been explored. However, the principle of representativeness also merits some consideration because it brought all relevant types of participants into the process, each of which altered the rule-making dynamic in different ways. As applied by the Communications Alliance, the principle of representativeness was inclusive. Consumer and public interest organisations, and industry participants could participate equally in working committee discussions even if they often disagreed about what was necessary to address the underlying regulatory problem. Moreover, the principle of representativeness brought together actors operating at different layers of the relevant supply chains. The presence of these market players often (although not always) enhanced the willingness of other industry participants to evaluate and address consumer and public interest concerns. As we saw in the MPS code case study, the structure of the MPS supply chain enabled MCSPs to force the aggregators to review the issues regulators, and consumer and public interest representatives raised. Aggregators then applied pressure to content providers. A similar but less powerful dynamic was at play in the IAF code case study.

III. The Procedural and Institutional Legitimacy of Part 6 Rule-making

The analysis of the procedural and institutional legitimacy of Part 6 rule-making that follows begins by assessing transparency and impartiality, as both are said to influence the quality and nature of deliberation, which is then considered. The section concludes with an evaluation of whether industry was accountable for the positions it adopted and the code rules that emerged from the process. Throughout the analysis, it is acknowledged that Part 6 rule-making challenges the traditional understandings of transparency, impartiality and accountability. It is therefore necessary in the analysis to revisit the purpose of each value in legislative and administrative law-making. By closely re-examining their objectives, it becomes possible to decouple each of these principles from the mechanisms that have been thought to achieve procedural and institutional legitimacy in traditional law-making processes. Moreover, the principles can be reframed so that they retain the underlying goals of these principles in traditional law-making while simultaneously accommodating the need for industry rule-making. If, as it is argued, this approach is correct, then it becomes conceivable that mechanisms other than those associated with legislative and administrative law-making—instruments that the study of the politic of Part 6 rule-making reveals—can collectively (if not individually) ensure that the principles of transparency, impartiality, deliberation and accountability are satisfied.

A. Transparency

In traditional legislative and administrative rule-making, transparency is valued because it is assumed it will improve deliberation. There is a 'presumption' that it minimises (even if it does not always avoid) the possibility that law-makers will act out of their own self-interest or become 'captured' by a particular set of stakeholders to the exclusion of others and consumer and public interest concerns.[34] It is assumed, as Bentham has stated, that 'the closer [they] are watched, the better [they] behave'.[35] The visibility of the law-making process is also important to accountability, another mechanism that seeks to ensure that law-makers remain responsive to all interested parties.[36] Transparency, so it is said, enables the general public and other interested parties to hold law-makers to account by giving them the information they need to evaluate their performance. As we saw in chapter three, reducing the risk of partiality and facilitating accountability underpinned many of the procedural and institutional features of traditional legislative and administrative rule-making: the permission of members of the general public to attend deliberative proceedings, accessing Hansard, consultation and disclosure of information.

By contrast, Part 6 rule-making is opaque. Apart from being given an opportunity to read and comment upon draft codes, the general public had no oversight of code development. Because of the obligation of confidentiality the Communications Alliance imposed on members of the working committee, private individuals could not attend working committee meetings. Discussions of working committee members were not recorded or transcribed; minutes of working committee meetings were prepared but not publicly disclosed. Private individuals had no (or limited) knowledge of the involvement of regulators, Ministers and other participants in the process. It may have been the practice of the Communications Alliance to notify respondents to public consultation if their comments had been addressed and, where appropriate, to give reasons why code modifications would not be forthcoming. However, no one (other than working committee representatives, the ACA or ACMA) was entitled to find out which individuals or companies commented on draft codes, what their comments were or the extent to which their concerns were addressed.[37]

[34] See, eg, PH May, 'Regulatory Regimes and Accountability' (2007) 1 *Regulation & Governance* 8, 11; M Lodge, 'Accountability and Transparency in Regulation: Critiques, Doctrines and Instruments' in J Jordana and D Levi-Faur (eds), *The Politics of Regulation: Institutions and Regulatory Reforms for the Age of Governance* (Cheltenham, Edward Elgar, 2004) 124, 128.

[35] M Lodge and L Stirton, 'Accountability in the Regulatory State' in R Baldwin, M Cave and M Lodge (eds), *The Oxford Handbook of Regulation* (Oxford, Oxford University Press, 2010) 349, 351–52 (quoting Bentham).

[36] R Mulgan, *Holding Power to Account: Accountability in Modern Democracies* (Basingstoke, Palgrave Macmillan, 2003) 21.

[37] The ACA and ACMA required the disclosure of all of this information as part of the code registration process. See ACA, *Developing Telecommunications Codes for Registration—A Guide* (October 2003) 16–18.

Nevertheless, it is argued that Part 6 rule-making was transparent in the sense that it achieved outcomes consistent with the rationales supporting the requirement of transparency. It is accepted that the process was not transparent to the general public. However, the transparency to the general public that is so prized within traditional legislative and administrative rule-making is arguably only a mechanism designed to ensure its two underlying objectives are satisfied: that an adequate amount and quality of information are disclosed by law-makers to the relevant individuals who hold them to account, and that deliberation is not compromised by the presence of the self-interests of law-makers. The extent to which industry was impartial (or otherwise) during the process and whether the criterion of deliberation was met given its confidentiality are considered below (see sections III.B and III.C). However, if transparency is understood as a requirement that sufficient relevant information must be disclosed by industry to enable others to hold it to account, then the process of Part 6 rule-making was transparent. Subject to some important caveats, a sufficient amount of information was disclosed between working committee members and other Part 6 participants that enabled them to hold industry to account (see further section III.D below). Moreover, in this instance, confidentiality supported the flow of information from industry to informed recipients—the regulators, and the consumer and public interest representatives who served on working committees of the Communications Alliance. This flow of information enhanced their ability to hold industry accountable. Rather than discouraging industry to impart information, the Part 6 process created a space where industry was able to be more open about its practices with others.

In all case studies, a significant amount of information, including knowledge of operational, technical and commercial processes, was exchanged between delegates. Reasons for decisions were given by industry, even if (as occurred in the MPS code) they were not always accepted without challenge or believed by consumer and public interest advocates. At the requests of committee chairs, proposals were frequently submitted in writing, often with some justification, in an effort to build consensus and resolve disputes. Moreover, many delegates (carriage service providers and consumers) involved in the development of the Consumer Contracts code emphasised sharing information and the importance of educating the other members of the working committee, even if the purpose of the latter was closely linked to their advocacy roles. Similarly, in the IAF code case study, the equipment suppliers, carriage service providers, and consumer and disability representatives interviewed described teaching as part of their function, even though consumer and disability representatives believed that fixed handset equipment manufacturers deliberately withheld information from them in the main working committee. Education was not emphasised by the delegates from the MCSPs interviewed for the MPS code case study, but industry did at least provide a rationale and some justification for its approach on various issues to consumer and public interest representatives, and the regulators. Moreover, they reported they spent quite some time teaching them about the structure of and participants in the MPS market.

The above analysis is, however, qualified in a number of important ways. First, absent direct observation of the rule-making process, it is not possible to know with absolute certainty the quality or quantity of information exchanged. The minutes and accompanying meeting papers of working committees reviewed certainly indicate industry provided and justified many of its positions, but they often do not record what was said in any great detail. Equally, it cannot be verified if committee members fully disclosed all relevant information but there is no evidence to suggest anyone acted in bad faith. Third, the three codes that were the focus of the case studies were developed many years before delegates were interviewed, and interviewees were not provided with copies of working committee documentation to refresh their memories before interview. Most delegates who were interviewed did not recall the specifics of committee decision-making. However, a consistent statement made by a number of representatives on the Consumer Contracts code committee was the relatively open and frank discussion concerning industry practices. Fourth, a source of tension between industry and consumer and public interest representatives in all three case studies was often the lack of real data to evaluate assertions by industry delegates that proposed rules were excessively costly. Accurately determining the cost of regulatory rules before implementation is not a problem unique to the telecommunications industry.[38] Some costs are just not easily quantifiable, as the Consumer Contracts code case study illustrates.[39] However, in many instances, for example when IT system upgrades or equipment testing were at issue, it does seem reasonable to expect industry to produce some quantitative data to facilitate discussion. Consumer and public interest representatives and regulators may not be able to verify that data but it would at least force industry to demonstrate that it had properly costed proposals before dismissing them.

If the qualified conclusion that the rule-making process broadly satisfies the criterion of transparency (defined as the disclosure of information necessary to hold industry to account) is correct, two questions arise. The first asks why. What made industry provide the information to working committee members (voting and non-voting) and others involved in the process? Disclosure of relevant information to the ACA and ACMA can perhaps be explained by its power to scrutinise codes prior to registration. However, other working committee members and Part 6 participants had no formal power to require disclosure of information. Why did industry reveal it? It is suggested here that the politic of Part 6 rule-making drove disclosure. The dynamic generated between all participants, the context in which codes were formulated, and the principles of representativeness and consensus that form part of the Communications Alliance's rule-making framework

[38] Similar difficulties arise in the food industry. See, eg, E Golan, F Kuchler and L Mitchell with contributions by C Greene and A Jessup, 'Economics of Food Labeling' (2001) 24 *Journal of Consumer Policy* 117.

[39] See s II.B of ch 5.

all went towards creating an atmosphere that necessitated that industry explain and justify its position to others. Absent these factors, it is doubtful if information would have flowed so relatively easily.

The second question, which follows from the first, queries the traditional 'presumption' that transparency is essential in the absence of any significant evidence that the obligation of confidentiality on working committee members somehow perverted the process itself. Certainly, some consumer and public interest representatives interviewed in the Consumer Contracts code case study suggested that confidentiality worked against consumer and public interest organisations, hindering their ability to solicit the views of their members who were not employees. However, even if valid, the quality and quantity of information industry disclosed to committee delegates does not appear to have been adversely affected as a result. It is true that there was nothing inherently confidential that was exchanged between working committee members. However, in the absence of any evidence that a lack of transparency corrupted the rule-making process, and in the face of indications that industry may not participate if the process were fully transparent to the public, it needs to be asked if confidentiality when coupled with a requirement of consensus and representativeness is akin to a form of parliamentary privilege[40] at the legislative level. Instead of hindering accountability, the requirement of confidentiality the Communications Alliance imposes appears to serve as a mechanism that facilitates the flow of information between all participants and hence enhances the quality of their deliberation, and expands the ability of non-industry participants to hold industry to account.

Despite determining (albeit with some qualifications) that the process of Part 6 rule-making satisfies the criterion of transparency, the analysis concludes with a note of caution about the impact that confidentiality may have on ACMA and the mechanisms traditionally used to hold it (and other independent regulatory authorities) to account. The code development process arguably gave ACMA scope to be less open with the public than it otherwise should have been. In the MPS code case study, for example, when the draft code was released, ACMA issued a press release encouraging members of the public and industry to comment on it.[41] However, it implied that the code was an industry-produced document. It was not indicated anywhere that ACMA had vetted the code before it was released in draft with ACMA's permission or that it was in direct negotiations with industry about the code's content. Hiding behind the cloak of industry is neither fair to industry nor an accurate reflection of ACMA's role in the process. Admittedly, in the MPS code case study, ACMA was not a member of the working committee; and therefore, the Communications Alliance's requirement of confidentiality did not

[40] See, eg, RFV Heuston, *Essays in Constitutional Law* 2nd edn (London, Stevens & Sons Ltd, 1964) 82–100.

[41] ACMA, 'ACMA Encourages Comment on Mobile Premium Services Code' (Media Release, 141/2008, 11 November 2008).

apply to it. The obligation of confidentiality to which it was subject arose because of Part 7A of the Australian Communications and Media Authority Act 2005 (Cth). Nevertheless, the case study raises wider questions about how regulatory bodies are held to account in the age of decentred regulation.[42]

B. Impartiality

The standard of impartiality seen as essential for robust discussion and deliberation by each of the three theories of representative democracy considered in chapter three—the disinterested decision-maker formulating rules in a neutral venue and acting in the best interests of consumers and the general public—was clearly not met. The industry members of working committees (whether representing themselves or their constituents) were clearly motivated by their own self-interests or the interests of their constituencies. Consumer, public interest and industry delegates cited venue neutrality as a factor critical to the emergence of the Consumer Contracts code. They also mentioned the importance of an independent chair. However, either or both elements were missing in the IAF and MPS codes. In the IAF code, the chair was not neutral; she was a representative from CTN, which, as argued in chapter six, worked (at least initially) to the advantage of consumer and disability representatives on that working committee. By the time the MPS code was developed, the Communications Alliance was also an advocate for industry. Although the Communications Alliance still retained the function of facilitating self-regulation, it, its staff and the lawyers it hired to help draft the code were no longer perceived by consumer and public interest delegates to be neutral. Indeed, there was a great sense of distrust between the Communications Alliance and the representatives from the Consumer and Disability Councils.

Asking if industry decision-makers were impartial is perhaps not the correct question. As conceived, Part 6 was an attempt to harness the knowledge and expertise of the telecommunications industry. Rather than requiring industry to act impartially in the best interests of consumers and the general public, it sought to reframe industry decision-making. Like many strategies of proceduralization, its aim was to channel self-interest by obligating industry to take into account the interests and concerns of all other participants in the process, in the hope that decisions in the public interest would follow.[43] Raising issues of impartiality is therefore not appropriate or at least does not advance the analysis very far. Industry will automatically fail any test of impartiality. Instead, the central question ought to be whether industry considered the relevant concerns of others before

[42] Similar questions have arisen in the context of negotiated rule-making. See, eg, CB Harrington and ZU Turem, 'Accounting for Accountability in Neoliberal Regulatory Regimes' in MW Dowdle (ed), *Public Accountability: Designs, Dilemmas and Experiences* (Cambridge, Cambridge University Press, 2006) 195.

[43] See, eg, Ayres and Braithwaite, above n 5, ch 3.

it reached its decisions: did it exercise some degree of independent judgement or did it dismiss proposals put forward by other Part 6 participants out of hand, without any sincere consideration of their underlying merits? Understood in this way, the test industry must satisfy overlaps to a significant degree with the concept of deliberation (discussed in section III.C below).

If, as argued, genuine appraisal of the ideas of others is the standard against which industry should be evaluated, it is quite clear that the politic of Part 6 rule-making forced industry-voting representatives to seriously consider and reflect on the concerns and proposals suggested by others, including consumer advocates and public interest groups. In many (if not all) cases, industry-voting members of working committees also re-evaluated their own positions in light of arguments made by participants within and outside of the working committee room. Assessment and re-assessment is seen most clearly in the Consumer Contracts code where industry interviewees highlighted the difficulties they had in determining what was in their employers' best interests. They used information gathered from working committee meetings to assist with the formulation of their internal positions on aspects of unfairness. However, assessment and reassessment are also present in the other two case studies. In the MPS code, industry evaluated and agreed to several measures proposed by ACMA (and supported by delegates from the Consumer and Disability Councils)—the provision of complaints data to ACMA, the online register for content service providers and an obligation on content service providers and aggregators to provide (and keep up-to-date) their contact details in a database maintained by the Communications Alliance. In the IAF code case study, mobile handset manufacturers and other equipment suppliers eventually considered the information that they could provide to carriage service providers, even if they were disengaged with the process at the outset. Evaluation and re-evaluation, of course, does not mean that industry assented to every request. Indeed, industry often did not agree to consumer and public interest demands as its refusal to create a code monitoring committee in the MPS code case study so graphically illustrates. However, it was forced to consider (at least in the three codes studied) the merit of the other side's argument and articulate reasons for taking the positions it adopted.

C. Deliberation

As we saw in chapter three, deliberation serves different purposes for theorists of representative democracy and legisprudential scholars, and therefore what is precisely required of law-makers to satisfy the criterion of deliberation varies. Republicans believe that the aim of deliberation is ultimately to shape preferences and enhance civic virtue. To achieve that end, debate must be 'reasoned' and 'informed'. Optimistic pluralists, on the other hand, have no interest in enhancing civic virtue. Deliberation, in their view, is a mechanism to resolve the conflict between competing interest groups. Although it may 'moderate' the views of interest groups, deliberation is primarily seen as a contest from which the 'best' ideas will emerge. For Waldron, deliberation is one of the 'principles of legislation' that gives law 'authority'.[44] It requires arriving at a 'sound view'[45] after consideration of diverse perspectives and the effects it may have on individuals and the society as whole. Yet, for Wintgens, law must be rationally justifiable. Deliberation—finding relevant facts, identifying problems, weighing alternatives and taking into account reasonably foreseeable effects into account—is central to ensuring that law-making is a logical exercise.[46] However, all emphasise (at a minimum) the exchange of 'information and opinions', and taking into account 'public-regarding reasons',[47] features that are manifest in the ordered debate of traditional legislative law-making and the structured decision-making of administrative rule-making. As a result, Part 6 rule-making has been evaluated with reference to the presence (or absence) of these two particular characteristics.

In each of the three case studies, there was some trading-off of interests (as republicans and others fear). For example, the issues of unilateral variation in the Consumer Contracts code, and the amount and type of information that equipment suppliers had to provide carriage service providers and end-users in the IAF code were ultimately resolved by bargaining and negotiation. In the MPS code case study, there appears to have been less deal-making within the actual working committee room; in part because much of the decision-making was taking place during meetings with ACMA. However, deal-making was taking place. Telstra's decision to adopt double opt-in to deflect political pressure is perhaps the best evidence of 'give and take' in that situation. The decision of MCSPs to implement call barring—when at least one MCSP interviewed indicated there was no evidence to suggest that the absence of call barring was causing customer service complaints—and the decision of the chair of the MPS working committee to cease discussion on code monitoring are other examples. However, prior to some form of agreement being reached on these issues, there was a significant amount of deliberation—information and opinion sharing—that took place within and outside of working committees among all Part 6 participants. Perhaps, most importantly, there was also discussion and consideration of proposals made by regulators, and consumer and public interest representatives within industry constituencies and internally within individual members of industry, as highlighted earlier in the discussion of the politic of Part 6 rule-making and the analysis of the criterion of impartiality.

[44] See, eg, J Waldron, 'Principles of Legislation' in RW Bauman and T Kahana (eds), *The Least Examined Branch: The Role of Legislatures in the Constitutional State* (Cambridge, Cambridge University Press, 2006) 15, 18, 27–28.

[45] ibid 23.

[46] LJ Wintgens, *Legisprudence: Practical Reason in Legislation* (Abingdon, Ashgate, 2012) 115–38; 294–302.

[47] A Vermeule, *Mechanisms of Democracy: Institutional Design Writ Small* (Oxford, Oxford University Press, 2007) 5.

Similarly, in the Consumer Contracts and IAF codes, agreement was often reached for reasons of pragmatism and/or fatigue. In the MPS code, industry, consumer and public interest representatives could not agree; consumer and public interest representatives walked out of the process. Nevertheless, in all three case studies, decisions were taken after the delegates shared information and discussed the relevant issues. In fact, a cause of fatigue in the Consumer Contracts code case study was the repetitive nature of the discussion. Delegates shared information about and discussed the same topics on numerous occasions. In the IAF code, consumer and disability representatives did not simultaneously discuss the various issues with fixed handset and mobile phone manufacturers. Discussion with fixed handset manufacturers occurred in the main working committee while the discussion with a mobile phone manufacturer occurred in the formal subcommittee. However, industry provided consumer and disability representatives considered responses in each forum; they gave them an explanation for their decisions. Their explanations may not have been as comprehensive as the explanations industry players gave in the Consumer Contracts and MPS code case studies, but an explanation was provided. In the MPS code, the decision of the Communications Alliance to cease further working committee discussions on the code monitoring and compliance provision was made after consumer and public interest representatives presented their proposals; and industry listened, evaluated and responded to them.

Again, without direct observation of the rule-making process within the working committee or elsewhere, it is not possible to know precisely how deliberation unfolded. At least on paper, however, it would appear that the criterion of deliberation was met. On the whole, decisions were taken after examination of the various views and each party had either amended its position or was better able to justify its original position in light of the material exchanged. As mentioned in the discussion on transparency, industry provided reasons for its decisions (at least to regulatory, consumer and public interest representatives on the working committees) and ultimately to the ACA or ACMA. Even if the reasons it gave were contested and/or took into account its own economic considerations, industry gave some explanation for the rules it was ultimately prepared to accept or reject. The distrust that clearly existed between industry, consumer and public interest representatives no doubt contributed to the robustness of the debate but the politic was the most significant factor. As explored earlier, the dynamic that was generated between the participants of Part 6 rule-making, the context in which it occurred and aspects of the Communications Alliance's rule-making framework all necessitated sharing of relevant information and evaluation of consumer and public interest concerns.

D. Accountability

The idea that law-makers must answer for their decisions is a quintessential value of representative democracy, and legislative and administrative rule-making.

However, despite universal agreement that 'accountability' is desirable, there continues to be some debate about what the term precisely means.[48] As Bovens has stated, 'Accountability is a contestable concept *par excellence*. Anyone studying accountability will soon discover that it can mean different things to many different people.'[49] Given there are multiple definitions of accountability that are used in a multiplicity of contexts and in different jurisdictions, it is not possible to survey all of them here. Rather, the focus will be on the 'core'[50] meaning of accountability because it underpins the conventional mechanisms of accountability incorporated into legislative and administrative law-making discussed in chapter three: voting, parliamentary oversight, and judicial review. In both rule-making contexts, accountability is seen as a 'relationship'[51] between a principal (the accountant or account-holder) and an agent (the accountee or accountor) 'involving [two] complementary rights on the part of the account-holder and obligations on the part of the accountor'.[52] By entrusting an agent with a particular responsibility, the principal is entitled to 'call' the agent to account: the principal may 'seek information, explanation and justification' from the agent about its conduct.[53] The principal also has a right to 'hold' the agent to account; it is empowered in some way to impose sanctions or has access to remedies if the agent has not acted in the best interests of the principal or complied with the principal's instructions.[54] As a consequence of these rights, the agent has two reciprocal duties to perform. He or she must inform, explain and justify behaviour to the principal, and accept whatever remedies and sanctions the principal may impose.[55]

To determine if a decision-maker is 'accountable' as defined above, analysis typically centres on different 'sets of accountability questions'[56] or what Mashaw refers to as the 'grammar of governance'.[57] Questions include, for example, 'who is accountable?'; 'to whom?', 'for what?';[58] 'why does an actor feel compelled to render account?';[59] 'through what processes is accountability assured?'; 'by what

[48] See, eg, Dowdle, above n 42; C Harlow and R Rawlings, 'Promoting Accountability in Multilevel Governance: A Network Approach' (2007) 13 *European Law Journal* 542, 545–46; M Bovens, 'Two Concepts of Accountability: Accountability as a Virtue and as a Mechanism' (2010) 33 *West European Politics* 946; T Willems and W Van Dooren, 'Coming to Terms with Accountability: Combining Multiple Forums and Functions' (2012) 14 *Public Management Review* 1012.

[49] M Bovens, 'New Forms of Accountability and EU-Governance' (2007) 5 *Comparative European Politics* 104, 105.

[50] ibid 107; Mulgan, above n 36, 7.

[51] Mulgan, above n 36, 11.

[52] ibid. See also CF Sabel and J Zeitlin, 'Learning from Difference: The New Architecture of Experimentalist Governance in the EU' (2008) 14 *European Law Journal* 271, 303.

[53] Mulgan, above n 36, 9.

[54] ibid 8, 9.

[55] ibid 10.

[56] C Scott, 'Accountability in the Regulatory State' (2000) 27 *Journal of Law and Society* 38, 41.

[57] JL Mashaw, 'Accountability and Institutional Design: Some Thoughts on the Grammar of Governance' in Dowdle, above n 42, 115, 115.

[58] Scott, above n 56, 41.

[59] M Bovens, 'Analysing and Assessing Public Accountability: A Conceptual Framework' (European Governance Papers No C-06-01, 16 January 2006) 15.

standards is the accountable behaviour to be judged?'; and 'what are the potential effects of finding that those standards have been breached?'[60] Depending on the answers to the questions of 'to whom?' or 'why?', accountability regimes then tend to be classified 'spatially'—vertically, horizontally or diagonally[61] and sometimes as 'upwards' or 'downwards'.[62] They may also be categorised variously as 'political', 'market', 'social',[63] 'administrative', 'bureaucratic', 'legal/judicial' and 'public/consumer' to list but a few of the different and numerous classifications used in the literature.[64]

In the analysis of accountability in Part 6 rule-making that follows, a different tack is adopted for the principal reason that even if deployed with modifications by some scholars in other non-traditional settings,[65] the traditional analytical framework has largely been developed in the context of traditional rule-making. It accepts three important premises of the 'traditional' definition of accountability that simply cannot be assumed in the context of industry code development. The first of these premises is the assumption that there is some form of hierarchy between a principal and an agent, ie, the principal has some kind of power, 'moral authority or priority'[66] over the agent. There are many different participants in the process of Part 6 rule-making (as the analysis of the politic of Part 6 rule-making highlighted) but it is difficult to label industry as an agent of Parliament given that Part 6 technically does not give it any power to make legally binding codes. Part 6 was drafted so that it is ACMA (not industry) who determines if a code is registered and hence acquires the force of law. Yet, it is also difficult to classify ACMA as an agent of Parliament in this context given that the process of Part 6 rule-making is clearly led by industry. Second, the traditional definition of accountability is premised on the ability of the principal to clearly specify goals.[67] However, Part 6 arguably does not give industry much (if any) direction about the content of codes. It provides a list of examples of matters that may be dealt with by industry, but the guidance is limited and falls well short of anything resembling 'precise instructions'[68] that the principal-agent model presumes. Moreover, as argued in chapter two, one of the reasons for permitting industry to formulate codes was the complexity of the telecommunications market—a market elected representatives did not understand and hence could not direct by way of command and control regulation. Third and as a consequence of the second premise, accountability (as traditionally defined) is 'retrospective';[69] it is a process that occurs after an agent has carried out (or otherwise) the particular task requested by the principal.

60 Mashaw, above n 57, 118.
61 Bovens, 'Analysing and Assessing Public Accountability', above n 59, 15.
62 Scott, above n 56, 42.
63 Mashaw, above n 57, 120–26.
64 For an excellent overview, see Mulgan, above n 36, 30–35.
65 See, eg, Marshaw, above n 57, 134–52.
66 Mulgan, above n 36, 11–12.
67 Sabel and Zeitlin, above n 52, 304.
68 ibid.
69 Harlow and Rawlings, above n 48, 545.

The process is retrospective because of the assumption that goals can be set and monitored. Yet as the three case studies of Part 6 rule-making highlighted, the process was in large measure an exercise in 'problem solving'[70] shared by all participants. No one, including industry, knew at the outset how underlying issues should or could be resolved.

Given the three underlying conditions on which the 'traditional' definition of accountability is based were not present in Part 6 rule-making, instead of focusing on traditional accountability questions, the approach used here concentrates on identifying mechanisms (if any) in the process that performed the same or equivalent function as traditional methods of accountability. It is not concerned with whether industry was accountable in the sense that it complied with the three Part 6 codes once the ACA or ACMA registered them. That issue is outside the scope of this book. Rather, it seeks to find tools that achieved the underlying goal of accountability in traditional rule-making processes—ensuring that industry answered for its decisions or explained itself to others. However, it explicitly recognises the possibility that the means by which this goal of accountability is achieved will necessarily be different in the context of Part 6 rule-making than in traditional and administrative law-making. Indeed, as we saw in each of the three case studies, there was no judicial review of Part 6 rule-making. Parliament had no oversight of the three codes. The general populace never voted on the content of the codes. Nevertheless, if the approach of functional equivalence is used, it can be argued that industry was accountable for its decisions. Information was sought from industry, which had to explain and justify its positions throughout the process in light of arguments put to it by numerous participants, including consumer and public interest organisations. Moreover, there were possible (and in some cases immediate) consequences for industry if it failed to act on the concerns raised by the various actors in the process.

As the analysis of the politic of Part 6 rule-making demonstrated, one of the chief characteristics of the process was discussion, a key aspect of which was the need for industry to explain why it was adopting particular viewpoints. In each of the case studies, questions on all sorts of matters were posed to industry, inside and outside of working committee meetings, from a variety of participants—members of supply chains, consumer and public interest organisations, the ACA, ACMA, the ACCC, the TIO, the CEO of the Communications Alliance and the Minister—who asked for and, in all cases, received some explanation of the particular stance industry was adopting. Recipients may not have been (and often were not) convinced by the arguments industry made. In many cases, they expressed their disagreement with them. However, the answers they received triggered further questions, explanations and discussions.[71] Throughout code development, industry was required to articulate reasons for its positions and, as the discussion of transparency highlighted, industry often justified them by sharing information

[70] Sabel and Zeitlin, above n 52, 304.

[71] This iterative process led to the prescriptiveness of code rules observed in ch 1.

about its operational, technical and commercial processes. All information and arguments were carefully scrutinised by the different actors and were the subject of intense debate, which was often heated and highly contested (as the case studies illustrate). Consequently, industry was often required to rethink its original views in their entirety; formulate alternatives that addressed the underlying issues raised; and/or buttress its existing position by developing more compelling reasons as to why it could not depart from the its initial stance. Unlike traditional accountability, accountability in this context was 'real-time' or what Sabel and Simon writing in the context of new governance have called 'dynamic accountability'.[72]

There were also possible consequences to industry in at least two of the case studies if it did not address issues raised by process participants. In the Consumer Contracts code case study, consumer and public interest organisations were able to act as an effective check against industry. They had a capacity to influence the process for two reasons: the principle of consensus and the ACA's willingness to exercise a big stick or a penalty default. Ultimately, if consumer and public interest organisations remained unconvinced by the rules that industry favoured or believed the arguments it put forward were so unreasonable in that case study, they could veto the code in its entirety. Consumer and public interest organisations had real power in that case study because industry needed a code to be adopted. Code formulation was very much seen as a test by the ACA and government that industry had to pass in order to retain its right to self-regulate and draft consumer codes. Although not raised expressly by interviewees involved with the MPS code, it is relatively clear that had industry not modified the code in accordance with ACMA's wishes then ACMA would not have registered the code. Assuming the Minister would have continued to apply pressure to see some form of regulatory action, ACMA would have had to pursue an industry standard with the resulting loss of regulatory control valued by industry. Independently, the ACCC could also pursue action under the Trade Practices Act 1974 (Cth). In the IAF code case study, it is less obvious what (if anything) industry stood to lose if a code were not adopted. Failure to adopt a code would have caused embarrassment to the Communications Alliance, and a possible loss of reputation and credibility; but ACMA was not proactively engaged and may not have pursued an industry standard.

IV. Conclusion

The politic of Part 6 rule-making appears to have ensured that code development was broadly consistent with the procedural and institutional principles of the rule of law (at least on the basis of the three codes studied). Subject to some caveats,

[72] CF Sabel and WH Simon, 'Epilogue: Accountability Without Sovereignty' in G de Burca and J Scott (eds), *Law and New Governance in the EU and the US* (Oxford, Hart Publishing, 2006) 395, 400.

the process accorded with the rationale supporting the principle of transparency. Representatives sitting on the three working committees (if not the general public) were able to hold industry (as well as other participants, including regulators, and consumer and public interest delegates) to account. No voting working committee member was impartial. However, the influence other actors involved had on the process created a dynamic that forced industry to exercise some degree of independent judgement when evaluating suggestions from non-industry participants, including representatives of consumer and public interest groups, who bore the brunt of the responsibility for putting the case to industry when the Consumer Contracts and IAF codes were developed. For similar reasons, most issues appear to have been seriously deliberated by working committee delegates. Industry was also required to give account, even if the mechanism by which it was held to account was different to those developed for traditional and administrative law-making. Industry had to explain and justify its conduct during and throughout the process to a variety of participants from the public and private sectors, including politicians. Collectively, these actors working within and outside of the working committee room gave rise to a 'system of checks and balances in which particular forms of [industry] behaviour [were] inhibited or encouraged by the overall balance in the system'.[73] As we have seen, Part 6 rule-making tests the boundaries of traditional procedural and institutional legitimacy; but the rules it produced were developed broadly in accordance with the principles of transparency, impartiality, deliberation and accountability.

The dynamic that existed occurred for more than reasons of serendipity as Jaffe implies in his seminal 1937 article entitled 'Law Making by Private Groups'.[74] Industry's willingness to evaluate consumer and public interest proposals was strengthened by what at first blush may seem some unlikely sources: internal corporate divisions, participants in the supply chain and the CEO of the Communications Alliance. In addition, consumer and public interest delegates were allowed to serve on working committees, a factor which can be explained, in large measure, by the way in which the Casualties of Telecom affair was handled. Participation by consumer and public interest representatives as well as regulators in industry rule-making was valued from the outset because Telecom struggled to regain credibility in the eyes of the general public and politicians; a heavy emphasis was placed on consultation and discussion among all interested parties as a result. From then on, consumer participation on working committees became a norm that continues to constrain the Communications Alliance process. Ministers and regulators also became involved, flexing their muscles of command and control as required from time to time, and the process was sufficiently permeable so that they could influence it, even if they were not voting members of the working committee. Some (but not all) of the principles of the Communications Alliance's

[73] Scott, above n 56, 55.
[74] LL Jaffe, 'Law Making by Private Groups' (1937) 51 *Harvard Law Review* 201, 250.

rule-making framework were also relevant. Representativeness determined in a significant way who became involved in the conflict; consensus gave consumer and public interest delegates an important right of veto, provided they remained in the process. Finally, the context in which rule-making occurred—the time pressures under which industry delegates worked, their inability to bind their employers in working committee meetings and the involvement of the leading industry players in a relatively small market—are likely to have contributed to industry's genuine assessment of consumer and public interest concerns.

9

The Responsiveness of Part 6 Rule-making

I. Introduction

This chapter considers if the process of Part 6 rule-making was 'responsive' to the 'practices and norms'[1] of all interested parties with a stake in its outcomes or if it was 'too responsive' to the needs of any one stakeholder. Regulatory scholars maintain that rule-making that is responsive to all interested parties is beneficial for several reasons, some of which were considered by policy-makers and legislators when Part 6 of the Telecommunications Act 1997 (Cth) was formulated.[2] It permits the state to mobilise the talents and knowledge of stakeholders. It leads to regulation that is more efficient, flexible, timely[3] and innovative.[4] It results in rules that are better targeted to the specific industry concerned and rules that are more reasonable yet more comprehensive.[5] Moreover, better-targeted and more reasonable rules are believed to increase the probability that industry will comply with them.[6] Most importantly, however, responsive rule-making makes it more likely that any rules that are adopted at the end of the process will effect change.[7] In other words, rule-making that is responsive increases the probability that the objectives of the regulatory system set by the state will be attained. For the Australian telecommunications sector, the state has set three main objectives: the promotion of the long-term interests of end-users of 'carriage services' or of services provided by means of carriage services; the efficiency and international competitiveness of the Australian telecommunications industry; and the

[1] C Parker and J Braithwaite, 'Regulation' in P Cane and M Tushnet (eds), *The Oxford Handbook of Legal Studies* (Oxford, Oxford University Press, 2003) 128.

[2] See s III of ch 2.

[3] C Coglianese and E Mendelson, 'Meta-Regulation and Self-Regulation' in R Baldwin, M Cave and M Lodge, *The Oxford Handbook of Regulation* (Oxford, Oxford University Press, 2010) 146, 152.

[4] I Ayres and J Braithwaite, *Responsive Regulation: Transcending the Deregulation Debate* (Oxford, Oxford University Press, 1992) 111. See also CF Sabel and J Zeitlin, 'Learning from Difference: The New Architecture of Experimentalist Governance in the EU' (2008) 14 *European Law Journal* 271.

[5] Ayres and Braithwaite, above n 4, 110–11; 112–13; Coglianese and Mendelson, above n 3, 152.

[6] Ayres and Braithwaite, above n 4, 110–16; Coglianese and Mendelson, above n 3, 152.

[7] K Yeung, *Securing Compliance: A Principled Approach* (Oxford, Hart Publishing, 2004) 30.

availability of accessible and affordable carriage services that enhance the welfare of Australians.[8] These are the ends that the process of Part 6 rule-making was designed to achieve. Responsive rule-making does not guarantee they were achieved. However, if the Part 6 process was not responsive to the interests of all of its stakeholders, then its ability to accomplish the goals of the Telecommunications Act 1997 (Cth) would have been compromised.

An initial hurdle in the analysis, however, is defining what responsiveness means (and hence requires) in a rule-making context. Braithwaite has described responsiveness as a 'democratic ideal'.[9] However, the term to date has not been clearly defined in the regulatory literature, which remains largely focused on enforcement and compliance.[10] Therefore, it is argued in this chapter that questions about what makes the process of industry rule-making responsive (and therefore more likely to be effective in meeting the public policy goals set by the state) should be understood as questions about its procedural and institutional legitimacy. Assuming that is correct, the principles of deliberation (the weighing up of alternatives and determination of what, on balance, meets the needs of all stakeholders), the exercise of some independent judgement, accountability and transparency among stakeholders, defined in chapter eight, clarify the meaning of responsiveness in the context of industry rule-making. This approach is justified for two principal reasons. First, these standards resonate with the three theories of democracy, which it has been suggested enable the regulatory state to normatively ground the instrumentalism of industry rule-making: republicanism, pluralism and deliberative democracy. Second, the principles are consistent with the conceptions of society and law that underpin strategies of proceduralization.

Section I of this chapter begins by defining responsiveness. It links the concept of responsiveness to republicanism, pluralism and deliberative democracy, arguing that the four principles of procedural and institutional legitimacy, as defined in chapter eight, are compatible with each of these theories. It then explains the assumptions that strategists of proceduralization make about society and the ramifications they have for law and the regulatory state. Section II of this chapter then applies the principles of deliberation, the exercise of some independent judgement, accountability and transparency between stakeholders. It evaluates if the process by which the Consumer Contracts, Information on Accessibility Features for Telephone Equipment (IAF) and MPS codes (discussed in chapters five, six and seven) were developed was responsive to the needs of consumers and other public interest stakeholders; or if it was 'too responsive' to industry participants. It argues that the process was, on balance, responsive to the needs

[8] Telecommunications Act 1997 (Cth) s 3(1).

[9] J Braithwaite, 'Responsive Regulation and Developing Economies' (2006) 34 *World Development* 884, 884.

[10] See, eg, VL Nielsen, 'Are Regulators Responsive?' (2006) 28 *Law & Policy* 395, 396–97, 406–07; R Baldwin and J Black, 'Really Responsive Regulation' (2008) 71 *MLR* 59.

of all interested parties because the 'politic' of Part 6 rule-making identified in chapter eight ensured that the four principles of procedural and institutional legitimacy were satisfied. The politic prevented the process from becoming too responsive to the needs of industry. The chapter concludes by arguing that the principles of procedural and institutional legitimacy provide some practical measures against which policy-makers and others with an interest in industry rule-making can evaluate responsiveness and predict the effectiveness of regulatory initiatives in the decentred state.

II. Defining Responsiveness

Adopting a definition of responsiveness for the process of rule-making that turns on whether the four principles of procedural legitimacy have been met has merit for three reasons. First, such an understanding is consistent with the republican principle of non-domination that implicitly underpins Ayres and Braithwaite's classic *Responsive Regulation: Transcending the Deregulation Debate.*[11] Second, the principles of deliberation, transparency, accountability and impartiality are also compatible with pluralism and deliberative democracy, the other theories of democracy that it has been suggested provide a normative basis for the regulatory strategy of proceduralization.[12] Finally, use of these standards is consistent with the conceptions of law and society assumed by strategists of proceduralization. Each argument is considered below.

A. Non-domination

To understand the connection between the four principles of procedural and institutional legitimacy, and the principle of non-domination on which Ayres and Braithwaite's four techniques of responsive enforcement—the pyramid, tripartism, enforced self-regulation and partial-industry intervention—is premised, one must first understand the meaning of domination in republican theory. Pettit, with whom Braithwaite has collaborated,[13] argues that domination against another occurs when someone (an agent) (1) has the 'capacity to interfere', (2) on an 'arbitrary basis', (3) 'in certain choices that the other is in a position to make'.[14]

[11] Ayres and Braithwaite, above n 4.

[12] J Black, 'Proceduralizing Regulation: Part I' (2000) 20 *OJLS* 597, 607.

[13] See, eg, J Braithwaite and P Pettit, *Not Just Deserts: A Republican Theory of Criminal Justice* (Oxford, Clarendon Press, 1990).

[14] Philip Pettit, *Republicanism: A Theory of Freedom and Government* (Oxford, Clarendon Press, 1997) 52.

Interference involves intentionally or negligently 'making things worse' in some way, by 'changing the range of options available, by altering the expected pay-offs assigned to those options, or by assuming control over which outcomes will result from which option and what actual payoffs, therefore, will materialise'.[15] Capacity to interfere requires an actual (not potential) ability to intervene, ie one that can be readily deployed. Arbitrariness is whimsy; interference occurs at 'the agent's pleasure.'[16] For Pettit, this happens if the exercise of power is made 'without reference to the interests, or the opinions of those affected' and those interests are relevant, meaning that they are 'shared' with others who are affected by a decision: they are not 'exceptional' or somehow unique.[17] Finally, for domination to arise, the person must have the capacity to interfere on an arbitrary basis with respect to at least one decision the other individual can make.[18] Non-domination is the opposite of domination—the situation where none of the above three conditions is satisfied.

As the previous paragraph indicates, whether non-domination arises turns to a great extent on the absence of arbitrariness or (phrased more positively) the presence of 'responsiveness' to the interests of others. However, Pettit asserts that arbitrariness is a procedural concept. Indeed, he refers to responsiveness as a 'proper' or 'decent hearing',[19] a term upon which he does not elaborate; although he suggests that in some circumstances, a 'proper' hearing may only be given if held privately. Arbitrariness is not concerned with whether the act of interference adversely affects (or 'disadvantages') the interests or values of the person(s) concerned. Nevertheless, it is inevitable that procedure and substance are linked (at least in the eyes of the individuals who are affected by an act of interference). Where a process refers to the interests of individuals and substantively addresses the concern(s) they raise, clearly domination does not arise. However, Pettit argues that arbitrariness and domination also do not materialise even when the outcome of a process does not work in favour of individual concerns. Why? How can a process that may genuinely consider but ultimately not address concerns still be non-arbitrary and hence non-dominating?

For Pettit, this question arises in two instances.[20] The first situation is when a concern raised by an individual is driven by a particular self-interest and it has been decided by another that it is inconsistent with an interest they both share with others. Provided the decision-making process follows the correct procedures (as understood by the relevant parties) or, in other words, a 'proper hearing'[21] has been given and the decision is made because of an interest the parties have in common, then there is no domination. An example Pettit provides involves a

[15] ibid 53.
[16] ibid 55.
[17] ibid 55–56.
[18] ibid 58.
[19] ibid 195 and 196.
[20] The following discussion is based on ibid 197–200.
[21] ibid 195.

group of residents opposed to having an airport being built in their neighbourhood. Ultimately they are unsuccessful: the airport is built. However, these citizens have not been dominated, in his view, if decision-making procedures are followed and the airport was built to further a shared interest in the ability of the community to travel by air. The second situation in which the problem of reconciling non-domination with an unfavourable outcome happens is when there is disagreement as to what is in the collective interest. In some instances, the difficulty is resolved because the person who is adversely affected accepts that people are likely to have different views. In those cases, non-domination is avoided if procedures are followed; the decision was taken in light of or in full 'awareness' of the data or concerns of the opposing individual; and the decision made involved 'a genuine attempt to determine the common interest'.[22] In the other (more difficult) cases where individuals care passionately about a particular issue and are not prepared to accept that views of the common interest may differ, how to preserve non-domination is not clear cut or well-delineated by Pettit. However, he suggests that the use of 'measures of conscientious procedural objection'[23] could assist.

What constitutes a 'fair hearing' is context-specific. In addition, the assertion that any common interests—'a set of values ... which is beyond, and even greater than, the aggregate of individual interests'—can exist most likely raises the ire of liberal theorists.[24] Nevertheless, what is noteworthy in Pettit's discussion is the emphasis he places on many (if not all) of the same principles that emerged from the discussion of what makes traditional law procedurally and institutionally legitimate. A hearing must ensure that the concerns of affected parties are fully conveyed, listened to and understood; and a bona fide attempt has been made to reach agreement or find common ground in an effort to address their concerns. Moreover, it is the presence of extensive discourse that mitigates the potential for arbitrariness with which republicanism is ultimately concerned.

By Braithwaite's own admission, his large body of work on responsive regulation has not emphasised what he calls the 'imperative of linking strategies of responsiveness to the normativity of a politics of non-domination'.[25] However, he has made clear that regulation which is responsive, ie regulation that 'seeks to achieve the collaboration and co-operation of those subject to regulation'[26] must have what he calls an 'ethical grounding' or it risks becoming 'a threat to the law's purposes'.[27] In other words, the degree to which regulation can be responsive to any stakeholder must ultimately be consistent with the values of law itself or law

[22] ibid 198.

[23] ibid 200.

[24] See generally ibid 3–31. See also M Feintuck, *'The Public Interest' in Regulation* (Oxford, Oxford University Press, 2004) 198–99.

[25] J Braithwaite, 'Relational Republican Regulation' (2013) 7 *Regulation & Governance* 124, 128. For criticism of this omission, see J Freigang, 'Is Responsive Regulation Compatible with the Rule of Law?' (2002) 8 *European Public Law* 463, 470–72.

[26] H Collins, *Regulating Contracts* (Oxford University Press, 1999) 65.

[27] Braithwaite, 'Relational Republican Regulation', above n 25, 129.

becomes 'captured'[28] and its coherence is undermined. Whether non-domination ought to serve as a basis on which to 'ground' responsiveness, as Braithwaite asserts, cannot be debated here. However, to the extent that non-domination can serve as a 'credible' way to anchor responsiveness, the conception of a fair hearing embedded within it is consistent with the principles of deliberation, transparency, accountability and impartiality, identified earlier in chapter three and defined for the purposes of the decentred state in chapter eight, that embody the procedural and institutional principles of legal legitimacy.

B. Consistency with Other Democratic Theories Underpinning Proceduralization

Non-domination is not the only democratic principle that could be used to marry the responsiveness of industry rule-making with the coherence of law. In addition to republicanism, Black has suggested that deliberative democracy and pluralism could provide a foundation for alternative conceptions of proceduralization. Deliberative democracy offers what Black calls a 'thick' conception whereas pluralism presents a 'thin' conception.[29] There are many different theories of deliberative democracy, but only two variants will be discussed here: Habermas' theory of 'communicative action' and the concept of directly deliberative polyarchy (DDP), developed by Cohen and Sabel.[30] Habermas' theory of communicative action has been selected because Black has suggested that it, along with the related idea of the 'ideal speech situation', could ground a thick conception of proceduralization.[31] DDP has been chosen because it underpins the concept of democratic experimentalism, a technique of proceduralization that has attracted significant attention in the US and the EU. The compatibility of these two theories of deliberative democracy with the four principles of procedural and institutional legitimacy (as refined) are considered first. An assessment of the compatibility of pluralism with the modified principles of procedural and institutional legitimacy then follows.

i. Deliberative Democracy

As Black states, Habermas' book *Between Facts and Norms*[32] offers a 'rich' and 'complex' account of law and democracy[33] that is deeply 'rooted in reason'[34] and

[28] G Teubner, 'After Legal Instrumentalism? Strategic Models of Post-Regulatory Law' in G Teubner (ed), *Dilemmas of Law in the Welfare State* (Berlin, Walter de Gruyter, 1986) 299, 311.

[29] Black, 'Proceduralizing Regulation: Part I', above n 12, 599, 606–08.

[30] J Cohen and C Sabel, 'Directly Deliberative Polyarchy' (1997) 3 *European Law Journal* 313.

[31] Black, 'Proceduralizing Regulation: Part I', above n 12, 599.

[32] J Habermas, *Between Facts and Norms: Contributions to a Discourse Theory of Law and Democracy* (William Rehg trans, Polity Press, 1996).

[33] Black, 'Proceduralizing Regulation: Part I', above n 12, 597, 607.

[34] J Cohen, 'Reflections on Habermas on Democracy' (1999) 12 *Ratio Juris* 385, 386.

discourse. However, the work in its entirety cannot be incorporated into a thick conception of proceduralization without some modification.[35] Black is, for example, critical of Habermas' assumption that the necessary conditions he specifies for 'legitimate law formation' can only be satisfied by legislatures and the courts.[36] Indeed, she states Habermas 'demonstrates very little imagination' about the decentred state or legal pluralism.[37] Equally, she believes that Habermas' work contains some significant oversights. In particular, she points out his failure to acknowledge that deliberation inevitably has to be mediated because 'blockages' in communication will arise.[38] Black does not suggest how differences between speakers could be overcome. However, she does believe that a comprehensive theory of thick proceduralization must address Habermas' omission. Despite these weaknesses, Black nevertheless maintains that two of Habermas' ideas that undergird his theory of deliberative democracy could form the building blocks of a thick conception of proceduralization: his notions of communicative action and the ideal speech situation.[39]

For Habermas, communicative action is in essence a theory of rationality.[40] It posits that through the use of language social actors can seek to coordinate their actions 'on the basis of a shared understanding that the goals [they will pursue] are inherently reasonable or merit-worthy'.[41] At the outset of dialogue, social actors will have competing and conflicting goals. However, the very purpose of entering into debate is to determine collectively the ends that should be followed.[42] From rational dialogue and reasoned debate, consensus, or what is mutually acceptable to all, can and will emerge.[43] However, there are certain pre-conditions that must be satisfied before 'rationally motivated agreement'[44] can be reached.[45] First and perhaps foremost, participants cannot be coerced. They must reach agreement without force. All participants must also be treated equally. For example, each participant must have an 'opportunity'[46] to present their arguments for and against a particular proposition. All participants are entitled to pose questions and seek clarification from others in order to evaluate the arguments presented to them and

[35] Black, 'Proceduralizing Regulation: Part I', above n 12, 599; J Black, 'Proceduralizing Regulation: Part II' (2001) 21 *OJLS* 33, 35–45.

[36] Black, 'Proceduralizing Regulation: Part II', above n 35, 35–36.

[37] Black, 'Proceduralizing Regulation: Part I', above n 12, 614.

[38] Black, 'Proceduralizing Regulation: Part II', above n 35, 38–45.

[39] Black, 'Proceduralizing Regulation: Part I', above n 12, 608–09.

[40] J Bohman and W Rehg, 'Jurgen Habermas' in EN Zalta (ed), *Stanford Encyclopedia of Philosophy* s 3.1 https://plato.stanford.edu/archives/fall2017/entries/habermas.

[41] ibid.

[42] M Rosenfeld, 'Law as Discourse: Bridging the Gap Between Democracy and Rights' (1995) 108 *Haravard Law Review* 1163, 1168–69; A Brand, *The Force of Reason: An Introduction to Habermas' Theory of Communicative Action* (Sydney, Allen & Unwin, 1990) 14–18.

[43] Black, 'Proceduralizing Regulation: Part I', above n 12, 609.

[44] Bohman and Rehg, above n 40.

[45] The following discussion is based on Black, 'Proceduralizing Regulation: Part I', above n 12, 609; Rosenfeld, above n 42, 1169 and Bohman and Rehg, above n 40.

[46] Rosenfeld, above n 42, 1169.

re-evaluate the reasons for their own position. Moreover, the participants must be committed to evaluating and rejecting arguments and making decisions solely on the basis of the 'force of the better argument'.[47] It is only in these circumstances that the normative requirements of the ideal speech situation are satisfied.[48]

By contrast, proponents of DDP assume that citizens have agreed (if only at a very high level) the public policy goals that society should pursue, but they are unable to agree the precise measures they should take to achieve them.[49] The inability to agree upon and adopt measures arises for the principal reason that existing constitutional structures within democratic societies centralise decision-making. As a consequence of centralisation, uniform responses to regulatory problems are mandated. However, uniformity can never be achieved (or at least is very difficult to achieve) because citizens have different backgrounds and hold various and conflicting values; and there is an ever increasing lack of certainty about how regulatory problems should be addressed, among central decision-makers and citizens alike, because of their growing complexity. Proponents of DDP argue therefore that 'local units'—groups consisting of citizens, industry bodies and/or other affected parties—should determine the means used to address mutually agreed public policy goals. However, in return for this discretion, local units are required to arrive at their decisions by satisfying two requirements. First, they must deliberate matters within themselves, taking into account all relevant information provided by their various members. Second, they must deliberate matters between themselves, which involves either taking into account pertinent information that other local units working to address comparable problems may provide; or explaining why their particular choices are preferable to those of other local units in the specific circumstances. The latter requirement is a form of 'benchmarking' that initially involves consideration of the rules or other decisions adopted by other local units and, where necessary, refinement and modification to the specific rules or other decisions proposed by a particular local unit. It also requires local units to continuously monitor and evaluate the effectiveness of their decisions after they have been taken in light of the experience of other local units. Where evidence emerges that there are more effective alternatives, local units are expected to act upon that information and revisit their initial decisions, again by deliberating matters within and between themselves. In a DDP, existing constitutional structures—governments, administrative agencies, legislatures and the courts—remain in place, but their functions are altered. Their purpose is to promote and support local units and their deliberative activities.

[47] Black, 'Proceduralizing Regulation: Part I', above n 12, 609.

[48] Bohman and Rehg, above n 40.

[49] The following discussion is based on Cohen and Sabel, above n 30, 326–33. See also MC Dorf and CF Sabel, 'A Constitution of Democratic Experimentalism' (1998) 98 *Columbia Law Review* 267; CF Sabel and J Zeitlin, 'Experimentalist Governance' in D Levi-Faur (ed), *Oxford Handbook of Governance* (Oxford, Oxford University Press, 2012) 169.

Although proponents of DDP emphasise deliberation within and between local units, the concept of DDP is not based on a theory of reason. On the contrary, its advocates have expressly rejected Habermas's concept of communicative action and the ideal speech situation as a suitable basis for a theory of democracy. Citizens, they argue, disagree about 'the nature and competence of reason'.[50] Instead, DDP is grounded in the Rawlsean concept of 'public reason.'[51] Before any rule or decision can be adopted, local units must be able to identify and articulate considerations that other reasonable citizens can accept as reasons.[52] DDP theorists have not fully delineated the arguments that might constitute the reasons that other reasonable citizens can accept, but they have suggested that not all reasons merit the same level of consideration by decision-makers within local units. 'Constitutional' considerations—reasons that affirm 'the standing of citizens as free and equal members of the political society'—carry significant weight.[53] Reasons that deny citizens such standing should be discounted. 'Policy reasons' are those reasons relevant to a particular issue but are 'neither required by nor incompatible with a conception of citizens as free and equal'.[54] The weight afforded to them is to be determined on a case-by-case basis.

It is not necessary here to evaluate the merits of Habermas' theory of communicative action or the ideal speech situation; or Cohen and Sabel's theory of DDP. Equally, it is unnecessary to consider if these theories ought to and can be carried over into the context of proceduralization. Certainly, many have questioned the premise of communicative action; if the 'counterfactual' of the ideal speech situation can ever be realised—even in the traditional legislative context of rule-making—and if Habermas' emphasis on rationality only serves to exclude certain groups from deliberative discussion.[55] Many have questioned the utility of the concept of public reason that underpins DDP.[56] Some have commented that DDP fails to provide clear criteria against which the process of 'learning' that the process of deliberation is intended to trigger can be evaluated;[57] or to adequately address the conditions required for learning.[58] Others have suggested that DDP necessitates a far greater level of social equality among participants of local units

[50] Cohen, above n 34, 387.

[51] ibid.

[52] Cohen and Sabel, above n 30, 327–28.

[53] ibid 327.

[54] ibid 328.

[55] See, eg, O Weinberger, 'Habermas on Democracy and Justice: Limits of a Sound Conception' (1994) 7 *Ratio Juris* 239.

[56] Jonathan Quong, 'Public Reason' in Edward N Zalta (ed), *Stanford Encyclopedia of Philosophy* s 7 https://plato.stanford.edu/entries/public-reason.

[57] See, eg, JE Fossum, 'Reflections on Experimentalist Governance' (2012) 6 *Regulation & Governance* 394, 395.

[58] See, eg, J Lenoble and M Maesschalck, 'Renewing the Theory of Public Interest: The Quest for a Reflexive and Learning-based Approach to Governance' in O de Schutter and J Lenoble (eds), *Reflexive Governance: Redefining the Public Interest in a Pluralistic World* (Oxford, Hart Publishing, 2010) 3, 16–20.

if it is to be successful.[59] However, if, as Black asserts, communicative action and the ideal speech situation could provide a democratic foundation for strategies of proceduralization; and if, as its proponents suggest, DDP could serve as a foundation for democratic experimentalism, a specific strategy of proceduralization, they resonate with the principles of procedural and institutional legitimacy (as refined) for the reasons explained below.

Accountability—the giving of reasons—is clearly essential for Habermas. Indeed, discussion and debate between law-makers could not take place without it. Further, he assumes that the decision-making process is transparent. In the same way that it has been argued in chapter eight that the process of Part 6 rule-making was transparent, deliberants are expected to disclose all relevant information pertaining to the topic for debate. Also, those participating in debate are expected to be impartial. Their participation is conditional on identifying the argument with the most force—the argument that is most responsive to the collective goals set by the regulatory state. Arguments that do not satisfy this criterion must be discarded, and it is assumed that deliberants are capable of setting aside arguments that may serve their own interests or otherwise may satisfy a criterion of decision-making not founded on rationality. Deliberation too is central for Habermas. All reasons, including 'public-regarding reasons', must be evaluated before any rule can be adopted.

Similarly, DDP is broadly consistent with the principles of procedural and institutional legitimacy (as refined). Ensuring local units answer for their decisions or explain themselves to others is fundamental to DDP. It is only through the process of explaining their decisions, and supporting them with reasons, that local units can 'teach' and 'learn' from each other—the two activities with which DDP and democratic experimentalism have become synonymous. Deliberation—the exchange of information and taking into account public-regarding reasons—is also central to DDP. Indeed, DDP has been described as 'the ebb and flow of reason giving'[60] and a 'form of information pooling'.[61] Importantly, during debate, members of local units must articulate and take into account only reasons that third parties will acknowledge as reasons. Considerations of self-interest and other reasons that may deny the freedom and equality of citizens must be discarded.[62] Proponents of DDP make no explicit reference to impartiality, but the idea of exercising some degree of independent judgement and/or sincerely considering the underlying merits of a particular matter is implicit in their understanding of deliberation. They presume that participating citizens are reasonable.

[59] See, eg, WE Scheuerman, 'Democratic Experimentalism or Capitalist Synchronization? Critical Reflections on Directly-Deliberative Polyarchy' (2004) 17 *Canadian Journal of Law and Jurisprudence* 101, 118; DA Super, 'Laboratories of Destitution: Democratic Experimentalism and the Failure of Antipoverty Law' (2008) 157 *University of Pennsylvania Law Review* 541.

[60] Dorf and Sabel, above n 49, 389.

[61] Cohen and Sabel, above n 30, 329.

[62] ibid 327.

Moreover, they assume that participants are able to identify and classify constitutional, public policy and other reasons; and properly evaluate the weight each should be granted during debate. The refined definition of transparency proposed in chapter 8 is arguably narrower than one proponents of DDP would adopt. There are references to 'public deliberation' and 'arenas open to citizens'[63] throughout the experimentalist governance literature. Sabel and Zeitlin have also stated in their writings about experimentalist governance in the EU that 'the citizen's right to know not just what the authorities are deciding but also the evidence and arguments motivating their decisions' is 'a necessary foundation for all forms of democratising destablisation'.[64] However, Dorf and Sabel have recognised that confidentiality can, in specific instances, serve as a 'corrective' and avoid 'distortions' of public policy debate.[65] They do not specify the circumstances when confidentiality may be necessary. They state only that those circumstances will need to be determined 'by experience and experiment'.[66] However, when confidentiality may be applied, the refined definition of transparency—the disclosure of sufficient relevant information to deliberants—must be satisfied. If the situation were otherwise, the deliberation within and between local units that proponents of DDP envisage would not and could not occur.

ii. Pluralism

Black does not explore in any detail the democratic theory of pluralism on which she asserts her thin conception of proceduralization could be based. It is not clear, for example, if she would subscribe to the 'optimistic' vision of pluralism sketched in chapter three. She states only that if pluralism were to serve as the democratic basis for proceduralization, it is not 'particularly novel' and offers 'little that is new'.[67] However, if the optimistic account of pluralism were adopted as the basis of a thin conception of proceduralization, it is compatible with the four principles (as refined) that legal legitimacy embodies. For optimistic pluralists, some form of obligation to be impartial is essential if rule-makers are to be able to 'umpire' the competition taking place in the 'marketplace of ideas'. Moreover, rule-makers (whoever they may be) must deliberate; decisions are to be taken after consideration of more than just their self-interests. Similarly, optimistic pluralists expect rule-makers to give account for their decisions: they must explain their decisions. Finally, the rule-making process must also be transparent. There must be at a minimum the disclosure of sufficient relevant information if it is to accord with the optimistic pluralist's conception of legitimate law-making.

[63] See, eg, ibid 313.
[64] Sabel and Zeitlin, above n 4, 313.
[65] Dorf and Sabel, above n 49, 373.
[66] ibid.
[67] Black, 'Proceduralizing Regulation: Part I', above n 12, 599.

C. The Decentred State and the Limitations of Law

Although there are important differences between them,[68] all strategies of proceduralization are premised on the notion that society is divided into a series of what Teubner calls 'sub-systems'[69] or what Braithwaite prefers to refer to as 'nodes of networked governance.'[70] Importantly, no one 'sphere' is superior to another. Rather, each is autonomous (or at least sufficiently autonomous so that it cannot be 'dominated' by others[71]) and derives its independence from its own particular way of thinking, which is different from the 'logics' adopted by other spheres.[72] For strategists of proceduralization, the autonomy that each sub-system, sphere or node enjoys has important implications for the way in which they can interact with each other. Because of their distinctive mechanisms of reasoning, different spheres of society cannot control (at least directly) what other nodes do. Their commands simply cannot and will not be understood by the other sub-systems that operate according to different rationales.[73] For this reason, the relationship between spheres is characterised by strategists of proceduralization as one of 'heterarchy' rather than 'hierarchy'.[74] In accordance with this conception of society, law is seen by strategists of proceduralization as one sphere, which together with the spheres of politics, the market and religion, for example, comprise social society.[75]

Adopting a 'fragmented' and 'decentred' conception of society has a number of important ramifications for law, however.[76] Most importantly, the function of law shifts from legitimating the exercise of state power to coordinating the 'impact'[77] that various sub-systems have on each other. Absent law that sets regulatory objectives, it is assumed that the different spheres will not consider the effect their conduct may have on others because they are primarily concerned with advancing their own goals as set and determined by their particular rationalities.[78] As Black explains, the purpose of law in this context is therefore to ensure that each sphere

[68] For example, Braithwaite disagrees with Teubner that the various sub-systems into which society is fragmented are or should be 'normatively closed.' Braithwaite, 'Responsive Regulation and Developing Economies', above n 9, 885.

[69] See generally G Teubner, *Law as an Autopoietic System* (Oxford, Blackwell, 1993). See also J Black, 'Constitutionalising Self-Regulation' (1996) 59 *MLR* 24, 44–45; Black, 'Proceduralizing Regulation: Part I', above n 12, 602–06.

[70] Braithwaite, 'Responsive Regulation and Developing Economies', above n 9, 885.

[71] ibid.

[72] Black, 'Constitutionalising Self-Regulation', above n 69, 46.

[73] ibid 44–45; Black, 'Proceduralizing Regulation: Part I', above n 12, 602; Braithwaite, 'Responsive Regulation and Developing Economies', above n 9, 885.

[74] Black, 'Proceduralizing Regulation: Part I', above n 12, 603.

[75] Black, 'Constitutionalising Self-Regulation', above n 69, 44.

[76] See Teubner, above nn 28 and 69. See also G Teubner, 'Juridification: Concepts, Aspects, Limits, Solutions' in G Teubner (ed), *Juridification of Social Spheres* (Berlin, Walter de Gruyter, 1987) 3.

[77] Black, 'Constitutionalising Self-Regulation', above n 69, 46.

[78] Teubner, above n 28, 307–08.

'takes into account in its own operations the effect of its externalities [on other systems or 'wider interests']'.[79] However, the ability of the regulatory state to achieve system integration is ultimately curtailed by law's own systemic limitations. Its ends cannot be achieved directly via substantive means because of the autonomy of other systems—the various systems cannot understand law's mindset. Instead, integration must be achieved indirectly via reliance on 'procedural' mechanisms that seek to encourage dialogue, participation and deliberation within and between different spheres.[80] Moreover, although use of such mechanisms has the potential to 'pattern decision processes, change organisational structures and alter power imbalances'[81] between systems, there is no guarantee (or indeed requirement) that 'democratization' will do so. This point is recognised explicitly in Ayres and Braithwaite's discussion of tripartism where they state:

> the way a democratic dialogue will ... resolve such a contradiction [between consumer and economic interests] is an open question ... The point is the virtue of struggling for principles of institutional design that do not seek to paper over these contradictions.[82]

The assumptions strategists of proceduralization make about law and society are contestable. However, if they are accepted, adoption of a definition of responsiveness to evaluate Part 6 rule-making that turns on the principles of deliberation, transparency, accountability and impartiality is clearly compatible with a conception of law in a democratic society that is limited to using procedural mechanisms to achieve its ends. Even though it is difficult to clearly distinguish between procedural and substantive means,[83] all four principles are directed to encouraging, stimulating and regulating the dialogue that it is hoped will cause regulatees to mitigate the effect their conduct has on others within society. Requiring decision-makers to be transparent in the sense of mandating them to provide pertinent groups with relevant information is likely to lead to a better-informed debate. Similarly, obligations to reflect on the concerns of all stakeholders (deliberation) and to re-evaluate proposed courses of action in light of them (impartiality) have the potential to trigger critical self-reflection. A duty to give reasons (accountability) also serves to enhance transparency and self-assessment; the latter of which is essential to the ultimate success of the proceduralization enterprise.

However, it must be made clear that even if the process of Part 6 rule-making were responsive as defined by reference to the four principles of procedural and institutional legitimacy, it is possible that industry will not comply with the rules

[79] Black, 'Constitutionalising Self-Regulation', above n 69, 44. Braithwaite refers to the importance of 'checking abuse' and serving 'human needs' but they are both captured by the idea of internalisation. Braithwaite, 'Responsive Regulation and Developing Economies' above n 9, 886.

[80] Teubner, 'After Legal Instrumentalism? Strategic Models of Post-Regulatory Law', above n 28, 309–13; Black, 'Constitutionalising Self-Regulation', above n 69, 45; Black, 'Proceduralizing Regulation: Part I', above n 12, 602–03; Braithwaite, 'Responsive Regulation and Developing Economies', above n 9, 885.

[81] Black, 'Constitutionalising Self-Regulation', above n 69, 47.

[82] Ayres and Braithwaite, above n 4, 97.

[83] HLA Hart, *The Concept of Law* 2nd edn (Oxford, Oxford University Press, 1994) 71–72.

that were produced. It is also possible (as the quotation from Ayres and Braithwaite highlights) that even if industry does comply with the code rules, the activity of developing them does not effect change or achieve the objects of the Telecommunications Act 1997 (Cth). Although legitimate, the process may not result in the internalisation of 'concern for the other player[s]'[84] or the externalities that sections of the telecommunications industry generate. Rather than address the imbalance of power between consumer and public interest groups and industry, 'tyranny of the minority' may be perpetuated. To evaluate whether Part 6 (as a technique of proceduralization) increases or decreases the likelihood of industry's compliance with rules and/or is effective in achieving the Act's objectives would necessitate consideration of a wide array of factors, only one of which will be procedural and institutional legitimacy. For example, compliance with rules is a process measure while the primary goal of Part 6 is to effect outcomes in ways that are consistent with achieving the purposes of the Act. Similarly, a factor in an evaluation of the effectiveness of Part 6 rule-making could include an analysis of what Braithwaite calls the 'effectiveness ideal' of responsiveness[85]—the extent to which industry has been responsive to consumer and public interests in a substantive sense, ie that industry has curtailed the behaviour the process was designed to address or has resolved an inequality between industry and consumer and public interests. In this context, the question of whether the principles of procedural and institutional legitimacy have been taken into account in rule formation is also relevant. However, the presence of procedural and institutional legitimacy does not dispose of the question of whether Part 6 rule-making has successfully 'irritated'[86] the sub-systems that comprise the telecommunications industry, such that conflicts between sectional interests are resolved. In short, the absence of mechanisms addressing the four principles of procedural and institutional legitimacy will render a process unresponsive but its presence is not determinative of the substantive question concerned with the effectiveness of Part 6 rules in achieving the public policy goals of the Telecommunications Act 1997 (Cth). It is also not determinative of the question of whether industry will comply with the rules that are produced.

D. Summary

Adopting the four principles of procedural and institutional legitimacy as measures of the responsiveness of Part 6 rule-making acknowledges the two important constraints imposed on law in a decentred and democratic society. Duties

[84] Ayres and Braithwaite, above n 4, 93.
[85] Braithwaite, 'Responsive Regulation and Developing Economies', above n 9, 886.
[86] Black, 'Proceduralizing Regulation: Part I', above n 12, 603.

of deliberation, accountability, impartiality and transparency seek to enhance exchange and dialogue between disparate groups—the procedural mechanisms law can use to achieve the purpose of internalising concern for others in the 'meta-regulatory' state. In addition, they enable the regulatory state to tie responsiveness to democratic principles, a task which is essential if law is to avoid losing its identity by 'surrendering'[87] itself to the other 'nodes', sub-systems and spheres of society. They are the principles central to the four theories of democracy that could provide a normative grounding for strategies of proceduralization. Without doubt, the Habermasean conception of deliberative democracy, DDP, the republican ideal of non-domination and pluralism differ. Each dictates that competing interests receive a 'hearing' but what is needed to satisfy that requirement varies. The conditions of the Habermasean ideal speech situation are perhaps the most onerous because they mandate equality between deliberants and the capacity of rule-makers to distance themselves from their personal interests before law can emerge. DDP is not as exacting as the ideal speech situation but its emphasis upon 'defending proposals by reference to considerations that others acknowledge as reasons'[88] nevertheless imposes a demanding requirement. The absence of arbitrariness emphasised by republicans arguably sets a lower threshold for a rule-making procedure to meet than deliberative democracy. With its emphasis on 'bargains and compromises', optimistic pluralism requires noticeably less of a hearing than the ideal speech situation, DDP or republicanism. However, the principles of procedural and institutional legitimacy (as refined) have much in common with these four competing conceptions of democracy. As we have seen, the need for deliberation involves actively listening to the concerns of others and genuinely formulating and evaluating proposals designed to address them; factors that are central to non-domination, both variants of deliberative democracy and optimistic pluralism. Accountability requires participants to provide reasons for their decisions, a point emphasised in all four conceptions of democracy. Only Habermas requires impartiality; but DDP, republicanism and optimistic pluralism assume the exercise of some independent judgement whereby participants can step back and listen to, and understand the views of those with competing interests; reconsider their own position in light of them; and take appropriate steps accordingly. Again, openness to the general public is not emphasised in the three theories. However, full and frank disclosure of information and views between participants directly involved in a particular rule-making or decision-making process is a hallmark of all of them. Indeed, direct participation in a process is said to render those individuals involved best able to hold the opposing side to account.

[87] Teubner, 'After Legal Instrumentalism? Strategic Models of Post-Regulatory Law', above n 28, 311.
[88] Cohen and Sabel, above n 30, 329.

III. The Responsiveness of Part 6 Rule-making

As seen in chapter one, industry rule-making has long been criticised for being too responsive to the needs of industry. Part 6 rule-making is no exception. Since the enactment of Part 6, consumer and public interest representatives who have sat on working committees of the Communications Alliance have expressed similar anxieties that the process is beholden to industry, and trumps consumer and public interest concerns. However, if as suggested that responsiveness in the context of industry rule-making is better understood as a question of procedural and institutional legitimacy, then it is not necessary to revisit the empirical questions of whether the process of Part 6 rule-making was responsive to the needs of various stakeholders or whether it was too responsive to the needs of particular participants in the process. As the analysis of the procedural and institutional legitimacy of Part 6 rule-making in chapter eight has highlighted, the code development process created, with some qualifications, a forum and a political dynamic where the needs of consumers and industry were canvassed. By no means was the process driven solely by the interests of industry; consumer and public interest advocates had their case heard, even if, as was seen in the MPS code case study, complete agreement between industry and consumer representations could not be reached. The politic ensured that industry listened to the concerns of consumer and public interest representatives; re-evaluated its position on matters of interest to them; and justified the stances it eventually took by providing and explaining the reasons that underpinned their decisions. On the whole, industry also shared enough pertinent information with all working committee delegates so they could both understand and critically evaluate why industry could not agree to consumer and public interest proposals. Equally, the dynamic of Part 6 rule-making ensured that public interest considerations did not supplant the legitimate interests of business. Delegates from consumer and public interest groups were forced to consider the needs of industry into their decision-making processes as well as to explain and give reasons for their positions to the relevant sections of the telecommunications industry.

Whether the three codes of practice developed by the working committees of the Communications Alliance and Part 6 rule-making met the effectiveness ideal of responsiveness—whether they were responsive to the wider interests of consumers and the general public and thus effected change within the telecommunications sector—is not a focus of this book. Nevertheless, it should be noted that consumer and public interest groups obtained some significant, substantive 'wins' as a result of the code development process. For example, consumer and public interest delegates secured provisions dealing with unfair contract terms in the Consumer Contracts code seven years before there was uniform Commonwealth and state legislation dealing with the issue.[89] The IAF code, one of

[89] Uniform legislation prohibiting unfair contract terms did not come into effect until 2011.

the first initiatives of its type worldwide, eventually led to the development of the Global Accessibility Reporting Initiative (GARI), a database with information about accessibility features for mobile phones and other devices that can now be accessed worldwide.[90] The revisions to the MPS code transformed the document so it could be more readily enforced by the state (if ACMA so chose). Additional measures were added to protect consumers from unscrupulous content providers and aggregators. Certainly, the imposition of obligations on various industry actors does not fully answer questions concerning the substantive responsiveness and effectiveness of Part 6 rule-making. A more comprehensive assessment of factors such as industry compliance with both the letter and spirit of the codes as well as their enforcement would at a minimum be necessary. However, the rules provide some evidence that Part 6 rule-making (as a regulatory tool) has some capacity to address power imbalances that previously worked in industry's favour.

IV. Conclusion

This chapter has explored whether the process of Part 6 rule-making was responsive to all of its stakeholders or whether it was 'too responsive' to the needs of participants from the telecommunications industry. It has concluded that the process of Part 6 rule-making was responsive to all interested parties for the same reasons that the process was found to be procedurally and institutionally legitimate in chapter eight: the politic that Part 6 rule-making generated.

The analysis in this chapter has ramifications that are not confined to the Australian telecommunications sector. If, as suggested, the concept of responsiveness has subsumed the concerns that procedural and institutional legitimacy is intended to address, the principles of transparency, impartiality, deliberation and accountability, as defined in chapter eight, provide measures that can be used to evaluate the responsiveness of industry rule-making across numerous business sectors. More fundamentally, the analysis has transformed the four principles of procedural and institutional legitimacy into important regulatory tools. Instead of erecting barriers to the '[fulfilment of] the collective goals justifying regulatory intervention'[91] as many regulatory scholars suggest (implicitly if not explicitly), they facilitate their achievement. As argued above, effectiveness encapsulates the presence of a number of elements, of which responsiveness is but one. However, if responsiveness is a mechanism to achieve effectiveness, as many regulatory scholars assert, then the standards of deliberation (the weighing up of alternatives and determination of what, on balance, meets the needs of all stakeholders),

[90] For more information about GARI, see R Garrett and G Astbrink, 'Are We There Yet? The Struggle for Phone Accessibility Information' (2010) 60(2) *Telecommunications Journal of Australia* 22.2, 22.5–22.6.

[91] Yeung, above n 7, 30.

the exercise of some independent judgement, accountability and transparency among stakeholders also provide some indicia of whether regulatory initiatives in the decentred state will be effective. Indeed, they are key components of effectiveness. They 'nurture'[92] the accomplishment of the regulatory goals set by the state. As this chapter has highlighted, the mechanisms used to ensure that the four principles of responsiveness and effectiveness are met will be different from the mechanisms used by the state to ensure that traditional legislative and administrative rule-making is legitimate. However, the goal of procedural and institutional legitimacy in the centred state and the aim of responsiveness (and therefore effectiveness) in the decentred state share in common the rationales that support the principles of transparency, impartiality, deliberation and accountability.

In addition, the analyses in this chapter and chapter eight, taken together, have identified a way to resolve the tension that has arisen between the responsiveness that regulatory scholars advocate to improve regulatory effectiveness and the principles of procedural and institutional legitimacy that are so cherished by the legal fraternity. They have shown that, if the rationale for industry rule-making is accepted, then the principles used to evaluate whether rule-making is procedurally and institutionally legitimate must, by necessity, be refined. Moreover, the principles can be refined in such a way that they remain true to the underlying goals of these principles in traditional rule-making. Further, the analyses have shown that industry rule-making can be procedurally and institutionally legitimate, even though the mechanisms used to facilitate procedural and institutional legitimacy in legislative and administrative rule-making are absent. Procedural and institutional legitimacy can be achieved by a variety of mechanisms—mechanisms seen in the Part 6 case studies. The analyses have also highlighted that procedural and institutional legitimacy is central to the instrumentalism of industry rule-making.

92 ibid 49.

10

Activating and Sustaining Legitimate and Responsive Industry Rule-making: The State of Play

I. Introduction

This study of Part 6 rule-making in the Australian telecommunications sector has argued that responsiveness, as a regulatory strategy to achieve public policy goals, and procedural and institutional legitimacy are not antithetical concepts. Procedural and institutional legitimacy may have originated in the centred state, and the notion of responsiveness in the decentred state. However, they share in common the rationales that support the principles of transparency, impartiality, deliberation and accountability. Industry rule-making certainly challenges our understanding of the principles of transparency, impartiality and accountability themselves. However, these three principles can be adapted in such a way that they can accommodate the need for industry rule-making yet still require it to be procedurally and institutionally legitimate. The adaptation of these principles also makes it possible for mechanisms other than those associated with traditional rule-making—mechanisms displayed in the three case studies of consumer code development by the Communications Alliance—to facilitate the achievement of procedural and institutional legitimacy. Further, these principles (as refined) embody responsiveness. They provide some concrete measures that can be used to evaluate if and when industry rule-making is responsive to the needs and priorities of its different stakeholders. Understood, respectively, as the weighing up of alternatives and determination of what (on balance) meets the needs of all stakeholders; the exercise of some independent judgement; ensuring all stakeholders explain themselves to others; and disclosure of the information necessary to hold industry and others to account, the principles of deliberation, impartiality, accountability and transparency are transformed into important regulatory tools that assist (rather than hinder) the realisation of public policy goals. The effectiveness of Part 6 rule-making and industry's compliance with Part 6 code rules have not been a focus of this book. However, if responsiveness is a mechanism by which public policy goals are achieved, then the principles of procedural and institutional legitimacy (as refined) also provide some signposts of when regulatory measures will be effective. In addition, these principles may be some of the factors industry takes into account when deciding whether to comply with legally binding industry codes of practice.

Having adapted the principles of procedural and institutional legitimacy to accommodate industry rule-making and having linked these principles (as refined) to responsiveness, this penultimate chapter reflects on what the three case studies of Part 6 rule-making teach us about activating and sustaining legitimate and responsive industry rule-making.

Section II of the chapter discusses the mechanisms observed in the three case studies that contributed to the procedural and institutional legitimacy of the process and its responsiveness to the public interest and the interests of all relevant stakeholders. It identifies a number of indicia that point to when industry rule-making is more likely to be simultaneously legitimate and responsive. Because of the relationship between responsiveness and effectiveness, the indicia also impliedly point to when industry rule-making is more likely to be effective. These indicia may assist legislators, policy-makers, regulators and others to determine if and when industry rule-making ought to be deployed in an effort to resolve the various regulatory problems that confront society and the state. They may also assist industries and industry associations that have been entrusted by legislatures and regulators to formulate rules to develop rule-making processes that can survive scrutiny from regulatory bodies and the general public.

Section III highlights that while the three case studies greatly inform our understanding of the legitimacy and responsiveness of industry rule-making, further in-depth study of industry rule-making in other industry sectors, and social and political contexts, needs to be carried out before we can fully understand how industry rule-making that is both legitimate and responsive can be activated and sustained.

II. The Indicia of Legitimate and Responsive Rule-making

To provide some form of structure to the discussion that follows below, the indicia have been grouped into four categories: the context of rule-making; rule-making participants and their characteristics; the rule-making framework; and the subject matter of rules.

A. The Context of Rule-making

The context in which industry rule-making occurs is important to legitimacy and responsiveness. Three factors need to be considered: the size and structure of the relevant industry, the geographical proximity of industry participants to relevant regulator(s) and others; and a culture within the industry of collaboration with regulators, and consumer and public interest organisations.

i. Industry Size and Structure

It was noted in chapter four that the Australian telecommunications industry is relatively small in global terms and in chapter eight that its size was likely to have contributed to the dynamic of Part 6 rule-making. Rule-making by smaller industries may therefore be more likely to be legitimate and responsive. However, the number of players within the relevant industry and their physical presence within the relevant jurisdiction where industry formulates rules that will be enforced are probably better indicators of legitimate and responsive rule-making than industry size. Industries that are made up of a vast number of small companies may find it difficult to generate and/or sustain the level of dialogue that occurred between the different members of industry and other rule-making participants in the three case studies. Adopting a rule-making framework that mandates working committee members and their delegates to act on behalf of similarly situated bodies rather than exclusively for themselves would, of course, facilitate discourse among a large number of companies.[1] It provides a means of funnelling the views of multiple contributors into the rule-making process. However, from a practical standpoint, there will be some limit beyond which it becomes impractical to coordinate that dialogue. Industry rule-making may therefore be more likely to be legitimate and responsive in industries where market power is concentrated within the hands of a few corporations. The importance of supply chains in the case studies also suggests that rule-making by industries comprised of vertically integrated firms may not be legitimate and responsive. The conflicts between interests are likely to be hidden and/or resolved by the corporate rules and procedures used by managers to regulate disputes in vertically integrated industries. Industries predominantly comprised of foreign-based companies that provide products and/or services to consumers in a relevant jurisdiction, but have no physical presence within it, are also unlikely to engage in any meaningful way with industry rule-making.

ii. Geographical Proximity to Regulator(s) and Others

Notwithstanding the availability of video and voice conferencing, face-to-face meetings are a vital aspect of the code development process. The physical proximity of industry to industry-regulators and other interested parties therefore plays a role in legitimate and responsive rule-making. In the case studies, all of the major providers of telecommunications services were headquartered and/or had offices in the same city as the regulator (the Australian Communications and Media

[1] See further s II.C.ii.a of this chapter (below).

Authority (ACMA)), the industry association (the Communications Alliance), and participating consumer and public interest organisations. The close physical proximity of these bodies to each other made travel to face-to-face meetings much easier and less costly.

iii. Collaborative Culture

Another relevant consideration is the history of some form of collaboration between the industry sector concerned, consumer and public interest organisations and regulators. As argued in chapter eight, a history of collaboration between industry, and consumer and public interest organisations, in particular, can establish powerful expectations that consumer and public interest organisations should be involved in industry rule-making. Had consumer and public interest organisations not been involved in the review of Telecom's privacy monitoring guidelines or the work of the Privacy Advisory Committee that followed the Casualties of Telecom affair discussed in chapter three, it is uncertain if consumer and public interest organisations would have become so intimately involved in Part 6 rule-making. Moreover, the Consumer Contracts and Information on Accessibility Features for Telephone Equipment (IAF) codes were developed when the government still had a majority shareholding in Telstra, the largest provider of fixed-line and mobile services in the Australian telecommunications market. The case study of the Mobile Premium Services (MPS) code suggests that industry rule-making can be legitimate and responsive, even when government is no longer a shareholder of a significant industry participant. However, the legacy of government-ownership will have contributed in some degree to the willingness of industry to work with regulators and Ministers.

B. Rule-making Participants and Their Characteristics

The organisations and individuals that participate in industry rule-making and their attributes are also important indicators of whether industry rule-making will be legitimate and responsive. Five types of organisations and individuals and their attributes are identified here: industry members and their delegates; industry forums and associations; consumer and public interest organisations; regulatory bodies; and the executive government.

i. Industry Members and Their Delegates

As one would expect, participation by the largest member(s) of the relevant industry is essential. However, the characteristics of the delegates they send to working committee meetings and other meetings with regulators are also important. The case studies suggest that delegates should be middle ranking employees who have worked for the relevant company for some period of time. With one exception, all of the delegates who served on the Communications Alliance working committees considered in this book were employed by the companies they represented. Management consultants and other independent contractors, for example, were notably absent from the rule-making process. Delegates also held relatively senior positions and/or had some 'clout' within the companies they represented. As a consequence, they were able to identify the relevant staff from the corporate divisions with a stake in the outcome of the rule-making exercise. In addition, they could trigger and maintain the internal discussion within and between those divisions that was central to the exercise of industry rule-making. However, the delegates were not high enough in the management structure of the companies concerned to bind the corporation on the spot. They had to go back and consult with their colleagues. Had more senior members of the corporate entities, such as CEOs and other board members, participated, they may have been able to bind their employers on the spot without internally consulting their staff. Lack of consultation with staff eliminates the prospect of organisational self-reflection and assessment, both of which are important to the legitimacy and responsiveness of industry rule-making.

ii. Industry Fora and Associations

The willingness of one or more industry fora or associations to embrace and/or assume responsibility for industry rule-making also appears to be necessary. They furnish the arena where rule-making occurs. They provide the physical space in which deliberation can be conducted. In addition, they adopt rule-making frameworks and other procedures that can lend support to the legitimacy and overall responsiveness of industry rule-making.[2] Further, they draw on their detailed knowledge of the relevant industry to determine the composition of working committees. Industry fora and associations may not be able to compel relevant members of industry to join the process but they have useful knowledge that it cannot be assumed that regulators have. Had ACMA (and not the Communications Alliance) determined the members of the working committee for the MPS code, it is likely that aggregators and content providers (important stakeholders) would never have been appointed. It will be recalled that ACMA initially wanted to impose all regulatory obligations on mobile carriage service providers as a result of its misunderstanding of the MPS industry.

However, the industry fora or associations concerned must have some form of reputation to uphold. As the three case studies show, the desire to protect the reputations of these fora or associations can motivate their CEOs to act in ways that contribute to the legitimacy and responsiveness of the industry rule-making process. The importance of reputation suggests that it is preferable for established industry fora and associations than newly formed industry fora and associations to become involved in and lead industry rule-making processes. Newly formed

[2] On the elements of the rulemaking framework, see s II.C of this chapter (below).

industry fora and associations that are less well established arguably have less to lose. Similarly, industry fora or associations with a small number of members and/or whose membership does not include at least one or more significant industry player may not be ideal to lead industry rule-making processes. All of the major players (and many of the smaller players) in the telecommunications services industry were members of the Communications Alliance when the three consumer codes were developed, and industry's support (financial and otherwise) for the Communications Alliance and its rule-making processes were important factors that contributed to the overall legitimacy and responsiveness of the rule-making process.

The relevant fora or associations do not have to be neutral in the sense that they cannot advocate for their industry members in other fora in order for the process to be consistent with the principles of transparency, impartiality, deliberation and accountability (as refined). Neutrality in other fora is one way of ensuring these principles are satisfied. In the Consumer Contracts and IAF codes, it assisted to allay the perceptions of consumer and public interest organisations that the process of industry rule-making was tainted and may have contributed to the robustness of the discussion that took place between the different stakeholders. However, it is not essential for a legitimate and responsive rule-making process. As the MPS case study illustrated, the presence of engaged politicians and regulators, media interest and industry supply chains can collectively (if not individually) serve the same function as neutrality.

iii. Consumer and Public Interest Organisations

The involvement of consumer and public interest organisations on industry working committees is another strong indicator of industry rule-making that is legitimate and responsive. By no means should the views of consumer and public interest organisations be seen as synonymous with the consumer and public interests. Industry is far too complex for the views of consumer and public interest organisations to be accepted without the input of other stakeholders. However, participation by consumer and public interest organisations in industry rule-making from the beginning of the process serves three important functions that are essential for legitimate and responsive rule-making. First, along with other interested parties, they challenge industry. They apply pressure to industry participants to provide reasons for their conduct. They coax industry to think through the actions it proposes to take in order to address the underlying regulatory problem. Second, they keep relevant regulatory bodies and Ministers 'honest'. They push regulatory bodies and Ministers to ask questions of and demand possible solutions from industry. The pressure from regulatory bodies and Ministers contributes to industry's willingness to listen to and consider the concerns of consumer and public interest organisations. Third, the involvement of consumer and public interest organisations in industry rule-making can bring members of industry to the negotiating table. As the case study on the IAF code illustrates, consumer and public interest organisations will fill the vacuum if industry fails to participate in rule-making. In industry's absence, the process will be illegitimate. Consumer and public interest organisations will draft rules that are likely to be too responsive to their own norms, and the fear of a process that is too responsive to consumer and public interest organisations will trigger industry engagement. This function of consumer and public interest organisations is not fully appreciated and is often overlooked.

However, in order for consumer and public interest organisations to participate in a meaningful way, they must be adequately funded either by government or by way of a levy on all relevant industry participants. At a minimum, the travel costs they incur because of their participation on industry working committees or in other activities related to industry rule-making should be paid. Consumer and public interest organisations that do not already receive funding from government to participate in industry rule-making activities should be entitled to recoup the costs of their time. Imposing these costs on industry may provide industry members with greater incentives to participate in industry rule-making from the beginning. Unnecessarily protracted processes, as seen in the IAF code case study, may be avoided. The importance of adequately funding consumer and public interest organisations means that the direct cost of industry rule-making will not necessarily be cheaper than traditional forms of rule-making. However, if consumer and public interest organisations are not financially supported during the rule-making process, there are risks that the dynamic of industry rule-making would be altered quite significantly to the detriment of the legitimacy and responsiveness of the rule-making process. Consumer and public interest organisations would be much less likely to participate. It is also doubtful if public consultation (at least in the form that it took in the three case studies) would serve as an adequate substitute. As the case studies illustrated, in order to contribute meaningfully to the debate, consumer and public interest organisations needed to be educated about the relevant sectors of the industry and their specific practices. Participation in the rule-making process provided that education, giving these organisations the opportunity to think through how consumer and public interests could be addressed in the specific—and often complex—market circumstances. Public consultation permits members of the public to make contributions to the process, and industry may respond in writing to these submissions. However, educating the wider public, thereby allowing its members to make informed contributions to the debate, is not a focus of public consultation. Moreover, public consultation does not provide members of the public with an opportunity to scrutinise industry's responses. It promotes an exchange of monologues rather than triggers any real dialogue.

The status and characteristics of the delegates that consumer and public interest organisations select to participate in industry rule-making is arguably of less importance than those of members of industry. All of the delegates of consumer and public interest organisations in the three case studies were senior employees within the organisations they represented, and the involvement of senior employees of consumer and public interest organisations in industry rule-making is likely to occur by default because their employers have a small number of staff. However, participation by more junior members would be acceptable, provided they are able to put their case to industry; evaluate what industry representatives tell them; and stimulate discussion among the members and employees of their respective consumer and public interest organisations.

iv. Regulatory Bodies

Others have previously suggested that the presence of a 'big stick' or a 'penalty default', such as the threat of an industry standard, is important if industry rule-making is to be responsive.[3] The empirical research carried out for this book supports that view. The Telecommunications Act 1997 (Cth) gives ACMA the power to adopt industry standards if industry fails to develop codes of practice in specific circumstances, including non-compliance with a formal request to develop a code. Industry formulated both the Consumer Contracts and IAF codes after receipt of formal requests to develop those codes from the Australian Communications Authority (ACA) (now ACMA), and the threat of industry standards developed by the ACA affected industry's willingness to engage with the Part 6 rule-making process. However, the research also suggests that the presence of a big stick or penalty default is necessary for the legitimacy of the process. In addition, the research suggests that a big stick or penalty default is important for legitimacy and responsiveness because it is used by other participants to their advantage in the process. In the three case studies, the big stick or penalty default provided the CEO of the Communications Alliance with a powerful rhetorical tool that she could (and did) use against the members of the industry organisation and its working committees. Moreover, the big stick or penalty default worked in conjunction with other (arguably smaller) regulatory sticks and penalty defaults. For example, in the MPS code case study, the Australian Competition and Consumer Commission (ACCC) had the power to take legal action against content service providers for misleading and deceptive conduct under the then Trade Practices Act 1974 (Cth). In the Consumer Contracts code case study, it had the ability to take legal action against carriage service providers for unconscionable conduct. Consumer Affairs Victoria enjoyed the power to enforce the provisions against unfair contract terms under the Fair Trading (Amendment) Act 2003 (Vic). Regulators, policy-makers and legislators therefore need to look beyond any sector-specific regulatory

[3] See, eg, I Ayres and J Braithwaite, *Responsive Regulation: Transcending the Deregulation* Debate (Oxford, Oxford University Press, 1992) ch 4; W Schulz and T Held, *Regulated Self-Regulation as a Form of Modern Government: An Analysis of Case Studies from Media and Telecommunications Law* (Eastleigh, University of Luton Press, 2004) 32, 99; CF Sabel and J Zeitlin, 'Learning from Difference: The New Architecture of Experimentalist Governance in the EU' (2008) 14 *European Law Journal* 271, 308.

arrangement (if applicable), and identify the presence of other regulators (state or federal) and any sticks or defaults they have that may be able to instigate and foster industry engagement in rule-making. The involvement of multiple regulators in industry rule-making may increase the direct costs of the process but it may bring regulatees to and keep them at the negotiating table.

The mere presence of big sticks and penalty defaults, however, will not lead to legitimate and responsive industry rule-making. The regulators who hold those sticks or who may impose those penalty defaults must be (and remain) engaged in the rule-making process. They must also be prepared to wield them. Regulators need not necessarily be as 'hands on' as staff and members of ACMA were in the MPS code case study. They could instead signal that industry agreement with consumer and public interest organisations will serve as a proxy for regulatory approval, as occurred in the Consumer Contracts case study. However, along with their senior management, they must be engaged. They must retain their 'meta-regulatory' responsibility to oversee and referee industry rule-making. Industry rule-making cannot work properly if regulators effectively delegate this important role in the process to industry by failing to become actively involved.

The importance of multiple regulatory sticks or penalty defaults and multiple engaged regulators may also suggest that industry rule-making is more suitable when industry regulators do not share concurrent powers with competition authorities to enforce competition and consumer protection legislation. Segmenting regulatory responsibility creates other regulatory voices whose views (along with those of other participants) must be reconciled by industry. It also renders transparent any conflicts and commonalities of opinion between the different regulatory divisions of a single regulator. These conflicts and commonalities may contribute to the legitimacy and responsiveness of the rule-making process. Again, the involvement of multiple regulators in industry rule-making may increase the direct costs of the process. However, these costs may be outweighed by the benefits of exposing any conflicts between regulators and forcing industry to reconcile them.

v. *The Executive Government*

Some degree of involvement by a Minister whose portfolio covers the relevant industry concerned is more likely to make industry rule-making legitimate and responsive. Similar to participation by regulatory bodies, the forms that Ministerial involvement take can be different. The Minister could be more peripheral to the process as Minister Helen Coonan was in the Consumer Contracts code case study. Equally, the Minister could be more actively involved as Minister Stephen Conroy was in the MPS code case study. However, some level of engagement is preferable. Ministers can apply pressure to discuss and consider the underlying issues, not only to industry but to regulatory bodies as well.

C. The Rule-making Framework

Legislators, policy-makers and regulators also need to be mindful of the framework used by industry to draft rules, as it plays an important role in the legitimacy and responsiveness of the rule-making process. The framework consists of the legislative requirements and/or obligations imposed by the relevant industry fora or associations that regulate industry rule-making. Regardless of whether the framework is set out in statute and/or the internal documentation of industry fora or associations, the three case studies suggest that it must contain certain elements in order for the rule-making process to be legitimate and responsive. Other elements are arguably less vital but their presence nevertheless contributes to the legitimacy and responsiveness of the process. Below, the essential elements are considered first. Consideration of the 'supplemental' elements then follows. The issue of whether some or all of these elements should be incorporated into legislation or are better left in the internal documentation of the relevant industry fora or associations is not discussed. However, it should be noted that the essential elements considered below formed part of the Communication Alliance's Operating Manual.

i. Essential Elements: Representativeness, Consensus and Confidentiality

Industry rule-making frameworks should contain requirements that working committees are 'representative' of all parties with an interest in the underlying rules being formulated. The meaning of representation in this context, however, is different from that used in legislative rule-making. In legislative rule-making, representation is typically understood as acting on behalf of others. Here representation means 'standing for' others, in the sense that working committee members have the same characteristics as the individuals, corporations and other organisations with an interest in the subject matter of the code rules. In other words, working committee members must be 'typical' of all relevant market participants.[4]

If applied correctly, the principle of representativeness ensures that consumer and public interest organisations are brought into the rule-making process and are present when proposed rules are discussed and drafted. It also brings at least one delegate from each member of the relevant industry supply chain (if one exists) to the negotiating table. As the case studies have highlighted, bringing together individuals from a diverse array of organisations and companies who must advocate in their best interests can trigger rigorous dialogue that fosters consideration of all relevant issues and perspectives, a dialogue that is central to legitimacy and the responsiveness endeavour.

[4] HF Pitkin, 'The Concept of Representation' in HF Pitkin (ed), *Representation* (New York, Atherton Press, 1969) 1, 10–11.

In addition to representativeness, industry rule-making frameworks should specify that the working committee operates by way of consensus and that the process must be kept confidential for the period the working committee is in existence.

The requirement to reach consensus confers an entitlement on all members of the working committee to be heard. It assists to negate the inequalities of resource, knowledge and skills that are likely to exist between members of industry, and consumer and public interest organisations. It also appears to neutralise any imbalance in market power that may exist between industry participants.

Making the rule-making process confidential provides industry with confidence to participate in the process. Without it, it is doubtful if industry would willingly become involved in rule formation. It also has the added benefit of reducing the cost of accessing confidential information when such information needs to be exchanged between working committee members, a problem that befalls traditional rule-making as well. However, the scope of any confidentiality provision the rule-making framework contains should not be so wide as to prevent the flow of working committee information within and between the constituencies of working committee members. Delegates from industry (as well as consumer and public interest organisations) should be able to speak freely to their internal staff and the members of their respective constituencies. It is essential they can exchange relevant information with them so informed input is funnelled into the process. As the case studies have shown, stimulating discussion that is wide in its breadth can only increase the number of issues that are brought to and resolved by working committees.

ii. *Supplemental Elements*

a. Role of Members and Their Delegates, Independent Chairs and Information Disclosure Rules

Three additional elements are likely to enhance the legitimacy and responsiveness of industry rule-making. They are: rules mandating that consumer and public interest organisations, and members of industry, once appointed to working committees as representatives, should act for other similar entities rather than exclusively for themselves; rules mandating that working committees be chaired by individuals who are truly independent of all members of the working committee; and rules mandating that members of industry must, where reasonably possible, support assertions that the cost of implementing rules is prohibitive.

Only the MPS code was developed by members of industry and public interest organisations that all acted for other similar entities rather than exclusively for themselves.[5] However, it is preferable that working committee delegates always

[5] Members of the DAB were represented indirectly by Tedicore in the IAF code. However, the other consumer and public interest groups directly represented themselves.

act on behalf of similar bodies, provided, of course, the similar bodies are known to the relevant industry association and/or they are willing to participate in rule-making in some way. Mandating such a role for delegates brings many more voices into the process, which can contest the views of other industry participants, as well as consumer and public interest representatives and regulators. The case studies of the Consumer Contracts and IAF codes certainly suggest that delegates acting solely in the best interests of their particular employers can facilitate legitimate and responsive rule-making. However, specifying delegates perform this role may be better suited to situations, such as the Consumer Contracts code, where the number of market participants or consumer and public interest organisations is relatively small. For markets with a greater number of competitors and situations where there are many consumer and public interest organisations with an interest in the rule-making proceedings, requiring delegates to act on behalf of all similarly situated entities is the only way to include them in the process in any meaningful way.

Two of the three consumer codes of practice—the IAF and the MPS codes—were developed by working committees led by chairs that were not independent or were not perceived to be independent of working committee members. Nevertheless, it was concluded in chapters eight and nine that for reasons unrelated to the actions of the working committee chairs, the processes by which these codes were adopted were procedurally and institutionally legitimate and responsive. It is difficult therefore to conclude that the independence of the working committee chair is essential for legitimate and responsive rule-making.[6] However, as the Consumer Contracts code illustrates, an independent chair can support the deliberative process in a way that chairs that are seen to be allied with the interests of industry or consumer and public interest organisations simply cannot. For this reason, use of an independent chair should be seen as an indicator of legitimate and responsive rule-making.

The suggestion that a rule that supports the disclosure of information (especially cost data) is indicative of the legitimacy and responsiveness of the rule-making process stems from the qualified conclusion in chapter eight that the Part 6 process was transparent. The conclusion was qualified, in part, because of the lack of data available to consumer and public interest delegates to evaluate industry assertions that proposed rules were too costly to implement and therefore could not be adopted. It has already been acknowledged that not all costs incurred as a result of the adoption of new regulatory rules can be quantified. However, for costs that can be quantified, a requirement that industry must demonstrate that

[6] On the role of independent chairs in corporate governance generally, see, eg, C Coglianese, 'Legitimacy and Corporate Governance' (2007) 32 *Delaware Journal of Corporate Law* 159, 162–64; ASX Corporate Governance Council, *Corporate Governance Principles and Recommendations* 3rd edn (2014) 14–18.

it has obtained quotations for the relevant work would arguably strengthen the legitimacy and responsiveness of the process. It would buttress the robustness of the dialogue between members of working committees and the ability of members to hold industry to account.

b. Public Consultation?

Public participation may be one of the easiest requirements for legislators, policy-makers and regulators to specify in the rule-making framework. However, public participation (at least in the form it took in the case studies) does not appear to play a significant role in the realisation of legitimacy and responsiveness. Legislators, policy-makers and regulators should therefore be wary of accepting arguments by industry that rule-making is legitimate and responsive because it permits members of the public to make written submissions on draft rules. Rates of written submissions in all three codes of practice studied were low. Moreover, even if the number of submissions from private individuals and organisations could be increased, the case studies suggest that any comments submitted would not contribute much (if anything) to the process unless they raised new arguments not previously considered by working committee members. This circumstance is likely to be relatively rare if private individuals are not given access to the information exchanged between working committee members before they make their written submissions. Perhaps, more importantly, written submissions do not permit private individuals to question industry in the same way that the delegates of consumer and public interest organisations were able to during working committee meetings. The limited form of scrutiny written submissions provide may have much greater significance in circumstances where consumer and public interests are not appointed to industry working committees. Altering its form so that there is a greater degree of interaction between the public and working committee members may also make public participation a good indicator of legitimacy and responsiveness. However, the case studies suggest that the involvement of consumer and public interest representatives is optimal for achieving these objectives.

D. The Subject Matter of Rules

Finally, the subject matter of the rules that industry is expected to draft may be an indicator of whether the underlying process that formulates them can be legitimate and responsive. As the MPS case study highlights, some subject matter is more likely to attract attention from the media, and the media can positively influence industry rule-making. They can encourage industry to begin the process of industry rule-making. They can also encourage industry, Ministers and regulators to continue and complete the necessary dialogue with each other, and consumer and public interest organisations.

III. Matters Requiring Further Empirical Investigation

The three case studies of Part 6 rule-making suggest that there are a number of elements that determine if industry rule-making will be simultaneously legitimate and responsive. However, legislators, policy-makers, regulators and others should be aware that the indicia the case studies reveal are by no means exhaustive. Before a comprehensive list of indicia could be drafted, more in-depth empirical study of industry rule-making is required. The particular matters necessitating additional investigation are considered below. They fall into two categories: questions that relate to activating legitimate and responsive rule-making; and questions that pertain to sustaining legitimate and responsive rule-making.

A. Activating Legitimate and Responsive Rule-making

The first (and perhaps the most important) issue relating to activating legitimate and responsive rule-making is whether the conditions that contributed to the legitimacy and responsiveness of the Part 6 process were unique; or if they can be reliably invoked in other instances of industry rule-making. In other words, are the conditions identified relevant only to the Australian telecommunications sector or do they have wider application to other industry sectors within Australia and/or different countries? Some conditions may be more relevant to particular industry sectors, and to different social and political contexts. Other conditions may be applicable to all industry sectors and in multiple countries.

Other important questions relating to the conditions that contributed to the legitimacy and responsiveness of the Part 6 process are: whether any particular indicator may be applied singularly and/or in combination with others; or whether the indicia must be applied cumulatively, in order for industry rule-making to be legitimate and responsive? These questions arise because the three case studies of Part 6 rule-making suggest that there is a pattern of interaction between the indicia that renders industry rule-making legitimate and responsive. Each of the factors identified above contributed in some way to the legitimacy and responsiveness of Part 6 rule-making. However, no one factor by itself made Part 6 rule-making legitimate and responsive. Again, the pattern of interaction between factors required for legitimate and responsive rule-making may differ depending on particular social and political contexts and the industry sector involved. Finally, are there mechanisms (other than the ones found in the Australian telecommunications context) that might contribute to the legitimacy and responsiveness of industry rule-making? If so, how do they contribute and in which circumstances?

B. Sustaining Legitimate and Responsive Rule-making

If confidentiality is essential to the legitimacy and responsiveness of industry rule-making, as suggested earlier, an initial question relating to sustaining legitimate and responsive rule-making is whether there is a risk that over time confidentiality will lead to a form of 'dishonest corporatism'[7] to the detriment of consumer and public interests. If collusion between consumer and public interest groups, industry participants and regulators is to be avoided, which mechanisms best stimulate and ensure legitimacy and responsiveness in the long run? For example, can the ability of individual consumers and small businesses to make complaints about industry service provision to ombudsmen, the media, local representatives and relevant ministers mitigate the risk of participants becoming captured by the rule-making process? Can provisions in the constitutions of consumer and public interest organisations help deter the possibility of capture by their working committee representatives? Can making government funding of consumer and public interest organisations conditional on periodic review also be used to reduce the possibility of capture of these organisations by industry interests? Can the decision-making structures of participating regulatory bodies, imposed by statute, contribute to minimising the risk of exclusion of relevant interests that confidential rule-making may bring about over time?

In addition to the issue of dishonest corporatism, two different but related queries arise. The first is whether industry can maintain the momentum for legitimate and responsive rule-making over longer time periods. The second is whether subsequent industry working committees 'learn'[8] from earlier industry working committees. Both concerns arise for the following reasons. First, the working committees of the Communications Alliance considered in the case studies were established on a case-by-case basis and generally in response to external factors, including formal requests to develop codes addressing the existence (or perception) of significant regulatory problems; or legislative change. Second, the rule-making framework of the Communications Alliance dictates that working committees are disbanded once a code of practice is adopted, and there is no apparent mechanism that enables or encourages industry working committee members to reflect on, or disseminate to others, any knowledge gained during the process of rule-making. Third, the individual industry representatives who were directly involved in rule-making may subsequently leave their employers, leading to a loss of corporate history and knowledge. The presence of each of these factors may decrease the likelihood that the momentum for legitimacy

[7] See, eg, M Shapiro, 'Dishonest Corporatism: Who Guards the Guardians in an Age of Soft Law and Negotiated Regulation?' in MK Landy, MA Levin and M Shapiro (eds), *Creating Competitive Markets: The Politics of Regulatory Reform* (Washington, DC, Brookings Institution Press, 2007) 319.

[8] See, eg, O De Schutter and J Lenoble (eds), *Reflexive Governance: Redefining the Public Interest in a Pluralistic World* (Oxford, Hart Publishing, 2010).

and responsiveness is sustainable after industry codes are adopted; and may limit opportunities for collective learning and/or capacity building within industry—opportunities that are essential according to democratic experimentalism (an influential strategy of proceduralization) and other theories of 'learning-based governance'.[9] ACMA has made periodic review of codes by bodies or associations representing sections of the telecommunications industry a condition of code registration under Part 6 since 1998,[10] and in each of the three codes studied, code review requirements were imposed by the relevant code working committees.[11] Moreover, the Communications Alliance has developed a 'document maintenance policy' that specifies the process by which Part 6 codes are reviewed.[12] However, detailed empirical study of the code review process; and the working committees (if any) established to revise Part 6 codes of practice (as well as comparable practices in other industries and countries) is needed before we can begin to properly address either question.

IV. Conclusion

When applying the indicia identified in this chapter, it is important to remember that the three case studies of Part 6 rule-making suggest that the indicia must be applied cumulatively rather than independently in order to stimulate industry rule-making that is legitimate and responsive. Each of the factors contributed in some way to the legitimacy and responsiveness of Part 6 rule-making, but no single factor rendered Part 6 rule-making legitimate and responsive. It is possible that the precise pattern of interaction between the factors required for legitimate and responsive industry rule-making will differ in other industry sectors and jurisdictions. However, the three case studies of Part 6 rule-making indicate that the presence of many of these factors may not be sufficient to ensure that industry rule-making processes are legitimate and responsive. All factors may need to be present. In addition, legislators, policy-makers, regulators and others should be aware that there may be mechanisms (other than the ones found in the Australian

[9] ibid xvi–xxiii.

[10] See, eg, ACA, *Registering Telecommunications Industry Codes—A Guide* (July 1998) 8.

[11] The Consumer Contracts code stipulated review two years from the date it was registered and subsequently every five years. The IAF code mandated the code had to be reviewed 18 months after the date of registration and then every five years; and the accompanying guidelines had to be reviewed 'at least annually'. It also stipulated that review of the accompanying guidelines had to be conducted by representatives of ACMA, equipment suppliers, carriage service providers and organisations representing people with disabilities. The MPS code required review 'after 1 July 2010 and every 5 years subsequently, or earlier in the event of significant developments that impact on the code, or as otherwise determined by the Communications Alliance'.

[12] See, eg, Communications Alliance, *Document Maintenance Policy and Process* (May 2008).

telecommunications context) that might simultaneously achieve legitimacy and responsiveness. They should not discount the possibility of factors, unique to their political and social contexts, and the specific industry sector(s) in question, which may help industry rule-making processes to satisfy the requirements of transparency, impartiality, deliberation and accountability (as refined). Legislators, policy-makers, regulators and others also need to be cognisant of the fact that mechanisms other than those identified in this chapter may be required to ensure that the legitimacy and responsiveness of industry rule-making can be maintained in the long run; and additional empirical research is needed to determine what they might be.

11

Conclusion

To conclude, three important points that are implicit in the book need to be made explicit, because they are central to its message and/or the lessons of the case studies. Readers are asked to keep them in mind when engaging with the ideas the book contains.

First, industry rule-making can at once be legitimate and responsive. However as this book has shown, the rationales that legitimacy and responsiveness share in common impose important conditions on industry rule-making processes. Moreover, satisfying those requirements involves a complex balancing act between an array of factors, some or many of which may not be present in the specific industry sectors where governments, legislatures and policy-makers are contemplating permitting or have already authorised industry rule-making. The book has also highlighted that while these factors may be sufficient to stimulate industry rule-making that is legitimate and responsive, they may not be enough to foster legitimate and responsive rule-making on a continuing basis. It is for this reason that governments, legislatures, policy-makers and others are urged to give greater attention to identifying, and understanding the interaction between, the non-traditional legal mechanisms that are likely to ensure that industry deliberates; discloses sufficient information to enable others to hold it to account; considers the relevant concerns of others before it reaches its decisions; and explains and justifies its positions.

Second, lawyers and others may find it difficult to accept the argument developed in chapter 8 that the mechanisms that are thought to ensure procedural and institutional legitimacy in legislative and administrative rule-making can be divorced from the four principles of procedural and institutional legitimacy—the principles of transparency, impartiality, deliberation and accountability. They may continue to hold the view that absent tools such as the hard look doctrine, judicial review, 'disinterested and professional'[1] administrative decision-makers and the other mechanisms identified in chapter three, industry rule-making can never be legitimate. However, to continue to tether the principles of procedural and institutional legitimacy exclusively to these traditional mechanisms not only allows tools that could be used (and are being used successfully) to promote the underlying rationales for transparency, impartiality, deliberation and

[1] LL Jaffe, 'Law Making by Private Groups' (1937) 51 *Harvard Law Review* 201, 248.

accountability in the industry rule-making context to be overlooked. It also runs the risk of making the four principles irrelevant to industry, because the mechanisms thought to ensure procedural and institutional legitimacy in legislative and administrative rule-making are not features of industry rule-making and are not likely to be. Such an approach is particularly dangerous in a forum where the procedural and institutional values of the rule of law remain as important as ever. As has been argued in chapter nine, the concept of responsiveness must be tied explicitly to the essential rationales of transparency, impartiality, deliberation and accountability. Otherwise, responsiveness simply becomes a word, devoid of meaning, that gives governments, legislatures and industry scope to assert they are being responsive while at the same time permitting consumer and public interests to be ignored. Ambiguity has surrounded the concept of responsiveness. However, by drawing attention to the link between responsiveness and the fundamentals of procedural and institutional legitimacy, it is hoped that governments, legislatures, policy-makers, industry and others will have a clearer set of standards to work toward when they design and evaluate industry rule-making processes.

Finally, the empirical study of industry rule-making and its capacity (or otherwise) to acknowledge and address consumer and public interests continue to deserve more attention from legal and regulatory scholars than they have received to date. As the case studies of Part 6 rule-making have illustrated, industry associations and other rule-making fora have become sites where public policy decisions with important ramifications for consumers and citizens are made. The significance of these fora is only likely to grow in the future, as governments, legislatures and administrative agencies increasingly turn to industry actors to find solutions to a raft of on-going, and often complex, regulatory problems. Moreover, unless industry rule-making bodies engage adequately with consumer and public interest concerns, the promise of enhanced regulatory effectiveness that prompts governments, legislatures and administrative agencies to experiment with industry rule-making will never be realised.

APPENDIX: METHODOLOGY

In order to assess whether the Part 6 rule-making process satisfied the procedural and institutional demands of the rule of law, a historical qualitative case study methodology was used in each of the three case studies. The methodology combined 'informal' document analysis[1] of the files, held by the Communications Alliance, of the first versions[2] of Consumer Contracts, Information on Accessibility Features for Telephone Equipment (IAF) and Mobile Premium Services (MPS) codes that had been registered by the Australian Communications Authority (ACA) or the Australian Communications and Media Authority (ACMA) but were no longer in force; and semi-structured interviews of individuals who had represented members of the relevant working committees. The files held by the Communications Alliance for each of the three consumer codes consisted of meeting agenda, details of the working committee members, all drafts of the relevant code, committee meeting papers, including the minutes of meetings, the original project proposal and the working committee's terms of reference.

As explained briefly below, the decisions to adopt a historical qualitative case study approach and to study the Consumer Contracts, IAF and MPS codes were dictated primarily by the confidentiality of the Communication Alliance's code development process; the record keeping of the Communications Alliance; and the confidentiality obligations with which ACMA must comply. These constraints certainly added to the concerns identified in chapter 3 that the process may not be procedurally and institutionally legitimate. Nevertheless, the historical qualitative case study methodology used provided robust data about the process of Part 6 rule-making that enabled sound conclusions about the procedural and institutional legitimacy of Part 6 rule-making (and industry rule-making more generally) to be drawn.

I. Choice of Methodology

An ethnographic study of Part 6 rule-making was not possible. Since April 2000 the Communications Alliance has made compliance with an obligation of

[1] A Peräkylä and J Ruusuvuori, 'Analyzing Talk and Text' in NK Denzin and YS Lincoln (eds), *The Sage Handbook of Qualitative Research*, 5th edn (Thousand Oaks, CA, Sage Publications, 2018) 669, 670.

[2] The term 'first version of a code' as used in this appendix means a code dealing with a particular subject matter that was addressed by a working committee of the Communications Alliance for the first time.

confidentiality an express condition of participation by working committee delegates.[3] The precise wording of the confidentiality obligation was slightly modified in 2007.[4] However, under both formulations, working committee delegates are in essence required to keep working committee discussions and documentation confidential unless they need to report to or seek approval from the organisations they represent. In June 2010, the CEO of the Communications Alliance invited me to observe the steering group and working committees responsible for the review of the Telecommunications Consumer Protection (TCP) code.[5] However, my ability to sit as an observer was made dependent upon the agreement of all members of the Steering Group, comprised of representatives from industry, regulatory bodies and one consumer organisation; and not all members agreed. One or more members of the Steering Group were 'uncomfortable' with the idea.[6]

As a result of the Steering Group's decision, it was decided the historical qualitative case study approach used would be adopted for several reasons. Qualitative case studies offer richness and specificity. Consumer and public interest representatives involved in the development of consumer codes of practice had made plenty of assertions about the difficulties they faced during the process. However, the statements made by these groups were often not supported by any detailed examples of why reform was necessary and/or did not address or consider possible explanations for industry's behaviour.[7] Moreover, even if plenty of anecdotes had been publicly available, they are, as Cheit argued in his study of technical standard-setting by public and private bodies in the US, of limited value if one is trying to fully understand the 'quasi-political'[8] process by which consumer codes are developed. They are 'impressionistic'[9] at best and often taken out of the context in which they arose. In addition, there was a perception that participants needed 'space' to comment frankly on the process. A review of publicly available information on code development had indicated that the process was contentious and polarising. Use of codes no longer in force was therefore thought to avoid

[3] See ACIF, *Operating Manual for the Development of Codes, Standards, Specifications, Guidelines and Other Supporting Arrangements* (April 2000) cl 4.8.3. Representatives may have been subject to an implied equitable obligation of confidentiality prior to April 2000.

[4] Communications Alliance, *Operating Manual for the Development of Industry Codes, Standards and Supplementary Documents and the Establishment and Operation of Advisory Groups* (June 2007) cl 3.2.

[5] Communications Alliance, *Industry Code C628:2007: Telecommunications Consumer Protections Code* (2007).

[6] Email from J Stanton, CEO, Communications Alliance, to author (24 June 2010).

[7] See, eg, Consumer Driven Communications Group, *Consumer Driven Communications: Strategies for Better Representation (Final Report)* (December 2004); D Wilding, 'In the Shadow of the Pyramid: Consumers in Communications Self-Regulation' (2005) 55(2) *Telecommunications Journal of Australia* 37, 42–44.

[8] RE Cheit, *Setting Safety Standards* (Berkeley, University of California Press, 1990) 6.

[9] Ibid 244 (note 12).

some of the sensitivities for the sections of the telecommunications industry, consumer and public interest representatives and regulatory bodies involved. Concentrating on first versions of codes was driven by a working hypothesis that initial code formation was more difficult than rule revision. Finally, it was anticipated that analysis of Communications Alliance code documentation alone (no matter how detailed) would only partially tell the story of the code development process. Therefore, interviews with working committee delegates and others involved in the process were also needed.

II. Selection of the Three Codes for In-depth Study

When the project was first being scoped in August 2007, I learned that, with the exception of the material related to the Consumer Contracts and IAF codes, the Communications Alliance did not have the files for the first versions of all consumer codes that had been registered by the ACA. (The MPS code was not drafted and registered with ACMA until 2009.) ACMA was contacted in April 2010 in the hope that it had the relevant documentation, as it was a non-voting member of the relevant working committees and it had its own files relating to the registration of all consumer codes. However, in May 2010, the then chair of ACMA, Chris Chapman, declined to assist with and/or participate in the research project, citing ACMA's obligations of confidentiality under Part 7A of the Australian Communications and Media Authority Act 2005 (Cth).[10] As a result of the chair's decision, I had to rely on documentation held by the Communications Alliance. As the Communications Alliance had files for the first versions of only the Consumer Contracts, IAF and MPS codes, these codes became the object of inquiry.

III. Identifying and Locating Interview Participants

The names of individuals who had served as representatives on working committees were identified from the Consumer Contracts, IAF and MPS codes, copies of which were publicly available on the websites of the Communications Alliance and the ACA or ACMA. Many individuals no longer worked for the companies

[10] Part 7A permits disclosure of information given in confidence to ACMA in connection with its statutory functions or obtained by ACMA as a result of the exercise of its statutory powers, including information obtained as a result of the exercise of its powers under Part 6 of the Telecommunications Act 1997 (Cth), only in specified circumstances.

they represented and some (but not all) were located after lengthy Facebook, LinkedIn and Internet searches. The Communications Alliance assisted in locating some participants. It forwarded a letter, prepared by me, inviting participation in the research project to those individuals who had served on one of the working committees for whom it had contact details. Regulatory delegates from the Australian Competition and Consumer Commission (ACCC) and Telecommunications Industry Ombudsman (TIO) were contacted once permission and support for the project from the ACCC and the relevant ombudsman were obtained. Interestingly, the ACCC, which is subject to confidentiality obligations similar to those of ACMA,[11] was willing to permit its staff to assist with the research project (if they so chose). No individual who represented the ACA and/or ACMA on the three relevant working committees was contacted about an interview because the chair of ACMA would not assist with the research.

IV. Conduct of Interviews

All interviews centred on an indicative list of questions provided to interviewees in advance. The questions were designed to solicit information that addressed the issues of participants, strategies and bias—the core elements of Schattschneider's theory of the scope of political conflict used to characterise the politic of Part 6 rule-making and explained in chapter four. Follow-up questions, tailored to what interview participants said, were posed. Interview participants were also given latitude to identify and discuss what they thought was relevant to an understanding of how and why a particular code emerged. Most of the interviews were conducted in person although one was carried out over the telephone and another via video-Skype. Most interviews lasted for approximately one hour but sometimes continued for two. All interviews were conducted on a one-on-one basis although two individuals from one organisation insisted they be interviewed together. Interviews were held after all documentation relevant to a particular code was reviewed and took place in a variety of locations throughout Australia. The interviews for the Consumer Contracts code took place in March and April 2011. Interviews for the IAF and MPS codes were held in February, March and April 2012. All individuals interviewed spoke in their individual capacities and their views were not necessarily shared by the organisations they represented. When interviews with delegates to the MPS code working committee commenced, the first version of the MPS code had been deregistered by ACMA. All interviewees therefore spoke about versions of codes that were no longer in force at the time of interview.

[11] Competition and Consumer Act 2010 (Cth) s 155AAA.

All interviews were also conducted after clarification was provided by the Communications Alliance that none of the questions to be posed to interviewees raised issues of confidentiality. Clarification was sought because various organisations and individuals involved in Part 6 rule-making held conflicting and inconsistent understandings of the scope and duration of the obligation of confidentiality owed by working committee delegates. Importantly, for the integrity of the research, the Communications Alliance did not ask for any topic to be added, deleted or amended.

V. The Limitations of the Research

All three case studies dealt with a particular subject matter that had been addressed by a working committee of the Communications Alliance for the first time and had been registered by the ACA or ACMA under Part 6. However, as was explained in chapter seven, the working committee established to draft the MPS code was tasked with revising the Mobile Premium Services Self-Regulatory (MPSI) Scheme, drafted by the Mobile Marketing Council of the Australian Direct Marketing Association (ADMA) and the Australian Mobile Telecommunications Association (AMTA), in 2006. Unlike the MPS working committee, the working committees for the Consumer Contracts and IAF codes drafted code rules from scratch. An argument could therefore be made that any comparison of the politic of the MPS code with the dynamic of the Consumer Contracts and IAF codes is not truly 'like for like'. Rather, the development of the MPS code is more akin to a review of an existing code first prepared by the Communications Alliance. While that may be true, it must be remembered that the central question that the case studies was seeking to answer was whether Part 6 rule-making was procedurally and institutionally legitimate. Neither the Communications Alliance nor the Telecommunications Act 1997 (Cth) makes any procedural distinction between codes that are developed for the first time and codes that are revised. The Communications Alliance requires all working committees to comply with the same rule-making model outlined in chapter three. Consequently, even though the context in which the MPS code was developed may differ, the case study still provides important and relevant data needed to answer the legitimacy question.

The three case studies relate to the drafting, public comment and content approval phases of code development. However, within the Communications Alliance, code development occurs in accordance with a five-stage procedure consisting of (1) a proposal phase; (2) a drafting phase; (3) a public comment phase; (4) a content approval phase, which involves formal voting by members of the relevant working committee; and (5) a process approval phase. As its name suggests, during the proposal phase, problems and issues to be addressed within a code are identified and internal approval for code development is obtained.

Historically, the board of the Communications Alliance gave permission for working committees to be established although, since 24 May 2005, the CEO determines if approval is granted. Working committee members are also selected during the proposal phase. The process approval phase, on the other hand, involves the CEO's submission of a code completed by a working committee to the board for its endorsement. During this phase, the board decides whether to submit the relevant code to ACMA for registration.

It was recognised that how issues are framed, who formulates them and how members of working committees are selected to resolve them could have important effects on the work committees undertake. However, it is the aspects of rule-making that encompass the drafting, public comment and content approval phases—the phases considered in the three case studies—that have been the principal focus of legal academic study of the procedural and institutional legitimacy of 'law-making' by legislators and administrative bodies. Further, the board plays a very limited role in code development. Although the central concern of the board in the process approval phase is whether the working committee has complied with the organisation's rule-making model, the board has generally just sought assurances to that effect from the CEO and/or the working committee itself rather than undertake its own review. If a procedural irregularity is identified, it has to direct the working committee to resume work from the stage where the procedural error occurred.[12] The board has no authority to amend the content of a code. It can only accept or reject a code in its entirety.[13] The three case studies therefore concentrate on those aspects of the rule-making process of the Communications Alliance that are central to a study of procedural and institutional legitimacy of Part 6 rule-making.

All documentation provided by the Communications Alliance for each code was examined. However, the minutes of each working committee proved to be the most useful, as they noted (in varying levels of detail) the substantive issues discussed by individual representatives as well as their specific concerns and respective positions. The minutes were drafted contemporaneously by the project manager assigned to each working committee by the Communications Alliance. There is a possibility that they contain some omissions and/or do not accurately reflect the full discussion of the subject matter by committee delegates. It is also conceivable that that they are biased towards the Communications Alliance and/or its members, as they were drafted by employees of the Communications Alliance. However, these risks were significantly reduced by the fact that project managers circulated draft minutes to all working committee members for their

[12] Communications Alliance, *Operating Manual for the Development of Industry Codes, Standards and Supplementary Documents and the Establishment and Operation of Advisory Groups* (June 2007) s 8.3.

[13] Ibid s 8.2.

comment and approval. It is documented in the minutes of one meeting of the MPS code working committee that a consumer and public interest representative was too busy to read the draft minutes of the previous meeting but approved them anyway. In addition, during interviews, some consumer and public interest representatives said there was a limit as to how much time and energy they could devote to minute review. Nevertheless, it was concluded that the possibility of the minutes containing serious errors or omissions that would detract from their reliability as a source of information for the book was remote. They were entirely consistent with statements made by working committee representatives who were interviewed from consumer and public interest organisations about the process.

Not all working committee representatives for each of the three codes were interviewed. In some instances, they could not be located; in other cases, they were contacted but declined to participate in the project. Every effort was made to interview at least one delegate from each member of the three working committees but again this was not possible because of difficulty tracking all delegates down and/or their wish not to become involved with the research. In the end, nine of the 22 individuals who represented the voting and non-voting members of the Consumer Contracts code; six of the 13 delegates to the IAF code and four of the six delegates to the MPS code were interviewed. Committee chairs and project managers were also interviewed. Despite the inability to interview all delegates, it was possible to interview some industry delegates and some individuals who had represented consumer and public interests for each code. Thus, the three case studies incorporate and reflect the perspectives of industry, consumer and public interest participants in the process. They provide a balanced account of the process from which sound conclusions about the procedural and institutional legitimacy of the Part 6 rule-making can be drawn.

With the exception of two individuals, all participants who agreed to be interviewed were willing to have the discussion audio-recorded thus ensuring an accurate record of the conversation. When permission was not given, handwritten notes were made during those interviews and additional memos were prepared immediately after them. Two individuals agreed to be interviewed provided that they had an opportunity to review a draft of the relevant case study and correct factual errors. One individual made minor comments, which have been incorporated into the relevant case study. The three codes studied were also prepared many years ago. The Consumer Contracts code was developed between May and December 2004 (seven years before interviews were conducted); the IAF code between April 2004 and November 2005 (again seven years before interviews were conducted) and the MPS code between April 2008 and March 2009 (three years before interviews were conducted). It was inevitable the recollections of delegates had waned and not all interview participants were able to answer all of the questions asked. No interviewees requested a copy of the relevant code development documentation in advance of interviews to refresh their memories. A copy of the documentation was also not offered to individuals before interviews; it was unrealistic to expect that busy professionals would be able to find the time to read it. However, all factual statements made by interviewees were corroborated, wherever possible, by the available documentation and/or other interviewees. Statements of fact that were blatantly inconsistent with the documentation were disregarded. It was also not possible to verify if everything interview participants said was truthful; however, there was nothing to indicate that any interview participant was dishonest.

SELECT BIBLIOGRAPHY

Articles/Books/Book Chapters/Conference and Working Papers

Abramson HI, 'A Fifth Branch of Government: The Private Regulators and Their Constitutionality' (1989) 16 *Hastings Constitutional Law Quarterly* 165

Adler MD and Dorf MC, 'Constitutional Existence Conditions and Judicial Review' (2003) 89 *Virginia Law Review* 1105

Airo–Farulla G and White S, 'Separation of Powers, 'Traditional' Administration and Responsive Regulation' (2004) 4 *Macquarie Law Journal* 57

Aman Jr AC, 'Globalization, Democracy, and the Need for a New Administrative Law' (2002) 49 *University of California at Los Angeles Law Review* 1687

Ansell C and Gash A, 'Collaborative Governance in Theory and Practice' (2008) 18 *Journal of Public Administration Theory and Practice* 543

Aranson PH, Gelhorn E and Robinson GO, 'A Theory of Legislative Delegation' (1982) 68 *Cornell Law Review* 1

Argument S, 'Delegated Legislation' in Groves M and Lee HP (eds), *Australian Administrative Law* (Cambridge, Cambridge University Press, 2007) 134–42

Arthurs HW, 'Rethinking Administrative Law: A Slightly Dicey Business' (1979) 17 *Osgoode Hall Law Journal* 1

Asimow M, 'Delegated Legislation: United States and United Kingdom' (1983) 3 *Oxford Journal of Legal Studies* 253

Ayres I and Braithwaite J, *Responsive Regulation: Transcending the Deregulation Debate* (Oxford, Oxford University Press, 1992)

Baggott R, 'Regulatory Reform in Britain: The Changing Face of Self–Regulation' (1989) 67 *Public Administration* 435

Baldwin R, 'Regulation: After 'Command and Control'' in Hawkins K (ed), *The Human Face of Law: Essays in Honour of Donald Harris* (Oxford, Clarendon Press, 1997) 64–84

——, *Rules and Government* (Oxford, Clarendon Press, 1997)

——, 'Legislation and Rule–making' in Cane P and Tushnet M (eds), *The Oxford Handbook of Legal Studies* (Oxford, Oxford University Press, 2003) 727–47

Baldwin R and Black J, 'Really Responsive Regulation' (2008) 71 *The Modern Law Review* 59

Baldwin R, Cave M and Lodge M, *Understanding Regulation: Theory, Strategy, and Practice* 2nd edn (Oxford, Oxford University Press, 2012)

Baldwin R and Houghton J, 'Circular Arguments: The Status and Legitimacy of Administrative Rules' (1986) *Public Law* 239

Baldwin R, Scott C and Hood C, *A Reader on Regulation* (Oxford, Oxford University Press, 1998)

Balleisen EJ, 'The Prospects for Effective Coregulation in the United States: A Historian's View from the Early Twenty–First Century' in Balleisen EJ and Moss DA (eds), *Government and Markets: Toward a New Theory of Regulation* (New York, Cambridge University Press, 2010) 443–81

Balleisen EJ and Eisner M, 'The Promise and Pitfalls of Co–Regulation: How Governments Can Draw on Private Governance for Public Purpose' in Moss D and Cisternino J (eds), *New Perspectives on Regulation* (Cambridge, MA, The Tobin Project, 2009) 129–51

Bamforth N, 'The Scope of Judicial Review: Still Uncertain' (1993) *Public Law* 239

Bamforth N and Leyland P (eds), *Public Law in a Multi–Layered Constitution* (Oxford, Hart Publishing, 2003)

Bar–Siman–Tov I, 'Legislative Supremacy in the United States?: Rethinking the "Enrolled Bill" Doctrine' (2009) 97 *Georgetown Law Journal* 323

——, 'Lawmakers as Lawbreakers' (2010) 52 *William and Mary Law Review* 805

——, 'The Puzzling Resistance to Judicial Review of the Legislative Process' (2011) 91 *Boston University Law Review* 1915

Beermann JM, 'Administrative–Law Like Obligations on Private[Ized] Entities' (2002) 49 *University of California at Los Angeles Law Review* 1717

Beisheim M, 'Private Governance: Private Rules for Privatization' in Von Weizacker EU, Young OR and Finger M (eds), *Limits to Privatization: How to Avoid Too Much of Good Thing* (London, Earthscan, 2005) 328–77

Berglund C and Matti S, 'Citizen and Consumer: The Dual Role of Individuals in Environmental Policy' (2006) 15 *Environmental Politics* 550

Biggins J and Scott C, 'Public–Private Relation in a Transnational Private Regulatory Regime: ISDA, the State and OTC Derivatives Market Reform' (2012) 13 *European Business Organisation Law Review* 309

Bingham LB, 'The Next Generation of Administrative Law: Building the Legal Infrastructure for Collaborative Governance' (2010) 2010 *Wisconsin Law Review* 297

Bingham T, *The Rule of Law* (London, Allen Lane, 2010)

Birkinshaw P, 'Corporatism and Accountability' in Cox A and O'Sullivan N (eds), *The Corporate State: Corporatism and the State Tradition in Western Europe* (Aldershot, Edward Elgar, 1988) 48–69

Birkinshaw P, Harden I and Lewis N, *Government by Moonlight: The Hybrid Parts of the State* (London, Unwin Hyman, 1990)

Black J, 'Constitutionalising Self–Regulation' (1996) 59 *The Modern Law Review* 24

——, *Rules and Regulators* (Oxford, Clarendon Press, 1997)

——, 'Reviewing Regulatory Rules: Responding to Hybridisation' in Black J, Muchlinski P and Walker P (eds), *Commercial Regulation and Judicial Review* (Oxford, Hart Publishing, 1998) 123–57

——, 'Proceduralizing Regulation: Part I' (2000) 20 *Oxford Journal of Legal Studies* 597

——, 'Decentring Regulation: Understanding the Role of Regulation and Self–Regulation in a "Post–Regulatory" World' (2001) 54 *Current Legal Problems* 103

——, "Proceduralizing Regulation: Part II' (2001) 21 *Oxford Journal of Legal Studies* 33

——, 'Critical Reflections on Regulation' (2002) 27 *Australian Journal of Legal Philosophy* 1

——, 'Constructing and Contesting Legitimacy and Accountability in Polycentric Regulatory Regimes' (2008) 2 *Regulation & Governance* 137

——, 'Legitimacy and the Competition for Regulatory Share' (Law, Society and Economy Working Paper No 14, LSE Law, 2009)

Black J and Rouch D, 'The Development of the Global Markets as Rule–makers: Engagement and Legitimacy' (2008) 2 *Law and Financial Markets Review* 218
Blankenburg E, 'The Poverty of Evolutionism: A Critique of Teubner's Case for "Reflexive Law"' (1984) 18 *Law and Society Review* 273
Bleischwitz R, '"Co–evolution" between State Regulation and the Private Sector' in von Weizacker EU, Young OR and Finger M (eds), *Limits to Privatization: How to Avoid Too Much of a Good Thing* (London, Earthscan, 2005) 341–47
Blount, F, 'Post–1997 Challenges' (October 1995) *Australian Communications* 58
Born G and Prosser T, 'Culture and Consumerism: Citizenship, Public Service Broadcasting and the BBC's Fair Trading Obligations' (2001) 64 *The Modern Law Review* 657
Borrie G, 'Laws and Codes for Consumers' (1980) *The Journal of Business Law* 315
——, 'The Regulation of Public and Private Power' (1989) *Public Law* 552
Bottomley S, *The Constitutional Corporation* (Burlington, VT, Ashgate, 2007)
Bovens M, 'Analysing and Assessing Public Accountability: A Conceptual Framework' (European Governance Papers No C–06–01, 16 January 2006)
——, 'New Forms of Accountability and EU–Governance' (2007) 5 *Comparative European Politics* 104
——, 'Two Concepts of Accountability: Accountability as a Virtue and as a Mechanism' (2010) 33 *West European Politics* 946
Bowrey K, *Law and Internet Cultures* (Cambridge, Cambridge University Press, 2005)
Bradley A, 'The Sovereignty of Parliament–Form or Substance?' in Jowell J and Oliver D (eds), *The Changing Constitution* 7th edn (Oxford, Oxford University Press, 2011) 35–69
Braithwaite J, 'On Speaking Softly and Carrying Big Sticks: Neglected Dimensions of a Republication Separation of Powers' (1997) 47 *University of Toronto Law Journal* 305
——, 'Responsive Regulation and Developing Economies' (2006) 34 *World Development* 884
——, *Regulatory Capitalism: How It Works, Ideas for Making It Work Better* (Cheltenham, Edward Elgar, 2008)
——, 'The Essence of Responsive Regulation' (2011) 44 *University of British Columbia Law Review* 475
——, 'Relational Republican Regulation' (2013) 7 *Regulation & Governance* 124
Braithwaite J and Pettit P, *Not Just Deserts: A Republican Theory of Criminal Justice* (Oxford, Clarendon Press, 1990)
Brand A, *The Force of Reason: An Introduction to Habermas' Theory of Communicative Action* (Sydney, Allen & Unwin, 1990)
Breyer S, *Regulation and Its Reform* (Cambridge, MA, Harvard University Press, 1982)
Brown I (ed), *Research Handbook on Internet Governance* (Cheltenham, Edward Elgar, 2013)
Brown I and Marsden CT, *Regulating Code: Good Governance and Better Regulation in the Information Age* (Cambridge, MA, The MIT Press, 2013)
Brown R, 'The Contagiousness of Conflict' (2010) 5 *Information, Communication & Society* 258
Bull MJ, 'The Corporatist Ideal–Type and Political Exchange' (1992) XL *Political Studies* 255
Büthe T, 'Engineering Uncontestedness? The Origins and Institutional Development of the International Electrotechnical Commission (IEC)' (2010) 12 *Business and Politics* 1
Büthe T and Mattli W, *The New Global Rulers: The Privatization of Regulation in the World* (Princeton, Princeton University Press, 2011)

Buttigieg E, *Competition Law: Safeguarding the Consumer Interest: A Comparative Analysis of US Antitrust Law and EC Competition Law* (Alphen aan den Rijn, Kluwer Law International, 2009)
Cafaggi F, 'New Foundations of Transnational Private Regulation' (2011) 38 *Journal of Law and Society* 20
Caldart CC and Ashford NA, 'Negotiation as a Means of Developing and Implementating Environmental and Occupational Health and Safety Policy' (1999) 23 *Harvard Environmental Law Review* 141
Calliess GP and Zumbansen P, *Rough Consensus and Running Code: A Theory of Transnational Private Law* (Oxford, Hart Publishing, 2010)
Campbell E, *Parliamentary Privilege* (Sydney, Federation Press, 2003)
Campbell H, 'Self–regulation—A Consumer View' (1999) 49 *Telecommunications Journal of Australia* 34
Cane P, 'Self Regulation and Judicial Review' (1987) 6 *Civil Justice Quarterly* 324
——, 'Accountability and the Public/Private Distinction' in Bamforth N and Leyland P (eds), *Public Law in a Multi–Layered Constitution* (Oxford, Hart Publishing, 2003) 247–76
——, 'Review of Executive Action' in Cane P and Tushnet M (eds), *The Oxford Handbook of Legal Studies* (Oxford, Oxford University Press, 2003) 146–63
Carr CT, *Delegated Legislation: Three Lectures* (Cambridge, Cambridge University Press, 1921)
Casey D and Scott C, 'The Crystallization of Regulatory Norms' (2011) 38 *Journal of Law and Society* 76
Cawson A, 'Varieties of Corporatism: the Importance of Meso–level Interest Intermediation' in Cawson A (ed), *Organized Interests and the State: Studies in Meso–Corporatism* (London, Sage Publications, 1985) 1–21
——, *Corporatism and Political Theory* (Oxford, Basil Blackwell, 1986)
Cheit RE, *Setting Safety Standards* (Berkeley, University of California, Press, 1990)
Coenen DT, 'A Constitution of Collaboration: Protecting Fundamental Values with Second–Look Rules of Interbranch Dialogue' (2001) 42 *William and Mary Law Review* 1575
——, 'The Rehnquist Court, Structural Due Process, and Semisubstantive Constitutional Review' (2002) 75 *Southern California Law Review* 1281
Coglianese C, 'Assessing Consensus: The Promise and Performance of Negotiated Rulemaking' (1997) 46 *Duke Law Journal* 1255
——, 'Is Consensus an Appropriate Basis for Regulatory Policy?' in Orts EW and Deketelaere K (eds), *Environmental Contracts: Comparative Approaches to Regulatory Innovation in the United States and Europe* (London, Kluwer Law International, 2001) 93–113
——, 'Empirical Analysis and Administrative Law' (2002) 2002 *University of Illinois Law Review* 1111
——, 'Legitimacy and Corporate Governance' (2007) 32 *Delaware Journal of Corporate Law* 159
Coglianese C, Kilmartin H and Mendelson E, 'Transparency and Public Participation in the Federal Rulemaking Process: Recommendations for the New Administration' (2009) 77 *George Washington Law Review* 924
Coglianese C and Mendelson E, 'Meta–Regulation and Self–Regulation' in Baldwin R, Cave M and Lodge M (eds), *The Oxford Handbook of Regulation* (Oxford, Oxford University Press, 2010) 146–68

Cohen D, 'The Role of the State in a Privatized Regulatory Environment' in Webb K (ed), *Voluntary Codes: Private Governance, the Public Interest and Innovation* (Carleton, CA, Carleton Research Unit for Innovation, Science & Environment, Carleton University, 2004) 35–55

Cohen J, 'Reflections on Habermas in Democracy' (1999) 12 Ratio Juris 385

——, 'Deliberation and Democratic Legitimacy' in Goodin RE and Pettit P (eds), *Contemporary Political Philosophy: An Anthology* 2nd edn (Oxford, Blackwell Publishing, 2006) 143–55

Cohen J and Sabel C, 'Directly–Deliberative Polyarchy' (1997) 3 European Law Journal 313

Collins H, *Regulating Contracts* (Oxford, Oxford University Press, 1999)

Collins R, 'Accountability, Citizenship and Public Media' in Price ME, Verhulst SG and Morgan L (eds), *Routledge Handbook of Media Law* (Abingdon, Routledge, 2013) 219–33

Corbett A, 'The (Self) Regulation of Law: A Synergistic Model of Tort Law and Regulation' (2002) 25 *University of New South Wales Law Journal* 616

——, 'Regulating Corporate Governance' in Parker C and others (eds), *Regulating Law* (Oxford, Oxford University Press, 2004) 60–81

Corbett A and Spender P, 'Corporate Constitutionalism' (2009) 31 *Sydney Law Review* 6

Corner S, 'Looking Beyond the Duopoly' (March 1995) *Australian Communications* 13

——, 'Predicting the Post–1997 Position' (May 1995) *Australian Communications* 15

Corones S and Clarke PH, *Australian Consumer Law: Commentary and Materials* 5th edn (Sydney, Thomson Reuters (Professional) Australia, 2015)

Cotterrell R, *The Sociology of Law: An Introduction* 2nd edn (London, Butterworths, 1992)

Cox GW, 'On the Effects of Legislative Rules' in Loewenberg G, Squire P and Kiewiet DR (eds), *Legislatures: Comparative Perspectives on Representative Assemblies* (Ann Arbor, MI, University of Michigan Press, 2002) 247–68

Craig P, *Public Law and Democracy in the United Kingdom and the United States of America* (Oxford, Clarendon Press, 1990)

——, 'Formal and Substantive Conceptions of the Rule of Law: An Analytical Framework' (1997) *Public Law* 467

——, *Administrative Law* 8th edn (London, Sweet & Maxwell, 2016)

Craven GJ, 'Legislative Action by Subordinate Authorities and the Requirements of a Fair Hearing' (1988) 16 *Melbourne University Law Review* 569

Crew G, 'The Australian Communications Industry Forum' (1997) 47(3) *Telecommunications Journal of Australia* 14

Creyke R, McMillan J and Smyth M, *Control of Government Action: Text, Cases and Commentary* 4th edn (Chatswood, NSW, LexisNexis, 2015)

Croley S, 'Making Rules: An Introduction' (1995) 93 *Michigan Law Review* 1511

——, 'Theories of Regulation: Incorporating the Administrative Process' (1998) 98 *Columbia Law Review* 1

Cuellar MF, 'Rethinking Regulatory Democracy' (2005) 57 *Administrative Law Review* 411

Daintith T, 'The Executive Power Today: Bargaining and Economic Control' in Jowell J and Oliver D (eds), *The Changing Constitution* 2nd edn (Oxford, Clarendon Press, 1989) 193–218

——, 'Political Programmes and the Content of the Constitution' in Finnie W, Himsworth CMG and Walker N (eds), *Edinburgh Essays in Public Law* (Edinburgh, Edinburgh University Press, 1991) 41–55

——, 'The Techniques of Government' in Jowell J and Oliver D (eds), *The Changing Constitution* 3rd edn (Oxford, Clarendon Press, 1994) 209–36

Daintith T and Page A, *The Executive in the Constitution: Structure, Autonomy and Internal Control* (Oxford, Oxford University Press, 1999)
Dal Pont GE, *Equity and Trusts in Australia* 6th edn (Sydney, Thomson Reuters (Professional) Australia, 2015)
Dicey, AV, *Introduction to the Study of the Law of the Constitution* (London, Macmillan Press, first published 1885, 1960 edn)
Deighton–Smith R, 'Regulatory Impact Assessment in Australia: A Survey of 20 Years of RIA Implementation' in C Kirpatrick and D Parker (eds), *Regulatory Impact Assessment: Towards Better Regulation?* (Cheltenham, Edward Elgar, 2007) 145–70
De Schutter O and Lenoble J (eds), *Reflexive Governance: Redefining the Public Interest in a Pluralistic World* (Oxford, Hart Publishing, 2010)
DeLong JV, 'Informal Rulemaking and the Integration of Law and Policy' (1979) 65 *Virginia Law Review* 257
DeNardis L, *The Global War for Internet Governance* (New Haven, Yale University Press, 2014)
Donnelly C, *Delegation of Governmental Power to Private Parties: A Comparative Perspective* (Oxford, Oxford University Press, 2007)
Dorf MC and Sabel CF, 'A Constitution of Democratic Experimentalism' (1998) 98 *Columbia Law Review* 267
Dunleavy P and O'Leary B, *Theories of the State: The Politics of Liberal Democracy* (Basingstoke, Macmillan Education, 1987)
Dworkin R, *Taking Rights Seriously* (London, Duckworth, 1977)
Eckert S and Börzel TA, 'Experimentalist Governance: An Introduction' (2012) 6 *Regulation & Governance* 371
Elliot R, 'Rethinking Manner and Form: From Parliamentary Sovereignty to Constitutional Values' (1991) 29 *Osgoode Hall Law Journal* 215
Epstein D and O'Halloran S, *Delegating Powers: A Transaction Cost Politics Approach to Policy Making Under Separate Powers* (Cambridge, Cambridge University Press, 1999)
Epstein RA, 'Beyond the Rule of Law: Civic Virtue and Constitutional Structure' (1987) 56 *George Washington Law Review* 149
Eskridge Jr WN, 'The Circumstances of Politics and the Application of Statutes' (2000) 100 *Columbia Law Review* 558
Eskridge Jr WN and Frickey PP, 'Legislation Scholarship and Pedagogy in the Post–Legal Process Era' (1987) 48 *University of Pittsburgh Law Review* 691
—— (eds), *Henry M Hart, Jr and Albert M Sacks, The Legal Process: Basic Problems in the Making and Application of Law (tent ed, 1958)* (New York, Foundation Press, 1994)
——, 'An Historical and Critical Introduction to *The Legal Process*' in Eskridge Jr WN and Frickey PP (eds), *Henry M Hart, Jr and Albert M Sacks, The Legal Process: Basic Problems in the Making and Application of Law (tent ed, 1958)* (New York, Foundation Press, 1994)
Eskridge Jr WN, Frickey PP and Garrett E, *Cases and Materials on Legislation: Statutes and the Creation of Public Policy* 3rd edn (St Paul, MN, West, 2001)
——, *Legislation and Statutory Interpretation* 2nd edn (New York, Foundation Press, 2006)
Eskridge Jr WN and others, *Cases and Materials on Legislation: Statutes and the Creation of Public Policy* 5th edn (St Paul, MN, West Academic, 2014)
Evan WM, 'Public and Private Legal Systems' in Evan WM (ed), *Law and Sociology: Exploratory Essays* (New York, Free Press of Glencoe, 1962) 165–184
Evans H and Laing R (eds), *Odger's Australian Senate Practice* 14th edn (Canberra, Commonwealth of Australia 2016)

Fallon Jr RH, '"The Rule of Law" as a Concept in Constitutional Discourse' (1997) 97 *Columbia Law Review* 1
Feintuck M, *'The Public Interest' in Regulation* (Oxford, Oxford University Press, 2004)
——, 'Regulatory Rationales Beyond the Economic' in Baldwin R, Cave M and Lodge M (eds), *The Oxford Handbook of Regulation* (Oxford, Oxford University Press, 2010) 39–63
Fell L, 'Shaping the Post–1997 Environment' (December/January 1994–95) *Australian Communications* 20
——, 'Austel—Evolution or Devolution?' (October 1995) *Australian Communications* 49
——, 'Interview with Anne Hurley' (2004) 54(3) *Telecommunications Journal of Australia* 37
Forbath WE, 'Habermas's Constitution: A History, Guide and Critique' (1998) 23 *Law and Social Inquiry* 969
Forsyth C, 'The Scope of Judicial Review: "Public Duty" Not "Source of Power"' (1987) *Public Law* 356
——, (ed), *Judical Review and the Constitution* (Oxford, Hart Publishing, 2000)
Fossum JE, 'Reflections on Experimentalist Governance' (2012) 6 *Regulation & Governance* 394
Fraser N, 'Rethinking the Public Sphere: A Contribution to the Critique of Actually Existing Democracy' (1990) 25/26 *Social Text* 56
Fredman S and Morris GS, 'The Costs of Exclusivity: Public and Private Re–examined' (1994) *Public Law* 69
Freedman JO, 'Crisis and Legitimacy in the Administrative State' (1975) 27 *Stanford Law Review* 1041
Freeman J, 'Collaborative Governance in the Administrative State' (1997) 45 *University of California at Los Angeles Law Review* 1
——, 'Private Parties, Public Functions and the New Administrative Law' in Dyzenhaus D (ed), *Recrafting the Rule of Law: The Limits of Legal Order* (Oxford, Hart Publishing, 1999) 331–69
——, 'The Private Role in Public Governance' (2000) 75 *New York University Law Review* 543
Freeman J and Langbein LI, 'Regulatory Negotiation and the Legitimacy Benefit' (2000) 9 *NYU Environmental Law Journal* 60
Freiberg A, *The Tools of Regulation* (Sydney, The Federation Press, 2010)
——, *Regulation in Australia* (Sydney, The Federation Press, 2017)
Freigang, J, 'Is Responsive Regulation Compatible with the Rule of Law?' (2002) 8 *European Public Law* 463
Frickey PP, 'Honoring Hans: On Linde, Lawmaking, and Legacies' (2007) 43 *Williamette Law Review* 157
Frickey PP and Smith SS, 'Judicial Review, the Congressional Process and the Federalism Cases: An Interdisciplinary Critique' (2002) 111 *Yale Law Journal* 1720
Friedman LM, 'On Regulation and Legal Process' in Noll RG (ed), *Regulatory Policy and the Social Sciences* (Berkeley, University of California Press, 1985) 111–35
Fuller LL, *The Morality of Law* 2nd edn (New Haven, Yale University, 1969)
Funk W, 'When Smoke Gets in Your Eyes: Regulatory Negotiation and the Public Interest–EPA's Woodstove Standards' (1987) 18 *Environmental Law* 55
——, 'Bargaining Toward the New Millennium: Regulatory Negotiation and the Subversion of the Public Interest' (1997) 46 *Duke Law Journal* 1351

——, 'Public Participation and Transparency in Administrative Law–Three Examples as an Object Lesson' (2009) 61 *Administrative Law Review* 171

Ganz G, 'Delegated Legislation: A Necessary Evil or a Constitutional Outrage?' in Woods T and Leyland P (eds), *Administrative Law Facing the Future: Old Constraints and New Horizons* (Oxford, Blackstone, 1997) 60–82

Garland MB, 'Deregulation and Judicial Review' (1985) 98 *Harvard Law Review* 505

Garrett E and Vermeule A, 'Institutional Design of a Thayerian Congress' (2001) 50 *Duke Law Journal* 1277

Garrett R and Astbrink G, 'Are We There Yet? The Struggle for Phone Accessibility Information' 60(2) *Telecommunications Journal of Australia* 22.1

Gelhorn E and Robinson GO, 'Rulemaking "Due Process": An Inconclusive Dialogue' (1981) 48 *University of Chicago Law Review* 201

Goggin G and Spurgeon C, 'Mobile Message Services and Communications Policy' (2005) 23 *Prometheus* 181

Golan E, Kuchler F and Mitchell L, 'Economics of Food Labeling' (2001) 24 *Journal of Consumer Policy* 117

Goldsworthy J, 'Legislation, Interpretation and Judicial Review' (2001) 51 *University of Toronto Law Journal* 76

——, *Parliamentary Sovereignty: Contemporary Debates* (Cambridge, Cambridge University Press, 2010)

Goodin RE, 'Institutions and Their Design' in Goodin RE (ed), *The Theory of Institutional Design* (Cambridge, Cambridge University Press, 1996) 1–53

Gordon M, 'The Conceptual Foundations of Parliamentary Sovereignty: Reconsidering Jennings and Wade' (2009) *Public Law* 519

Grabosky P, 'Using Non–Governmental Resources to Foster Regulatory Compliance' (1995) 8 *Governance: An International Journal of Policy and Administration* 527

——, 'Beyond *Responsive Regulation*: The Expanding Role of Non–state Actors in the Regulatory Process' (2013) 7 *Regulation & Governance* 114

Grace C and Wilkinson P, *Sociological Inquiry and Legal Phenomena* (London, Collier Macmillan, 1978)

Graham C, 'Self–Regulation' in Richardson G and Genn H (eds), *Administrative Law and Government Action: The Courts and Alternative Mechanisms of Review* (Oxford, Clarendon Press, 1994) 189–209

——, *Regulating Public Utilities: A Constitutional Approach* (Oxford, Hart Publishing, 2000)

Grant A, 'Industry Structure and Regulatory Bodies' in Grant A and Howarth D (eds), *Australian Telecommunications Regulation* 4th edn (Sydney, CCH Australia Ltd, 2012) 3–47

Grant A and Raiche H, 'Consumer Protection and Universal Service' in Grant A and Howarth D (eds), *Australian Telecommunications Regulation* (Sydney, CCH Australia Ltd, 2012) 357–404

Gunningham N and Grabosky P, *Smart Regulation: Designing Environmental Policy* (Oxford, Oxford University Press, 1998)

Gunningham N, Kagan RA and Thornton D, 'Social License and Environmental Protection: Why Businesses Go Beyond Compliance' (2004) 29 *Law and Social Inquiry* 307

Gunningham N and Rees J, 'Industry Self–Regulation: An Institutional Perspective' (1997) 19 *Law and Policy* 363

Gunningham N and Sinclair D, 'Designing Environmental Policy' in Gunningham N and Grabosky P (eds), *Smart Regulation: Designing Environmental Policy* (Oxford, Oxford University Press, 1998) 375–453

——, 'Integrative Regulation: A Principle–Based Approach to Environmental Policy' (1999) 24 *Law and Social Inquiry* 853

Gurvitch, G, *The Sociology of Law* (New Brunswick, NJ, Transaction Publishers, first published 1947, 2001 edn)

Gutmann A and Thomson D, *Why Deliberate Democracy?* (Princeton, Princeton University Press, 2004)

Habermas J, *Between Facts and Norms: Contributions to a Discourse Theory of Law and Democracy* (Rehg W tr, Cambridge, Polity Press, 1996)

Hachez N and Wouters J, 'A Glimpse at the Democratic Legitimacy of Private Standards: Assessing the Public Accountability of Global G.A.P.' (2011) 14 *Journal of International Economic Law* 677

Haines F, Reichman N and Scott C, 'Problematizing Legitimacy and Authority in Law and Policy' (2008) 30 *Law and Policy* 1

Hall C, Scott C and Hood C, *Telecommunications Regulation: Culture, Chaos and Interdependence Inside the Regulatory Process* (London, Routledge, 2000)

Hallström KT, 'ISO Enters the Field of Social Responsibility: Construction and Tension of Global Governance' in Schuppert GF (ed), *Global Governance and the Role of Non–State Actors* (Baden–Baden, Nomos, 2006) 117–56

Hamilton RW, 'The Role of Nongovernmental Standards in the Development of Mandatory Federal Standards Affecting Safety or Health' (1978) 56 *Texas Law Review* 1329

——, 'Prospects for the Nongovernmental Development of Regulatory Standards' (1982) 32 *American University Law Review* 455

Hanks P, Gordon F and Hill G, *Constitutional Law in Australia* 3rd edn (Chatswood, NSW, LexisNexis, 2012)

Harden I and Lewis N, *The Noble Lie: The British Constitution and the Rule of Law* (London, Hutchinson Education, 1986)

Hardy C, McAuslan M and Madden J, 'Competition Policy and Communications Convergence' (1994) 17 *University of New South Wales Law Journal* 156

Harlow C, '"Public" and "Private Law": Definition without Distinction' (1980) 43 *The Modern Law Review* 241

Harlow C and Rawlings R, *Law and Administration* 2nd edn (London, Butterworths, 1997)

——, 'Promoting Accountability in Multilevel Governance: A Network Approach' (2007) 13 *European Law Journal* 542

Harrington CB, 'Regulatory Reform: Creating Gaps and Making Markets' (1988) 10 *Law & Policy* 293

——, 'Howard Bellman: Using "Bundles of Input" to Negotiate an Environmental Dispute' in Kolb DM (ed), *When Talk Works: Profiles of Mediators* (San Francisco, Jossey–Bass, 1994) 105–47

Harrington CB and Turem ZU, 'Accounting for Accountability in Neoliberal Regulatory Regimes' in Dowdle MW (ed), *Public Accountability: Designs, Dilemmas and Experiences* (Cambridge, Cambridge University Press, 2006) 195–219

Hart H, *The Concept of Law* 2nd edn (Oxford, Oxford University Press, 1994)

Harter PJ, 'Negotiating Regulations: A Cure for Malaise' (1982) 71 *Georgetown Law Journal* 1

——, 'The Political Legitimacy and Judicial Review of Consensual Rules' (1983) 32 *American University Law Review* 471
Haufler V, *A Public Role of the Private Sector: Industry Self–Regulation in a Global Economy* (Washington, DC, Carnegie Endowment for International Peace, 2001)
——, 'Globalization and Industry Self–Regulation' in Kahler M and Lake DA (eds), *Governance in a Global Economy: Political Authority in Transition* (Princeton, Princeton University Press, 2003) 226–52
Hay C, *Political Analysis: A Critical Introduction* (Basingstoke, Palgrave, 2002)
Hayhurst J and Wallington P, 'The Parliamentary Scrutiny of Delegated Legislation' (1988) *Public Law* 547
Heuston RFV, *Essays in Constitutional Law* 2nd edn (London, Steven & Sons, 1964)
Lord Hewart of Bury, *The New Despotism* (London, Ernest Benn Ltd, 1929)
Hitchens L, 'Commercial Broadcasting–Preserving the Public Interest' (2004) 32 *Federal Law Review* 79
——, 'Citizen Versus Consumer in the Digital World' in Kenyon AT (ed), *TV Futures: Digital Television Policy in Australia* (Melbourne, Melbourne University Publishing, 2007) 343–63
Horrocks S and Hill R, 'Protecting the Consumer Interest in Network Standards and Operations Codes of Practice' in Communications Research Unit (ed), *Communications Research Forum: Proceedings* (Canberra, DCITA, vol 4, 1999) 527–57
Horwitz RB, *The Irony of Regulatory Reform: The Deregulation of American Telecommunications* (Oxford, Oxford University Press, 1989)
Inoue T, 'The Rule of Law as the Law of Legislation' in Wintgens LJ (ed), *Legislation in Context: Essays in Legisprudence* (Aldershot, Ashgate, 2007) 55–74
Jack M (ed), *Erskine May: Parliamentary Practice* 24th edn (Chatswood, NSW, LexisNexis 2011)
Jackson M, 'Data Protection Regulation in Australia After 1988' (1997) 5 *International Journal of Law and Information Technology* 158
——, *Hughes on Data Protection in Australia* 2nd edn (North Ryde, NSW, LBC Information Services, 2001)
Jaffe LL, 'Law Making by Private Groups' (1937) 51 *Harvard Law Review* 201
——, 'An Essay on Delegation of Legislative Power: I' (1947) 47 *Columbia Law Review* 359
——, 'An Essay on Delegation of Legislative Power: II' (1947) 47 *Columbia Law Review* 561
Jennings WI, *The Law and the Constitution* 5th edn (London, University of London Press, 1959)
Joerges C, Schepel H and Vos E, 'The Law's Problems with the Involvement of Non–Governmental Actors in Europe's Legislative Processes: The Case of Standardisation under the "New Approach"' (Working Paper No 99/9, European University Institute, 1999)
Joseph R, 'Politics and Telecommunications Deregulation' (1996) 46(1) *Telecommunication Journal of Australia* 9
——, 'The Redefinition of Australian Telecommunications Policy: An Historical Overview' (1996) 46(2) *Telecommunication Journal of Australia* 51
——, 'Analysing the Telecommunications Deregulation Process in Australia' (1996) 46(3) *Telecommunication Journal of Australia* 49
Jowell J, 'The Rule of Law and Its Underlying Values' in Jowell J and Oliver D (eds), *The Changing Constitution* 7th edn (Oxford, Oxford University Press, 2011) 11–34

Kagan RA, *Adversarial Legalism: The American Way of Law* (Cambridge, MA, Harvard University Press, 2001)
Kahan DM, 'Democracy Schmemocracy' (1999) 20 *Cardozo Law Review* 795
Kay A, 'A Critique of the Use of Path Dependency in Policy Studies' (2005) 83 *Public Administration* 553
Keeton GW, *The Passing of Parliament* (London, Ernest Benn Limited, 1952)
Keith R, 'Judicial Intervention in Parliamentary Proceedings: The Implications of *Egan v Willis*' (2000) 28 *Federal Law Review* 549
Kernaghan K, 'Towards a Public–Service Code of Conduct–and Beyond' (1997) 40 *Canadian Public Administration* 40
Kerwin CM and Furlong SR, *Rulemaking: How Government Agencies Write Law and Make Policy* 4th edn (Washington, DC, CQ Press, 2011)
Kingsbury B, Krisch N and Stewart RB, 'The Emergence of Global Administrative Law' (2005) 68 *Law and Contemporary Problems* 15
Kingsford Smith D, 'Beyond the Rule of Law? Decentered Regulation in Online Investing' (2004) 26 *Law & Policy* 439
——, 'Governing the Corporation: The Role of 'Soft Regulation'' (2012) 35 *University of New South Wales Law Journal* 378
Kinley D, 'Constitutional Brokerage in Australia: Constitutions and the Doctrines of Parliamentary Sovereignty and the Rule of Law' (1994) 22 *Federal Law Review* 194
Kirk J, 'Constitutional Implications from Representative Democracy' (1995) 23 *Federal Law Review* 37
Kleinwachter W, 'Multistakeholderism, Civil Society, and Global Democracy: The Case of the World Summit on the Information Society' in Drake WJ and Wilson III EJ (eds), *Governing Global Electronic Networks: International Perspectives on Policy and Power* (Cambridge, MA, The MIT Press, 2008) 535–82
Koppell JG, 'Pathologies of Accountability: ICANN and the Challenge of "Multiple Accountabilities Disorder"' (2005) 65 *Public Administration Review* 94
Krent HJ, 'Fragmenting the Unitary Executive: Congressional Delegation of Administrative Authority Outside the Federal Government' (1990) 85 *Northwestern University Law Review* 62
Krygier M, 'Four Puzzles About the Rule of Law' in Fleming JE (ed), *Getting to the Rule of Law: Nomos L* (New York, New York University Press, 2011) 64–104
Kunkel DL, Castonguay JS and Filer CR, 'Evaluating Indusry Self–Regulation of Food Marketing to Children' (2015) 49 *American Journal of Preventive Medicine* 181
Ladeur KH, 'The Changing Role of the Private in Public Governance—The Erosion of Hierarchy and the Rise of a New Administrative Law of Cooperation' (Working Paper No 2002/9, European University Institute, 2002)
Lane PH, *Lane's Commentary on the Australian Constitution* 2nd edn (North Ryde, NSW, Lawbook Co, 1997)
Langbein LI and Kerwin CM, 'Regulatory Negotiation versus Conventional Rule Making: Claims, Counterclaims, and Empirical Evidence' (2000) 10 *Journal of Public Administration Research and Theory* 599
Lawrence DM, 'Private Exercise of Governmental Power' (1986) 61 Indiana Law Journal 647
Lee K, 'Creating a Level Playing Field or Expanding the Nanny State? Regulating the Content of Premium Rate SMS/MMS and Walled–Garden Services in Australia' (2006) 11 *Media and Arts Law Review* 99

——, 'Counting the Casualties of Telecom: The Adoption of Part 6 of the *Telecommunications Act 1997* (Cth)' (2009) 37 *Federal Law Review* 41
Lee K and Prime J, 'US Telecommunications Law' in Walden I (ed), *Telecommunications Law and Regulation* 4th edn (Oxford, Oxford University Press, 2012) 187–274
Lee M, 'Minister Promises Lower Prices and Better Service' (1994) 2 *Telecommunications Law and Policy Review* 103
Lenoble J and Maesschalck M, 'Renewing the Public Interest: The Quest for a Reflexive and Learning–based Approach to Governance' in de Schutter O and Lenoble J (eds), *Reflexive Governance: Redefining the Public Interest in a Pluralistic World* (Oxford, Hart Publishing, 2010) 3–21
Levine ME and Forrence JL, 'Regulatory Capture, Public Interest, and the Public Agenda: Toward a Synthesis' (1990) 6 *Journal of Law, Economics, and Organization* 167
Lewinsohn–Zamir D, 'Consumer Preferences, Citizen Preferences and the Provision of Public Goods' (1998) 108 *Yale Law Journal* 377
Lewis N, 'Who Controls Quangos and the Nationalized Industries?' in Jowell J and Oliver D (eds), *The Changing Constitution* 1st edn (Oxford, Clarendon Press, 1985) 198–228
——, 'Regulating Non–governmental Bodies: Privatization, Accountability and the Public–Private Divide' in Jowell J and Oliver D (eds), *The Changing Constitution* 2nd edn (Oxford, Clarendon Press, 1989) 219–45
——, 'Corporatism and Accountability: The Democratic Dilemma' in Crouch C and Dore R (eds), *Corporatism and Accountability: Organized Interests in British Public Life* (Oxford, Clarendon Press, 1990) 63–101
Liebmann GW, 'Delegation to Private Parties in American Constitutional Law' (1975) 50 *Indiana Law Journal* 650
Linde HA, 'Due Process of Lawmaking' (1976) 55 *Nebraska Law Review* 197
——, 'Structures and Terms of Consent: *Delegation, Discretion, Separation of Powers, Representation, Participation, Accountability*?' (1999) 20 *Cardozo Law Review* 823
Livingstone S and Lunt P, 'Representing Citizens and Consumers in Media and Communications Regulation' (2007) 611 *The Annals of the American Academy of Political and Social Science* 51
Livingstone S, Lunt P and Miller L, 'Citizens and Consumers: Discursive Debates During and After the Communications Act 2003' (2007) 29 *Media, Culture & Society* 613
Lodge M, 'Accountability and Transparency in Regulation: Critiques, Doctrines and Instruments' in Jordana J and Levi–Faur D (eds), *The Politics of Regulation: Institutions and Regulatory Reforms for the Age of Governance* (Cheltenham, Edward Elgar, 2004) 124–44
Lodge M and Stirton L, 'Accountability in the Regulatory State' in Baldwin R, Cave M and Lodge M (eds), *The Oxford Handbook of Regulation* (Oxford, Oxford University Press, 2010) 349–70
Luban D, 'The Publicity Principle' in Goodin RE (ed), *The Theory of Institutional Design* (Cambridge, Cambridge University Press, 1996) 154–98
Lubbers JS, 'Achieving Policymaking Consensus: The (Unfortunate) Waning of Negotiated Rulemaking' (2008) 49 *South Texas Law Review* 987
Lutz DS, *Principles of Constitutional Design* (Cambridge, Cambridge University Press, 2006)
Macassey L, 'Law–Making by Government Departments' (1923) 5 *Journal of Comparative Legislation and International Law* 73
MacNeill K, 'Self Regulation: Rights and Remedies—the Telecommunications Experience' in Finn C (ed), *Sunrise or Sunset? Administrative Law in the New Millennium: Papers*

Presented at the 2000 National Administrative Law Forum (Canberra, Australian Institute of Administrative Law, 2000) 249–66

Majone G, 'Two Logics of Delegation: Agency and Fiduciary Relations in EU Governance' (2001) 2 *European Union Politics* 103

——, 'Delegation of Regulatory Powers in a Mixed Polity' (2002) 8 *European Law Journal* 319

Malcolm D, 'The Limitations, if Any, on the Powers of Parliament to Delegate the Power to Legislate' (1992) 66 *The Australian Law Journal* 247

Marsden CT, *Internet Co–Regulation: European Law, Regulatory Governance and Legitimacy in Cyberspace* (Cambridge, Cambridge University Press, 2011)

Marshall G, *Constitutional Theory* (Oxford, Clarendon Press, 1971)

Marshall TH, *Sociology at the Crossroads and Other Essays* (London, Heinemann, 1963)

Mascini P, 'Why Was the Enforcement Pyramid So Influential? And What Price Was Paid?' (2013) 7 *Regulation & Governance* 48

Mashaw JL, 'Accountability and Institutional Design: Some Thoughts on the Grammar of Governance' in Dowdle MW (ed), *Public Accountability: Designs, Dilemmas and Experiences* (Cambridge, Cambridge University Press, 2006) 115–56

Mattli W and Büthe T, 'Setting International Standards: Technological Rationality or Primacy of Power?' (2003) 56 *World Politics* 1

——, 'Accountability in Accounting? The Politics of Private Rule–making in the Public Interest' (2005) 18 Governance: An International Journal of Policy, Administration, and Institutions 399

May PJ, 'Regulatory Regimes and Accountability' (2007) 1 *Regulation & Governance* 8

McAuslan P and McEldowney JF (eds), *Law, Legitimacy and the Constitution: Essays Marking the Centenary of Dicey's Law of the Constitution* (London, Sweet & Maxwell, 1985)

McDonald L, 'The Rule of Law in the '"New Regulatory State"' (2004) 33 *Common Law World Review* 197

McGarity TO, 'Some Thoughts on "Deossifying" the Rulemaking Process' (1991–1992) 41 *Duke Law Journal* 1385

Meidinger E, 'The Administrative Law of Global Private–Public Regulation: the Case of Forestry' (2006) 17 *The European Journal of International Law* 47

Meyerson D, 'Rethinking the Constitutionality of Delegated Legislation' (2003) 1 *Australian Journal of Administrative Law* 45

Michael DC, 'Federal Agency Use of Audited Self–Regulation as a Regulatory Technique' (1995) 47 *Administrative Law Review* 171

Michelman F, 'Law's Republic' (1988) 97 *Yale Law Journal* 1493

——, *Brennan and Democracy* (Princeton, Princeton University Press, 1999)

Mitnick BM, *The Political Economy of Regulation: Creating, Designing, and Removing Regulatory Forms* (New York, Columbia University Press, 1980)

Molina O and Rhodes M, 'Corporatism: The Past, Present, and Future of a Concept' (2002) 5 *Annual Review of Political Science* 305

Monypenny P, 'A Code of Ethics as a Means of Controlling Administrative Conduct' (1953) 13 *Public Administration Review* 184

Moran M, *The British Regulatory State: High–Modernism and Hyper–Innovation* (Oxford, Oxford University Press, 2003)

Morgan B, 'Regulating the Regulators: Meta–regulation as a Strategy for Reinventing Government in Australia' (1999) 1 *Public Management: An International Journal of Research and Theory* 49

——, 'The Economization of Politics: Meta–Regulation as a Form of Nonjudicial Legality' (2003) 12 *Social & Legal Studies* 489
——, *Social Citizenship in the Shadow of Competition: The Bureaucratic Politics of Regulatory Justification* (Aldershot, Ashgate, 2003)
Morgan B and Yeung K, *An Introduction to Law and Regulation: Text and Materials* (Cambridge, Cambridge University Press, 2007)
Morrison J, 'Models of Democracy: From Representation to Participation?' in Jowell J and Oliver D (eds), *The Changing Constitution* (Oxford, Oxford University Press, 2004) 144–67
Mulgan R, *Holding Power to Account: Accountability in Modern Democracies* (Basingstoke, Palgrave Macmillan, 2003)
Murphy WT, 'Systems of Systems: Some Issues in the Relationship Between Law and Autopoiesis' (1994) V *Law and Critique* 241
Navot S, 'Judicial Review of the Legislative Process' (2006) 39 *Israel Law Review* 182
Nielsen VL, 'Are Regulators Responsive?' (2006) 28 *Law & Policy* 395
Northfield D, *The Information Policy Maze: Global Challenges—National Responses* (Melbourne, RMIT University Press, 1999)
Ogus A, 'Rethinking Self–Regulation' (1995) 15 *Oxford Journal of Legal Studies* 97
——, (ed), *Regulation, Economics and the Law* (Cheltenham, Edward Elgar, 2001)
——, *Regulation: Legal Form and Economic Theory* (Oxford, Hart Publishing, 2004)
Oliver D, 'Common Values in Public and Private Law and the Public/Private Divide' (1997) *Public Law* 630
——, *Common Values and the Public–Private Divide* (London, Butterworths, 1999)
Oliver PC, *The Constitution of Independence: The Development of Constitutional Theory in Australia, Canada and New Zealand* (Oxford, Oxford University Press, 2005)
Omarova ST, 'Wall Street As Community of Fate: Toward Financial Industry Self–Regulation' 159 *University of Pennsylvania Law Review* 411
Osborne D and Gaebler T, *Reinventing Government: How the Entrepreneurial Spirit is Transforming the Public Sector* (New York, Plume, 1992)
Page AC, 'Self–Regulation and Codes of Practice' (1980) *Journal of Business Law* 24
——, 'Self–Regulation: the Constitutional Dimension' (1986) 49 *The Modern Law Review* 141
Page EC, *Governing by Numbers* (Oxford, Hart Publishing, 2001)
Paiement P, 'Paradox and Legitimacy in Transnational Legal Pluralism' (2013) 4 *Transnational Legal Theory* 197
Pannick D, 'Who is Subject to Judicial Review and in Respect of What?' (1992) *Public Law* 1
Parker C, *The Open Corporation: Effective Self–Regulation and Democracy* (Cambridge, Cambridge University Press, 2002)
——, 'Regulating Self–Regulation' in Bell S (ed), *Economic Governance and Institutional Dynamics* (Oxford, Oxford University Press, 2002) 244–61
——, 'Regulator–Required Corporate Compliance Program Audits' (2003) 25 *Law & Policy* 221
——, 'Introduction' in Parker C and others (eds), *Regulating Law* (Oxford, Oxford University Press, 2004) 1–12
——, 'Restorative Justice in Business Regulation? The Australian Competition and Consumer Commission's Use of Enforceable Undertakings' (2004) 67 *The Modern Law Review* 209

——, 'Twenty Years of Responsive Regulation: An Appreciation and Appraisal' (2013) 7 *Regulation & Governance* 2
Parker, C and Braithwaite J, 'Regulation' in Cane P and Tushnet M (eds), *The Oxford Handbook of Legal Studies* (Oxford, Oxford University Press, 2003) 119–45
Parker, C and others (eds), *Regulating Law* (Oxford, Oxford University Press, 2004)
Pearce D and Argument S, *Delegated Legislation in Australia* 5th edn (Chatswood, NSW, LexisNexis Butterworths, 2017)
Pengilley W, 'Competition Law and Voluntary Codes of Self Regulation: An Individual Assessment of What Has Happened to Date' (1990) 13 *University of New South Wales Law Journal* 212
Pennock JR, *Administration and the Rule of Law* (New York, Farrer and Rinehart, 1941)
——, 'Political Representation: An Overview' in Pennock JR and Chapman JW (eds), *Representation: Nomos X* (New York, Atherton Press, 1968) 3–27
Peters A, Koechlin L and Zinkernagel GF, 'Non–state Actors as Standard Setters: Framing the Issue in an Interdisciplinary Fashion' in Peters A and others (eds), *Non–state Actors as Standard Setters* (Cambridge, Cambridge University Press, 2009) 1–32
Peters BG, Pierre J and King DS, 'The Politics of Path Dependency: Political Conflict in Historical Institutionalism' (2005) 67 *The Journal of Politics* 1275
Pettit P, *Republicanism: A Theory of Freedom and Government* (Oxford, Clarendon Press, 1997)
Pitkin HF, *The Concept of Representation* (Berkeley, University of California Press, 1967)
——, 'The Concept of Representation' in Pitkin HF (ed), *Representation* (New York, Atherton Press, 1969) 1–23
Posner RA, 'Theories of Economic Regulation' (1974) 5 *The Bell Journal of Economics and Management Science* 335
——, 'Review of Jeremy Waldron, *Law and Disagreement*' (2000) 100 *Columbia Law Review* 582
Priest M, 'The Privatization of Regulation: Five Models of Self–Regulation' (1998) 29 *Ottawa Law Review* 233
Prosser T, 'Towards a Critical Public Law' (1982) 9 *Journal of Law and Society* 1
——, 'Regulation, Markets and Legitimacy' in Jowell J and Oliver D (eds), *The Changing Constitution* 5th edn (Oxford, Oxford University Press, 2004) 351–73
——, 'Regulatory Agencies, Regulatory Legitimacy and European Private Law' in Cafaggi F and Muir–Watt H (eds), *Making European Private Law: Governance Design* (Cheltenham, Edward Elgar, 2008) 235–53
——, *The Regulatory Enterprise: Government Regulation, and Legitimacy* (Oxford, Oxford University Press, 2010)
Punder H, 'Democratic Legitimation of Delegated Legislation–A Comparative View on the American, British and German Law' (2009) 58 *International & Comparative Law Quarterly* 353
Raiche H, 'A Telecomms Privacy Committee at Last' (1994) 1 *Privacy Law and Policy Reporter* 101
——, 'The Policy Context' in Grant A (ed), *Australian Telecommunications Regulation* 3rd edn (Sydney, University of New South Wales Press, 2004) 1–21
Ramsay I, 'Consumer Law, Regulatory Capitalism and the "New Learning" in Regulation' (2006) 28 *Sydney Law Review* 9
——, *Consumer Law and Policy: Text and Materials on Regulating Consumer Markets* 3rd edn (Oxford, Hart Publishing, 2012)

Rauterberg GV and Verstein A, 'Assessing Transnational Private Regulation of the OTC Derivatives Market: ISDA, the BBA and the Future of Financial Reform' (2013) 54 *Virginia Journal of International Law* 9

Raz J, *The Authority of Law: Essays on Law and Morality* 2nd edn (Oxford, Oxford University Press, 2009)

Reeder C, 'Regulation by Contractors: Delegation of Legislative Power to Private Entities in Texas' (2004) 5 *Texas Tech Journal of Texas Administrative Law* 191

Regini M, 'The Conditions for Political Exchange: How Concertation Emerged and Collapsed in Italy and Great Britain' in Goldthorpe JH (ed), *Order and Conflict in Contemporary Capitalism* (Oxford, Clarendon Press, 1984) 124–42

Richardson G and Genn H, *Administrative Law and Government Action: The Courts and Alternative Mechanisms of Review* (Oxford, Clarendon Press, 1994)

Rose–Ackerman S, 'Consensus Versus Incentives: A Skeptical Look at Regulatory Negotiation' (1994) 43 *Duke Law Journal* 1206

Rosenfeld M, 'Law as Discourse: Bridging the Gap Between Democracy and Rights' (1995) 108 *Harvard Law Review* 1163

Rowland M, 'ACIF Boycott Raises Self–Regulatory Questions' (2002) 5 *Telemedia* 121

Rubin E, 'Law and Legislation in the Administrative State' (1989) 89 *Columbia Law Review* 369

——, 'It's Time to Make the Administrative Procedure Act Administrative' (2003) 89 *Cornell Law Review* 95

Ryan MH and Cloke S, 'Significant Market Power (SMP) and Other Conditions' in Conradi M (ed), *Communications Law Handbook* (Haywards Heath, Bloomsbury Professional, 2009) 53–69

Sabel CF and Simon WH, 'Epilogue: Accountability without Sovereignty' in de Burca G and Scott J (eds), *Law and New Governance in the EU and the US* (Oxford, Hart Publishing, 2006) 395–411

Sabel CF and Simon WH, 'Minimalism and Experimentalism in the Administrative State' (2011) 100 *The Georgetown Law Journal* 53

Sabel CF and Zeitlin J, 'Learning from Difference: The New Architecture of Experimentalist Governance in the EU' (2008) 14 *European Law Journal* 271

——, *Experimentalist Governance in the European Union: Towards a New Architecture* (Oxford, Oxford University Press, 2010)

——, 'Experimentalism in the EU: Common Ground and Persistent Differences' (2012) 6 *Regulation & Governance* 410

——, 'Experimentalist Governance' in Levi–Faur D (ed), *Oxford Handbook of Governance* (Oxford, Oxford University Press, 2012) 169–83

Saunders C and Le Roy K, 'Perspectives on the Rule of Law' in Saunders C and Le Roy K (eds), *The Rule of Law* (Sydney, Federation Press, 2003) 1–20

Sawer G, 'The Separation of Powers in Australian Federalism' (1961) 35 *The Australian Law Journal* 177

Schattschneider E, *The Semisovereign People: A Realist's View of Democracy* (New York, Holt, Rinehart and Winston, 1960)

Schepel H, *The Constitution of Private Governance: Product Standards in the Regulation of Integrating Markets* (Oxford, Hart Publishing, 2005)

Scheuerman WE, 'Democratic Experimentalism or Capitalist Synchronization? Critical Reflections on Directly–Deliberative Polyarchy' (2004) 17 *Canadian Journal of Law and Jurisprudence* 101

Schiller RE, 'Enlarging the Administrative Polity: Administrative Law and the Changing Definition of Pluralism, 1945–1970' (2000) 53 *Vanderbilt Law Review* 1389

Schmitter P, 'Reflections on Where the Theory of Neo–corporatism Has Gone and Where the Praxis of Neo–corporatism May Be Going' in Lehmbruch G and Schmitter PC (eds), *Patterns of Corporatist Policy–Making* (London, Sage Publishing, 1982) 259–79

——, 'Democratic Theory and Neocorporatist Practice' (1983) 50 *Social Research* 885

——, 'Neo–corporatism and the State' in Grant W (ed), *The Political Economy of Corporatism* (London, Macmillan, 1985) 32–62

——, 'Corporatism' in Krieger J (ed), *The Oxford Companion to Politics of the World* 2nd edn (Oxford, Oxford University Press, 2001) 175–77

Schneier E, *Crafting Constitutional Democracies: The Politics of Institutional Design* (Lanham, MD, Rowman & Littlefield Publishers, 2006)

Schoenbrod D, *Power Without Responsibility: How Congress Abuses the People Through Delegation* (New Haven, Yale University, 1993)

——, 'Delegation and Democracy: A Reply to My Critics' (1999) 20 *Cardozo Law Review* 731

Schuck PH, 'Delegation and Democracy: Comments on David Schoenbrod' (1999) 20 *Cardozo Law Review* 775

Schudson M, 'The Troubling Equivalence of Citizen and Consumer' (2006) 608 *The Annals of the American Academy of Political and Social Science* 193

Schulz W and Held T, *Regulated Self–Regulation as a Form of Modern Government: An Analysis of Case Studies from Media and Telecommunications Law* (Eastleigh, University of Luton Press, 2004)

Schwarcz SL, 'A Fundamental Inquiry into the Statutory Rulemaking Process of Private Legislatures' (1995) 29 *Georgia Law Review* 909

——, 'Private Ordering' (2002) 97 *Northwestern University Law Review* 319

Scott C, 'The Proceduralization of Telecommunications Law' (1998) 22 *Telecommunications Policy* 243

——, 'Accountability in the Regulatory State' (2000) 27 *Journal of Law and Society* 38

——, 'Analysing Regulatory Space: Fragmented Resources and Institutional Design' (2001) *Public Law* 329

——, 'Speaking Softly Without Big Sticks: Meta–Regulation and Public Sector Audit' (2003) 25 *Law & Policy* 203

——, 'Regulation in the Age of Governance: The Rise of the Post–Regulatory State' in Jordana J and Levi–Faur D (eds), *The Politics of Regulation: Institutions and Regulatory Reforms for the Age of Governance* (Cheltenham, Edward Elgar, 2004) 145–74

——, 'Self–Regulation and the Meta–Regulatory State' in Cafaggi F (ed), *Reframing Self–Regulation in European Private Law* (Alphen aan den Rijn, Kluwer Law International, 2006) 131–59

——, 'Regulating Private Legislation' in Cafaggi F and Muir–Watt H (eds), *Making European Private Law: Governance Design* (Cheltenham, Edward Elgar, 2008) 254–68

——, 'Beyond Taxonomies of Private Authority in Transnational Regulation' (2012) 13 *German Law Journal* 1329

Scott C and Black J, *Cranston's Consumers and the Law* 3rd edn (London, Butterworths, 2000)

Scott C, Cafaggi F and Senden L, 'The Conceptual and Constitutional Challenge of Transnational Private Regulation' (2011) 38 *Journal of Law and Society* 1

Sebok AJ, 'Reading the Legal Process' (1996) 94 *Michigan Law Review* 1571

Seidenfeld M, 'A Civic Republican Justification for the Bureaucratic State' (1992) 105 *Harvard Law Review* 1511

——, 'Demystifying Deossification: Rethinking Recent Proposals to Modify Judicial Review of Notice and Comment Rulemaking' (1997) 75 *Texas Law Review* 483

Selznick P, *Law, Society, and Industrial Justice* (New York, Russell Sage Foundation, 1969)

Shapiro M, *Who Guards the Guardians? Judicial Control of Administration* (Athens, University of Georgia Press, 1988)

——, 'Dishonest Corporatism? Who Guards the Guardians in an Age of Soft Law and Negotiated Regulation?' in Landy MK, Levin MA and Shapiro M (eds), *Creating Competitive Markets: The Politics of Regulatory Reform* (Washington, DC, Brookings Institution Press, 2007) 319–30

Sharma LL, Teret SP and Brownell KD, 'The Food Industry and Self-Regulation: Standards to Promote Success and to Avoid Public Health Failures' (2010) 100 *American Journal of Public Health* 240

Sinclair D, 'Self-Regulation Versus Command and Control? Beyond False Dichotomies' (1997) 19 *Law & Policy* 529

Smismans S, 'Reflexive Law in Support of Directly Deliberate Polyarchy: Reflexive-Deliberative Polyarchy as a Normative Frame for the OMC' in De Schutter O and Deakin S (eds), *Social Rights and Market Forces: Is the Open Coordination of Employment and Social Policies the Future of Social Europe?* (Brussels, Bruylant, 2005)

Smith W, 'Ensuring a Consumer Voice Beyond 1997' (1994) 44(3) *Telecommunications Journal of Australia* 25.

Snyder DV, 'Private Lawmaking' (2003) 64 *Ohio State Law Journal* 371

Solomon JM, 'Law and Governance in the 21st Century Regulatory State' (2008) 86 *Texas Law Review* 819

——, 'New Governance, Preemptive Self-Regulation and the Blurring of Boundaries in Regulatory Theory and Practice' (2010) 2010 *Wisconsin Law Review* 591

Steinfield E and Maisel JL, *Universal Design: Creating Inclusive Environments* (Hoboken, NJ, John Wiley & Sons, 2012)

Stellios, J, *Zines's The High Court and the Constitution* 6th edn (Sydney, Federation Press, 2015)

Stewart RB, 'The Reformation of American Administrative Law' (1975) 88 *Harvard Law Review* 1667

——, '*Vermont Yankee* and the Evolution of Administrative Procedure' (1978) 91 *Harvard Law Review* 1805

Stigler GJ, 'The Theory of Economic Regulation' (1971) 2 *The Bell Journal of Economics and Management Science* 3

Stone A, 'Disagreement and an Australian Bill of Rights' (2002) 26 *Melbourne University Law Review* 478

Stone B, 'Administrative Accountability in the "Westminster" Democracies' (1995) 8 *Governance: An International Journal of Policy and Administration* 505

Strauss PL, 'Disqualifications of Decisional Officials in Rulemaking' (1980) 80 *Columbia Law Review* 990

Streeck W, 'The Study of Organized Interests: Before "The Century" and After' in Crouch C and Streeck W (eds), *The Diversity of Democracy: Corporatism, Social Order and Political Conflict* (Cheltenham, Edward Elgar, 2006) 3–45

Streeck W and Schmitter PC, 'Community, Market and State—and Associations? The Prospective Contribution of Interest Governance to Social Order' in Streeck W and Schmitter PC (eds), *Private Interest Government: Beyond Market and State* (London, Sage Publications, 1985) 1–29
Stuhmcke A, 'The Rise of the Australian Telecommunications Industry Ombudsman' (2002) 26 *Telecommunications Policy* 69
Suchman MC, 'Managing Legitimacy: Strategic and Institutional Approaches' (1995) 20 *Academy of Management Review* 571
Sunstein CR, 'Interest Groups in American Public Law' (1985) 38 *Stanford Law Review* 29
——, 'Beyond the Republican Revival' (1988) 97 *Yale Law Journal* 1539
——, *After the Rights Revolution: Reconceiving the Regulatory State* (Cambridge, MA, Harvard University Press, 1993)
——, *Designing Democracy: What Constitutions Do* (Oxford, Oxford University Press, 2001)
Super DA, 'Laboratories of Destitution: Democratic Experimentalism and the Failure of Antipoverty Law' (2008) 157 *University of Pennsylvania Law Review* 541
Susskind L and McMahon G, 'The Theory and Practice of Negotiated Rulemaking' (1985) 3 *Yale Journal of Regulation* 133
Swinton K, 'Challenging the Validity of an Act of Parliament: The Effect of Enrolment and Parliamentary Privilege' (1976) 14 *Osgoode Hall Law Journal* 345
Sylvan L, 'Self–Regulation—Who's in Charge Here?' (Australian Institute of Criminology's 'Current Issues in Regulation: Enforcement and Compliance' Conference, Melbourne, 2 September 2002)
Taggart M (ed), *The Province of Administrative Law* (Oxford, Hart Publishing, 1997)
——, 'The Nature and Functions of the State' in Cane P and Tushnet M (eds), *The Oxford Handbook of Legal Studies* (Oxford, Oxford University Press, 2003) 101–18
Tamanaha BT, 'A Concise Guide to the Rule of Law' in Palombella G and Walker N (eds), *Relocating the Rule of Law* (Oxford, Hart Publishing, 2009) 3–15
Tambini D, Leonardi D and Marsden C, *Codifying Cyberspace: Communications Self–Regulation in the Age of Internet Convergence* (London, Routledge, 2007)
Taylor JA and Frey LT, 'The Need for Industry and Occupation Standards in Hospital Discharge Data' (2013) 55 *Journal of Occupational and Environmental Medicine* 495
Talesh SA, 'The Privatization of Public Legal Rights: How Manufacturers Construct the Meaning of Consumer Law' (2009) 43 *Law and Society Review* 527, 528.
Teubner G, 'Substantive and Reflexive Elements in Modern Law' (1983) 17 *Law and Society Review* 239
——, 'After Legal Instrumentalism? Strategic Models of Post–Regulatory Law' in Teubner G (ed), *Dilemmas of Law in the Welfare State* (Berlin, Walter de Gruyter, 1986) 299–325
——, 'Juridification: Concepts, Aspects, Limits, Solutions' in Teubner G (ed), *Juridification of Social Spheres: A Comparative Analysis in the Areas of Labor, Corporate, Antitrust and Social Welfare Law* (Berlin, Walter de Gruyter, 1987) 3–48
——, *Law as an Autopoietic System* (Oxford, Blackwell, 1993)
Tomkins A, 'Delegated Legislation in the English Constitution' in Andenas M and Turk A (eds), *Delegated Legislation and the Role of Committees in the EC* (The Hague, Kluwer Law International, 2000) 101–25
Tushnet M, 'Judicial Review of Legislation' in Cane P and Tushnet M (eds), *The Oxford Handbook of Legal Studies* (Oxford, Oxford University Press, 2003) 164–81

Tusikov N, 'Transnational Non–state Regulatory Regimes' in Drahos P (ed), *Regulatory Theory: Foundations and Applications* (Canberra, ANU Press, 2017) 339–53
Urbinati N and Warren ME, 'The Concept of Representation in Contemporary Democratic Theory' (2008) 11 *Annual Review of Political Science* 387
Vandenbergh M, 'The Private Life of Public Law' (2005) 105 Columbia Law Review 2029
——, 'The New Wal–Mart Effect: The Role of Private Contracting in Global Governance' (2007) 54 *University of California at Los Angeles Law Review* 913
Verkuil PR, 'Public Law Limitations on Privatization of Government Functions' (1986) 84 *North Carolina Law Review* 397
Vermeule A, 'Judicial Review and Institutional Choice' (2002) 43 *William and Mary Law Review* 1557
——, 'The Constitutional Law of Congressional Procedure' (2004) 71 *The University of Chicago Law Review* 361
——, *Mechanisms of Democracy: Institutional Design Writ Small* (Oxford, Oxford University Press, 2007)
Wade, ECS, 'Introduction' in Dicey, AV, *Introduction to the Study of the Law of the Constitution* (London, Macmillan Press, first published 1885, 1960 edn)
Wade HWR and Forsyth CF, *Administrative Law* 11th edn (Oxford, Oxford University Press, 2014)
Waldron J, *The Dignity of Legislation* (Cambridge, Cambridge University Press, 1999)
——, *Law and Disagreement* (Oxford, Oxford University Press, 1999)
——, 'Legislating with Integrity' (2003) 72 *Fordham Law Review* 373
——, 'Principles of Legislation' in Bauman RW and Kahana T (eds), *The Least Examined Branch: The Role of Legislatures in the Constitutional State* (Cambridge, Cambridge University Press, 2006) 15–32
——, 'Legislation and the Rule of Law' (2007) 1 *Legisprudence* 91
——, 'Representative Lawmaking' (2009) 89 *Boston University Law Review* 335
——, 'The Rule of Law and the Importance of Procedure' in Fleming JE (ed), *Getting to the Rule of Law: Nomos L* (New York, New York University Press, 2011) 3–63
Walker N, 'The Idea of Constitutional Pluralism' (2002) 65 *The Modern Law Review* 317
Webb K (ed), *Voluntary Codes: Private Governance, the Public Interest and Innovation* (Carleton, CA, Carleton Research Unit for Innovation, Science and Environment, Carleton University 2004)
Weimer DL, 'The Puzzle of Private Rulemaking: Expertise, Flexibility, and Blame Avoidance in U.S. Regulation' (2006) 66 *Public Administration Review* 569
Weinberg J, 'ICANN and the Problem of Legitimacy' (2000) 50 *Duke Law Journal* 187
Weinberger O, 'Habermas on Democracy and Justice: Limits of a Sound Conception' (1994) 7 *Ratio Juris* 239
Westerman P, 'Who Is Regulating the Self? Self–Regulation as Outsourced Rule–making' (2010) 4 *Legisprudence* 225
——, 'Pyramids and the Value of Generality' (2013) 7 *Regulation & Governance* 80
Wilding D, 'In the Shadow of the Pyramid: Consumers in Communications Self–Regulation' (2005) 55(2) *Telecommunications Journal of Australia* 37
——, 'The Debate About Self–Regulation' [2005] (167) *Communications Update* 8
Wilkinson M, 'Three Conceptions of Law: Towards a Jurisprudence of Democratic Experimentalism' (2010) 2010 *Wisconsin Law Review* 673

Willems T and Van Dooren W, 'Coming to Terms with Accountability: Combining Multiple Forums and Functions' (2012) 14 *Public Management Review* 1012
Williams SF, '"Hybrid Rulemaking" under the Administrative Procedure Act: A Legal and Empirical Analysis' (1975) 42 *University of Chicago Law Review* 401
Williamson PJ, *Corporatism in Perspective: An Introductory Guide to Corporatist Theory* (London, Sage Publications, 1989)
Wintgens LJ, 'Legislation as an Object of Study of Legal Theory: Legisprudence' in Wintgens LJ (ed), *Legisprudence: A New Theoretical Approach to Legislation* (Oxford, Hart Publishing, 2002) 9–39
——, 'Rationality in Legislation—Legal Theory as Legisprudence: An Introduction' in Wintgens LJ (ed), *Legisprudence: A New Theoretical Approach to Legislation* (Oxford, Hart Publishing, 2002) 1–39
——, 'Legisprudence as a New Theory of Legislation' in Wintgens LJ (ed), *The Theory and Practice of Legislation* (Abingdon, Ashgate, 2005) 3–25
——, *Legisprudence: Practical Reason in Legislation* (Abingdon, Ashgate, 2012)
Woolf H and others, *De Smith's Judicial Review* 7th edn (London, Sweet & Maxwell, 2013)
Wright BC (ed), *House of Representatives Practice* 6th edn (Canberra, Commonwealth of Australia 2012)
Yeung K, *Securing Compliance: A Principled Approach* (Oxford, Hart Publishing, 2004)
Zeitlin J, *Extending Experimentalist Governance: The European Union and Transnational Regulation* (Oxford, Oxford University Press, 2015)

Communications Alliance Documentation

The website of the Communications Alliance has been archived by the National Library of Australia in October each year since 2002. Go to pandora.nla.gov.au for more information.

For recent Communications Alliance documentation, go to www.commsalliance.com.au.

INDEX